# YOUR CHILDREN ARE VERY GREATLY IN DANGER

# YOUR CHILDREN ARE VERY GREATLY IN DANGER

## SCHOOL SEGREGATION IN ROCHESTER, NEW YORK

JUSTIN MURPHY

CORNELL UNIVERSITY PRESS
*Ithaca and London*

First published 2022 by Cornell University Press

Printed in the United States of America

Library of Congress Cataloging-in-Publication Data

Names: Murphy, Justin (Educational journalist), 1985– author.
Title: Your children are very greatly in danger : school segregation in Rochester, New York / Justin Murphy.
Description: Ithaca [New York] : Cornell University Press, 2022. | Includes bibliographical references and index.
Identifiers: LCCN 2021020725 (print) | LCCN 2021020726 (ebook) | ISBN 9781501761867 (hardcover) | ISBN 9781501761874 (pdf) | ISBN 9781501761881 (epub)
Subjects: LCSH: Segregation in education—New York (State)—Rochester—History—20th century. | Segregation in education—New York (State)—Rochester—History—21st century. | Segregation in education—New York (State)—Rochester—Case studies. | Education, Urban—Social aspects.
Classification: LCC LC212.522.N48 M87 2022 (print) | LCC LC212.522.N48 (ebook) | DDC 379.2/630974789—dc23
LC record available at https://lccn.loc.gov/2021020725
LC ebook record available at https://lccn.loc.gov/2021020726

*For Millie and Woody*

# Contents

*Preface* *ix*

Introduction: The Question of Questions 1

1. The African School 18
2. Nowhere Else to Go 41
3. Willing Combatants 72
4. Six Rugged Years, All Uphill 99
5. From Charlotte to *Milliken* 132
6. Considering the Metropolis 157
7. The Urban-Suburban Program 183
8. The Age of Accountability 205

Conclusion: Three Steps toward Change 231

*Acknowledgments* *241*

*Notes* *245*

*Note on Sources* *283*

*Index* *287*

# Preface

As a journalist covering the Rochester City School District, I often find myself the audience for lengthy treatises regarding the dire, seemingly irredeemable state of urban education here and across the nation. These explanations land most frequently on a few common culprits, none of them mutually exclusive. A self-serving school board, inept and overzealous. Tuned-out teachers, uninterested in the plight of the city and content to coast from paycheck to paycheck until their pensions vest in full. Paunchy administrators holed up in a downtown office building doing God knows what, far removed from the children they're meant to serve. Parasitic charter school operators, in league with their cabal of corporate school reformers, leeching money from "real" public schools. Lazy, stupid parents and—this part is usually left unsaid—their lazy, stupid kids.

It has become increasingly apparent to me that these pat formulations of the problem, even in combination, are ultimately insufficient. They lack context in two important ways. First, any assignment of blame to entirely local factors—Adam Urbanski's forty-year reign over the Rochester Teachers Association, for instance, or the unusually high salaries that Rochester school board members draw—fails to explain why every urban school district in the United States suffers from the same ills as Rochester to a greater or lesser extent. Second, and related, these short-sighted explanations ignore the critical historical context of how urban schools in Rochester and elsewhere arrived at their present pitiable state and how it fits into a broader history of discrimination and oppression. Education policy in the United States has been slouching away from the standard of *Brown v. Board of Education* for long enough that most educators and policymakers, not to mention children and parents, cannot readily conceive of any other approach to the issue. My goal here has been to provide that missing context.

I hope readers will recognize in this book not only a recitation of racist actions but also—peeking out intermittently from behind the clouds of bigotry and violence and fear—the joy of learning that is possible when children from different backgrounds meet in the classroom on equal terms and under the guidance of teachers who respect them. Joy is not a typical metric in reform-based school accountability. Many students and teachers who spent time in such classrooms in Monroe County described their experiences with that word, though, and I have visited enough schools to appreciate its presence. The Children's School of Rochester and Rochester International Academy in the city school district come to mind. So do schools I have visited in East Irondequoit, Gates Chili, Rush-Henrietta, and other diverse suburban school districts. These schools are not perfect, but they seem to have fostered a richness of relationship-building and respect that more homogenous schools seldom manage to attain.

This effect, it seems to me, is often dismissed as extraneous to the actual business of education or seen as ephemeral and essentially random. I hope readers of this book will keep their minds open to a different premise: that every school could be dynamic and joyful if only adults would commit to building the proper foundation of anti-racism rather than racism; faith rather than fear; integration rather than segregation.

This approach constitutes not simply a rescue mission for Black city children but a rethinking of public education everywhere. Parents of children in well-regarded school districts may find this unnecessary. But though the harm done to Black students through two hundred years of segregation is obvious and easily observed through nearly any metric, white students have by no means gone unscathed. It was this psychic harm that James Baldwin had in mind in the 1964 essay from which this book takes its title. In it he addressed white parents directly about the insidious effect of racial separation on all children, in particular their own:

> I know you didn't do it, and I didn't do it either, but I am responsible for it because I am a man and a citizen of this country and you are responsible for it, too, for the very same reason: as long as my children face the future they face, and come to the ruin that they come to, your children are very greatly in danger, too.
>
> They are endangered above all by the moral apathy which pretends it isn't happening. This does something terrible to us. Anyone who is trying to be conscious must begin to be conscious of that apathy and must begin to dismiss the vocabulary which we've used so long to cover it up, to lie about the way things are.[1]

Rochester, like many places in the United States, has deep familiarity with "the moral apathy which pretends it isn't happening." As will be seen in the introduction and conclusion of this book, I believe our community can end its dangerous, racist game of make-believe only by dismantling the physical and political barriers of segregation. My hope is that the history contained in this book will illuminate our community's way in the quest for new ideas, new strength, and a new resolution to stop lying about the way things are.

# YOUR CHILDREN ARE VERY GREATLY IN DANGER

# Introduction
## The Question of Questions

"Please don't get your feet wet," the grown-ups kept saying. But it was an unusually sunny day in January 2020 and as the first- and third-graders walked in front of Anna Murray Douglass Academy School 12 they could not resist kicking the clumps of dirty snow, sending them splattering across the sidewalk. They forded the snow drifts piled in the landscaping and tramped up to the Frederick Douglass statue in the front of the building, rubbing their fingers along the ridges of his coat and hands and hair to see what they felt like.

This short walk—a perimeter of the Frederick Douglass Community Library, the Anna Murray Douglass Academy, and the Frederick Douglass Recreation Center—likely contains more Douglass artwork than any other acre on the planet. The Douglass family lived at the site until their house burned, or was burned, in 1872. "He used to go to our school," a girl whispered, pointing. Her sneakers lit up in blue neon lights when she kicked snowballs. Now they were wet. One of the older children overheard her comment and corrected her: "No, he used to *live* at our school."

School 12 was renamed for Anna Murray Douglass in 2018. The Rochester school board decided to do so after a fourteen-year-old boy named Trevyan Rowe walked away from the school one morning earlier that year without anyone noticing and drowned in the Genesee River. Teachers at the school had marked him present even though he never showed up for class that day. The new name, said the school board president, Van White, would be "an opportunity to talk about a different, more positive future, given what happened to Trevyan." About 85 percent of the students at Anna Murray Douglass Academy are Black or Latino, and the same number qualify for free or reduced lunch. A few decades ago, the opposite was true. Djinga St. Louis took a bus there in the 1980s from her home in southwest Rochester's 19th Ward and was one of the very few Black children in the school's gifted program. "I'll never forget, I didn't know if I was in a city school or a suburban school, because there were so many white kids around me," she said.[1]

Ideally, Anna Murray Douglass Academy would be at neither demographic extreme but instead enroll a more racially and socioeconomically diverse population. To achieve that, the Rochester City School District (RCSD) and the Brighton Central School District, just a mile away, used about $100,000 in state desegregation funding to create a joint program based on School 12's popular bilingual program. The effort fell apart, however, when it became clear that the Brighton children would have to enroll in the city school. The prospect of that happening was remote. The squandered grant was chalked up as a learning experience.[2]

"Did Frederick Douglass learn how to read in school?" a girl asked.

The Anna Murray Douglass Academy children were back in the classroom and sitting on the carpet, cross-legged or splayed out on the floor. Douglass's stern, middle-age face beamed out from the smart board. The image was low resolution and distorted, squished horizontally so that his bushy, graying hair spread across the screen like purslane. The second "s" was missing from his name.

The teacher pursed her lips admiringly. This was a good question—the kind that might earn a kid a few Douglass dollars to spend on pencils or stickers or candy.

"No, because slaves couldn't go to school. It was against the law. Is that fair?"

The girl frowned and shook her head, the white plastic beads on her braids clacking against her skull.

Frederick Douglass would not approve of any of this.

He would not appreciate that all three of the schools named after him and his family in his adopted hometown have been deeply segregated. He would not be happy that one of them, the NorthSTAR program, closed in 2020 after being described as "sub-par at best," with "virtually no instruction occurring" and 85 percent of students chronically absent. The other tribute, Frederick Douglass Junior High School, was built in 1968 as part of a wide-reaching desegregation program that white Rochester residents derailed through protests, voting, and throwing rocks at Black children until their parents reluctantly conceded that racial integration was an unwise goal. Douglass would not like that, either.[3]

Douglass earned his own liberty and education after the harshest possible ordeal and then devoted his life as a free man to securing those rights for others—not only by abolishing slavery but by working to erase the stain of racism altogether. Such a lofty goal could only be accomplished, he believed, through integration, especially among the young. "Let colored children be educated and grow up side by side with white children, come up friends from unsophisticated and generous childhood together," he wrote, "and it will require a powerful agent to convert them into enemies."[4]

Again and again, Douglass returned to the necessity of an equal, integrated education if Black children were to become full-fledged citizens of the fractured nation. It was, in his words, "the question of questions for the colored people of this place." When his own daughter was forced to sit by herself in a classroom closet away from her white classmates, he excoriated the school in an open letter published across the country. When the Black trustees at African Methodist Episcopal (AME) Zion Church offered in 1849 to lease their basement for Rochester's Black-only school, he blasted them as "stupid creatures . . . servile tools of their own proscription and degradation" and organized a protest against the move.[5]

"There is no reason, nor can there be a reason why a colored child should not be taught in the same schools with white children," Douglass wrote. He could not have foreseen Rochester as it stands today, segregated by a municipal line that did not have the same force during his lifetime. His words nonetheless are prescient: "It is evident that colored people will continue to form a part of this community; and that their influence in it, for good or for evil, will be considerable. They may either contribute to its prosperity, virtue and happiness, or they may become a serious drawback upon all these. To elevate and improve the colored people, is but contributing to the general good of the whole community . . . [and] would be a noble example of justice and liberality worthy of the city of Rochester."[6]

Which is the path of justice and liberality in the matter of public education? How well have Rochester and other US cities followed it, and what has been the effect on their communal prosperity, virtue, and happiness? The current woeful state of schooling in Rochester and the educational disparities across the metropolitan area are attributable to explicit racial segregation and discrimination dating back to Frederick Douglass's age and beyond. That segregation was enacted through both government action and personal bigotry, and every attempt to dislodge it has been defeated by those same factors.

Once the exodus of white and middle-class families to the suburbs became irreversible, the topic of school segregation came to be seen as passé. Instead Rochester and other US cities have invested billions of dollars in the hope that technical fixes to school structure, governance, and pedagogy, together with sporadic bursts of federal funding, will relieve them of the obligation to confront the stark racial and socioeconomic divisions in their communities. The hope, in other words, is to operate separate but equal schools for mostly white and mostly nonwhite children. The fact that they are not equal—and have never been equal in any metropolitan area in the country in any meaningful sense for any meaningful period of time—is taken not as a refutation of the fundamental premise but rather as a sign that the conditions of the separation still need some adjusting.

This idea, of course, is best known from *Plessy v. Ferguson*, the 1896 US Supreme Court case that upheld states' right to provide racially segregated facilities. But it was not born with *Plessy*. And though *Plessy* arose from a case in Louisiana, the idea had currency far north of the Mason-Dixon line. One of its most forceful expressions, in fact, came from an 1883 New York school-segregation case that the *Plessy* court later used to support its argument. The New York case, *People ex rel. King v. Gallagher*, had to do with a twelve-year-old Black girl who was barred from a public school in Brooklyn. The New York Court of Appeals ruled in the school's favor. "The attempt to enforce social intimacy and intercourse between the races, by legal enactments, would probably tend only to embitter the prejudices . . . which exist between them, and produce an evil instead of a good result," the majority wrote in upholding the girl's exclusion. "It is believed that no sincere friend of [Black] people could . . . wish any other result than that which should sustain them in the enjoyment of those institutions specially organized for their benefit and advantage."[7]

Dissenting from the majority opinion was George F. Danforth, a judge from Rochester. In his dissent he inadvertently predicted *Plessy* and foreshadowed its reversal fifty-eight years later by *Brown v. Board of Education*.

> With equal plausibility it might be said that the city of Brooklyn could provide parks, streets and sidewalks exclusively for persons of color. . . . It would not answer in either case to say all these things are equal or even better in degree than those [for white people]. This would still be discrimination against the race, and so with the school, the main business of which is to prepare a youth for his future duties as a citizen

in his various relations toward the State, the performance of obligations due to other citizens, and possibly even forbearance and conduct toward opposing races.[8]

Time would prove that Danforth was correct; *Brown*, which follows his logic, is rightly upheld as a high mark in US history. And yet when one looks at schools in Rochester and across the country, it is impossible to escape the conclusion that *Plessy* has prevailed in spirit. The mechanisms behind school segregation were not local inventions but rather repeated in cities across the country. Rochester stands as a sorrowful archetype. In each chapter of this book, the reader will see evidence of political and social trends at the state and national level. Some of these forces—the insidious, underrecognized effect of racial discrimination in hiring, for instance—did particular damage in Rochester, but none bypassed it entirely. A reader outside western New York can take this book as a case study. Rochesterians, meanwhile, should bear in mind that the inequity they see in their community is the product of far-reaching influences. Purely local reform-based solutions—firing the superintendent, cutting teacher salaries, voting out the school board—fail to acknowledge the full scale of the problem.

This book proceeds in roughly chronological fashion with occasional detours to follow important issues. Chapter 1 begins with the earliest local educational opportunities for Black children and the first long fight to desegregate the public school system. Chapter 2 departs from a close focus on education to explain the Great Migration in Rochester and subsequent patterns of housing discrimination, for the action of the Civil Rights era cannot be understood without that background. Some of the most flagrant housing policies in the early to middle twentieth century included massive federal subsidies for which Black families were ineligible, targeted disinvestment by banks and real estate agents, and exclusionary restrictive covenants upheld by neighborhood associations and individual white homeowners. At a time when most children in the United States attended school within walking distance of home, these policies led inevitably to racially segregated schools.

At the same time, local school officials were not innocent. As will be seen in chapter 3, they drew school attendance boundaries and sited new construction to reinforce and extend residential housing segregation. When budget or physical space got tight, schools in Black neighborhoods suffered the first and deepest cuts, contending with shortened school days, loss of nonessential opportunities, and portable classrooms parked on ballfields.

The distinction between accidental and intentional segregation on which the courts relied so heavily during the Civil Rights era was a lie and a con.

Chapters 4 and 5 examine in detail the Civil Rights era fight to desegregate Rochester schools. It included several major district proposals, half a dozen federal lawsuits, public protests involving tens of thousands of students and no small amount of bloodshed. Ultimately it was unsuccessful. Chapter 6 reviews various attempts over the last century to implement metropolitan-level solutions for Rochester's educational ills, while chapter 7 deals exclusively with the most prominent of these, the Urban-Suburban Inter-District Transfer Program. Chapter 8 brings the historical narrative to the present day, illustrating the flaws inherent in the school reform model that has dominated national education policy for nearly forty years. The conclusion offers three recommendations for the people of Monroe County, where Rochester is located, to combat school segregation now.

Many other important subjects are discussed only in brief, or not at all. This book is neither a history of Black education in Rochester nor a history of education more generally. It touches only lightly, therefore, on topics that deserve a fuller treatment, such as the advent of common and secondary schools in the late nineteenth century or the explosive growth of charter schools in the early twenty-first century. It also is not an exhaustive account of the Black community in Rochester, the discrimination it has faced, or its resistance and activism. Rich subjects such as housing and job discrimination and disparities in criminal justice and health care are discussed only as context for education.

Three main themes will recur in this story. One is persistent white opposition to racial integration throughout the history of education in Rochester. This opposition has been based largely on several enduring fears. One is the fear of violence, including sexual violence. The Rochester school board in 1849 declined to close its separate school for Black children in part because, as one board member said, "no citizen would want a colored boy sitting in school beside his daughter." One hundred twenty years later, the school board president and antibusing leader Louis Cerulli insisted that the district investigate a purported increase in "shakedowns, beatings and attempted attacks on girls in the schools," in particular at the high schools where Black enrollment was increasing. The resulting study occupied a special committee for several months but ultimately showed no such trend. "Violence in the schools has been overplayed and used as a smokescreen," said Franklin Florence, the president of the local Black Power organization FIGHT. "The real issue is, black kids are not learning in inner-city schools."[9]

Another persistent fear is that the quality of education for white children will be degraded or that they will lose resources to their Black peers. National research has consistently shown this fear to be unfounded—schools that desegregate usually see an increase in funding, and Black children benefit educationally while white children suffer no harm and benefit in important nonacademic ways. Neither this research nor appeals to equity have reduced white parents' anxiety. A group of parents at all-white School 30 sued the district in 1964 over a plan to add some students from the overcrowded, all-Black School 3. "Is this going to take the roots from under my little girl?" one white mother asked the school board. "If she suffers, will this board pay her psychiatry bills?" In 2014, as the Spencerport school district to Rochester's west was considering joining Urban-Suburban, some residents protested on the grounds that their own children would lose academic scholarships or spots on the basketball team if more Black children were brought in.[10]

Despite these protests, the Spencerport school board voted unanimously to adopt Urban-Suburban, and several other districts followed suit in 2015 and 2016. These actions, beneficent on their face, highlight the second recurring theme in the history of segregated education in Rochester. White opposition to integration has tended to soften only where it would benefit white families in some way, in particular financially. Suburban school districts rushed to join Urban-Suburban only after it became apparent that Rochester students represented a significant untapped revenue stream and a way to prop up declining enrollment. Similarly, the Rochester school board closed the segregated Black school in 1856 only after the cost of educating a handful of Black children in their own separate building became intolerable. In the context of higher education, the University of Rochester in 1939 finally agreed to admit Black medical students not in response to complaints from the local Black community but because the state threatened to strip its tax-exempt status if it did not.[11]

The emergence of a converging financial interest for white families, though, does not suffice to explain these and other instances of racial progress. Rather, such victories were earned through the long advocacy of Black parents to improve their children's educational opportunities, most often through desegregation. This is the book's third theme. Black parents organized a series of school boycotts in the mid-nineteenth century to press for an end to formal desegregation. They flocked to Rochester and other northern cities from the segregated South throughout the twentieth century in part so their children could attend nonsegregated schools. They organized and joined lawsuits during the Civil Rights era, pressing for integration with white students—not for the privilege of those students' company, but because of the resources that attached to them. As the journalist Nikole Hannah-Jones wrote: "Parents demanded integration only after they realized that in a country that does not value black children the same as white ones, black children will never get what white children get unless they sit where white children sit." The constancy of Black activism is an important through line in the history of segregated education in Rochester and provides a hopeful lens for the future.[12]

The argument of this book is that the effects of intentional segregation can be addressed only through intentional desegregation—and, ultimately, true integration. Any such appeal immediately must reckon with the fact that many Black community leaders in Rochester and elsewhere are opposed to such a strategy. This opposition may reflect political calculation but is nonetheless deeply grounded in experience, dating back in Rochester to 1832, when Black parents petitioned for a separate school where their children would not be "despised, called negroes, and completely discouraged by the white children." It was evident at the height of the desegregation movement in the late 1960s as well, when a group of disillusioned Black community leaders switched course and called for greater local control of mostly Black schools in Rochester through "community school councils" rather than integration. "We're not looking to build a separate black world for our children," FIGHT's president, Bernard Gifford, said then. "All we're saying is that we're sick and tired of black children being used as pawns."[13]

Rochester Mayor Lovely Warren is among those who support improvements within the current segregated paradigm rather than explicit desegregation efforts.* This position is guided by her family history. Her grandfather, Cecil McClary, dropped out of school in Kingston, South Carolina, in 1933 at the age of seven because he was ashamed not to have shoes to wear to class. In 1964 he moved with his wife and eight children to Rochester, where his wife's sister was already living. The first generation, indigent and thickly accented, struggled to fit in and were taunted as "Geechies." But McClary saved carefully from his job as a security guard and began to buy property to rent. His children graduated from school, got jobs, and provided greater opportunity for their own children. One of those second-generation Rochesterians was Warren, who was elected mayor of the city in 2013 and took the oath of office in her grandfather's hospital room just days before he died.[14]

"My mom and her older siblings . . . were stable, middle-class, taking care of their families," Warren said in a 2019 interview. "Every Sunday getting

*Faced with a felony indictment on campaign finance charges as well as the outcry over the March 2020 death of Daniel Prude at the hands of Rochester police, Lovely Warren lost the Democratic primary in June 2021 for what would have been her third term as mayor. She was defeated by city councilman and former RCSD school board member Malik Evans.

together at my grandparents' house for dinner, everyone going to church together. . . . That's what I grew up knowing." That stable family proved an important safety net when her father became addicted to drugs when she was a teenager. So, too, did her teachers and administrators at Wilson Magnet High School, who kept her from dropping out. Because of this deep faith in the value of intact, vibrant communities Warren has spent much of her time and political capital as mayor on community schools, arguing for more and better resources in existing neighborhoods rather than integration. "There's something [about] the connection between the school and the neighborhood you go to school in—it's a sense of family and belonging," she said. "There is something in that style of educating the child that matters."[15]

What has gone wrong, then, in Rochester and other cities? Warren believes it to be a combination of two main factors. First, traditional school attendance patterns where the buildings serve as neighborhood anchors have declined. More broadly, that has led to decreased stability at schools, with higher teacher and administrator turnover as well as weaker connections between the school and other neighborhood institutions. Second, according to Warren, teacher quality has declined, and among white teachers in particular the belief persists that "students are too poor to learn, and that poverty is an excuse for their failure." She referred approvingly a number of times to the way things "used to be." When asked to identify that time period, exactly, she said it referred to both her own education—she graduated from high school in 1995—and the segregated South before *Brown v. Board of Education*. "There was something about teaching as a noble profession, that the top-tier folks—the people who become doctors and lawyers—back in the day they would become teachers," she said. "You still had that sense of leadership."[16]

Warren's primary objection to the pursuit of racial integration is pragmatic. Racism, she said, is something children are taught. She notes that her daughter attends a relatively diverse private school, and that she herself benefited from diversity at Wilson Magnet and elsewhere. "Do I think my daughter is better off for having a diverse classroom? Absolutely," she said.

But, she continued:

> We know, the suburbs and the city—they don't want a metro school district. That's just politically not going to happen. So why come up with solutions that politically won't happen? That's why I'm saying, deal with the situation you have. . . .
>
> You can't force people's feelings to change. Just because you put Black kids and white kids together doesn't mean things are going to change. It just doesn't happen that way.[17]

Derrick Bell makes a more formidable case against pursuing integration. The eminent legal theorist, one of the architects of critical race theory, spent the early years of his career with the National Association for the Advancement of Colored People (NAACP) Legal Defense and Educational Fund, where he supervised hundreds of school desegregation cases. As white resistance persisted and lasting improvements proved scarce, Bell began to question the very premise of integration. He came to believe that the NAACP's single-minded focus on desegregating schools put too much faith in judicial intervention and underestimated the "near-seamless national web of constitutional injury" of which segregated schools were only a part: "Zealous faith in integration blinded us to the actual goal of equalizing educational opportunities for black children, and led us to pursue integration without regard to, and often despite, its ultimate impact on the well-being of students."[18]

To flesh out his argument, Bell went as far as to draft an alternate Supreme Court decision in *Brown*, imagining a scenario where the justices upheld the separate but equal holding in *Plessy v. Ferguson*, motivated in large part by foreseeable white resistance. "The 'separate' in the 'separate but equal' standard has been rigorously enforced. The 'equal' has served as a total refutation of equality," Bell wrote in his hypothetical ruling:

> The Court recognizes these cases as an opportunity to test the legal legitimacy of the "separate but equal" standard, not as petitioners urge by overturning *Plessy*, but by ordering for the first time its strict enforcement. . . .
>
> A decision overturning *Plessy*, while it might be viewed as a triumph by Negro petitioners and the class they represent, will be condemned by many whites. Their predictable outraged resistance could undermine and eventually negate even the most committed judicial enforcement efforts.[19]

Bell's imagined ruling included strict and specific standards for equality in both resources and academic achievement as well as a restructuring of school boards to ensure minority representation. All of this would be done with court oversight. If this plan failed, or if a judicial panel were to discover "actions intended to subvert or hinder the compliance program," it might issue an order to "promptly desegregate," just as the *Brown* plaintiffs initially requested.[20]

Effort spent on desegregation will inevitably be wasted, Warren and Bell believe, as white Americans rise in opposition. History shows that even the *Brown* ruling, one of the most momentous decisions in US history, was insufficient to overcome this hostility. The same energy, they argue, would be better invested in improving the situation already existing in urban schools without attempting to address directly the racial and socioeconomic differences compared to their suburban counterparts.

A great deal of historical evidence supports argument; indeed, much of it is gathered in this book. The rebuttal to it is based not on naïve trust in postracial harmony but rather in examination of the academic and lifelong outcomes for students who have attended desegregated schools. The road to opening such schools has been fraught, to say the least. When they are opened, though—what happens then? The academic literature on this point is vast. Some studies focus on long-term outcomes for students who attended forcibly desegregated schools from the late 1960s to the early 1990s; other studies examine contemporary differences among schools, school districts, and metropolitan areas. The consensus from this rigorous, large-scale research is clear: desegregation and integration offer the greatest opportunity to improve population-level educational and economic outcomes for children of color in the United States.

The argument for desegregation was synthesized neatly during the 2007 US Supreme Court case *Parents Involved in Community Schools v. Seattle School District No. 1*. The Court in that case was asked to decide whether race could serve as a meaningful factor in schools' student placement policies; the broader question was whether desegregation efforts based on race would still be tolerated, if not encouraged, half a century after *Brown*. A coalition of 553 social scientists who supported desegregation summarized the existing body of academic research with three points: "(1) Racially integrated schools provide significant benefits to students and communities, (2) racially isolated schools have harmful educational implications for students, and (3) race-conscious policies are necessary to maintain racial integration in schools."[21]

Two studies based on massive data sets, one contemporary and one longitudinal, are useful synopses of the research consensus in 2022. The first was an analysis led by sean reardon of the Stanford University Center for Education Policy Analysis of standardized test results over eight years for all public schools in the United States. It found "a very strong link between racial school segregation and academic achievement gaps," with the gaps growing even wider in the most segregated systems. This was not owing directly to race, however, but rather to the way race was used to sort students socioeconomically: "We find that the association between racial school segregation and achievement gaps appears to operate entirely through differences in exposure to poor schoolmates. Once we control for racial differences in school poverty, racial segregation is no longer predictive of achievement gaps or the growth in the gaps. . . . Racial segregation matters, therefore, because it concentrates black and Hispanic students in high-poverty schools, not because of the racial composition of their schools, per se."[22]

The economist Rucker Johnson, meanwhile, created a unique data set by merging an inventory of judicial desegregation orders with corresponding student academic records as well as the findings of the Panel Study of Income Dynamics, the longest running longitudinal household study in the world. He was able to create matched pairs of students, similar in all ways except for their exposure to desegregation measures. Comparing the resultant control and experiment cohorts yielded startlingly clear advantages for Black students who had attended desegregated schools for their entire K-12 education compared to those who did not:

- an additional 1.5 years of average educational attainment and a 30 percent increase in likelihood to graduate
- a 30 percentage-point decrease in both the likelihood of ever being incarcerated and the likelihood of living in poverty as an adult
- a 30 percent increase in wages earned as an adult between ages twenty and fifty
- an 11 percentage-point increase in the likelihood of reporting very good or excellent health as an adult

Importantly, these effects grew more pronounced as students spent more years in a desegregated school rather than a segregated one. And in no case did white students suffer as their nonwhite classmates gained. Johnson concluded: "Integration, when implemented in a holistic fashion, has the power to break the cycle of poverty and can benefit all groups, regardless of race and ethnicity. Like the vaccines that have saved millions of lives in the medical field . . . integration is an unmitigated good."[23]

What is more, Johnson's data shows that Black students who were affected by desegregation orders saw immediate benefits that had nothing to do with race: a 20 percent increase in funding at the schools they attended and a drop in average class size from twenty-seven to twenty-three over just three years. This echoes reardon and coauthors' finding and lends support to the popular adage among desegregation supporters that "green follows white." As Gary Orfield put it: "Simply sitting next to a white student does not guarantee better educational outcomes for students of color. Instead, the resources that are consistently linked to predominately white and/or wealthy schools help foster real and serious educational advantages over minority segregated settings." Money is the most tangible of these resources but not the only one. Equally important is inclusion in the broad and deep social networks of mostly white middle-class families and exposure to what sociologist Robert Putnam called their "savvy" around higher education and professional employment. A great deal of longitudinal research demonstrates that Black students who attend desegregated schools set higher career goals for themselves and benefit later in life from wider professional social networks and higher rates of professional employment. "The social networks of more affluent, educated families amplify their other assets in helping to assure that their kids have richer opportunities," Putnam wrote. "[This builds] their capacity to understand the institutions that stand astride the paths to opportunity and to make those institutions work for them."[24]

The reardon et al. and Johnson studies also illustrate an important paradox in desegregation research. Those studies and many others like them were conducted over many years or even decades. And though such long-term research has strengthened the case for desegregation among experts, the absence of clear short-term effects has proven to be a confounding factor in making the case to the public. Journalists and policymakers are more attuned to immediate feedback; by the time a ten-year study is available, the original political environment inevitably will have shifted. This was certainly the case in Rochester, where the only serious attempt at widespread desegregation was repealed after a single school year. The conclusion that it had failed was based not on the long-term effects for students, but rather the tumult it caused in the community. As Frank Ciaccia, elected to the school board in 1971 on an antibusing platform, said: "If you're in that situation and you see all this massive busing going around, and neighborhoods are upset and parents are upset, and violence and riots in the schools—I don't know how anybody in their right mind can say, 'This is a good thing. We've got to keep this going.'"[25]

There was relatively little research on student outcomes resulting from the Rochester City School District's evolving experiments with desegregation from 1963 to 1971. The only noteworthy study was conducted by the district's own research division and published in 1968. It compared several groups of Black students, including some at all-Black School 3, where class sizes were significantly smaller than elsewhere in the district and extra support teachers were added, against some others at School 2, where students joined desegregated classes with mostly white classmates. The Black students in the desegregated School 2 classrooms were the clear winners. Their learning outpaced that of their peers at School 3 even though their classrooms had about ten additional students in them and fewer adults. "The integrated situation surpassed the one that had the massive compensatory programs," Superintendent John Franco summarized at a US Senate hearing in 1971. "The school that had reduced class size with a full-time teacher and all kinds of support of personnel was extremely expensive. . . . They made some gains, they did. But not in comparison to the other."[26]

The political counterargument to integration has an additional component: even if white families would consent to significant racial desegregation, Black families do not want it either. "When you ask people in poverty today if they want to move to the suburbs, 99 percent say, 'No, I want my neighborhood to be better,'" Lovely Warren said, capturing the same sentiment in an adjacent context. This reluctance to leave the neighborhood, or neighborhood school, is again perfectly well grounded in history. There are many thousands of nonwhite people still living in the United States whose entry as children into previously white spaces triggered jeers, slurs, spit, and rocks. "Busing has laid our children open to unfamiliar and hostile environments," Alberta Cason of FIGHT said in 1969. "They have been treated like lepers in these receiving schools." The first Black students to ride a bus to the previously all-white Charlotte High School in the late 1960s saw the words "n—— go home" spray-painted on the façade of their new school and a Black effigy hanging from a tree outside. Racist incidents in mostly white suburban schools today are perhaps less vivid but persist nonetheless.[27]

Yet the fact remains that Black families historically have pursued desegregation opportunities with enthusiasm, a trend that continues two decades into the twenty-first century. The first such initiative in Rochester, a 1963 open enrollment program where Black students could enroll in a neighboring, mostly white school, drew interest from 35 percent of eligible families versus the 2 percent the district had anticipated.[28] Later open enrollment offers throughout the 1960s were consistently oversubscribed. The cross-district Brockport Center for Innovation in Education and the Metropolitan World of Inquiry School, discussed in chapter 6, drew intense interest from Black families in the city and white families in the suburbs alike. Urban-Suburban today typically draws ten applicants for every open slot, even though it is well known that only the most qualified, easiest-to-educate students are typically accepted into participating suburban schools, and even though the program does no marketing and does not translate its application into languages other than English but rather garners interest strictly through word of mouth.

Polling, too, shows strong support in the Rochester area for desegregation measures, including a countywide school district. Polls conducted by the Siena College Research Institute in 2012, 2015, and 2018 showed that a countywide school district had the support of about 60 percent of Rochester

*Table 1* Opinion Poll Results for Desegregation Initiatives, 2018–19

| QUESTION | TOTAL | CITY | SUBURBS | WHITE | BLACK | HISPANIC |
|---|---|---|---|---|---|---|
| Believe children in city have same educational opportunity as those in suburbs | 23% | 21% | 23% | 25% | 13% | 36% |
| Support countywide schools | 53% | 60% | 49% | 47% | 78% | 63% |
| Support expanding charter schools | 65% | 65% | 65% | 63% | 76% | 68% |
| Support expanding Urban-Suburban program | 67% | 69% | 63% | 61% | 88% | 89% |
| Support expanding affordable housing in suburbs | 79% | 79% | 79% | 79% | 82% | 87% |

Source: *Democrat and Chronicle*/Rochester Area Community Foundation/Siena College Research Institute poll, Dec. 18, 2018, to Jan. 2, 2019 (seven hundred respondents, margin of error +/– 4.8 percent), available at https://www.documentcloud.org/documents/20986622-rochester-siena-poll-monroe-1218-crosstabs.

residents and more than 75 percent of Black residents throughout Monroe County. Even higher percentages of city residents and Black respondents favored the expansion of affordable housing in the suburbs.[29] In a separate 2016 poll, the overwhelming majority of urban respondents said they would send their child to a specialty magnet school where about half the children were low-income and the rest were middle-class—even if their own child were a racial minority, and even if it entailed a thirty-minute bus ride. Significantly, more than 60 percent of suburban parents also showed strong support for the above concept.[30]

The same finding is true on a national level. A 2019 Gallup poll, for instance, showed 78 percent Black support for government action toward desegregation. "Although there is a great deal of diversity of thought within the Black community, substantial majorities of Black respondents in recent surveys see segregation as providing inferior opportunities and view diversity as an important goal, and they favor a variety of policies to increase integration to access stronger schools," Gary Orfield and Danielle Jarvie wrote in 2020, summarizing the latest research.[31]

This is all to say that desegregation works as an educational strategy and has significant support among both white and nonwhite families and both in the city of Rochester and in the suburbs. The structural obstacles to cross-district desegregation, though, are formidable. Among other things, any nonjudicial attempt to revise the placement or effect of school district boundaries would require state legislation and buy-in from some or all of the school districts themselves. Two of the three recommendations offered in the conclusion of this book are aimed at this problem. The first calls for a comprehensive study of metropolitan solutions to inequality in education and other arenas in the Rochester area. Such a study has never been done despite nearly a century of debate over the merits of countywide schools, police, and government. The second recommendation is to use the existing framework of Urban-Suburban to increase equity immediately. The third and final recommendation is for extensive education for children and adults around the history and effects of racist discrimination and segregation, both locally and nationally. This root cause of inequality, racism, stretches back beyond the founding of our country and remains firmly in place today. It inevitably will derail any political or structural reform unless it is addressed directly. Confronting stubbornly entrenched racism head-on is, in the words of sociologist Dan Dodson, an opportunity for "education to bear down and do the job that it was expected to do in our historical heritage."[32] Successful antiracism work, with interest accruing from one generation to the next, is at heart the difference between desegregation and integration.

Dodson, a white man, was born in 1907 in the backwater ghost town of Panther's Chapel, Texas. He rose improbably to become one of the nation's foremost proponents of racial equality, helping broker Jackie Robinson's groundbreaking contract with the Brooklyn Dodgers, among other achievements. In a 1965 speech he described the difference between desegregation and integration by referring to Jesus's words in the Sermon on the Mount: "Whosoever shall compel thee to go a mile, go with him twain." The first mile, he said, is desegregation: "In this first or forced mile, we are dealing not with compassion or reconciliation, but with simple justice. . . . The law does not say that the superintendent of schools or the teachers have to love minority children sufficiently that they will allow them to come to the schools they run."[33]

This first mile of structural desegregation, Dodson conceded, "sounds harsh and foreboding," but cannot be passed over. Instead, he said, it must be used "as the springboard from which to demonstrate the tremendous power which America believes education possesses." This demonstration—the second mile—is integration, where students are not just sitting together but also learning and living together in a true community. "The great challenge which education faces is that of this second mile in which we can erase the existing footnotes to the American creed," Dodson said. He continued: "This is the mile in which education must intervene purposively in the lives of all children to the end that circumstance of birth, race, creed or color shall not deprive the lowliest of his chance. It calls upon the school to be a dynamic institution which takes all the children, erases the trauma of heritage, closes the academic gaps, and brings them into full scale participation."[34]

The history contained in this book provides an essential roadmap for the second mile of integration. Indeed, it is mere trivia unless brandished in the ongoing fight for justice. Phebe Ray, Walter Cooper, and Lillian Colquhoun serve as an inspiration to stand with integrity in the face of opposition. Lucy Colman, Jerome Balter, and Norman Gross show the importance of white allies demonstrating their commitment to equality. The blood spilled fifty years ago in front of Charlotte, Jefferson, and Franklin High Schools is a reminder that change does not come easily.

Fifty-five years after Dodson spoke, his words can be recast with cautious optimism. He took for granted fierce, near-unanimous white opposition to desegregation as was seen at the time in the South, but white, justice-minded parents and community members can make their voices heard. He assumed desegregation would happen under the supervision of white educators inside "the schools they run," but such a change today could happen—must happen—with leadership from all affected communities. He described "the trauma of heritage," but good educators in the twenty-first century know that Black students' heritage is much richer than that. This book contains many horror stories about racial desegregation, but we are not obligated to continue reenacting those stories in our own time.

As noted above, there are many who do not take integrated education as their goal. For them, too, the story of how Rochester schools arrived at their current state is deeply relevant. It is important to understand the past working of racial discrimination so we can recognize it in the present. It is important to honor those who fought for their children's equal education in the past, no matter the outcome of their efforts. It is important to memorialize those efforts and the forces that opposed them and hold both up to historical scrutiny, even if we doubt whether our community today has the courage to act. One day, perhaps, it will.

# Chapter 1

# The African School

The man's name is lost, but his question reverberates.

Why, he asked, should his taxes go to support a school from which his children were excluded? It was January 1841. The unnamed man addressing the Rochester Board of Education was, of course, Black.

It could have been the farmer Solomon Dorsey or the barber Elijah Warr. It could have been Nelson or Richard Picket, two brothers and blacksmiths boarding together on High Street, or George Dixon, who waited tables at the Rochester House hotel. It could have been Samuel Brown or William Earl or Charles Thurell or any of the other dozens of common laborers crowded into the Black section of the Third Ward in flimsy, hastily built wood-frame houses, kindling waiting for a fire to come along and reduce them to ashes. It is no surprise that the petitioner's name is lost; the surprise is that his question was recorded at all. It was one of only a handful of times in the city's first generation of public schooling that the input of Black families was noted. More often they were ignored and left to whatever teacher and whatever room could be obtained for the lowest price, if public money had to be dedicated at all. Better yet if they could be "aided by the munificence of their friends."[1]

When such munificence fell through, as it did more than once, the trustees did not upend their budget to replace it. That is why the unnamed man was at the meeting in the first place. Nine years after the trustees had first affirmed their responsibility to educate Rochester's few Black children, there existed no public school to receive them. The absence apparently had escaped notice, and the father's petition left the school trustees red-faced. They referred it to a committee and the committee referred it to John Spencer, the state superintendent of common schools.

"It is certainly desirable that this unfortunate class should have all the benefits of instruction," Spencer responded. "The laws contemplate their instruction and provision must be made for it." But he elaborated: "There must, however, be some discretion by the Trustees. Persons having infected diseases—idiots—infants, incapable of receiving any benefit from the school—and persons over 21, who may be deemed too old—may be excluded. . . . The admission of colored children is in many places so odious, that whites will not attend. In such cases the Trustees would be justified in excluding them, and furnishing them a separate room."[2]

In the nineteenth century as in the centuries that followed, segregation in Rochester schools took a number of different forms. There was a time when Black children had essentially no access to public schools, followed by a period of explicit segregation written into local law, then a gradual unsanctioned spread of Black children into neighborhood schools. Throughout the period preceding the Black school's final closure in 1856, parents such as the unnamed Black father of 1841 had a difficult task in advocating for their children. Hardly any of the adults were themselves educated; many had escaped slavery or been emancipated. With few exceptions, the men worked as laborers and the women as servants in the homes of the white well-to-do. Black residents were outnumbered fifteen to one by white residents of the city and effectively unrepresented on the board of education. Still, the credit for desegregation is theirs. They petitioned and organized and, in the last resort, withheld their children from school rather than expose them to what they believed were unsafe conditions and prejudiced instruction. When the Black school closed in 1856, Rochester was the first city in New York with fully desegregated schools. Black families then did not know, of course, that the greater fight for desegregation would remain active more than 150 years later.

The story of Black education in Rochester begins with Austin Steward, the city's first prominent Black resident. His arrival in the city in turn illustrates the circumstances of Black life in Rochester in the early nineteenth century. Steward was born into slavery in Prince William County, Virginia, about 1793, and was sold with his family at age seven to William Helm, a penurious minor landholder with a penchant for violence and gambling. Helm was related to William Fitzhugh, one of Rochester's founding fathers.[3]

Helm sold his Virginia property in about 1801 and relocated to Sodus Bay, forty miles east of Rochester, entirely unprepared for the rigors of life in what Steward called "almost an unbroken wilderness." He ordered the Black people he owned to clear the dense forest without horses, nearly starving them in the process. At one point, Steward wrote in his memoir, "we were now obliged . . . to gather up all the old bones we could find, break them up fine and then boil them; which made a sort of broth sufficient barely to sustain life." Within two years Helm had relocated to Bath, Steuben County, where he hired Steward out to serve as a carriage driver for an equally devilish man named Joseph Robinson: "He was cross and heartless in his family, as well as tyrannical and cruel to those in his employ; and having hired me as a 'slave boy,' he appeared to feel at full liberty to wreak his brutal passion on me at any time, whether I deserved rebuke or not. . . . He would frequently draw from the cart-tongue a heavy iron pin, and beat me over the head with it, so unmercifully that he frequently sent the blood flowing over my scanty apparel, and from that to the ground, before he could be satisfied."[4]

This experience with Robinson caused Steward to suffer from debilitating headaches for the rest of his life but ultimately led to his liberation. New York's gradual abolition law of 1799 prohibited hiring out enslaved people as Helm had done. Steward learned of the violation in 1815, declared himself free with the help of a manumission society in Canandaigua and went to work for the Quaker abolitionist Otis Comstock.[5] Immediately after gaining his freedom and collecting his first wages, Steward enrolled in an academy in Farmington. He arrived there, age twenty-three, "yet to learn what most boys of eight years know," and continued to attend classes for three winters. In the spring of 1817 he moved to Rochester and soon opened a meat market—the community's first Black-owned business, and the immediate target of vandalism and other "unmanly proceedings." Less than a year later, in the summer of 1818, he began teaching a Sunday school for "the neglected children of our oppressed race." He wrote in his memoir: "For a while it was well attended, and I hoped to be able to benefit in some measure the poor and despised colored children, but the parents interested themselves very little in the undertaking, and it shortly came to naught. So strong was the prejudice then existing against the colored people, that very few of the negroes seemed to have any courage or ambition to rise from the abject degradation in which the estimation of the white man had placed [them]."[6]

Steward's 1818 effort marked the first formal educational opportunity for Black children in Rochester. It was apparently fleeting, however; he makes no further mention of it in his memoir. He later joined with school master Zenas Freeman to teach another Sunday school for young Black students. One of his pupils was early Rochester's other leading Black citizen, Thomas James. Born into slavery in Canajoharie in 1804, James escaped about 1819 and settled in Rochester in 1823. "As a slave I had never been inside of a school or a church, and I knew nothing of letters or religion," he wrote. "The wish to learn awoke in me almost from the moment I set foot in the place." He enrolled in Steward and Freeman's school on Buffalo Street and supplemented this basic formal education with lessons from the clerks at the warehouse where he worked. He joined the African Methodist Episcopal Society in 1823, then began teaching a school for Black children on Favor Street, the later site of AME Zion Church, in 1828. He purchased the lot for the church in 1830 and was ordained as a minister in 1833. "I had been called Tom as a slave, and they called me Jim at the warehouse," he wrote. "I put both together when I reached manhood, and was ordained as Rev. Thomas James."[7] AME Zion received substantial financial support both from individual white clergy in Rochester and from the various Sunday school associations that had sprung up in the city. Given James's emergence as a civic leader and Steward's departure for the Wilberforce colony in Canada in 1831, it seems likely that the Favor Street Sunday school was the primary educational option for Black children and adults prior to 1832.

One drop-out from this time period left a brief record of his educational experience. Austin Reed, perhaps named after Austin Steward, was born in Rochester in 1823. His book, *The Life and Adventures of a Haunted Convict*, is the earliest known prison memoir from an African American writer. Reed completed it in 1858 while between stints at Auburn State Prison, having "broke[n] through the restraints of my mother and [fallen] victim to vice and crime." Reed began his story with the death of his father when he was five years old and pinpointed the moment that his education, likely under Steward's tutelage, went sideways. "[My mother] then gave me a severe whipping and sent me off to school," he wrote. "On my way to school I met several boys who ask me to join their company that day, that they was goin' to have some fun. I stuff my book into my pocket and joined their company."[8]

The establishment and initial development of schools for Black children in Rochester coincided with two other important trends, one local and one national. The first was the growth of Rochester itself, both commercially and as a hotbed of evangelism. The second was the advent in the United States of common schools, publicly funded and widely accessible.

Rochester's explosive expansion in the early nineteenth century, from a crude mill town on the western frontier to a bustling commercial port and nexus of regional civic activism, was one of the most remarkable and remarked-on stories in the young United States. A traveler to Rochester marveled in 1819: "Nothing I have heard of or seen . . . can boast of so rapid growth as the village of Rochester." The population increased from 331 in 1815 to 7,669 in 1826 and then to 12,252 in 1834, the year the city was incorporated, making it the fastest-growing municipality in the country during that time.[9] Even more dramatic was the growth in commercial production, particularly wheat. Output from Rochester mills increased from 65 barrels of wheat in 1823 to 460,000 in 1835, due entirely to the greater ease of getting goods to market on the newly built Erie Canal. Concomitant advances occurred in every sphere, from manufacturing and service industries to infrastructure and housing. Rochester, in short, was "a place of enchantment," a visitor wrote in 1825, "and [you] can scarcely believe your own senses, that all should have been the work of so short a period."[10]

The canal's role in the maturation and spread of the social movements for which the region became renowned was no less significant. As historian Whitney Cross wrote: "In matters religious and moral, [the canal's opening in 1825] separates the period of scattered, episodic eccentricities from the era of major, significant enthusiasms."[11] The greatest of these enthusiasms came with the preaching of the young firebrand Charles Grandison Finney. The name "Burned-Over District" refers to the belief that, by the time of Finney's arrival, western and central New York had been so thoroughly plowed by earlier waves of evangelists that there was scarcely anyone left to convert. As the population around the Genesee Valley swelled in the decade after the completion of the Erie Canal, though, Finney gave the lie to that claim and invested the term with an entirely different meaning. From September 1830 to March 1831, Finney preached nearly a hundred times in Rochester and met ceaselessly with "anxious sinners" eager to hear his message of salvation through faith and works. The local Protestant churches gained hundreds of members. At one overcrowded meeting in the First Presbyterian Church the walls and ceiling began to crumble, causing a stampede from the building, including out the windows into the Erie Canal.

The spiritual energy that Finney unleashed in Rochester and elsewhere soon translated to the promotion of social causes, principally abolitionism and temperance. As historian Milton Sernett wrote: "For those in the

Burned-over District who had pledged to seek good and shun evil, it was a small step from thinking in terms of individual regeneration to concluding that there needed to be a national conversion on the question of slavery."[12]

While the Erie Canal and the ideas that traveled its length were redefining upstate New York, towns and cities across the country were grappling with a changing sense of their obligation regarding the education of children in their communities. For the first half century of the independent United States, and certainly during the colonial period, there was no single recognizable educational paradigm. Opportunities varied dramatically based on geography, social class, race, and gender. Young male aristocrats, particularly in the Northeast, might learn from a private tutor and then advance to a preparatory academy before attending an early university. Girls might spend several years in a school of their own learning etiquette, dancing, and French—skills meant to help in marriage, if not in a career. Black children would be lucky if a local church sponsored an "African school" providing some rudimentary education, and poor children of any race might be excluded from school altogether if their families relied on them for income.

Just as important, the current distinctions between public, private, and parochial models were yet to be established. As the education historian Lawrence Cremin wrote about academies, one component of the educational ecosystem of the early nineteenth century: "[They] came in every size, shape and form, and under every variety of sponsorship. . . . Some were tied to local communities, some to church assemblies, some to government agencies. Some were supported by endowments, some by taxes, some by subscriptions, some by tuition rates, and most by some combination of the four. . . . [They] seemed infinitely adaptable to particular needs and opportunities."[13] Sunday schools such as those founded by Steward and James in Rochester were an important element in the mix of educational models. They emerged in the beginning of the nineteenth century as a way to provide basic, low-cost (the teachers were largely volunteers) schooling to children and adults, white and Black, who would have been excluded from more prestigious opportunities. From the perspective of the brahmin class, they also provided a means of control over the poor by preaching religion, humility, and temperance. Lessons were mostly limited to learning to read, particularly the Bible. A Sunday school teacher in Geneva, New York, bragged that a young Black girl in her class had recited 709 verses of Scripture in a single session. Steward called the Sunday school "that most useful of institutions, [where] you may learn without loss of time or money, that of which none should be ignorant—to read."[14]

Out of this stew, replicated in cities across the country, slowly developed some common ideas about public education and the purpose it should serve. "Never will wisdom preside in the halls of legislation, and its profound utterances be recorded on the pages of the statute book, until common schools . . . create more far-seeing intelligence and a purer morality than has ever yet existed among communities of men," Massachusetts Board of Education Secretary Horace Mann, the person most associated with the common schools movement, wrote in 1848. Crucially, these common schools would largely wipe clear the current class-based hierarchy, which had one track of schooling for aspiring scholars and another for everyone else. The common school, Cremin wrote, "would be common, not as a school for the common people . . . but rather as a school common to all people." It would cut across "all creeds, classes and backgrounds," though the implications for Black students specifically were left unenumerated.[15]

Along with Massachusetts, New York made some early strides toward creating common schools. Its regents described to the legislature in 1795 how common schools "must enrich the *pastures of the wilderness* and cause the *little hills* to rejoice on every side." Later that year the state put aside its first funds dedicated to "the encouragement and maintenance of elementary schools," requiring a local match. A permanent fund was established in 1805, and the first Act for the establishment of Common Schools was passed in 1812. This came just in time for Rochester, where the first public schoolhouse was built on Fitzhugh Street in 1813.[16]

Both the social reforms of the Burned-Over District and the movement toward common schools were pursued according to high ideals of personal and civic good. In each realm, though, a significant gap existed between theory and practice as far as people of color were concerned. If the goal of universal education was the creation of a responsible electorate, then Black children (and white girls) needed not be considered. Regarding higher education for Black children, one New York City newspaper asked: "What benefit can it be to a waiter or coachman to read Horace, or be a profound mathematician?" Advocates there pointed to the disparity between the "splendid, almost palatial edifices" where white children studied while Black children were "painfully neglected and positively degraded . . . pent up in filthy neighborhoods, in old and dilapidated buildings, held down to low associations and gloomy surroundings."[17]

To be sure, white progressives played a critical role in the rise of abolitionism and in establishing Rochester as an important center for various nationally significant social movements. In the thirty-year fight to desegregate the city's schools, however, white protagonists were scarce. As will be seen, entreaties from Rochester's few Black families for access to quality, integrated schools were by turns ignored, sidestepped, and delayed. When change did come, it was in response to a powerful set of pressures: families' protests, the mounting financial strain of operating additional schools, and several years of persistent public criticism from one of the most famous men in the country at that time.

"Prejudice is found also, in many of our schools—even in those to which colored children are admitted," Steward wrote in the 1850s, having observed the state of Black education in Rochester for more than three decades. "There is so much distinction made by prejudice, that the poor, timid colored children might about as well stay at home, as go to a school where they feel that they are looked upon as inferior, however much they may try to excel."[18]

For the first full generation of Black children to grow up in Rochester, the provision of simple lessons was a matter of private charity rather than of the public interest. The initial small step toward change came on January 23, 1832, when a group of thirty-two parents petitioned the state legislature to fund the establishment of a separate Black school: "The fact is too notorious, that [our] children are despised, called negroes, and completely discouraged by the white children. We do humbly believe that if the prayer of our petitions be granted, our children might be encouraged to learn: and although they are black, they may be made comely members of society—there they could enjoy Sunday-school privileges, and many other blessings might flow from such an institution, and we, their parents, would forever feel ourselves under the most solemn obligation."[19]

The petition was cosigned by the local commissioner of common schools, John McDonald. He also sent a separate note to the legislature adding that the petition had the support of "a very respectable portion of the other inhabitants of the place." He continued:

> Under the present organization our schools are open to all, and yet it is obvious that in them the literary and moral interests of the colored scholar can scarcely prosper. He is reproached with his color; he is taunted with his origin, and if permitted to mingle with others in the joyous pastimes of youth, it is of favor, not of right. Thus the law which may declare him free, now or in prospect, may be a dead letter. His energies are confined; his hopes are crushed; his mind is in chains; and he is still a slave.

> The situation of our colored population generally, not only interests our sympathies, but demands our exertions for its melioration; and your committee are unanimous in the opinion, that the interests of this unhappy class would be most promoted by granting the prayer of the petitioners, and constituting them a separate school.[20]

McDonald's note implies that at least some Black children had been admitted to the half-dozen or so existing common schools before 1832. It should continually be kept in mind in any case that from Rochester's first settling until well into the twentieth century, its Black residents made up a tiny fraction of the population. In 1834 there were about 360 Black people in Rochester, less than 3 percent of the overall population. That included about a hundred school-age children, of whom eighty-three were recorded as having attended at least some school in the winter of 1833–34, the second year of operation for the publicly funded school. The majority before then were surely limited to Sunday school, meaning that any Black children who crossed the thresholds of mostly white public school buildings would have been a brave few indeed.[21]

Rochester would not have been the only community in New York where schools were segregated in fact if not in policy. The state superintendent of schools had reported in 1824 that, "from habit or prejudice, or from some other cause," few if any Black students attended public schools, though there was no law prohibiting them from doing so.[22] Black residents of Lockport requested funds to open a segregated school because "the customs of the county do not permit us—neither indeed do we desire to join in society with those of a different complexion." In Buffalo, a nominal tuition fee barred poor Black families from public schools.[23]

The state legislature quickly approved the 1832 petition and provided an unknown sum of money for "the children of color in the village of Rochester to be taught in one or more separate schools." The local common school commissioners were enlisted as trustees, suggesting that the school had graduated from a charity interest to a governmental function. The distinction remained unclear, though. The schoolhouse itself, at Spring and Sophia Streets in the Third Ward, was purchased and refitted "by the assistance of a few friends of the colored people." A Black man, William Bishop, was hired to teach.[24]

The legislature did not finalize its work until April 1832, meaning that the school likely opened the following fall. In February 1833, trustees Elihu Marshall and James W. Smith toured the new school and reported that though the students' proficiency was "beyond our anticipation," parents were unable to continue to pay the teacher's salary.[25] As a result the school closed one year later, in March 1834. According to the local abolitionist newspaper, *The Rights of Man*: "The teacher was a colored man; possessing a very respectable English education, and all the qualifications of a teacher of a common school. . . . But he has now closed it for two reasons—first, the house, which was rented, has been sold and has gone into other hands for a school for the more favored and wealthy whites, and second, for the want of funds; the colored people being too poor to pay him for his services, even with the aid of the public money."[26]

No new Black school was opened after the Sophia Street school closed for want of space and funds; the introduction of public money had proven insufficient to maintain a school for the hundred or so school-age Black children. Those children again had to depend on charity for their education until the establishment of the Rochester Board of Education in 1941.

There are a few reasons why education for Black children may have fallen by the wayside in the mid-1830s. Rochester was officially incorporated as a city in April 1834, just a month after the Black school closed. The administration of schools was then transferred from the towns of Brighton and Gates to the new city's common council, which may have lacked enthusiasm for the subject or at least neglected to take it up promptly among its other responsibilities. The still-small Black community was also undergoing a leadership transition. Thomas James left Rochester in 1835 to establish a church in Syracuse and did not return for twenty-one years. Austin Steward, who had moved to Canada in 1831, returned to Rochester in 1837 but stayed only a few years before relocating permanently to Canandaigua in 1842. He remained a prominent businessman and antislavery advocate in the region but necessarily had a lesser role in Rochester itself.[27] Frederick Douglass, meanwhile, did not arrive in Rochester until 1847 (having been encouraged to do so by James, among others). Thus, as in the earlier period, Rochester's Black churches continued to be the primary locus for Black education. *The Rights of Man* reported in 1834 that there were three Black churches in the city, including two, Abyssinian Baptist and AME Zion, with Sunday schools.[28]

Seven years passed before the next recorded public protest against the lack of schools for Black children. It came in January 1841 from the unidentified Black father who asked for tax relief as long as his children were barred from the common schools.[29]

The board of education established a committee to investigate the question and asked John Spencer for guidance. He responded in February 1841 that, though the council was required to provide some instruction for "this unfortunate class," it was not obligated to admit Black students to the general public schools. The council followed this advice and instructed the school trustees, "for the moral good as well of the colored as of the white population . . . to make provisions for the said children in a school separate by themselves, and when such provisions are made to reject them from [the white students'] school house."[30]

This resolution, unanimously passed on February 11, 1841, made school segregation the law for the first time in Rochester's history. The white community's position on its responsibilities regarding the education of Black children was clear. Guidance from the state education department and school leaders' own internal deliberations had established that Black schools must be operated as part of the public education system. At the same time, the state and city governments had definitively decided that the two systems, Black and white, should be separate. It did not take long, however, for the newly constituted board of education to realize it would be much more expensive to build a separate school for so few Black children than to disperse them among more than a dozen already existing schools throughout the city.

In July 1841 the board received an estimate of $1,500 to build a separate Black schoolhouse and promptly deemed that expenditure "inexpedient." It opted instead to rent space in the Third Ward for the Black school. A white man, Leonard Risingh, was appointed as teacher after an unsuccessful search for a Black teacher. Austin Steward, temporarily back in the city, was named a school trustee along with prominent Black merchant and abolitionist Jacob Morris and tailor John Bishop.[31] In its 1850 review, the board of education recorded: "The school went on, for aught the committee can discover, quietly and successfully," until the next legislative action was taken in 1845. This avowed ignorance is indicative of the value the white community placed on Black education at the time, and no record exists of the school trustees reporting to the board as they were charged to do. The 1844 city directory shows that 152 students attended the Black school in a rented space on Spring Street with Samuel Boothby, a white man, serving as principal.[32]

In 1845 the board passed a pair of local laws affirming its duty to provide public schools for Black children and exempting them from taxation until such schools were provided. At the same time it again formally barred Black children from white schools, "except with the consent of the Board of Education." That last provision had the unintended consequence of drawing a request for the very consent it mentioned. In March 1846, a Black woman named Phebe Ray asked that her children be allowed to attend the public school on Chestnut Street, nearest her home on Mechanic's Alley. The request was referred to a committee and resurfaced the following month as a report from the legal committee. It was promptly tabled and abandoned.[33]

In May 1846 the district opened its second Black school, this one in a building on Washington Street rented from the Female Charitable Society and taught by a white woman named Mary Conning "while funds last." After that Conning was to "continue it by subscription until another appropriation"—again showing the holes in the public support for education of Black children. The two-school arrangement only lasted one school year; the Washington Street building remained open, with Conning staying on as teacher. The school continued at that location until 1849.[34]

In the meantime Black parents continued to protest the condition in which their children were kept. In March 1846 a gathering of Black residents produced a lengthy resolution decrying the "almost insurmountable difficulties" to the children's advancement: "Our children, however great pains we may take to have them neat and tidy in their persons, and respectful in their demeanor, are, in most parts of this, as well as other states, in which we are nominally free, excluded from the benefit of common schools, either through the prejudice of teachers, trustees, boards of education, or of the children of many whites, who, by disgusting exhibitions of abuse toward the colored child, show that they have derived but little benefit from the more favorable circumstances in which they have been placed."[35]

Comparatively little information is available about whether Black children were allowed in the region's various private schools in the mid-nineteenth century. There is evidence that at least one of them was desegregated. The Clover Street Seminary, at Clover Street and Elmwood Avenue in Brighton, was established in 1838 by Isaac Moore, with his sister-in-law Celestia Bloss, a member of a prominent local abolitionist family, as teacher and eventually principal. Bloss's brother William was a close confidant of Frederick Douglass and later played a role in desegregating the Rochester public school system. One of the teachers at Clover Street Seminary was Myrtilla Miner, a white woman who went on to found the Normal School for Colored Girls in Washington, DC, in 1851. Her stay in Rochester was brief (1843–44) but profound, according to a later profile: "In the Rochester school . . . were two free colored girls, and this association was the first circumstance to turn her thoughts to the work to which she gave her life."[36]

Black education in Rochester prior to 1849 was an inconsistent institution, advancing and receding according to political circumstances and the presence or absence of prominent advocates like Steward and James. Bursts of advocacy from Rochester's early Black residents in 1832, and perhaps again in the 1840s, returned real but short-lived gains. Phebe Ray's Black children were better off educationally in 1846 than she would have been as a child, but they were hardly any closer to the status of the city's white students.

The next, boisterous period of change can be dated to October 28, 1847. On that date, a friend then living in Boston wrote a letter to the Quaker abolitionist Amy Post:

> My dear Amy,
>
> I have finally decided on publishing the North Star in Rochester, and to make that city my future home. I am now buying type and all the little etc. of a printing establishment. I shall probably be able to issue my first number as early as the middle of November—any delay can only do the enterprise harm—I have therefore resolved to commence at once. . . .
>
> Yours sincerely,
> F Douglass[37]

Frederick Douglass was born into slavery in Maryland in 1818. As a child he acquired some basic reading skills from Sophia Auld before her husband, Douglass's master Hugh Auld, put a stop to it:

> Mr. Auld found out what was going on, and at once forbade Mrs. Auld to instruct me further, telling her, among other things, that it was unlawful, as well as unsafe, to teach a slave to read. . . . "Now," he said, "if you teach that n—— (speaking of myself) how to read, there would be no keeping him. It would forever unfit him to be a slave."
>
> These words sank deep into my heart, stirred up sentiments within that lay slumbering, and called into existence an entirely new train of thought. . . . I now understood what had been to me a most perplexing difficulty—to wit, the white man's power to enslave the black man. It was a grand achievement, and I prized it highly. From that moment, I understood the pathway from slavery to freedom. . . . I set out with high hope, and a fixed purpose, at whatever cost of trouble, to learn how to read.[38]

From that slight spark Douglass rose to become one of the greatest men of American letters of the nineteenth century. His primary focus, of course, was the abolition of slavery. He escaped in 1838 by boarding a train heading north with borrowed identification documents and the help of his wife Anna. Among the innumerable other topics that captured his attention, though, was education for Black children—including his own. His own experience had taught him its importance, not only in freeing the enslaved but in preparing them for a life of liberty. "Colored men and women, who in view of the circumstances surrounding them, fail to appreciate the worth of [education] . . . cannot be regarded as otherwise than enemies to themselves, to the class with whom they are identified, and to the God who created them," he wrote. His arrival in Rochester in late 1847 gave new life to native-born Black Rochesterians' work in the area of public education for their children. Using his talents as a journalist, community organizer, and public speaker, Douglass helped bring about the end of formal segregation in the city's schools, even if the change occurred too late for some of his own children.

He was primed for the work through his own experience in slavery. He also served an importance apprenticeship of sorts in New Bedford, Massachusetts, where he settled just weeks after fleeing Baltimore in 1838. The New Bedford public schools had been desegregated that year, and he shortly struck up a relationship with the abolitionist William Henry Garrison, who in the following decade was to devote much energy to the integration of schools in the North. During Douglass's time in Massachusetts, the state witnessed the country's most intense battle on the topic of school segregation to date.[39]

Frederick and Anna Murray Douglass arrived in Rochester with four young children. The following summer they arranged for their oldest, nine-year-old Rosetta, to attend Seward Seminary, the city's most prestigious academy for girls. Sarah Seward had founded her school immediately after moving to Rochester in 1833 and two years later relocated from Spring Street to a newly constructed building on a five-acre lot on Alexander Street, then the city's eastern border. The school attracted from seventy-five to a hundred girls each year, many coming from elsewhere in New York, other states, and even Canada. Seward married in 1841 and leadership of the school fell to the head teacher, Lucilia Tracy.

In 1849, the girls' curriculum consisted largely of the "ornamental branches"—for example, the growing and arranging of flowers in place of biology. It qualified nonetheless as the city's best educational option for girls and, for Rosetta Douglass, had the advantage of being located just a few minutes' walk from her home. It would be the first school experience for Rosetta, who to that point had boarded and studied in Albany with Abigail and Lydia Mott, Quaker abolitionists and cousins of Lucretia Mott.[40]

Douglass was away from Rochester when the school year began. He returned to find that Rosetta, instead of being seated with the rest of the class, "was merely thrust into a room separate from all other scholars, and in this prison-like solitary confinement received the occasional visits of a teacher appointed to instruct her." Tracy, the principal, told him the board of trustees had objected to his daughter's presence and that she didn't feel free to disregard their wishes, having "remembered how much they had done for her in sustaining the institution." She offered, though, that if he and Rosetta could tolerate the treatment for a semester or so, "the prejudice might be overcome, and the child admitted into the school with the other young ladies and misses."[41]

While Douglass deliberated with his wife, Tracy went back to her students and asked them each individually whether they objected to Rosetta's presence. The way she phrased the question, Douglass wrote, was "well calculated to rouse their prejudices," yet each of the girls, "thanks to the uncorruptible virtue of childhood and youth, . . . [said] they welcomed my child among them, to share with them the blessings and privileges of the school, and when asked where she should sit if admitted, several young ladies shouted, "By me, by me, by me." Tracy then took the question to each of the girls' parents, asking whether they were comfortable having a Black child in the school. Of them, according to Douglass, only one objected: Horatio Gates Warner, the influential Democratic lawyer and editor of the Rochester *Daily Advertiser*.

If Warner had hoped his objection would be confidential, he soon learned otherwise. Douglass wrote a blistering three-page open letter to Warner in the *North Star*; it was later reprinted in full in newspapers across the country:

> If this were a private affair, only affecting myself and my family, I should possibly allow it to pass without attracting public attention to it; but such is not the case. It is a deliberate attempt to degrade and injure a large class of persons, whose rights and feelings have been the common sport of yourself, and persons such as yourself, for ages, and I think it is unwise to allow you to do so with impunity. Thank God, oppressed and plundered as we are and have been, we are not without help. We have a press, open and free, and have ample means by which we are able to proclaim your wrongs as a people, and your own infamy, and that proclamation shall be as complete as the means in my power can make it.

Three other Seward Seminary students, Douglass reported, left the school as a result of the controversy over his daughter, and another three changed their plans to begin there "because it has given its sanction to that antidemocratic, and ungodly caste." Rosetta, meanwhile, was accepted into another school, "quite as respectable and *equally* Christian to the one from which she was excluded."

Douglass concluded his letter to Warner, who by this point surely regretted his earlier stance: "Now I should like to know how much better you are than me, and how much better your children than mine? We are both worms of the dust, and our children like us. We differ in color, it is true (and not much in that respect), but who is to decide which color is most pleasing to God, or most honorable among men? But I do not wish to waste words or argument on one whom I take to be as destitute of honorable feeling, as he has shown himself full of pride and prejudice."[42] This incident, which occurred less than a year after Douglass moved to Rochester, illustrates the tension he endured throughout his twenty-five years in the city. When purchasing his house on Alexander Street, he had already faced opposition from white neighbors. Then, as at the Seward Seminary, children showed the most acceptance and affection, gathering to hear him sing and play the violin on his porch on warm evenings. Even as Douglass's wife Anna worked tirelessly with him in hosting countless Black people escaping slavery on their way to Canada, she found that racism "ran rampant" in Rochester and made few friends in the city. The final blow came in 1872, when the Douglass home on South Avenue was burned to the ground, an apparent arson, while they were away. "My pathway was not entirely free from thorns in Rochester," Douglass wrote in retrospect. "The vulgar prejudice against color, so common to Americans, met me in several disagreeable forms."[43]

Warner never responded publicly to Douglass, but neither did he or the school relent. Rosetta never returned to Seward Seminary. The experience was not the family's only personal brush with racism in Rochester schools. Douglass wrote in his *Life and Times* that his children were barred from the nearby public school but instead would have had to attend the "inferior colored school" in the Third Ward. "I hardly need say that I was not prepared to submit tamely to this proscription, any more than I had been to submit to slavery, so I had them taught at home for a while, by Miss Thayer," he wrote. Phebe Thayer was a Quaker governess and a relative of Amy and Isaac Post.[44] This dispute was likely in the fall of 1849; Frederick Douglass Jr., then seven years old, later recalled that "the colored children attending public schools were sent home on account of their color," returning several months later after sustained agitation from his father. Douglass argued the case to Superintendent Reuben Jones and several trustees in a private meeting in 1850, Jones later recalled, making "an address which I do not believe was ever excelled. . . . I felt at the time that I wished the whole city of Rochester might hear the argument, and I have often regretted that it is lost to the world."[45]

At different times the five Douglass children attended both School 15, near their Alexander Street house, and School 13, on Hickory Street, nearer to the South Avenue home to which they moved in 1852.[46] Only the eldest, Rosetta, ever attended college. Jones in later years called her "one of the brightest [students] in any of the schools of the city." The other children received more practical training, partly at the suggestion of their mother. They were kept home from school one day a week to help with the printing and distribution of Douglass's newspapers and subsequently stopped attending altogether once their father could find them apprenticeships in typesetting or some other trade. For Frederick Douglass Jr., this occurred at age twelve; for Charles Remond Douglass, age sixteen.[47]

Even after the schools were desegregated, the Douglass children, like other Black children, faced intense social opprobrium. Charles Remond Douglass described the experience of his sister Annie before her early death in 1860: "The taunts of the school children whose parents were pro-slavery made the further attendance at No. 13 school of my youngest sister Annie and myself intolerable, so mother took her out of school at the age of eleven and sent her to a private teacher."[48]

Caution is required in drawing a straight line between Rosetta Douglass's rejection from Seward Seminary and her father's subsequent participation in the campaign to integrate the public schools. For one thing, Seward Seminary was private, not public, and her dismissal from it did not mark the end of the family's woes with Rochester schools. For another, school segregation had been an important cause for Douglass even before he moved to Rochester and likely would have drawn his energy in any case. The episode did, however, serve to publicize the matter dramatically and perhaps increased the urgency with which the public school authorities considered their own situation.

The debates over school segregation of 1848–51 proceeded along a number of contested fronts. Douglass's arrival helped energize and give voice to Rochester's Black community, whose protests during that time were more forceful and effective than they had ever been previously. They were supported by a growing number of white people. The abolition movement had gained great momentum by 1848. Two antislavery societies had been established in Rochester in 1833 and the State Convention of the Colored Citizens of New York was held in the city in 1843 and again in 1846.[49] Social progressives, including on the school board, were perhaps finding it harder to overlook discrimination in their own community while moralizing against southern slave owners. "Our white countrymen [once] could say the negro ought to be free [and] they felt they had uttered a radical and philanthropic sentiment," Douglass wrote in 1849. "Something more than the mere act of emancipation is now thought to be due to this long neglected and deeply injured people." Last, and perhaps decisively, the school board suffered increasingly under the financial burden of operating a separate building for the city's few Black students, who otherwise could easily have been accommodated in the common schools. This fiscal crisis was fostered in turn by boycotts and other protests of the Black community.[50]

All these pressures were evident in August 1849 as the school board members deliberated on whether to open a second school for Black children on the east side of the city. A budget analysis showed that educating Black students separately at a second building would cost at least three times more per pupil than educating students in the common schools. This alone, they believed, was enough to foreclose the idea of keeping the segregated schools open. More generally, they continued:

> If then, as we trust, we have shown that the system of exclusive schools for colored children cannot be maintained upon the grounds of economy nor *utility*, upon what ground, then, was the system first established, and why has it been maintained? We answer, it was first conceived and has been maintained solely . . . in order to gratify a morbid public sentiment against the colored race. . . .
>
> But we trust that the enlightened, generous and philanthropic portion of the citizens of Rochester are as willing to open the doors of their "Free Schools" to those whose only impediment is their color, as they are and ever have been to the poor, destitute and degraded of other nations and climes. Why should we close the doors of our schools upon those who can boast that they are *American* citizens, created by the same overruling Providence, children too who "hunger and thirst" for the blessings of knowledge and education—who have as much natural right to enjoy the beneficent effects of our "Free Schools" as those of a lighter hue?[51]

Writing in the following week's *North Star*, Frederick Douglass wholeheartedly approved the Committee on Colored Schools' recommendation, saying that it would be "a noble example of justice and liberality worthy of the city of Rochester." He warned, though, against a scheme to circulate a petition among Black residents asking for the preservation of at least one Black school. "We should feel the most intense mortification if, while many of the most respectable white people of this city should be in favor of admitting our children to equal privileges in the use of our common schools, a single colored man should be found opposed to the measure," he wrote.[52]

Nonetheless, the resolution—to close the sole Black school and disperse its students among the common schools—was not adopted. Several board members raised objections. One, John Quinn, noted that gender barriers had only recently been taken down and pointed out that "no citizen would want a colored boy sitting in school beside his daughter." Instead, an east-side Black school, just north of Main Street between St. Paul Street and Clinton Avenue, was opened, and the board went scouting for alternate sites for a west-side school, as the current school's North Washington Street site apparently had become untenable.[53]

The board committee returned in November 1849 with the recommendation of renting space in the basement of AME Zion Church, and the plan was quickly adopted. From Douglass's perspective, the city's Black citizens had not only lost the present integration battle but had taken a major step back in finding themselves in the "low, damp and dark cellar" of the church. He heaped scorn on the "stupid creatures who officiate as Trustees in Zion Church" for providing a lifeline to the segregated system:

> For some time past [the school trustees] have been at a loss to find a place whereon to build a school-house for colored children; when almost wearied out in the pursuit, and almost ready (from sheer necessity) to admit colored children into the district schools, where they have a right to be, we record with shame and confusion the scandalous fact that *the trustees of the Zion Methodist Church, for the paltry consideration of two hundred dollars*, offered the use of the cellar of their meeting-house, and have thus become the servile tools of their own proscription and degradation. For such base and cringing servility we have no language sufficiently strong to express our indignation and contempt. . . . The cellar of that church is about as fit for a school-house for tender children as an *icehouse* would be, and we have been credibly informed that *that* has been the use to which this *cellar* has been put.[54]

Douglass concluded, for the moment, by noting that the fight for integrated schools was "just now, the question of questions for the colored people of this place" and calling for loud resistance. The school board's decision was all the more harmful because, as soon as the east-side school opened, all Black students living in that part of the city were ejected from the common schools they had been attending. A large group of residents, both Black and white, heeded his call and met at the courthouse in protest. They signed a resolution stating that "the people of Rochester may justly share the reproach of slavery in South Carolina if they give countenance to this wrong."[55]

In January 1850 the board again declined to vote for formal desegregation. Nonetheless, cracks in the official policy continued to emerge. The new east-side school was plagued by boycotts; it had only seven or eight Black students as well as a dozen or so "ragged white children" who lived nearby, Douglass reported. And the school board noted in March that, of seventy-three school-age Black children in Rochester, twenty-four were attending their local common schools, with half of them at School 15 on Alexander Street, near Douglass's house. By contrast, average attendance at the west-side Black school was thirty-eight students. Black parents continued to boycott the east-side school, leading to its closure in the fall of 1851, and Superintendent Reuben Jones recommended a policy whereby children would only attend the Black school if they "[could] do so without great inconvenience." Desegregation was a fact in the classroom, if not in the law or the school board room. Still, the board—at least what Douglass called the "pro-slavery Irish faction"—would not admit defeat. It pointed to the petitions of 1832 and 1849, both purporting to show support among the Black community for a segregated school that would provide "a place of refuge for colored children who would not be kindly received in other schools."[56]

The record of Douglass's advocacy goes silent in 1851. That may have been a result of him shifting his attention to his more typical sphere of national affairs after the passage of the Fugitive Slave Act of 1850; it may also be that his later writing on the subject was lost when his house (and many of his papers) burned in 1872. The Black community nevertheless continued its fight, protesting again in 1854 when the teacher at the Black school, a white man named William Barnes, was rehired by the board over the wishes of both the parents and "60 or 70 other respectable white citizens." Barnes, the protesters wrote, had "manifested his love of the intellectual improvement of the colored race, by closing the door and pocketing the key, to prevent young men of color from meeting to improve their minds." What was more, the board had agreed to pay Barnes $650 annually, $50 more than the Black families' preferred candidate had requested. He was an unidentified Black man "who has labored for those with whom he is identified, as a letter-writer, as a lecturer, and as a poet," and who was unable to work at another trade because of disability. The board's choice of Barnes had been "actuated by narrow prejudice against color, unworthy of them as men, and a disgrace to the city and age in which we live," the Black parents protested. "We will agitate and agitate, until our rights are respected and our wrongs are redressed." The episode reinforces how otherwise unknown Black parents, rather than Douglass or any other prominent individual alone, provided the energy and activism for desegregation.[57]

In fact, the board had already considered and rejected an even more economical option for the school. Barnes was rehired only after the board insisted on a male teacher. A minority of the board members would have preferred "a competent female teacher [who] could be employed at half the cost [and] who would do equal justice to the pupils of the school." The board again studied the question of closing the Black school in January 1855 and again declined to act despite calculating that continuing to educate Black students separately was increasing expenses fourfold. Attendance had dropped yet again, down to twenty-six students per day on average. Superintendent Jones blamed Black parents for this dilemma, criticizing them for having "shown so little appreciation of the advantages thus offered."[58] The school's ballooning expense persuaded the board to follow its original plan of hiring a cheaper, female teacher in place of Barnes. Their choice was Lucy Colman, a thirty-nine-year-old abolitionist at the beginning of a long career in social activism. She was given $350 for the year but, as she admitted later, "I had an object in view in taking that school, which I accomplished, other than earning my living." As she later recalled in her memoir:

> I took the situation, determining in my own mind that I would be the last teacher, and that the school should die. It died in just one year. I persuaded the parents in the different districts to send the more advanced children to the schools in their own districts, suggesting that they always see to it that they went particularly *clean*, and to impress upon the pupil that his or her behavior be faultless as possible. I then advised the trustees of the church to withdraw the permission for any further use of the building, save for church purposes. When the time came for the opening of the new year's school, there were neither scholars nor school-house. The death was not violent. No mention was made of the decease in the papers, and I presume there were not ten persons in the city that knew, or if they had known would have cared, that the disgrace was abolished.[59]

AME Zion did not actually withdraw approval for use of the building but rather increased the rent, requesting a sum beyond the board's already waning appetite. The new superintendent, John Atwater, commented again on the futility of maintaining the Black school in March 1856. Prejudice was the only barrier to change, he noted, "and experience proves this is not a very serious obstacle, for in most of the Schools of the city there are already more or less colored children, and in some instances they are among the best and most intelligent scholars in our Schools."[60]

The *coup de grace*, as Colman noted, came quietly. A committee reported to the school board in July 1856 that it had been "entirely unable to procure a suitable room" for the Black school. As a result, the board announced that it would close the school "for the present term." That unheralded announcement marked the end of explicit racial segregation in Rochester schools. It came twenty-four years after the city first acknowledged at least partial responsibility for "this unhappy class," and thirty-eight years after Austin Steward conducted the first formal classes for Black children in 1818.[61]

As long as the struggle had been, Rochester was the first large school district in New York to fully desegregate. A similar campaign in Buffalo went on unsuccessfully for more than a decade before some Black students were grudgingly admitted to their neighborhood schools beginning in 1855, then given free choice of schools in 1872. Buffalo's Black School only closed in 1880, after a lawsuit based on Reconstruction-era legislation. Many other cities—Albany, Geneva, Troy, Poughkeepsie, and Schenectady—declined to act until the 1873 passage of a state law that prohibited segregation by race in public facilities, including schools. New York City, like Buffalo, maintained a designated Black school long after allowing Black students to attend the common schools. As late as 1900, the state's top court upheld the legality of separate but equal schools under both state and federal law, and laws providing for separate education were not entirely repealed until 1938.[62]

In a preface to Lucy Colman's memoir, Amy Post claimed that Colman, "by her own exertions, without help from any one, removed from our city of Rochester the blot of the *colored* school."[63] This, of course, was not true. But why did Rochester achieve the distinction of having the first desegregated school system in New York? Some credit goes to the white residents, including those on the school board, who inveighed against segregated schooling for years. Douglass had certainly brought the issue to its greatest prominence, first through the Seward Seminary affair and then as an organizer and publisher of the *North Star.*

The most significant contribution—and the one most likely to escape documentation—surely came from Black parents, their names mostly lost to history, who advocated over decades for their children. The unidentified father who asked in 1841 why he should pay taxes for schools from which his children were barred. Phebe Ray, the domestic servant, who petitioned the board in 1846 for access to a closer school. And the groups of Black parents—perhaps a majority of those in the city at the time—who attended a series of protests in the late 1840s and again in the mid-1850s, then boycotted the Black school until its final demise. Their energetic activism made Rochester, at least for a time, the most progressive city in the state in terms of the opportunities it afforded its children.

The parallels between Rochester's first desegregation effort and its second one—still uncompleted and now mostly abandoned—are plain. As long as nineteenth-century Black children attended school separately, they found themselves in subpar buildings, subject to eviction and with little attention given to their proximity to home. Public officials were swayed more easily by financial considerations than moral ones. The wishes of white families in proximity were given outsized consideration. Black families' advocacy was most effective when corralled by a charismatic leader such as Frederick Douglass, but otherwise regularly silenced or ignored.

Why were white citizens, in Rochester and elsewhere, reluctant to welcome small numbers of Black children into public schools? As Douglass's Maryland slave-master, Thomas Auld, put it, education would unfit them for slavery. The logic of that unfitting led Douglass to a conclusion that troubled most white antebellum Americans. "It is very clear to us that the only way to remove prejudice, and to command the respect of our white fellow citizens, is to repudiate, in every form, the idea of our inferiority, by maintaining our right to civil, social and political equality with them," he wrote. Civil, social, and political equality for Black people—even for Rochester's purportedly liberal white populace, the idea was almost unthinkable. Even Douglass, the most respected Black man of the century, harbored real bitterness at the treatment he received. Perhaps it was in a fit of optimism that he wrote, "The only source from which we have reason to expect opposition . . . [is] that low vulgar herd of whites, whose chief sense of their own consequence is derived from their ability to abuse and insult with impunity those whom they are pleased to term 'n——s.'"[64]

Douglass saw formal school desegregation in Rochester, even in time for some of his own children to benefit. The greater work—"to remove prejudice, and to command the respect of our white fellow citizens"—was hardly begun.

# Chapter 2

# Nowhere Else to Go

Jessie James's life in Sanford, Florida, contained a contradiction that she never understood.

Weekdays were for school. Her parents were educated and active in the local Black community, including the NAACP. Jessie and her five younger siblings were encouraged to read the newspaper and Bible and to become leaders wherever they went. Education was a highly prized commodity. After school was out, though, they dropped their books and headed for the fields to pick beans or cut celery, to plant and to harvest, year after year through the relentless summer heat.

"There were many questions raised in my mind as a child, and as I worked after school and when school was out during the summer," she said. "I asked myself why I would complete high school when there were no jobs available and I would have to continue to work on the farm." She graduated high school in 1952 and already was engaged to be married. One day she and her fiancé were discussing their future plans. "He said to me, as soon as we were married I was going to go into the celery field," James said. "I did not want to spend the rest of my life on the farm. . . . So the marriage was out."[1]

Instead, James packed her bags and embarked on what was already a well-traveled route from Sanford to Rochester. Like thousands of Floridians, Mississippians, and South Carolinians before and after her, she weighed the apparent certainty of a lifetime of farm labor in the South against the prospect, however dim, of a better life in the unknown North, and chose the latter. James arrived in the summer of 1952 and within two days found a job as a maid at Rochester General Hospital. Just as quickly, she was confronted with a new, nebulous type of racial discrimination, different from the stark Jim Crow laws of the South but no less pernicious. She sought to buy a house on the west side of the city, only to learn that she had inadvertently strayed over Genesee Street, a bright red line that Black people could not cross. She asked for information on a program to become a nurse but found it was not available to her. Instead she took second and third jobs cleaning, cooking, mending clothes, operating a telephone switchboard, and working in a canning plant. On weekends she picked potatoes. "Many of us coming off the migrant farms had little knowledge, little skill and little interest in what was going on," she said. "We were constantly trying to make it from day to day with what little pennies we had." James eventually earned bachelor's and master's degrees and spent seventeen years working as an administrator at Rochester Institute of Technology, helping coordinate the college's programming with community needs. She was involved in school integration efforts and small business assistance for minorities.[2]

James's path to New York and her early struggles here, as well as the focus of her professional life, reflect a momentous cultural and demographic shift in Rochester in the decades after the end of World War II and its far-reaching impact on the arrangement of work, housing, and educational opportunities in the area. As late as 1940, Rochester's 2,700 Black residents made up just 1 percent of the total city population. Although the majority of Black families lived in the Third Ward, others were scattered across the rest of the city without too much outward friction with white neighbors.[3] Over the next half century, the city's Black population grew by more than 2,000 percent while the white population fell by more than half. This constituted a clear threat to the established social order in both the white and Black communities. The conflict was first apparent in the issue of housing; only later did it manifest most strikingly in the city's educational system. Racial segregation in twenty-first century schools cannot be understood without reference to the Great Migration and in particular the systemic discrimination Black people faced in their search for housing.

In the early twentieth century, most of Rochester's Black community descended either from residents who had been present since the city's founding or those who had been had been drawn by the presence of Frederick Douglass and the city's broader reputation as what he called the "most liberal of northern cities."[4] A third source was a stream of Black migrants who had come from Culpepper, Virginia, via Mumford, southwest of

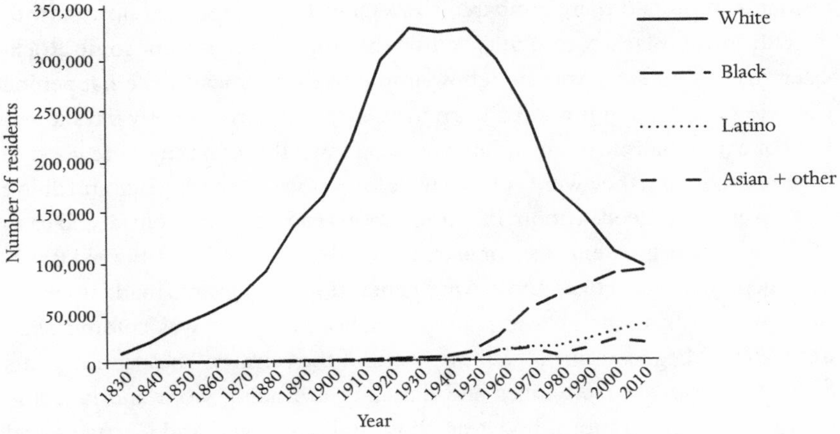


**FIGURE 2.1.** City of Rochester population by race and ethnicity, 1830 to 2010.
Source: US Census data, 1830 to 2010.

Rochester, after the end of the Civil War. This "Culpepper Connection" was forged by Benjamin Franklin Harmon, a Mumford-area native and captain in the 140th New York Volunteer Infantry Regiment. Harmon was stationed at Culpepper Courthouse at the close of the war and saw an opportunity in the mass of those recently emancipated from slavery. "He knew the need of farm hands at home and offered to send up . . . a car load of slaves," his niece later recalled. "They were the first colored people to come to this community and formed the [basis] of the colored population now here. It was a [hard] job to train them to use horses . . . but with patience they finally became trusted servants."[5] About twenty-five Black Culpepper families eventually settled in the Mumford area and their presence in turn helped facilitate a flow of migrant farm workers for the next several decades. As in Rochester, Black residents both permanent and migrant were largely hemmed in by the prejudice of their white neighbors—Harmon himself told his mother he was worried "that you should be left alone with those darkies," and Black people were carefully segregated into camps or certain sections of town—but it was nonetheless a more congenial environment than the one they'd left, with higher wages for farm work and the ability to attend school and buy land.[6]

Even with the infusion from Culpepper, the early twentieth-century Black population in Rochester was small compared to those of other northern cities. As late as 1950, Black residents in Rochester made up just 2 percent of the overall population; the proportion in Buffalo, New York City, and Chicago by then had risen to 6, 9, and 14 percent, respectively. There were 36,600 Black residents in Buffalo then compared to 7,600 in Rochester. This slow start to growth in the Black community led to the impression among some Rochesterians that the city was somehow immune to the racial strife happening elsewhere. As Evelyn Brandon, born in 1917, put it, "In the early days it was kind of a paternalistic town. White people in town thought they were good to their negroes, and they were good to us as long as we stayed in place and didn't make waves."[7] Indeed, a boom in immigration from Italy and central and eastern Europe was greater cause for alarm from the perspective of the old Rochester gentry. By 1890 first- and second-generation immigrants made up more than two-thirds of the growing city population, and that was before Italian immigration began in earnest after the turn of the century. These immigrants faced a great deal of prejudice and difficulty in finding work and housing. Within a few generations, however, those Italians, Poles, and Germans had been more or less folded into the evolving category of "white." This happened just as immigration from the South began to spike after World War II.[8]

Thus an uneven and occasionally uneasy détente developed in early twentieth-century Rochester regarding the proper geographical, social, and economic place for Black residents. Because the conceptual bounds of the Black community were well understood, and as long as its size posed no great threat to the white power structure, there was relatively little outward racial tension in Rochester, and Black leaders seldom saw fit to agitate publicly (though there were occasions when they did so). The city's genteel brand of racism kept most Black people in tight physical quarters and menial jobs but nonetheless fostered the slow growth of a stable Black community. This community was compact and constrained but, by the same token, proud and nearly self-sufficient. Nearly every member of the Third Ward enclave who

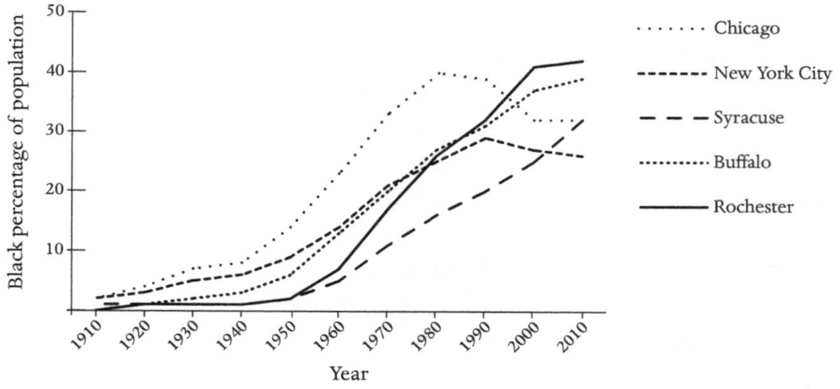


**FIGURE 2.2.** Percentage of Black residents in selected US cities, 1910 to 2010.
Source: US Census data, 1910 to 2010.

ever went on to document his or her experience could recite the names of all the Black doctors, dentists, teachers, morticians, and lawyers in the city. Chief among them was Charles Lunsford, Rochester's first Black doctor and an active member of the local NAACP chapter. Barbering, too, was a common and respected profession for men. "We knew every colored family in town and they knew us," Evelyn Brandon recalled. "There was a sense of strength and support. It was an extended family, as it were. . . . You didn't have to worry about if you got stuck downtown and you didn't have a nickel for the streetcar. Someone would always take care of you."[9]

Of course, this was not the same as equality. "To all appearances, Rochester is the perfect Northern city," R. Nathaniel Dett, a local Black leader, wrote in 1936. "The discrimination as practiced here is of a subtle kind, to which I sometimes feel that certain of our so-called Negro leaders are party." The situation was particularly striking for those arriving in Rochester from elsewhere. A visiting Black politician observed in 1934 that Rochesterians, Black and white, "live in a whirlpool of prejudice. . . . I must add that the Rochester Negro is far behind other cities in social, economic and political progress." A migrant who arrived in Rochester after World War II later told a state investigator: "When we first came here we were under the impression that most whites in Rochester had never seen Negroes who could read and write, and that one who could was automatically in a favored position. Evidently the long-term Negro residents have never asserted themselves, so that a pattern has grown up in which they are—without realizing it—deprived of their normal rights and privileges."[10]

To fully explore why Rochester lagged in Black racial consciousness and as a destination for southern Black migrants would require a much fuller treatment than belongs here. In general, though, migration was spurred chiefly by the opportunity for a better quality of life—in regard to housing and education, yes, but most importantly in regard to jobs. In Rochester, the distribution of good, secure jobs with generous benefits was closely concentrated in the hands of a select few industrialists, an arrangement that did not prevail to the same extent in larger cities. And up until the Civil Rights era, the Eastman Kodak Company, Xerox, Bausch and Lomb, and other major employers almost never hired Black people.

The 1939 State Commission on the Colored Urban Population showed that Black employment at major factories in upstate New York, particularly Rochester, was "practically non-existent":

> In Rochester, for example, our survey showed that of 35,120 employees in private firms, only 70 were Negroes. The largest firm, [Eastman

> Kodak], employing 16,351 persons, reported *one* Negro porter and 19 construction workers engaged by a subsidiary corporation. Another firm manufacturing optical goods reported 3,000 employees—*no* Negroes; two clothing manufacturers reported 4,000 employees and *not one Negro* because they "are supplied with workers by the union upon requisition." . . . Your Commission was at a loss to understand how Negroes in these and other communities in the up-State region managed to make a living and avoid starvation.[11]

None of those few business elites were more important than George Eastman of Eastman Kodak. The self-made inventor was an admirer of Booker T. Washington and gave generously to Washington's Tuskegee Institute, believing strongly in "proper education of the Hampton Tuskegee type, which is directed almost wholly toward making [Black people] useful citizens through education on industrial lines." In at least one case he protested that racial discrimination "would not be tolerated for an instant" in his realm of control.[12] And yet despite the magnificent legacy of philanthropy that Eastman and his namesake company left in Rochester and abroad, his record on racial equity in hiring was woeful. In the decades before the Black Power movement arrived in dramatic fashion at the company's iconic State Street headquarters, Black residents knew better than to bother seeking anything but the most menial employment at Kodak. One Black job seeker described the common reception at the hiring office: "We don't have any colored jobs. [We] got some jobs, but nothing for you." Eastman, like many white industrialists of his age, was an enthusiastic supporter and major financial contributor to the racist eugenics movement. He confided to friends that he wished for "some humane way of eliminating the hopelessly insane and fourth-offender criminals." His one significant Black employee was his longtime valet, Solomon Young, a North Carolinian who was hired at age twenty-five after Eastman advertised at one of the Black schools he supported that he needed "a good boy to go north and work." Young would later tell his niece, Alice Young: "George Eastman was a lot of good things, but it was never his intent that African-Americans would be working in a factory in Rochester."[13]

Two incidents from 1924 neatly encapsulate the point, as well as the way local Black leaders found themselves powerless to object to discrimination. In the first, a Black person attempting to purchase a ticket for a show at the Eastman Theater was told he could only sit in the balcony. When the issue was brought to the local NAACP, the leaders there decided to let it slide.

The local leader Franklin Bock wrote, summarizing a joint decision: "If the matter is not [dropped], the monied interests, of which Mr. Eastman is the leader, may make it tremendously hard for all the colored people in the city whether they are involved in this controversy or not."[14]

At about the same time, Bock and the local NAACP received a letter from a Black Massachusetts dentist named Irving Gray, who explained that he had signed a contract to become an internist at Eastman's Rochester Dental Dispensary but was strongly encouraged to look elsewhere once the clinic director, Harvey Burkhart, learned his race. "[Burkhart] proceeded to try to discourage me by relating a sad story of their past experiences with a colored man who was . . . mistreated by his fellow internists. They also say that colored people do not come there in sufficient quantities to keep a colored doctor busy." Charles Lunsford and Van Levy, the only Black dentist in the city at that time, immediately recognized the "sad story" as a lie—they surely would have heard about another Black physician in town. Nonetheless, they advised Gray to take Burkhart's advice and try his luck elsewhere. Burkhart, they noted, served on the New York Board of Dental Examiners, and so "it would not be wise for us to do anything that would make it difficult for colored men to pass the State Board Examination."[15]

Bock, a white man, boldly summarized both situations in a letter to national NAACP Secretary Walter White: "It is very easy to explain. Mr. Eastman controls the Dental Dispensary as he does the Eastman Theater." The theater manager and Burkhart, he wrote, "have been informed by some very prejudiced person that if they do not curb the colored people in this way they will overrun the town. . . . So far it is very difficult to get a direct statement from Mr. Eastman about his own attitude toward the matter." Bock sought, but never obtained, an audience with George Eastman himself, and both matters were dropped. He wrote to White: "The colored people are not many here in Rochester and our financial interests bow so completely to Mr. Eastman's judgment that it would be disastrous to get his severe enmity."[16]

Multiple similar situations occurred over the next several years. In 1927, a Black medical school candidate from South Carolina was "told flatly by Dean [George] Whipple that Negroes and Japanese would not be admitted." In 1930, a Black female student was ejected from the dormitories at the Eastman School of Music once the dean realized her race. "As you must certainly know, this University, as well as many institutions in this city, is dominated by George Eastman," Lunsford and other local NAACP members wrote pointedly to the national branch. Walter White tried to get an audience with

Eastman but was told by George Burks, then the acting NAACP branch secretary: "I have been very much in doubt as to whether there could be any one here in our City who could possibly be in touch with Mr. Eastman." White then wrote to Eastman directly and received a curt reply: "I am sorry that I am unable to meet your wishes in regard to an interview because the work of your organization is outside the scope of my activities."[17]

This racist legacy persisted at Kodak after Eastman's death. The company inserted racially restrictive covenants into property deeds through its employee realty corporation and would face a public reckoning after Rochester's racial uprising in 1964. The University of Rochester (UR), which Eastman had helped grow into a world-class institution, was equally culpable. Over its early history it consistently discouraged Black students from applying for admission.

The acclaimed singer and Rochester native William Warfield was an exception. He enrolled in the University of Rochester in 1936 and professed to having experienced racial harmony. He acknowledged, though, that he "may have missed some unpleasantness, too, through sheer obliviousness . . . I didn't know until years later that I had been recommended for the music fraternity, Phi Mu Alpha Symphonia, and turned down because I was black. 'Don't you remember that time we all resigned from Phi Mu Alpha?' a former classmate later asked me. 'There was a clique that didn't want to pledge a Negro, and a bunch of us resigned in protest.' Now that he mentioned it, I did remember that there had been a batch of resignations; at the time I didn't focus on it."[18]

In a prominent 1937 case, the local NAACP protested against the university's medical school, saying that it "consistently discourage[d] the admission of Negro students" either as doctors or as nurses, and that it did not allow those who were admitted to serve as interns or residents at Strong Memorial Hospital. This was no idle conjecture. The dean, George Whipple, had a form letter he sent to Black applicants informing them that they would not be allowed to work at Strong. "Under the circumstances, therefore, we feel it would be much wiser for you to apply to several of the schools who can, and do, give adequate clinical training to Negro students," the letter read. The protesters, led by Lunsford, attempted to persuade the city council not to renew a contract for UR to run the municipal hospital unless it changed the policy. The city councilors instead heeded the advice of Whipple, who recommended that they not "get mixed up with politics."[19]

The issue resurfaced two years later during a hearing before a state commission on racial discrimination. Whipple, a close personal friend of George Eastman's who for many years dined once a week at his mansion, told the commission that Black doctors and nurses working at the hospital "would cause wholesale objection on the part of white patients" and would lead all the white students to quit. The commission responded in its report:

> When informed of the fact that a Negro woman had been admitted to the Nurses' Training School of the Buffalo Municipal Hospital, not very far from Rochester, and that not one student nurse had resigned or even voiced an objection, these officials could do no more than shrug their shoulders. And, when further confronted with the testimony that in the city of Rochester itself there were three Negro physicians whose practices were 60 per cent, 75 per cent and 95 per cent white—involving all types of cases including obstetrics—these officials were at a loss for a reasonable explanation of their opinions. Obviously these were simply conjectures, and the entire situation is an example of flaunted discrimination against Negroes.[20]

The report recommended stripping the university of its tax-exempt status if it didn't change the policy, and the threat had its desired effect. Four years later, Lunsford and the NAACP hailed UR for having admitted one Black student each in the medical and nursing schools, thereby "recognizing its interracial responsibilities." Most in the Black community, though, saw that the problem persisted. "When I first arrived in Rochester [around 1949], I wouldn't even think of going to the University of Rochester," James Christian, a Black man, said. "Unless I was a person who was just extraordinary and outstanding, they wouldn't even consider me." In 1958 the UR's NAACP campus chapter was obligated to protest a whites-only clause in the charter of the Sigma Chi fraternity. The UR president, Cornelius de Kiewiet, said he was "distressed" by the publicity resulting from the protest and advised the student chapter to "confine [themselves] to quiet intra-campus activities."[21]

Episodes like the fight over admission to the medical school were the exception to nearly a century of mostly listless race relations. The city's few thousand Black residents were reasonably well situated in the growing but stable Black neighborhoods in the Third and Seventh Wards. If their prospects were dimmer for being Black, the situation was at least tolerable. By necessity they were accustomed to staying clear of the white power structure and knew to pick their fights judiciously. For several generations, staying in place and not making waves was a viable strategy.

The seeds of change were planted in 1929, when brothers Hal and George Fish traveled from their farm in Wayne County, east of Rochester, to Sanford, Florida, looking for labor to expand their celery crop. They met a man named John Gibson and asked whether he could pull together a local crew to help them harvest in New York in the summer.[22]

Sure, he told them.

Across the United States, farmers like the Fishes were converging on the same concept in response to common economic factors. As historian Dorothy Nelkin wrote:

> With industrialization, the local labor supply in rural areas, once able to handle the harvests, was drained into urban industries. At the same time, southern workers became available as a result of economic and technological changes during the Depression—in particular, the decline of the share-crop system and the mechanization of cotton picking. The migrant labor system as it gradually evolved was also affected by increased development of technology in agriculture, which limited labor needs to brief but highly intensive manpower-demand periods.[23]

Migrant farm workers traveled by the thousands along established South-North circuits, hopscotching from farm to farm as crops came ready for harvest. They came to the Rochester area as part of the Atlantic Coast Stream, harvesting beans in Florida in February, strawberries in Virginia and North Carolina in June, tomatoes in Maryland in August, and potatoes and apples in New York in September.[24] The exact itinerary depended on the crew leader, who served northern farmers and southern laborers as a contractor, chaperone, and go-between of uncertain scruples. Many weary itinerants eventually "settled out," leaving Florida for good and starting a new life in a northern town or city they'd come to know.

These agricultural workers were one strand of what became known as the Great Migration, the most monumental domestic demographic shift in US history. Tens of millions of Black men, women, and children left their mostly rural southern homes for the economic and social promise of the increasingly urban North. The movement was at heart a search for work and progressed in distinct pulses when jobs in northern industries were plentiful, particularly during the world wars. Migratory connections in specific northern cities were established via word of mouth from friends and family who had already made the move, with the result that some southern Black communities were essentially reconstituted in new cities thousands of miles away. "A time was in the 1950s, if you met a Black person downtown, the chances were two to one that they'd be from one of a few communities in Florida," longtime Rochesterian Walter Cooper recalled.[25]

Seasonal migrant workers had been coming to the agricultural region surrounding Rochester ever since emancipation and transportation technology made it feasible, and particularly once the Culpepper natives had established a foothold. As early as 1904 the *Democrat and Chronicle* made note of the departure of dozens of farmhands returning to Virginia at the end of the growing season. A brief surge of migration to Rochester itself occurred during World War I. "The problem was solved automatically, so to speak," the Rochester *Post Express* wrote, when those jobs dried up after the armistice.[26] It took many decades before significant numbers of those migrants began to settle down in upstate New York and then to transition from agricultural work to industrial or service jobs in the city of Rochester.

Wayne County's evolution into the pre-eminent fruit-producing region in the Northeast began thirteen thousand years ago with the final retreat of ice-age glaciers and the slow draining of Glacial Lake Iroquois. A thick layer of silt was deposited on the land between the southern boundary of that glacial lake, now roughly marked by New York State Route 104, and the current southern shore of Lake Ontario. The Cayuga Indians were the first to plant apple and cherry orchards; by the early 1800s they had been largely supplanted by European settlers who in time expanded from small family operations to spacious plantations with thousands of trees. Farther south, bottomlands between the glacial drumlins along the Clyde River were drained beginning in the 1880s, leaving rich humus well suited for growing vegetables. By 1970 over thirty thousand acres were devoted to fruit, mostly apples, and another thirteen thousand to vegetables, more than anywhere else in New York.[27] The entire operation was "a never-failing source of wonderment," journalist Arch Merrill said: "To the north . . . there are thousands of bushels of cherries, apples, peaches, pears, apricots, plums and other fruits to be picked. To the south, there are the mammoth crops of an amazing variety of vegetables to be taken from the rich, black muck land."[28]

The job of harvesting this huge amount of produce quickly surpassed the capacity of the local workforce. German prisoners of war were put to work picking apples during World War II.[29] A more reliable vein of workers, though, was found in Black migrants from the South. One such laborer, Alex Brown, arrived in Wayne County in 1945, finished with school in Florida at age sixteen and looking for something new in life. He came north with his father and the rest of a migrant worker crew, driving two days in the back of a truck, huddled beneath a canvas tarp to keep off the rain. When they arrived they were housed in a renovated chicken coop and paid from ten to twenty cents per bushel of apples, picking from dawn until the sun went down. "It was terrible to raise a family when you's in the migrant stream," he said. "Sometimes the conditions you be living in would be unsanitary. . . . We didn't have any social activities at all unless we know some people and we visit them at their camp, and some Sundays we go to a church occasion."[30]

Brown settled in Wayne County after 1948 and became an organizer for the AFL-CIO on behalf of migrant workers. He carried a gun for his protection and documented evidence of Ku Klux Klan activities while teaching apple- and cherry-pickers their rights under the law. It took decades for this persistent and courageous work to yield practical results. In the meantime, the annual cycle for the typical southern migrant worker remained the same. The season started in April or May with a local Black entrepreneur, the crew leader, selling a fresh pack of lies: Fifty or seventy-five cents for every bushel of produce picked, with the fruit already hanging ripe on the vine. A string of reputable farms mapped out on the seasonal itinerary, each with renovated housing and schools for the children. Reliable transportation for the thousand-mile journey from Florida to upstate New York and back. Fiction, all of it, in the majority of cases.

In fact, the contract between the farmer and the crew leader was usually not signed until the broken-down bus of fifty or more migrants arrived, having left whatever minimal bargaining power they started with back home in Florida. Housing was often a converted chicken coop or barn with little protection from the elements and no indoor plumbing. The crew leader was paid for the number of bodies he brought and had no incentive to insist on fair wages or conditions for his workers. They, in turn, had no recourse of any kind—no transportation, no money, no effective protection under local, state, or national law. As Julius Amaker, a farm agent with the US Department of Agriculture, put it: "It's a sin on every one of our lives to permit human beings to live the way migrants do."[31]

Dale Wright, a Black journalist who spent a summer as a migrant laborer, concluded: "The illiterate, unskilled migrant farm worker exists to be cheated, overworked, underpaid, and exploited for work honestly done. . . . The body of minimal laws designed to govern the operations of crew leaders are chronically, purposefully ignored, frequently with the knowledge and approval of farmer-employers and just as frequently with the tacit permissiveness of the authorities charged with their administration and enforcement."[32] Wayne County, with its vast apple orchards and proximity to markets in Rochester and Syracuse, received more migrant workers than any other county in the state. Overall, the farming communities surrounding

Rochester took in more than ten thousand migrant workers each summer at hundreds of camps, licensed and unlicensed. These camps regularly lacked flush toilets, either indoor or outdoor; adequate cooking facilities; clean water for handwashing, bathing or drinking; and housing in line with state health and building regulations for size, safety, and construction. "Shacks of squalor," a newspaper reporter called them, "revolting in their ugliness and inadequacy, [violating] any but the basest concepts of the dignity of man. . . . The tales and records of personal hygiene and health bring chills to the squeamish."[33]

Growers consistently balked at demands to improve their facilities, citing both economic necessity and the purported preferences of the workers themselves. "Most growers and officials insist that migrants do not know how to use flush toilets, do not want them, and destroy them when they are provided," one investigator wrote. "This argument is not supported by the observed facts." In the fields where workers spent most of their days, there often were not even outdoor privies; instead people were forced to relieve themselves in the open air beside the crops they were picking.[34]

Ruby McCants Ford was born in Haines City, Florida, in 1956, and first came to Wayne County to pick apples in 1965. She recalled her family of nine sleeping in one room on two beds—one for her parents, one for the seven children.

> Back in the old days, before they started inspecting camps, the farmers, to me, really didn't care what you slept on. They went out there and found a mattress some child done pissed on or whatever, drag it on in there. Your mama beat it out and try to sort it out the best she can and throw a sheet on it, and you get in it. . . .
>
> Sometimes we used to find rats' beds in the mattress in our bed, little pink baby rats. . . . It would be a hole with a nest in it with the cotton all out of it, and they just flipped the mattress over. You can't throw it away; if you throw it away, you ain't got none.[35]

In 1941, journalist Howard Coles had gone with his family to Mumford for a few weeks to escape the bustle of the city and to do some writing. He came upon a number of migrant bean pickers from South Carolina and asked them to show him where they lived:

> What a place for human habitation! From the physical appearance of the place, one got the impression that the first good wind storm would blow it down like a deck of cards. Even inside, one found little protection from the elements, for through large cracks in the walls,

> I could see the men moving around outside. All the window panes were broken out and most of the rooms were without doors. The floors swayed and creaked under our weight; dust, dirt and an accumulation of cobwebs were much in evidence and the whole place reeked with mustiness and the dampness of decay.[36]

Even the white residents of the village had become alarmed, Coles wrote, because the men "appeared to be not hungry, but weak and ill." It turned out their crew leader had not paid the grocery bill and the men had been reduced to panhandling. They wouldn't drink from the pump near their ramshackle house because they believed it to be contaminated, and they didn't have coal for the stove on which they relied for cooking and heating. This, in return for a promise of thirty cents an hour to pick beans. Perhaps because their squalor had spilled over into the rest of the town, the farm owner in question was reported to the state and arrested for operating a labor camp without the proper permits. In the meantime, a number of the men were hustled into a van and driven back south where they came from without being paid their wages or given a chance to collect their clothes.[37]

More frequently the official response to abject housing and health conditions, illegal employment practices, and unpaid wages was silence. Workers were prevented from accessing social services because of a lack of transportation and a well-founded distrust of the northern power structure. The people responsible for code enforcement in northern rural communities were often the friends and neighbors of the farmers and contractors themselves and had little desire to scrutinize the situation too closely. As a Rochester-area planning agency wrote: "[The migrant worker's] abilities are needed but he is not wanted, and the sooner he moves on the better the local community likes it."[38]

Predictably, the consequences were worst for children. The educational experience for migrant children in upstate New York farming communities presaged their later experience in the city of Rochester in several ways. During the short time the children were in northern schools, they quickly became accustomed to overt and implicit discrimination from white teachers and administrators, who were a novel change from the strictly segregated professional staff in southern schools. The students' race was just one strike against them and conceivably could have been overcome; their transience and ostracized position in the community were, in many cases, insuperable.

As important, being on the move for as much as eight months a year meant that the students missed an enormous amount of time in school. As one observer wrote of a woman he interviewed: "Her children have attended school, at various times, in Florida, Virginia, Delaware, New York, New Jersey and Connecticut. . . . Her daughter and her sons have gone to elementary schools in those states and stayed in those schools maybe a few weeks, maybe only a few days, then moved on to another school, or to no school 'for a while,' even though during the period of time called 'for a while' other children all over the country are at school."[39] Such inconsistent education did not encourage students to persevere through graduation, particularly when their parents had little experience with education and no resources to advocate for it. Boys often transitioned into full-time farm labor before they reached adolescence; girls were under pressure to care for younger siblings in the absence of quality childcare or else had children of their own. "If a girl in the muck can get past 13 or 14 without getting pregnant, then she is doing all right," one young mother said.[40]

The most significant effect of migratory farm work on children—one that persists to the present generation—was constant exposure to emotional and physical trauma. A more harmful environment could hardly have been engineered. Children of poor, uneducated parents, removed from any sense of community, were shuffled, mostly unsupervised, through a never-ending procession of unsafe living conditions embedded in hostile, culturally foreign communities, without benefit of the educational and social services provisions on which they might otherwise have relied. The psychiatrist Robert Coles found the "essence" of migrant labor to be "the wandering, the disapproval and ostracism, the extreme and unyielding poverty." A child living under these conditions for months or even years at a time, he wrote, would inevitably form "a self-image . . . of life's hurts and life's drawbacks, of life's calamities—which in this case are inescapable and relentless and unyielding."[41]

Early childhood education was almost nonexistent. Childcare facilities and prekindergarten classes were rare, and rarely of high quality, until after the southern migrant labor movement had mostly concluded. A 1944 survey of more than a hundred labor camps found just seventeen nurseries. Parents were occupied working in the fields all day and in any case were in no position to provide the stable environment necessary for normal child development. "Frequently no one patiently answers a migrant child's questions; he does not have toys, books and scribbling paper," one observer wrote. "No one in the family gives him basic instruction about sounds, shapes or colors."[42]

Basic social services, especially health care, were largely inaccessible. Applying for welfare usually meant traveling into town to fill out the application, and most migrant workers lacked the wherewithal, time, and transportation to do so. Local officials, meanwhile, had no motivation to increase their own social service expenditures on nonlocals who would be moving on to the next job within a few weeks.[43] Laborers were paid piece-rate and seldom had access to workers' compensation, two powerful disincentives to missing work to seek medical care. Illness, injury, and lack of appropriate clothing or other resources, in addition to the barriers discussed above, caused children to miss school.

This intensely negative experience with the mechanisms of governmental and social assistance was not unique to migrant workers, even if it was more concentrated than in other industries. It goes a long way toward explaining a cultural skepticism in the Black community of the medical profession, for instance, that continues with powerful consequences to this day. Ivory Simmons worked on Wayne County farms as a child and recalled watching his mother die delivering a child at home after being denied at a hospital for lack of insurance. "The doctors would not take my mother in the hospital because we didn't have money, so she stayed home and tried to have a baby and she died of childbirth," Simmons said. "That day, that time never left me—and therefore that experience made me hate doctors, and made me hate hospitals."[44]

Focusing only on migrant workers' deficits risks neglecting traits of resilience that the same difficult conditions often instilled: self-sufficiency, for example, or work ethic. Still, a growing body of research shows that traumatic experiences in childhood, particularly early childhood, cause greater damage than previously understood. An unstable living situation costs a child more than a few nights' sleep; physical abuse from an adult leaves more than physical scars. These experiences interfere with the development and functioning of the brain. Without appropriate intervention, children who face such trauma are likely to grow into adults who struggle to control their impulses, concentrate on work, or properly raise children of their own. As Robert Coles warned in 1967: "I fear it is no small thing, a disaster almost beyond repair, when children grow up, literally, adrift on the land, when they learn as a birthright the disorder and early sorrow that goes with virtual peonage, with an unsettled, vagabond life. In other words, I fear I am talking about millions of psychological catastrophes."[45]

Even as the use of southern migrant labor peaked in the 1950s and 1960s, it was obvious to observers that the men, women, and especially children in question faced potentially disastrous long-term harm. Eyewitness accounts crowded the front pages of northern newspapers and the programs of sociology and public health conferences. In 1967 US Senators Robert Kennedy and Jacob Javits toured two Wayne County camps and declared the conditions "deplorable." Housing at one consisted of twelve immobilized buses with no running water. The owner appeared with a shotgun and accused the senators and their coterie of "do-gooders" of trespassing. The poor conditions, he said, were the migrants' own fault.[46]

Sustained pressure from religious and civil rights organizations as well as the Black and mainstream newspapers eventually resulted in incremental improvements, including better access to health care and education and closer attention to sanitary code violations and unfair employment practices. At the same time, the advance of farm technology and other market forces led to a decreased need for migrant workers. In any case, much of the prospective labor pool had relocated to Rochester or other cities by the late 1960s and was not likely to return to the road.

That overwhelming generational experience of isolation and uprootedness—now mostly shifted onto people from Mexico and Central America—had a profound impact on the people who would come to constitute the majority of Rochester's Black population in the last quarter of the twentieth century. With conditions on Wayne County farms as hopeless as they were, southern migrant workers inevitably looked to the small, respectable Black community in Rochester as a step up. That second leg of the Great Migration, from farm to city, accelerated after World War II as industrial and service jobs—still low-paying, but at least better than itinerant stoop labor—abounded. One migrant later recalled his decision to move from Wayne County to the city as a simple one: "Who wants to work on somebody else's farm for nothing anyway? I knowed the place [Rochester]. The farms was close by. . . . I thought I could make a good start here."[47]

More than seventy years after Black migration to Rochester first gained steam, it is easy to overlook the multilayered dissonance that the arrival en masse of Black southern migrants created in the city. To northern Black people, the new arrivals from the rural South seemed backward and unsophisticated, a threat to their already tenuous social status in a majority-white city. A social worker captured in a few poignant words the horror of established Black families: "They are beginning to be classified again as Negroes."[48]

Conversely, the migrants found their new northern neighbors distant and aloof, lacking in hospitality at precisely the moment the migrants badly needed experienced social guides. A white reporter summarized, shortly after World War I: "The Southern negro still found music in the mouth organ and the banjo and pleasure in clog dances. The Northern negro had a piano in his home and perhaps his son or daughter played the violin, and he and his family were well dressed—high toned and 'stuck up' from the standpoint of his Southern compatriot."[49]

A 1951 master's thesis by the University of Rochester sociology student Laura Root gives a fascinating illustration of the dynamic as it played out geographically, with the older, more stable Black population in the Third Ward and many of the newly arriving migrants in the Seventh Ward, including in the Baden-Ormond neighborhood. In dozens of interviews, residents from each territory portrayed the other with disdain and downright hostility. "(These) newcomers are a bunch of rough loose living n——s whose actions reflect upon our status in Rochester," one Third Ward, or west-side, resident said. Another added: "Those loose livers coming in here will make it troublesome for us who (have) lived here a long time. We have decent names and people respect us."[50]

The Seventh Ward "bean pickers," meanwhile, derided the self-proclaimed Black gentry as "biggities" obsessed with social status and white mores. They noted that the same white and Black moralists who clucked their tongues at the rampant organized vice in Baden-Ormond could often be seen partaking in it on Saturday nights. Regarding the charge that they underappreciated the need for education, they noted that many of those maligned Baden-Ormond sex workers had arrived in Rochester with college degrees but been unable to find suitable employment. "They're so damn smart with their silly clubs," one Baden-Ormond resident said of the Third Ward. "They're just trying to act like white folks and they're n——s same as me. Everything the white man does, they try to do."[51]

White residents, meanwhile, observed both factions with growing alarm and a rapidly changing perspective on what was delicately referred to as "the negro question." Throughout Root's interviews, the white gaze was never far from the surface. "This is the crux of the conflict," she wrote. "West Siders desire to maintain their superior reputation in the eyes of the White population of the city, and the [Seventh Ward] folk are indifferent to what the Whites think, since they are not striving to achieve 'respectability.'"[52]

Bobby Johnson, a Rochester poet and journalist, was born in the city in 1929 and thus watched the southern migration with the perspective of the existing social hierarchy. Still, he recalled: "There were always some people who said, 'There's no racism here, everything's fine; the only problem is these ignorant bean pickers coming from the South. They're the ones that make everything bad, but otherwise it's fine.' That was not true at all. Almost any Black person could take up the Sunday newspaper, look at the want ads for apartments for rent—a great, big, thick paper—and you try to find an apartment, and when you [call], they weren't available."[53]

In just a few decades the carefully tended equilibrium of pre–World War II Rochester was blown to pieces. One scholar wrote: "The Negro migrant was strange; soon he became the object of ridicule. Ultimately he was feared."[54] This fear manifested principally in the matter of housing.

If the Great Migration was the signal demographic event of the twentieth century for northern US cities like Rochester, the dissolution of a comparatively equitable housing pattern was its most significant consequence. It opened the way for targeted disinvestment both public and private, calcified prejudice on a personal level, and facilitated later, damaging criminal justice measures. Housing segregation was established and enforced by a series of mechanisms ranging from defiant neighbors and deceitful landlords to official policies of the federal government. Local and personal opposition to Black homeowners in white neighborhoods was codified by real estate boards and, crucially, given the strength of law by the Federal Housing Administration. By the time these racist practices were formally disavowed in the 1968 Fair Housing Act, several generations of discriminatory groundwork had already been laid. And at a time when nearly every child in the United States walked to school, segregated housing inevitably meant segregated education.

Rochester's Third Ward has been an identifiable Black neighborhood since before the city's founding, yet housing segregation did not achieve its current severity until well into the twentieth century. As late as 1950, no census tract had more than 50 percent Black residents.[55] This was because of common technological and socioeconomic factors hindering strict segregation in cities across the United States. As the historians Douglas Massey and Nancy Denton wrote:

> In most cities, to be sure, certain neighborhoods could be identified as places where blacks lived; but before 1900 these areas were not predominantly black, and most blacks didn't live in them. . . . Land use was not highly specialized, real estate prices were low, and socially distinctive residential areas had not yet emerged. In the absence of structural steel, electricity and efficient mechanical systems, building densities were low and urban populations were distributed uniformly. Such an urban spatial structure is not conducive to high levels of segregation by

> class, race or ethnicity, and the small African American population that inhabited northern cities before 1900 occupied a niche in the urban geography little different from that of other groups.[56]

Policies of segregation did not bear full fruit in Rochester until Black migrants began arriving en masse after 1950, but the segregative structure was in place well before. Journalist Howard Coles, one of the most prominent figures in local Black history in the twentieth century, sounded the earliest alarm. Coles was born in 1903 in Belcoda, a hamlet near Mumford, and raised among the Culpepper contingent there. His grandfather, Rev. Clayton Coles, had been born in slavery in Tennessee and served as body servant to the famous Confederate general Thomas "Stonewall" Jackson during the Civil War before arriving in Mumford in 1888 and starting a church for its Black residents. After high school Howard Coles left home and worked as a messenger and delivery man for the *Herald Tribune* in New York as well as a waiter at a Long Island seafood restaurant, studying journalism and sales at the YMCA in his free time. On a trip to Chicago he visited the newsroom of its monumental Black newspaper, the *Defender*, an event that helped form in his mind the idea of founding his own newspaper for Rochester's Black community. He returned to Rochester in 1934 and published the first edition of the *Voice*, later renamed the *Frederick Douglass Voice*. The newspaper's name signaled his enduring devotion to Douglass; he also pushed for a US Postal Service stamp commemorating Douglass and organized memorial events at his statue in Highland Park. "I always felt like Frederick Douglass lived with us, because my father talked about him so much and [his picture] was everywhere," Coles's daughter, Joan Coles Howard, said.[57]

In 1938, Coles and the *Voice* undertook a survey of housing conditions encompassing several hundred Black residents. The houses surveyed were in large part damp, overcrowded, and underserved with gas and electricity. Many people lacked furnaces and relied on their cooking stoves for heat. Damp earthen cellars, leaky roofs, and communal toilets for a dozen people or more were common, particularly in the Seventh and Eighth Wards. "In many cases, we found that the houses were unfit to live in," Coles wrote. "The majority of places surveyed need major repairs to the stairways, floors and walls; also the plumbing was bad. . . . Rats, mice, roaches and bed-bugs were found in many homes, even large and offensive sewer rats." Coles's findings could hardly be dismissed as partisan allegations. A 1940 municipal survey largely supported them, showing for example that more than 40 percent of residential buildings in the Portland Avenue area lacked central heating.[58]

**FIGURE 2.3.** Howard Coles was publisher of the *Frederick Douglass Voice* and a licensed realtor in Rochester. From the Howard W. Coles Collection, Rochester Museum and Science Center, Rochester, NY.

Incredibly, Coles's survey also found that despite these fetid conditions Black Rochesterians often paid more rent than white tenants. This was strictly a matter of supply and demand, as Coles described it:

> Here as in other cities similar to Rochester, the Negro population is severely handicapped in respect of its housing problem not only with lack of income, which of course is basic, but also with a strictly practiced policy on the part of realtors and renting agents of segregating Negroes in the most undesirable and deteriorated districts as well as with uniformly high and exorbitant rents . . .
>
> In the Seventh Ward, a great number of ramshackle houses and outmoded apartments are rented to the Negro people that are not fit for human beings at any time. Yet rents of $2.75, $4.00, $5.00 and $5.50 are charged weekly. We have cases proving that one pretext or another is used to raise rents, when landlords know that Negro tenants must submit due to having nowhere else to move.[59]

The policies that caused these conditions were created and upheld by the most powerful layers of society, including the local and federal governments. The most visible instruments of segregation were real estate agents and moneylenders, who quickly arrived at a common understanding of their professional and social responsibility when it came to Black people buying houses. Real estate agents, as a rule, refused to sell houses in white neighborhoods to Black families. A local NAACP investigator wrote in 1960 of the Nothnagle Realty Company, the largest firm in the city: "They are firmly committed to a policy most likely to incur and retain the good will of the general Rochester house-buying public, the bulk of which is white—ergo, their tendency toward evasiveness, duplicity and subterfuge designed to dissuade Negro families from penetrating any farther into the whitelands than a safe 'fringe' area." John Nothnagle ran for the Rochester school board in 1961 and sat for an interview with an NAACP committee that pressed him on his service as "a silent and active participant in the Rochester brand of apartheid." He responded, according to the committee's report, with "the time-worn argument that whites were fearful of their neighborhoods being invaded by wife-beating, knife-wielding, illiterate Negroes."[60]

Real estate agents may have blocked Black homeownership out of personal prejudice or social pressure; perhaps most important, they did so on threat of expulsion from their professional organization. The National Association of Real Estate Boards in its official code of ethics declared: "A Realtor should never be instrumental in introducing into a neighborhood . . . members

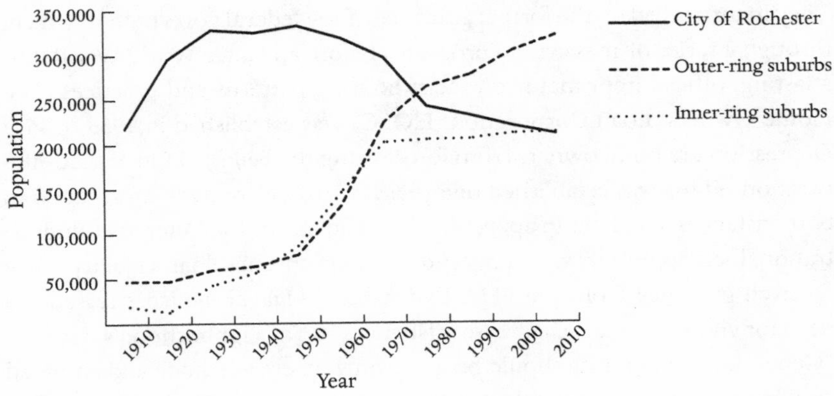


**FIGURE 2.4.** Monroe County population by geographic area, 1910 to 2010.
Source: US Census data; "Monroe County Population by Municipality and Decade," Pete Nabozny, December 12, 2018, www.petenabozny.com.

of any race or nationality, or any individuals whose presence will clearly be detrimental to property values in that neighborhood." In case any confusion remained, in an educational text the association gave as an example of an objectionable presence "a colored man of means who was giving his children a college education and thought they were entitled to live among whites."[61]

In addition to his career as a journalist, Howard Coles was also a licensed realtor, giving him unique insight into both housing conditions for the Black community in Rochester and the real estate practices that helped sustain them. He ended up resigning from the Rochester Real Estate Board in protest in 1960:

> These are my reasons for resigning: I am tired of winking at shady deals and of being asked to sell through third parties; I am tired of being asked to show houses at night; I am tired of trying to sell houses that are priced three and four thousand dollars [above] their true value; I am tired of telling falsehoods to people about where they can and cannot buy; I am tired of selling old houses and of never being able to sell new houses to the people with whom I am identified. . . . Most of all, I am tired of supporting American prejudice that is rampant here in Rochester in this necessary field.[62]

If a real estate agent faltered in his or her professional obligations, banks and other lending institutions remained as a bulwark against Black encroachment.

They in turn relied on the formal guidance of the federal government, which, through a series of massive aid programs before and after World War II, put a lasting, official imprimatur on racist housing patterns and practices. The Home Owners' Loan Corporation (HOLC) was established in 1933 to save Depression-era homeowners from foreclosure; the Federal Housing Administration (FHA) was established one year later to insure bank mortgages. In both instances, and later in appraising home loans for the Veterans Administration, local appraisers were engaged to rate properties' loan viability. They received guidance from the FHA *Underwriting Manual*, which stressed the need for vigilance against "adverse influences" on a neighborhood's stability: "Generally, a high rating should be given only where adequate and enforced zoning regulations exist or where effective restrictive covenants are recorded against the entire tract, since these provide the surest protection against undesirable encroachment and inharmonious use. . . . Restrictions should [prohibit] . . . the occupancy of properties except by the race for which they are intended."[63] In regard to schools in particular, the underwriting manual warned appraisers that neighborhoods should be viewed as "far less stable and desirable" where children would be "compelled to attend school where the majority or a considerable number of the pupils represent a far lower level of society or an incompatible racial element." The relationship between housing and school discrimination, then, was self-perpetuating, even at this early stage.[64]

The brightly colored maps that HOLC appraisers produced stand as striking visual documentation of federal participation in housing segregation. White-only Rochester neighborhoods in Maplewood, Charlotte, the southeast quadrant, and the developing suburbs were coded green or blue, the safest for investment. Most of the city was coded yellow, or "definitely declining." The worst rating, red, was reserved for the areas just southwest and northeast of downtown where the small but growing Black population was concentrated. Banks categorically refused to lend in those redlined communities, driving crippling disinvestment. The written descriptions of certain neighborhoods were more specific in their assessment. Talking about Corn Hill and the Third Ward, the appraisers wrote: "Negroes have come into the area and today it is the poorest section of the entire city. Pride of ownership is lacking. . . . The most that can be said for [the neighborhood] is that it is convenient." Comments in other cities were even more explicit. In Camden, New Jersey, for instance, appraisers wrote of one mostly Polish neighborhood: "Negro district on edge of section, but splendid cooperation of all residents in this section will always prevent spread." Eighty years later, the redlined Rochester tracts are part of the area known as "The Crescent" and stand as the most impoverished and unsafe neighborhoods in the city. They were the location of the 1964 uprising and, as of 2022, have some of the lowest performing schools in New York.[65]

Another, related line of defense for white homeowners came in the form of deed restrictions and racial covenants. Both real estate agents and banks encouraged homeowners to insert clauses into their deeds and to join covenants with their neighbors, setting restrictive terms on future use or sale of the property. These were enforceable contracts that prevented sales to purchasers of a targeted race, most often Black people. They were in effect on much of the development happening throughout the Rochester metropolitan area from the 1920s to the mid-1940s. Even governmental entities, including Monroe County, the town of Gates, and Gates School District No. 1, wrote restrictive clauses for property they sold or occupied. Major economic and political organizations, including the Roman Catholic Diocese of Rochester and Eastman Kodak, did the same. They used a thinly veiled code in advertising to alert potential white buyers: "rigid restrictions" were in place to ensure only "particular people" would be considered—those whom "you would enjoy having as neighbors." The Gannett newspapers carried countless such advertisements and reinforced the message from an editorial perspective as well. Not until 1948 did the US Supreme Court invalidated racially restrictive covenants. They remain visible on countless deeds in the Monroe County clerk's office and in government repositories across the country.[66]

Rochester's growing suburbs were particularly inaccessible to would-be purchasers or renters of color. Realtors declined to show properties there and the towns themselves stiffened zoning restrictions, reinterpreting their previously liberal codes to prevent poor Black people from moving in. Black people seeking to buy houses in the suburbs were regularly confronted with slurs, death threats, and petitions demanding that they go away. "The voices were different but the message was always the same,'" one Black man said in 1960. "'N——, go back where you belong. . . . Go back to [the slums] where all n——s belong." The Rev. Quintin Primo, an Episcopal pastor who served as president of the NAACP in the late 1950s, faced a petition from more than a hundred angry residents of Irondequoit, a Rochester suburb, when they learned the church was planning to purchase a rectory in the town for him and his family to live in. "His children are unruly and uncontrollable," the petition read. "The Primos plan to throw all-night, weekend drinking parties; our neighborhood and properties will be destroyed!"[67]

Black families were thus penned into an artificially restricted, systematically neglected geographical area—a ghetto—at the same time that the Black population was booming, particularly in the Seventh Ward around Joseph Avenue. The only way to accommodate the new arrivals was to subdivide the existing housing stock even as buildings and neighborhoods deteriorated through overcrowding. "Today we have twenty-four thousand Negro people crowded into two major ghetto areas which once housed seven thousand people," a local Congress of Racial Equality representative reported in 1962. John and Constance Mitchell recalled seeing twenty mailboxes outside one former single-family home across the street from their house in the Third Ward. Overcrowding became a chronic condition in the Third Ward in particular, as urban renewal in the Baden-Ormond neighborhood northeast of downtown had pushed many Black families to the southwest. As one researcher put it rather floridly: "Block after block of regal ruins inadequately house a tumescent humanity whose very proliferation causes outrageous crises, not the least of which are elementary sanitary problems."[68]

The roach-ridden tenements in the Third and Seventh Wards could only be subdivided so many times, though, and still Black migrants kept coming from the South. Spillover into previously exclusive white enclaves became inevitable and it, too, was managed by real estate agents and banks for maximum profit. Their practice was known as blockbusting and was common throughout the United States. Real estate agents knocked on doors in a white neighborhood, cautioning families to flee before a Black invasion began. Nellie King was eight years old when her family moved from the Clarissa Street area to Frost Avenue, farther in the southwest quadrant. They were the third Black family on the block, but more would soon arrive. "The real estate agents started coming through all that area—Woodbine, all those streets—and they started [telling people], 'The n——s are coming,'" she said. "So those people started giving away those houses in the 19th Ward." In 1969, the Nothnagle Realty Company sent a letter to homeowners on Warwick Avenue in the 19th Ward, "introducing" them to a Black couple who had recently bought a home on the street. The letter continued: "While negotiating this transaction, we received a number of inquiries from qualified buyers who desire to locate in your area, ONE OF WHOM MAY BE INTERESTED IN YOUR HOME!"[69]

White homeowners almost invariably took the hint, often selling their homes for less than market value. The agent could then turn around and resell the house at a significant markup to Black families desperate for safe, respectable accommodations. This engineered panic was predicated on what Coles called "the octopus, color prejudice," and it worked. "I remember well the 1960s mindset of 'impending doom' in the parish as the racial makeup began to change," a parishioner at the mostly white St. Augustine Church in the 19th Ward recalled. "The flight to the suburbs—and truly it was a flight, a fleeing, motivated chiefly by fear. I wonder what was gained and what was lost by all those flights. And what was there to be afraid of?"[70]

When all other barriers failed, violence against Black homeowners remained as a fallback option, in the form of a well-aimed gob of spit, brick, or bullet. Because Rochester's Black population began to expand later than that of Chicago, Detroit, and other northern cities, it was spared the horrific violence that swept across them in the years following World War I. Nonetheless, Black families who crossed the color line reported vandalism and threats of violence; the first Black family on Genesee Park Boulevard was greeted by a burning cross on their front lawn.[71]

James and Alice Young sought to buy a house in the 19th Ward but were denied, and their real estate agent faced death threats. Instead the Youngs had white friends buy the house, hold it for a month, and then transfer it to them. Before moving in they would visit after work; one day they decided to bring their baby's crib and set it up in their new home. "That was Thursday night," Alice Young recalled. "Friday we got there after work, and in the mailbox was this letter: 'You G—D—N—s have two weeks to move out of this neighborhood or else the house will be destroyed by fire [elisions in original].'" It was signed, "the Ku Klux Klan of Millbank Street."[72]

The Ku Klux Klan was indeed active in Rochester and its suburbs. The organization boasted of having more than two thousand members in the city in 1926, and as many as nineteen thousand people gathered that year at a Klan rally in East Rochester. Jasper Huffman recalled being in class at Monroe High School in the early 1960s when a white teacher explained that the Klan simply advocated for the rights of white people and didn't deserve its negative reputation. A Black classmate sat at her desk, crying. "She stood up and said, 'The Klan killed my father. Don't tell me anything about that,'" Huffman said. He stood up as well, in support of the girl; he believes it cost him the final half credit he needed to graduate. As late as 1980 Black residents in Rochester and the suburbs of Chili, Henrietta, and Irondequoit were confronted with cross burnings, harassment, and racist graffiti, and Klan recruitment signs were posted at Monroe Community College. After a cross was burned on the front yard of the only Black family on one street in Chili in 1980, police and neighbors concluded it was a "late-adolescent mindset that's probably behind this," rather than racism.[73]

Of course, some Black people did succeed in purchasing houses in white, middle-class neighborhoods. Many did so like James and Alice Young, through subterfuge and the assistance of sympathetic white friends who would purchase a house in their own name then transfer it to them. William Jacob Knox was a Harvard- and Massachusetts Institute of Technology–educated chemist who had been instrumental in the top-secret Manhattan Project. He came to Rochester in 1945 as a research scientist with Kodak. When he sought a house for his family, a real estate agent offered only an abandoned brothel on Joseph Avenue in the heart of the growing Black ghetto. Knox eventually succeeded in purchasing a house in a middle-class neighborhood after giving power of attorney to a white Kodak colleague.[74]

More commonly, the combined opposing forces to quality housing for Black people translated as an incontrovertible social norm. It didn't particularly matter whether the sale of a certain property might be blocked by a restrictive covenant, a real estate agent, or a bank. A 1968 Urban League report, summarizing scores of housing complaints it had brought to the state Division of Human Rights, concluded that housing discrimination was "less direct, more subtle" in Rochester than in other cities, indicating "an advanced state of perpetuation of discrimination."[75] Black people knew better than to go house-shopping in the white Maplewood or Highland Park neighborhoods in the first place.

The city of Rochester did attempt one solution other than subdividing and blockbusting: urban renewal, a term encompassing a generously funded national strategy of clearing aging, mostly nonwhite neighborhoods and replacing them with either bleak housing projects or highways, convention centers, or other inducements for white residents. In Rochester, the first urban renewal project razed a wide swath of the Seventh Ward, the Baden-Ormond neighborhood, to the ground and built in its place a set of seven public housing towers, seven stories each, at a cost of $5 million. They were called Hanover Houses and opened to their first tenants in December 1952 following years of debate over the creation of a public housing authority. "It's a turning point," said Irving Kriegsfeld, director of the Baden Street Settlement, a social services provider, eighteen months before the first unit was even occupied. "This neighborhood had been given up for lost. It is no longer lost." The towers had 392 apartments ranging from $39 to $48 a month, all "tastefully decorated" and outfitted with new appliances. "The public had a right to be impressed with what it saw," a reporter concluded after an open house to show off "the slum-clearance magic that has been wrought in a once substandard area."[76]

The original problem in the Baden-Ormond neighborhood, of course, had not been the fault of the houses themselves, and the city failed to act to address the worsening effects of poverty and segregation. Within five years a grassy courtyard in the Hanover Houses had been paved over, leaving children with nowhere to play but the hallways and elevators. These stank of urine because there were no bathrooms on the ground floor and young children couldn't make it back upstairs in time. As early as 1958, a consultant hired by the city reported: "Hanover Houses can scarcely escape the impact of its neighborhood, and many of its problem arise from the environment." The housing project was at the center of the 1964 uprising and afterward rapidly deteriorated into what housing authority officials conceded to be "a vertical ghetto." Tenants went on a rent strike in 1969 and succeeded in obtaining some improvements, but these did not prevent an exodus of all but the most destitute residents. A FIGHT publication in the early 1970s described the site as "characterized by rats, roaches, broken benches, falling fences, asphalt playground, inoperative elevators, stopped-up sinks, exposed wires, . . . unsecurable windows seven stories above ground level and exposed steam pipes." One longtime Rochester real estate agent put it succinctly: "No one in their right mind would give consideration to tenancy in Hanover Houses."[77]

Luis Burgos grew up in Hanover Houses, the son of two Puerto Rican transplants among many in northeast Rochester. Their apartment overlooked Joseph Avenue; Burgos recalled watching through the window as National Guard troops marched down the street in 1964. His father worked in a bakery on Joseph Avenue before becoming the first Puerto Rican to work in the city parks department in January 1959, two months before Luis was born. He often cut grass as part of his job and would sometimes take his children with him to different parts of the city. To them—seven children living with two adults in a three-bedroom apartment—the modest single-family houses they saw became the stuff of dreams. "We'd go to these homes that were just beautiful, and we really realized what it was like for other people, more fortunate people financially," he said. "For children who lived in that kind of environment to see one of those little residential streets off East Ridge Road—those little Cape Cod houses seemed like mansions to us."[78]

Even given serious poverty and progressively worsening housing conditions, people who grew up in Hanover Houses' during the buildings' earlier years described a sense of community that had not yet faded. "For me,

[Hanover Houses] was like a huge community of people who just helped one another," said Velverly Caldwell, who lived there for several years as a child in the early 1960s. "We did things together with all the neighbors; we played together; the adults cooked together during the holidays." Burgos recalled the same feeling of community support, particularly around the nearby Baden Street Settlement, but also described seeing three men bleeding from gunshot wounds while he played outside with his friends at about age seven. "It was a terrible, violent thing for a child to see," he said. "I'm not looking back at it with rose-colored glasses. There were aspects of the poverty that weren't good."[79]

The result of all the events described in this chapter—the unprecedented migration of Black people from the South, the shifting and hardening of racial prejudice, the restrictions on the Black housing market, motivated by racism and supported at the highest level of government—was, by 1960, a city more segregated and unequal than at any time since, perhaps, the abolition of slavery in New York in 1827. Black families were stacked in oppressive high-rises or jammed into unsanitary subdivisions, penned into two neighborhoods on threat of violence. This was happening at the same time that white families were enjoying an unprecedented array of federal subsidies aimed at helping them into the middle class and beyond. That disparity would lead to, among other things, the deadly unrest of 1964.

Clarence Ingram arrived in Rochester in 1953 with a bachelor's degree, four years in the US Army and a well-paying job under his belt. He recalled inquiring about an apartment he had seen advertised for rent on Clifton Street, on the western boundary of the Third Ward:

> The lady answered the door and when I mentioned what I was there for she immediately closed the door in my face and said she didn't have anything that she wanted to rent to me. . . . I can remember that face. I can remember that lady very, very, very well.
>
> The same lady owned a grocery store down on the corner of Prospect and Clifton street. I remember I went out on Sunday morning following the Saturday night of [the 1964 uprising], just looking at all the area. I approached that particular store and she was sitting out in front of the store with all the rubbish and spoiled food and torn-up trash, and she was in a very despondent mood, she was crying, and wondered why this would happen to her. She cited the number of years she'd been in the community, the type of person she was, and didn't understand why it would happen to her. Immediately I remembered the face

> that had closed the door in *my* face when I went to the apartment. I can imagine how these sorts of things over the years create problems and brought us to this explosive point.[80]

Worsening residential segregation was, of course, reflected in the neighborhood schools. By the 1962–63 school year there were five elementary schools with more than 80 percent minority children, led by School 3 in the Third Ward with 95 percent. At the same time, twenty-three elementary schools had 1 percent minority children.[81] The premigration status quo was irreparably broken.

# Chapter 3

# Willing Combatants

When Rosetta Crutchfield and her two young children arrived in Rochester from Sanford, Florida, in 1948, the city and its Black community had not yet undergone their great transition. Jobs were still available, and she found one immediately as a nurse's aide. The housing market in the Third Ward, though strongly discriminatory, was not as predatory as it soon would become. The nearby School 3, where her children enrolled, was not yet marked by strict segregation. "We were active; I was happy," her second daughter, Nellie King, said. "If anyone had a problem it was not mine. A lot of my Black friends couldn't understand me, but I just couldn't see making problems where there wasn't any."

Rosetta felt the same way. Their house was strictly "race-neutral," her daughter recalled, to the point that Nellie and her siblings were not allowed to mention people as Black or white. Nor did they discuss how they came to be one of the first Black families on Frost Avenue when they moved there in the 1950s, or how their white neighbors fled shortly thereafter. When Nellie was in middle school and a teacher suggested the white students would soon be forced to bring baseball bats with them to bed—that was not discussed, either. "We just had a way of living so we didn't deal with it," she said. "She did not want to talk about race issues."[1]

It was an old strategy for the old Black Rochester, but times were changing. By the early 1960s, Nellie had unleashed her neatly pressed hair into its natural state. On a class trip to New York City she found African clothing to wear and discovered that not all Black women "had to girdle up our booties." She recognized the way people like her had been caricaturized and made to feel less than human. "It was awesome, absolutely awesome, to learn I didn't have to go through this process of changing my hair to look white; to look as non-Black as possible," she said. She joined the NAACP Youth Council and the Young Democrats and dreamed up African names for the children she would have.

Her mother, too, began to change. She took a job as a teacher's aide at School 19, where she observed the steady increase in migrant children from the South—children like her own—and the way their education differed from the norm for white children, with portable classrooms taking up half the space on the playground. She watched as Rochester police brought dogs to a dance her children and other Black teenagers were attending. She recalled the oppressive racism and menial factory work she'd fled in Sanford. And when someone came through the neighborhood seeking plaintiffs for a potential NAACP class action lawsuit against the Rochester City School District for racial discrimination, Rosetta Crutchfield signed up. "That was out of character," Nellie said. "Mom wasn't really an activist. She became involved when she thought she needed to be involved." In Rochester and across the country, more and more Black men and women were making the same calculation.[2]

The sense of urgency embodied by Rosetta Crutchfield only emerged as Rochester's Black population grew. Certainly Black residents in city schools had faced discrimination before the Great Migration; what they lacked were the numbers to fight it consistently. Black children in the city were so few as to escape the attention of the press and other chroniclers except in unusual instances. In 1938, for instance, Black children made up 1 percent of the overall enrollment of 47,000. Even at School 3 in the Third Ward, where by far the largest number attended, they made up only 14 percent of the student body. As a result, from 1856, the year the Black school closed, until the first stirrings of the Civil Rights era a hundred years later, accounts of the growth of the school district omitted Black students entirely or mentioned them only in passing—unless there was trouble.[3]

Few Black residents from the early twentieth century left recollections of their time in Rochester schools. One who did was William Warfield, who found his singing voice while attending Washington High School. He wrote in his autobiography of growing up in "a climate of tolerance and remarkable good will" in Rochester in the 1920s and 1930s:

> Rochester was such an egalitarian environment that my youngest days were untainted by any of those psychologically damaging encounters

> with racism that too often blight the young lives of adult children elsewhere. . . .
>
> We all still believed in the idea of America as a melting pot, and my high school, like my neighborhood, was a real healthy cauldron. If some of the other ethnic groups didn't always take to Negroes all that well, it was rarely a cause of unpleasantness. If there were any problems I wasn't aware of them.[4]

Elsie Scott, an early Black nurse in Rochester who graduated from East High School in 1926, recalled that "from a very young age, until perhaps the issue of dating arose, she [was] accepted socially on equal terms with the other youngsters in her class. They were all in and out of each other's homes, attending school functions together, walking home together." Her career was temporarily blocked, however, when she applied for nursing school and was rejected at every local hospital.[5] Joseph and Pauline Moore had ten children attend School 31 and then East High School. One of their daughters, Joan Moore, recalled: "The teachers knew the family and had great respect for the family. Prejudice came not from the teachers but from people in the neighborhood." Still, she described getting into a fight with a white classmate after the great boxer Joe Louis won the heavyweight title in 1937; he told her that Louis had won the fight "because 'he was a n——' and that's all we know how to do."[6]

Even in desegregated schools, Black students often had to contend with teachers' harmful biases, ranging from paternalism to outright bigotry. "There is, on the part of the teachers, a marked lack of interest in, sympathy with, and understanding of Negro pupils," a set of statewide investigators reported in 1939. "They do not properly advise or encourage the pupils with respect to their continuation beyond the compulsory school ages."[7]

A prominent controversy occurred in 1895 when Susan B. Anthony appeared alongside the antilynching activist Ida B. Wells during a speaking event at Rochester's First Baptist Church. When a combative audience member asked why more Black people did not move to the North if conditions in the South were so bad—this was before the Great Migration—Anthony answered that it was because "they get no better treatment in the North than they do in the South." To illustrate the point, she described a recent incident in which School 3 had barred a Black girl from attending a school dance on the grounds that her presence would keep all the other students away. "I consider that the outrage on the feelings of that colored girl was the result of the same spirit that inspires the lynchings of the South," Anthony concluded.[8]

Reporters found the teacher in question at her home to hear her side of the story. As she explained it, she simply had told the fourteen-year-old girl "in as kind of a manner as possible" that "the other pupils, being neighbors and friends, would naturally dance [only] with each other, and that if they did that she would not be able to learn, and consequently would not get the worth of her [admission]." It had all been smoothed out, she said, the girl "smiling and apparently contented," until Anthony got wind of it.[9]

Even a small number of Black teachers would surely have helped ameliorate conditions for Black students. Alas, such teachers did not exist. The first known Black teacher in Rochester (other than at the Black-only school prior to 1856) was Florence Sprague, who appears to have been a niece of Nathan Sprague, husband of Frederick Douglass's daughter Rosetta. She was appointed in July 1889 and spent the 1889–90 school year as a "supply teacher," or building-wide substitute teacher, at School 24. She also served briefly as the superintendent of the Sunday school at AME Zion Church, then trained as a stenographer and went on to serve as the executive secretary to Booker T. Washington at the Tuskegee Institute.[10] The next Black teacher in the city was Viola Van Buren, a 1916 graduate of West High School and the Rochester Normal School teacher training program who taught at School 10 beginning in 1918.[11] Helen Sellers, also a graduate of the normal school, followed in about 1923. The first Black teacher to make a lasting impact was Bessie Walls, who was appointed in 1928 and remained for more than thirty years until her death in 1962. "Back in those days a black teacher had to be very, very well qualified to work in the schools," one of Walls's classmates, Marie Daley, said. Even as the Black population began to inch upward, Walls remained the district's only Black teacher for many years. She was joined in 1948 by Letha Ridley, a North Carolina native who later became the district's second Black principal and worked until 1973.[12]

Van Buren, Sellers, and Walls were three of only four Black teachers to graduate from the city's teacher preparatory school by 1939. The fourth apparently was instructed "through oral oath" not to seek a job in the city school district after graduation, and many others were discouraged from applying in the first place. "These conditions leave grave suspicions that there exists a practice of racial discrimination in Rochester," state investigators found in 1939. "And, it has been reported that in some instances, such discouragement has been fortified with threats and in fact the deliberate failure of some of these students."[13]

One of the most memorable figures in Black education in the early twentieth century was Isabella Dorsey, who operated outside the school system altogether. She and her husband Thomas Dorsey had no children of their own but instead, beginning in 1910, took in a number of Black foster children. Rochester Police Chief Joseph Quigley learned of their efforts and arranged some private financial support, helping Dorsey purchase a site in the Forest Lawn area of the Lake Ontario shoreline in 1916. Owners of nearby vacation cottages quickly raised an objection, at which point supporters raised $15,000 to purchase a twenty-six-acre farm at South Clinton and Elmwood avenues, the current site of McQuaid Jesuit High School.[14]

The Dorsey Home for Colored Children opened there in 1918 with about twenty-five Black orphan children up to age sixteen; a later expansion increased capacity to thirty-five. Thomas Dorsey ran the farm and Isabella Dorsey oversaw the kindergarten and orphanage. The older children attended School 24 on the other side of Pinnacle Hill, walking in good weather and going by sleigh in the snow. As a result, that school had the greatest Black enrollment of any in the city during that period with the exception of School 3 in the Third Ward.[15] Once a year they joined other disadvantaged Rochester children in the Orphans' Day parade, riding in convertibles up to Manitou Beach for festivities including dancing, games and—specifically for the Black children—a watermelon-eating contest.[16]

**FIGURE 3.1.** Isabella Dorsey, seen here in 1921, cared for Black orphans in Rochester at the Dorsey Home for Colored Children from 1910 to 1922. Photo by Albert Stone, from the Albert R. Stone Negative Collection, Rochester Museum and Science Center, Rochester, NY.

Dorsey left the home in 1922 to oversee an industrial boarding school for older Black children in Cattaraugus County. The orphanage came under the auspices of the Rochester Community Chest, which continued to run it until 1928. By that time the majority of the children came from elsewhere in the state, as there were few other similar institutions outside New York City. The Community Chest determined it could no longer sustain the expense. The children were dispersed back into foster care and the land was sold, with the proceeds going into a fund for the education of Black orphan children. Dorsey died three years later in June 1932. "It is said that having to surrender this work preyed upon Mrs. Dorsey and she failed steadily from the time she left the school," the *Democrat and Chronicle* wrote.[17]

Dorsey and her pupils aside, Black education in the pre–Civil Rights period made the news only when controversy arose. In 1951, for example, the local NAACP chapter complained to the school board about use of the children's book *Little Black Sambo* in elementary schools. The title character is South Asian, not African American, but is drawn in a racially exaggerated "pickaninny" style. Such books, chapter secretary Walter Bonner wrote, "are to some children their first introduction to Negroes [and] strengthen the conclusion among the uninformed and prejudiced that Negroes are all the same."[18]

Superintendent James Spinning said he was unaware of the negative connotation but acceded to the request nonetheless. The decision set off a furious debate in the newspapers' letters to the editor sections. "Doubtless next they will be banning Shakespeare because those of English descent will find that some of his works poke fun at the English," one person wrote. Another, taking a textual approach, noted that Sambo in fact carries the day in the story against three hungry tigers and concluded, "The dark-skinned peoples could not ask for a better ambassador of good will."[19]

Demographic change was not the only factor contributing to the growing restlessness of Black people in northern cities like Rochester. The four years the United States spent fighting in Europe and Asia had been, for its Black citizens, a dissonant and ultimately catalytic time. Over and over they saw their country fail to live up to the principles it supposedly was defending. Blood donated to the War Department was processed through segregated blood banks to prevent "contamination." Domestic military bases, mostly located in the South, were strictly segregated, and northern Black soldiers were shocked at the treatment they received when they ventured off-base, including lynching and other racist violence. Military jobs were often sorted by race, with Black enlistees consistently being assigned the lowest paid, most menial duties.[20]

At the same time, the massive wartime propaganda apparatus extolling the American values of liberty and opportunity had proven inconvenient when it came to Black citizens requesting the same. For Black Americans both at home and abroad, the disconnect between the government's democratic propaganda and their own lived experience was impossible to overlook. "If it was cause for international weeping that Jews were beaten in Berlin and scourged into a loathesome ghetto in Warsaw, what about a tear for black ghettos in America?" Roy Wilkins, later president of the NAACP, asked in 1944: "Hitler jammed our white people into their logically untenable position. Forced to oppose him for the sake of the life of the nation, they were jockeyed into declaring against his racial theories. . . . But the irritation at having to say these things in their extremity, and the anger at the literal interpretation of them by the belabored Negro, made our white people angrier and angrier in their insistence upon the status quo."[21]

US cities saw a wave of race riots in 1943 as questions about access to work, housing, and basic civil liberties exploded into violence. The most devastating was in Detroit, where a fistfight at an amusement park developed into three days of rioting with dozens killed. Scores of lesser incidents were reported across the country, and though Black Americans made few tangible gains as a result, these events again made evident to white Americans that racial tension would not defuse itself. The pioneering Black educator Mary McLeod Bethune compared a riot in Harlem to the Boston Tea Party and connected Black Americans' grievances with those of the oppressed in China and Russia: "Along with other good Americans the Negro has been . . . fighting now on land and sea and in the air to beat back these forces of oppression and tyranny and discrimination. Why, then, should we be surprised when at home as well as abroad he fights back against these same forces?"[22]

At the same time, a more comprehensive effort was underway to harness and expand the increasingly powerful Black vote in northern cities. In cities on the leading edge of the Great Migration, such as Chicago, Detroit, and New York, painstaking voter registration efforts were helping the Black community wrest concessions from white candidates in exchange for their support—and, eventually, putting Black candidates into office. By 1956 there were three Black Congressmen and about forty Black state legislators across the country as well as a growing allotment of judges, school trustees, and city council members.[23] In the North as in the South, registering Black people to vote and helping them secure housing and work was a labor-intensive job undertaken by myriad individuals and local organizations. Increasingly in the postwar years, those advocates worked under the aegis of the NAACP. Founded in 1909, the NAACP had by then emerged as the pre-eminent national organizing force in voter registration, political advocacy, and civil rights litigation. National membership exploded from about 51,000 in 1940 to more than 500,000 in 1946 and the national leadership undertook an aggressive desegregation policy.[24] This included lawsuits and protests regarding public transportation and housing but eventually had the greatest impact in education—to be specific, the education of a young Kansas girl named Linda Brown.

Whereas de facto segregation in northern schools had mostly disappeared by the mid-twentieth century, it was alive and well in the former Confederacy and bordering states. Not only were the races kept strictly segregated but every conceivable objective and subjective measure showed plain inequality, despite purported laws to the contrary. Georgia, Alabama, and Mississippi in 1930 spent five times as much per pupil on white schools compared to Black schools; South Carolina spent ten times as much.[25] Countless Black children had the humiliating experience of passing a well-appointed white school on their way to their own dilapidated building or seeing a bus full of white children zoom past as they made their way on foot. "Nothing rode the bus but the whites," one former student of a Black school in Macon County, Alabama, recalled. "And they would ride and throw trash, throw rocks and everything at us on the road and hoop and holler, "n——, n——, n——," all up and down the road. We weren't allowed to say one word back to them or throw back or nothing, because if you threw back at them you was going to jail."[26]

Segregation in the South, and particularly in southern schools, rested on a seemingly firm legal foundation. The truest bedrock was the 1896 case *Plessy v. Ferguson*, in which the Supreme Court had heard a complaint from Homer Plessy, a Louisiana "octaroon" who protested being barred from first-class train accommodations on the basis of his race. The Court upheld the ban and introduced into the legal lexicon the term "separate but equal." It recognized that the Fourteenth Amendment had ensured "absolute equality of the two races before the law," but did not go further to require "a commingling of the two races upon terms unsatisfactory to either." *Plessy* was followed by three cases from 1899 to 1927 that upheld and extended its logic.[27] Together they cemented segregated schools as "an inviolable institution," the historian Richard Kluger concluded: "And since the South encountered neither moral pangs nor legal obstacles when it allocated to black schools only a fraction of the funds it gave to the white ones under the so-called separate-but-equal doctrine, the Southern Negro faced exceedingly bleak prospects in hoping his children might obtain a better education than he himself had been permitted."[28] Even so, the prospect of imminent change was apparent to those who looked for it. "The great majority of Southern conservative white people do not see the handwriting on the wall," the Swedish sociologist Gunnar Myrdal wrote in his influential 1944 study of race in the United States. "[Yet] not since Reconstruction has there been more reason to anticipate fundamental changes in American race relations, changes which will involve a development toward the American ideals."[29]

*Brown v. Board of Education*, the realization of that change, was itself the culmination of twenty years of groundwork by NAACP-backed advocates, both in courtrooms and in Jim Crow cities, towns, and villages throughout the South. Starting in the 1930s, the NAACP and its energetic counsel, Thurgood Marshall, laid out a plan of attack on segregated institutions and, eventually, the institution of segregation itself. "I think we've humored the South long enough," Marshall said. "It's only by lawsuits and legislation that we'll ever teach reactionaries the meaning of the 14th Amendment."[30]

A series of federal court decisions regarding equal access to colleges, particularly graduate programs, created a new set of integrationist precedents to contend with the harsh facts of *Plessy*. Important incremental progress was achieved thanks to related demands by Heman Sweatt, a mail carrier from Houston, Texas, seeking admission to the University of Texas's law school, and George McLaurin, a veteran Black teacher who applied for a doctoral program at the University of Oklahoma. Sweatt was placed into a hastily created, poorly supported "law school" for Black students consisting of four rented rooms in an office building near the state capitol; McLaurin was admitted under court order but kept physically separated from white students in the classroom, library, and cafeteria.

In both cases, decided on the same day in 1950, the Supreme Court found that *Plessy's* "separate but equal" standard had not been met. The *Sweatt v. Painter* decision in particular was encouraging. Not only were the physical accommodations and library holdings unequal, the unanimous Court held, but the white school "possess[ed] to a far greater degree those qualities which are incapable of objective measurement but which make for greatness in a law school"—things such as reputation in the community and the value of alumni connections. What is more, segregating Black would-be lawyers from white people—i.e., "85 percent of the population of the State, [including] most of the lawyers, witnesses, jurors, judges and other officials with whom petitioner will inevitably be dealing when he becomes a member of the Texas Bar"—made it impossible for their education to match what offered at the University of Texas.[31]

*Sweatt v. Painter* and *McLaurin v. Oklahoma Board of Regents* left the doctrine of "separate but equal" in place but contained important logical inferences about what equality entailed. Without saying as much, the Court suggested that a segregated Black institution embedded in an avowedly white supremacist culture could scarcely meet the standard of *Plessy*, no matter the circumstances. Still, the applicability of that point to the much more controversial question of public K–12 education was far from evident. "The legal gap between the *Sweatt* and *McLaurin* cases on the one hand and an outright destruction of the *Plessy* precedent appeared to be appallingly wide, and [Marshall] and his colleagues were not at all sure they could cross it," historian Alfred Kelly, a friend of Marshall's, wrote.[32]

Doubtful or not, the NAACP legal team moved to capitalize on the opening by building cases in Delaware, Kansas, South Carolina, Virginia, and the District of Columbia where students faced a gantlet of challenges: lack of bus transportation and school supplies, outdated facilities and overcrowded classrooms, poorly paid teachers, and no extracurricular activities. In Clarendon County, South Carolina, white students got more than three times the per-pupil funding of Black students, who were forced to clean their building themselves in the absence of paid janitors. The science lab at one Washington, DC, school for Black children consisted of a Bunsen burner and a goldfish bowl.[33]

*Brown v. Board of Education* comprised five different cases, each a variation on the inadequacy of segregated public education for Black children. Linda Brown, whose name was listed first alphabetically among the plaintiffs, had to walk across a railroad switchyard to get to the all-Black Monroe School in Topeka, Kansas, even though the white Sumner School was closer to her house. Unlike in some southern cities, though, Topeka's white schools were only marginally newer and better resourced than the Black ones. Class sizes and teacher experience were roughly equal, and course offerings were similar. Indeed, many school districts in the South and elsewhere had taken hasty but significant steps to create parity between their white and Black schools, hoping to forestall more consequential judicial intervention of the kind the NAACP was attempting. Brand-new buildings for Black students were referred to derisively as "Supreme Court schools." This was a critical point for the plaintiffs, and one that followed directly from *Sweatt* in particular; new facilities or well-trained teachers alone do not make for equitable education. As an expert witness put it during the preliminary *Brown* litigation: "If the colored children are denied the experience in school of associating with white children, who represent 90 percent of our national society in which these colored children must live, then the colored child's curriculum is being greatly curtailed."[34]

The NAACP's key expert at the trial was Kenneth Clark, a young Columbia University psychologist who had earned the half-joking nickname "the doll man." He and his wife, Mamie Clark, had done interesting research on the self-image and self-esteem of young children by showing them white and Black dolls and asking which was "good," which was more attractive, and which looked like them. Black children, particularly those raised in highly segregated communities, consistently showed a preference for white dolls, which the Clarks interpreted as an expression of low self-esteem acquired via corrosive anti-Black prejudice. Many both within the NAACP legal team and in the opposition dismissed the Clarks' work as squishy social science, less convincing than the hard facts of classroom sizes or teacher salaries. But on May 17, 1954, when Chief Justice Earl Warren announced the Court's unanimous finding in favor of Linda Brown and the other Black petitioners, the impact of the Clarks' research was apparent. "To separate [Black children] from others of similar age and qualifications solely because of their race generates a feeling of inferiority as to their status in the community that may affect their hearts and minds in a way unlikely ever to be undone," Warren wrote. The NAACP had invited the Court to abolish the "separate but equal" standard and the Court did so emphatically.[35]

The *Brown* decision dropped like a bomb in the South. The cherished institution of segregated education was outlawed, even if many reactionary politicians quickly coalesced around a strategy that came to be known as "massive resistance." The seeds of the decades-long fight for integration—or, at least, desegregation—were contained in four fateful words in the Court's 1955 follow-up decision relating to the implementation of the historic ruling. School districts themselves were responsible for devising solutions, the Court ruled, and should do so "with all deliberate speed."[36] This speed proved to be deliberate indeed.

In Rochester, newspaper editorial boards praised the decision at a marked distance but called for patience in its implementation. Most striking in retrospect is their certainty, too obvious to require explication, that the ruling in *Brown* was something for the South to grapple with alone. The legality of school segregation in Kansas and South Carolina had no more to do with cities like Rochester, the editors believed, than the buses in Berlin or the weather in Warsaw. It was a foreign policy matter to pontificate on—to congratulate, in this case—in the assurance that its reverberations would peter out far short of the Genesee Valley. And indeed, as long as de jure segregation had remained in place, the de facto variety in Rochester and cities like it went mostly unmolested. After *Brown*, that changed.[37]

When the *Brown* decision was announced in 1954, Anne Micheaux had just turned three, still two years away from joining her older sister, Lydia, at School 3, just down the street from their home in Rochester's Third Ward. The ruling had no immediate effect on either girl, but in time they would become principal actors in the resultant local drama. For that, they could thank their mother, Katherine Jordan Harris, and her father, Anthony Jordan, upstairs of whose medical office the family lived.

Jordan, a native of Guyana and graduate of the Howard University College of Medicine, opened his practice in Rochester in 1932 and quickly became known as the doctor for the poor, making house calls even for those who couldn't afford to pay. Instead, he said, "Tell the Lord about me; there'll be no charges."[38] He demanded that his children and grandchildren follow in his footsteps, and his daughter, Katherine, became a social worker. "She was just born with a strong feeling of right from wrong and a willingness to speak that truth," Anne Micheaux said. "[She was] a willing combatant—at least as far as my own formative years are concerned." As Anne and her sister progressed through school, that sometimes meant heated parent-teacher conferences during which Harris protested her daughters being excluded from advanced-track courses and "teacher evaluations that had more to do with expectations due to race than strictly my performance."[39]

The Jordan family was gentry on Adams Street, but the community around them was changing. From 1940 to 1950 the Black population in Rochester grew by 133 percent. The following decade it grew by another 211 percent, to 23,586 in 1960. The continuous arrival of migrants from Florida, South Carolina, and other points south had many lasting implications for white and Black residents alike; chief among them, the city's two traditional Black neighborhoods swelled to bursting. A 1958 study of mid-sized upstate cities by the State Commission against Discrimination showed that the housing market in Rochester was uniquely hostile to Black buyers and renters. Sellers and banks were unwilling to deal with Black people and white neighbors undertook coordinated resistance efforts.[40]

Included in the wave of new arrivals was a small but influential cadre of young civil rights activists who greeted the *Brown* decision with enthusiasm. Many were scientists and engineers hired by Kodak during or after World War II, seeking opportunity in housing and education commensurate with their hard-earned professional status. They were known informally as the Young Turks; for a time, they organized through the Monroe County Non-Partisan Political League and other groups. All were emboldened by the gains made in federal desegregation cases and eager to see them translated in Rochester. This early cohort of Black NAACP-aligned activists—the Kodak chemist Walter Cooper, the Urban League president (and later school board member), Laplois Ashford, the Rochester Congress of Racial Equity president, Hannah Storrs, the Monroe County Non-Partisan League president, Obadiah Williamson, and John and Constance Mitchell—was responsible for moving Rochester from the relative conservatism of Charles Lunsford and old Black Rochester into the faster waters of the early Civil Rights era.[41]

Although the arrival of agricultural migrants had shaken the established Black community, these skilled Black newcomers represented a more subtle challenge to the status quo for respected Black citizens who had in large part attained their positions through longevity and service rather than advanced technical education. A 1958 survey of upstate cities showed great nuance within their small but growing Black communities:

> The older residents often look upon the highly-skilled newcomers as rash upstarts with pretensions far greater than merited by their pedigrees . . . and with attitudes toward present social patterns which may undo all the progress which has been made. The new professionals, on the other hand, tend to look upon the "oldsters" as persons of inferior training, with questionable reasons for pride in their lineage, and with a tendency toward inertia and acceptance of the status quo. . . .
>
> Neither group, however, appears to have much contact with the great mass of the Negro population, with whom they have little in common and for whom they often have little respect. Many representatives of both may, in fact, associate more with whites than with other Negroes.[42]

Frank McElrath arrived in Rochester from West Virginia in 1953 to work at Kodak as a chemist. He observed in the existing Black community a "minuscule professional class . . . [who] had a vested interest in things not getting too far out of hand, because they'd paid a terrible price to achieve what they had achieved." With that middle-class group effectively sidelined, McElrath said, leadership at the dawn of the national Civil Rights era was left to new arrivals:

> A good deal of Black people felt they'd gone as far north as possible to go without swimming, and here they stand: "We must do something about the problem here or live forever with it." And no one was willing to live forever with it. . . .
>
> The people who should have been the natural leaders of the Black community turned out to have too much of a vested interest in the

community. . . . Consequently, the leaders turned out to be people who were more radical, newer to the city of Rochester, somewhat less caring about who is who and what is what in Rochester. And consequently, it was perhaps ordained when those people were forced to take leadership that we'd have a violent confrontation sooner or later.[43]

The Young Turks were seen as the "rash upstarts" in the community for only a decade or so. After the 1964 uprising they were largely eclipsed by an even more aggressive faction typified by Franklin Florence and FIGHT, but not before winning important political gains—and setting into motion a prominent attack on school segregation in the city.

The children crammed into the Third and Seventh Wards had to go to school somewhere, of course. The strict neighborhood school model led to the emergence of schools where, for the first time, the majority of students were Black. In 1928 School 3 had 14 percent Black students, by far the largest percentage in the city; in 1963 it was one of five schools with more than 90 percent Black students, and Rochester had more mostly Black schools than any upstate district except Buffalo.[44]

As the demographics changed, enrollment rose. Two kindergarten classes at School 3 with forty students each were held together in a single large hall, and teachers were forced to conduct classes in portable classrooms. When even those measures did not suffice, the school in 1959 rented additional classroom space in the basement of the neighboring Corn Hill Methodist Church. It is not recorded whether anyone in the school was aware of the grim historical analogy; racial segregation had forced the "African School" in the same neighborhood into the basement of AME Zion Church 114 years earlier, something Frederick Douglass had blasted as an act of "degradation (and) cruelty." School board candidates in 1959 proclaimed themselves "shocked" and "aghast" at the overcrowding but despaired at finding a way to transport the School 3 children to the nearby, mostly white School 17, where an entire eight-classroom wing of the building was empty.[45]

In 1960 the school board approved spending $1.3 million to build a new, 750-student school on Reynolds Street, School 2. Officials hoped the location would draw from both white and Black neighborhoods, creating a fairly integrated building. It would not be ready until September 1961, though, so in July 1960 the RCSD administration put forth a plan to double-shift some students at mostly Black Schools 3, 4, and 19, shortening students' school day by seventy-five minutes in the process. Superintendent Howard Seymour endorsed the proposal as "the least unwieldy" possible. Opponents, led by the

NAACP's Walter Cooper and parent Jeannette Woodland, wondered why the students couldn't instead transfer to mostly white schools nearby. Woodland, who gathered more than two hundred petition signatures, said that the proposal "reflects time-honored discriminatory practices which have led to the deterioration of intergroup relations." Cooper said the shortened school day would "follow these youngsters as a serious handicap throughout their lives and will serve to perpetuate the frustrations and bitterness which characterize many of their parents."[46] The only reason the schools were overcrowded, they pointed out, was that Black residents were barred from moving out of the part of southwest Rochester where the schools were located.

The district and school board protested the characterization: "Discrimination is the last thing in the wide world this board can be accused of," the school board president, Jacob Gitelman, said. Nonetheless, the following week the district rescinded the plan, saying it would instead rent space or put up more temporary classrooms for the five hundred or so students in question. It also adopted a resolution addressing the root concern: "The area served by these three schools is crowded because many of its residents are unwelcome in other parts of the city. . . . These children should not be penalized for a condition that exists in our community." Already in 1959 the district predicted that School 2 would not be sufficient to solve the issue of overcrowding in the Third Ward schools when it opened in 1961, and indeed it was not.[47] The double-shifting plan, short-lived as it was, proved in retrospect to be the first salvo in the Rochester City School District's desegregation battle.

Two important factors favored the NAACP activists as the matter moved toward the courtroom in early 1962. First, the state's Board of Regents was heading in a similar direction. In 1960 it published a position paper on "intercultural education" and set up an advisory council on educational segregation. Racially homogenous schools, the regents wrote, were "socially unrealistic" and "wasteful of manpower and talent, whether this situation occurs by law or by fact."[48] More decisive state action in the matter was still to come, but already by 1962 it was apparent that state education leaders were ready to address the question of racial segregation in some way.

Before the executive branch could move any further, the judicial branch sprang into action with a landmark decision in the downstate city of New Rochelle. In 1960, eleven families in its Lincoln Elementary School, 94 percent Black, sued over their assignment to a school that was effectively segregated by race. As in Rochester and other northern cities, the unsubtle pressures on Black residents of New Rochelle had herded them into strictly segregated neighborhoods. The situation was exacerbated by the way school enrollment lines in the city were gerrymandered to keep Black children together along with a transfer-out mechanism provided almost exclusively for white children. The result was a system of "neighborhood schools" where, somehow, Black and white children living on the same block were sent to different schools.

In a groundbreaking ruling in federal court, Judge Irving Kaufman ordered the district to create a desegregation plan, using sweeping language to extend the obligations of *Brown* in a way northern school districts had not foreseen: "[*Brown*] was premised on the factual conclusion that a segregated education created and maintained by official acts had a detrimental and deleterious effect on the educational and mental development of the minority group children. . . . With these principles clear in mind, I see no basis to draw a distinction, legal or moral, between segregation established by the formality of a dual system of education, as in *Brown*, and that created by gerrymandering of school district lines and transferring of white children as in the instant case."[49] It was the first major school segregation case in the North. All-Black Lincoln was shuttered two years later as part of the New Rochelle school board's reluctant response. The more significant reverberation, though, was in turning integration advocates' attention north of the Mason-Dixon line. As Rochester activist Glen Claytor wrote: "If it is sustained by higher courts, the New Rochelle decision will provide a fulcrum with which to pry loose the adherence to the artificial school district boundaries now common in many northern cities—including our own."[50]

Indeed, 1961–62 was a period of changing focus for the NAACP. As Executive Secretary Roy Wilkins said: "After the 1954 court decision, we concentrated on the South, where we felt it very important, psychologically and politically, to score victories. Those victories have been won, even if on a token basis, and we now feel it's time to turn our attention northward." By the end of 1962 the organization had filed scores of desegregation lawsuits in Western and Northern school districts, including sixteen in New York and ten each in New Jersey and Illinois. "Public schools segregated in fact in the North and West no longer can be accepted through tradition or custom, or excused as the inevitable result of segregated housing," the NAACP's June Shagaloff wrote. "The fight against them will be pressed despite resistance from some educators, white parents . . . or real estate and political interests intent on maintaining the status quo."[51]

One major contributor to the Rochester integration movement in the late 1950s was the chairman of the NAACP's education committee, Walter Cooper. He was born in 1921 in Clairton, Pennsylvania, a small industrial city outside Pittsburgh to which his parents had migrated from the agricultural South. The schools there were tenuously integrated, and though his parents were barely educated themselves, they insisted on perfect attendance from their children. Cooper absorbed from his mother what he called his fundamental philosophy: "You have a deep and abiding faith in your humanity . . . and you stand for what's right no matter the circumstances. She said, 'You'll pay a heavy price, but you must do it.'" Already in high school he led student protests against the racist curriculum and, as a star of the football team, organized a well-timed walkout to integrate the cheerleading squad.[52] Cooper graduated as high school salutatorian in 1946 and attended nearby Washington and Jefferson College on a football scholarship. After graduating and spending two years as a teaching assistant at Howard University, he came to the University of Rochester in 1952 for a PhD program in chemistry.

Although the university had yet to shake its reputation for hostility to Black students, the campus NAACP chapter had attracted a core of Black and white students committed to social justice. There Cooper became active in the local civil rights movement, first as chairman of a scholarship committee for Black students, then, after earning his degree in 1957, as education chairman and a spokesman for the local NAACP. Inspired in part by the New Rochelle lawsuit, Cooper organized a study of segregative practices in Rochester schools showing, among other things, that majority-Black schools often received the least funding—and that funding tended to decrease as enrollment shifted toward minority students.[53]

Compelling as the pattern of segregation was, Cooper found the way to legal action blocked. Quintin Primo, pastor at St. Simon's Episcopal Church, was president of the local NAACP branch in 1961 and in many ways continued the conservative leadership style of Lunsford. By the late 1950s he was coming under increasing criticism for, as Cooper called it, "playing footsie with the white power structure."[54] One particular flashpoint was the siting of a low-income public housing project, Chatham Gardens, in an already poor neighborhood against the wishes of its residents.[55] Primo in 1961 declined to endorse the school-segregation study for possible action from the NAACP, but it proved to be one of the last decisions he made. Several months later he retired under pressure, leaving for Chicago where he eventually became an Episcopal bishop.

In his absence, Cooper's project gained steam. Primo's replacement, Reuben Davis, announced in late March the NAACP was studying the issue of school segregation with an eye toward "approach[ing] local authorities with it and . . . [doing] something about it in light of the New Rochelle case."

The school board discussed the question in April but settled only on conferring with the Monroe County Human Relations Commission. In early May, Davis said a lawsuit was imminent: "We are almost positive—in view of the fact that the board of education has done nothing—that we will take legal action." The school board president, Frances Cooke, complained that he was being hasty: "I thought we had made it plain that we were proceeding with the problem. . . . I am sure every member of the board recognizes the problem and I am certain we are going to deal with in the best possible way we can."[56]

Cooke's protest was fruitless. The lawsuit was filed on May 28, 1962, in the federal Western District of New York. It was brought in the names of twenty-two children in ten families, the first listed of whom was six-year-old Allen Aikens, a student at School 2.[57] They included, too, the children of Rosetta Crutchfield and Katherine Jordan Harris.

The brief complaint alleged that the district and school board had violated the plaintiffs' rights under federal law by operating racially segregated schools and upholding that segregation through school placement policies. The plaintiffs asked for an injunction against the district to prevent it "from continuing to enforce rules, regulations and procedures which effect and result in the maintenance of segregated schools in Rochester." They requested a desegregation plan to be submitted to the court, and, in a double negative, asked that the district "be further enjoined from failing to adopt the establishment of boundaries of schools for the purpose of creating and perpetuating positive racial integration patterns rather than perpetuation of racial segregation patterns."[58]

There were two noteworthy aspects to the *Aikens* lawsuit, one of them unique in the nation. First, unlike in New Rochelle, the complaint did not allege that the defendants had taken specific actions to cause segregation. "Our contention is simply that it exists," Davis said. "Whether it is intentional or unintentional, the result, an inferior situation, is the same." Second, for the first time in the North or South, the plaintiffs included both Black and white children. In other words, it held that white children's constitutional rights were being violated by being kept separate from Black children, as well as the converse.[59]

Among the white parents holding that opinion were Jerome and Ruth Balter, who lived with their three children on Cedarwood Terrace in the Browncroft neighborhood. Both Balters grew up in New York City and shared a sharp sense of social justice and a willingness to fight for it. Jerome was more effective as an organizer, whereas Ruth was "the one who was a very critical thinker," their youngest son, David, said. In 1955 they came to Rochester, where Jerome Balter worked as an industrial engineer. They made friends in the Black community and sent their children to the Frank Fowler Dow School 52. The Balters were among a handful of liberal Jews in a generally conservative white neighborhood and school. "It was growing up in a contrarian setting. . . . [like] a little bit of a siege mentality," David Balter recalled. "I would go with [my parents] down Joseph Avenue for leafletting or something like that." His father and brother attended the March on Washington in 1963, and his mother missed traveling to the historical march on the Edmund Pettis Bridge in Selma only after a jar fell from a kitchen cabinet and hit her on the head just before she was to leave home. The Balter children, David, Joseph, and Kathe, made up one of four white families to join the *Aikens* lawsuit. Ruth Balter recalled that her husband Jerome was active in recruiting plaintiffs for it. Participating, she said, "seemed very obvious to us at the time. . . . We understood the importance of it for our kids as well as for all kids. It wasn't just a do-good attitude—we frankly were concerned about what kind of exposure our own kids had."[60]

Another of the white plaintiff families had recently relocated to Rochester as well. Mark and Susan Faegre arrived from Washington, DC, in 1960; their father had gotten a job at the University of Rochester. The Faegres, too, attended the March on Washington in 1963. "They were just really socially active," Susan (Faegre) deFay said. "We were raised in that household just feeling like that's how it's supposed to be." Her brother said it was in Rochester's Cobbs Hill Park, playing with the neighbors, that he first heard the N-word used. "We were getting ready to play some kind of game and we did an eenie-meenie-meiny-moe and [a girl] said, 'Catch an N-word by the toe,'" he recalled. "I said, 'That's not how it goes.' And she said, 'That's how it goes around here.'"[61]

Leading the NAACP legal team were two lions of civil rights litigation, Jawn Sandifer and Robert L. Carter. Sandifer, chairman of the state NAACP legal redress committee, had successfully argued before the Supreme Court *Henderson v. United States*, an important precursor to *Brown v. Board of Education*. Carter had succeeded Thurgood Marshall as national NAACP chief counsel and played an important role in *Brown* itself, helping recruit Kenneth Clark as an expert witness. The local counsel was Reuben Davis, one of the few Black lawyers in the city. Born in Mississippi in 1920, Davis was drafted into the Army during his senior year of college at Virginia State University. He landed at Omaha Beach in France and took part in the Battle of the Bulge but, like so many other Black soldiers, could not escape the sting of prejudice back home. After finishing basic training in South Carolina he took a train to visit his family in Mississippi. The conductor walked him all the way down the track, past German prisoners of war sitting in second-class, to a cattle car where Black passengers were expected to ride. After the war Davis went to Boston University for law school and then moved to Rochester in 1955. His son, Mark Allan Davis, said becoming a lawyer was "a survival thing for him," a way to hold fast to right and wrong. "In terms of processing social justice in his own life—he could say, 'The law is concrete. This is what's right,'" Davis said. He later became the first Black City Court judge, serving in that role for twenty-two years. In early 1962, he was in private practice when he succeeded Primo as leader of the local NAACP.[62]

Despite the long wind-up, the RCSD superintendent, Robert Springer, said that the timing of the NAACP lawsuit had come as a surprise. He had expected the organization to bring the results of its study to the board with some sort of proposal.[63] The Gannett newspaper editorial pages, in the meantime, stepped forward to defend the community's leisurely pace toward equity for its growing Black population. The *Democrat and Chronicle* called the lawsuit "a slap" and alleged without evidence that Black parents sought to place their children in integrated schools "merely to satisfy their . . . status ambitions." It continued: "Rochester has always welcomed newcomers of all races, but the problems thus created cannot be solved overnight. Probably no city in the country has approached the challenge of assimilating its non-white population with more determination and sincerity than Rochester. . . . Could anything be less timely and more disturbing at this sensitive point in progress than a lawsuit which seems to impugn the integrity and good faith of the community?"[64]

The newly appointed school board president, Louis Cerulli, had made little secret of his preferred pace of change when it came to school integration. In April 1962 he predicted that segregation "would solve itself in time." Upon being sworn in as president, he cautioned, "Many things we would like to do for our schools and for our city . . . cannot be done immediately." And three days after the lawsuit was filed, Cerulli said that fellow board member Gitelman and Arthur Curran, the district's attorney, should step aside from the defense of the lawsuit because they belonged to the NAACP (both declined to do so, though Curran delegated most of the legal work to a deputy).[65]

A week after the suit was filed, the board announced it would seek guidance from a newly formed state advisory body on racial imbalance. At the same time it responded in court with a vigorous denial of the charges. It avoided answering the question of de facto segregation directly, saying all schools in Rochester were integrated, given that children of any race were technically permitted in them as long as they lived in the appropriate attendance zone. Parents who wanted a more balanced racial mix in their children's schools, the district said, had an obligation "to establish residency in an area not predominated by a homogenous racial group." Davis dismissed the response as "specious at most," ignoring the system's "positive obligation to integrate the schools."[66]

RCSD had taken another, more immediate step in response to the suit. The day it was filed, thirty-eight-year-old Alice Holloway Young was announced as the new principal of School 24 on Meigs Street. When she began the following September she became the first Black building leader in the city's history. Young was born in 1923 in Warren County, North Carolina, just two generations removed from slavery. Her father never received an education, but her mother had graduated from the Hampton Institute in 1906 and became a schoolteacher. Alice's school only went to eleventh grade, but a teacher recommended her to the admissions office at nearby Bennett College, where she enrolled at age sixteen with a single pair of shoes and a four-year work scholarship: scrubbing the floors, washing the windows, and polishing the brass on the thick oak doors. Her mother had taught her that any job she did was worth doing well; one day the college president called for the person responsible for shining the brass door plates. "They sent for me and I went down there shaking, poor little me," she recalled. "And he said: 'Miss Holloway, I never seen the brass on the door shine the way [it's] shining now.'"[67]

She graduated in 1944 and took a job with the American Baptist Home Missionary Society teaching lessons in a migrant worker camp in Madison County, east of Syracuse. It was her first job off the farm and college campus and her first time teaching. The lessons typically began and ended with children and adults, weary from travel and billeting in converted cow barns, learning how to write their names. The experience propelled her toward a career in education that lasted forty years. She began in 1952 as a teacher at School 9, then became the district's first "supervising teacher," or assistant principal, in 1958. She also was one of the founding trustees of Monroe Community College when it opened in 1961. "[Superintendent Robert Springer] called me down and said, 'I want you to go to School 24 on Meigs [Street] as a principal,'" Young recalled decades later. "And he said, 'And I am going to be watching you.' And I said, 'Yeah, and so many others will be watching me, but you'll like what you see.'"[68]

Qualified as Young was, her appointment had every appearance of a diversionary tactic on the part of the district. Her selection as principal was announced two weeks after the board made the decision at a closed-door meeting. The *Democrat and Chronicle* ran a story about her ascent with a headline large enough to compete with the story of the lawsuit. It noted that she belonged to the NAACP but was not active, and she declined to

**Figure 3.2.** Alice Young, seen here in 1976, became the first Black person to serve as a school principal in Rochester in 1962. Photo by David Cook, courtesy of the *Democrat and Chronicle*.

comment on the lawsuit, saying she hadn't known about it in advance. As Walter Cooper said: "When the status quo is under attack, there's always the technique of pulling one Black person in to show it's not as bad as you think it is." Young stayed at School 24 for three years before being promoted once again, this time to lead the newly established Title I program in charge of distributing federal antipoverty funding.[69]

Underlying all the segregation-related tumult of the 1960s in Rochester and other northern cities, was a significant, long-unchallenged assumption about the historical record leading to school segregation. Integration foes insisted repeatedly that racial imbalance derived wholly from discrimination in housing and not at all from particular actions on the part of schools. "The North is troubled in many schools by a lack of integration, as opposed to contrived segregation," the *Democrat and Chronicle* editorial page stated. "The Northern situation evolved spontaneously in the construction of schools in locations best serving children of various ethnic groups. It was not a conspiracy that segregation resulted." Robert Springer said it more precisely in 1963: "No decision, ruling or school boundary has ever been made by the Board of Education or the administration which affects adversely or discriminates against any pupil because of race, color or religion." It was therefore unfair, RCSD and community leaders held, to lay on the educational system the primary responsibility for rectifying the problem; RCSD could only hope to act in concert with progressive steps in other areas of government. Thus did the legal phrases *de jure*, meaning "by law," and *de facto*, referring to a pattern that developed without any official stimulus, enter the vernacular of even casual observers.[70]

It is true that housing discrimination was the greatest factor in the development and persistence of segregated schools in Rochester. Perhaps because housing discrimination was so blatant, desegregation activists, including the NAACP in its 1962 legal challenge, did not challenge the district on its claim of perfect innocence. Throughout the 1960s and beyond, the key question was not whether RCSD bore blame for racial imbalance in its schools, but how much responsibility it had to proactively overturn residential patterns in its placement procedures.[71]

In fact, there is ample evidence that RCSD, beginning at least as early as the 1940s and continuing until the early 1960s, took steps to protect and expand on the effects of housing discrimination in the city's schools. The strategies it used to do so were later recognized by courts in cities throughout the country. They included placing school facilities and drawing attendance zones in careful coordination with established residential segregation patterns; using optional attendance areas, which allowed white students an escape hatch in rapidly changing neighborhoods; and deploying mobile classrooms to accommodate overflowing population at Black schools rather than shifting some students to nearby, underutilized white schools. "It has become clear to me that the old bugaboo . . . of de facto [segregation] is a fraud," US Department of Health, Education, and Welfare Secretary Leon Panetta said in 1969. "There are few if any pure de facto situations. Lift the rock of de facto and something ugly and discriminatory crawls out from under it."[72]

One striking example came in 1962, when RCSD sought to alleviate overcrowding at majority-Black School 4 on Bronson Avenue. The school board authorized busing four classes of fourth-graders to the nearby, mostly white School 44—but kept them segregated within that building rather than interspersing all the children together. Springer defended the arrangement, saying that students "were grouped by ability and achievement." He then went further, claiming that advocates' accusation of unequal education, rather than any differences between schools, threatened to have "a detrimental effect upon the aspirational levels of the children . . . in those schools."[73] The decision to keep Black and white students separate was protested by the Citizens' Committee on School Integration and also by Franklin Florence, whose son happened to be among those affected. The School 4 students were "over there on loan just like a group of cattle," he said. "And if [that] isn't racial isolation in its ugliest form, I don't know what is."[74]

Another common response from the district when faced with overcrowding in mostly Black schools was the use of portable classrooms. Nowhere was this tactic employed more often than at School 3 in the Third Ward. The school board authorized the use of portable classrooms there four times in a seven-year period in the 1950s; on two other occasions it rented space at nearby churches. In 1963–64, 25 percent of the portable units in use in the district were located at mostly Black schools, even though such schools made up only 14 percent of all elementary schools in the city.[75]

RCSD built a number of new schools in the 1960s, both to accommodate the influx of Black migrant children and to replace its aging stock. All five of the buildings that opened from 1961 to 1966 were in areas of nonwhite population growth or adjacent to them, creating a prime opportunity to redraw attendance lines. Indeed, the district promised to do so. By the time the buildings opened, though, four of the five were deeply segregated—two with at least 90 percent nonwhite children and two with 99 percent. The problem was partly beyond RCSD's control—the siting and racial makeup of the Chatham Gardens housing complex, for instance, was an unforeseeable complication—but in other places the cause was clear. School 6, for example, was built close to an established racial boundary, where a broad east-west swath of the Black

Seventh Ward met up with a white section to the north. The School 6 zone was drawn to match the Black neighborhood, stretching widely from east to west. A student living just two blocks north of the school, meanwhile, would walk more than a mile to attend all-white School 36.[76]

The full picture of intentional segregative action is often, by its nature, buried in the monotony of monthly legislative meetings over the course of many years. Much of this evidence is nearly impossible to recreate from historical records—for instance, when an attendance zone line was changed but the specific details were not recorded in the board minutes. Happily, a thorough analysis of those actions in Rochester does exist, albeit in fragmentary form. It was completed by Jonathan Steepee, a University of Rochester graduate student working at the direction of Walter Cooper. Steepee's analysis was apparently the basis of the local branch decision to organize the *Aikens* lawsuit. Infighting among local leadership and Cooper's suspicions of President Quintin Primo resulted in Steepee's study being misplaced and not used as evidence in *Aikens*. Cooper told national NAACP leaders he didn't have a copy of the study to give to them, but somehow a partial, draft version of it ended up in the organization's voluminous papers at the Library of Congress.[77] Taken together, Steepee's study along with the more easily accessible records present a robust picture of explicit school board and district action to create and maintain segregated schools.

In particular Steepee traced the development of placement patterns in accordance with the racial makeup of neighborhoods. The clearest case had to do with the opening of the new East High School building in 1959. Before then, East had drawn elementary students from Schools 9 and 14, both with large proportions of Black children, among others. When the new building opened, it lost both those schools from its feeder pattern and gained in return students from Schools 27 and 31—but not all of them. School 27's attendance zone, for instance, was strictly split, with Black families living on the west side and mostly Italian families on the east side. The dividing line was the unassuming Hebard Street, just a third of a mile long. The next street to the west of Hebard was Scio, nearly 100 percent Black; the next street to the east, Union, was 100 percent white. When the school district reconfigured the attendance zone for its brand-new high school, the white students east of Hebard Street made the cut and the Black students to the west of it did not. A similar vivisection was performed on the School 31 attendance zone, with Black neighborhoods carefully excised.[78]

Both Robert Springer and his successor, Herman Goldberg, insisted that schools in Black neighborhoods received no fewer resources than those in white schools. In his 1963 report to the New York State Education

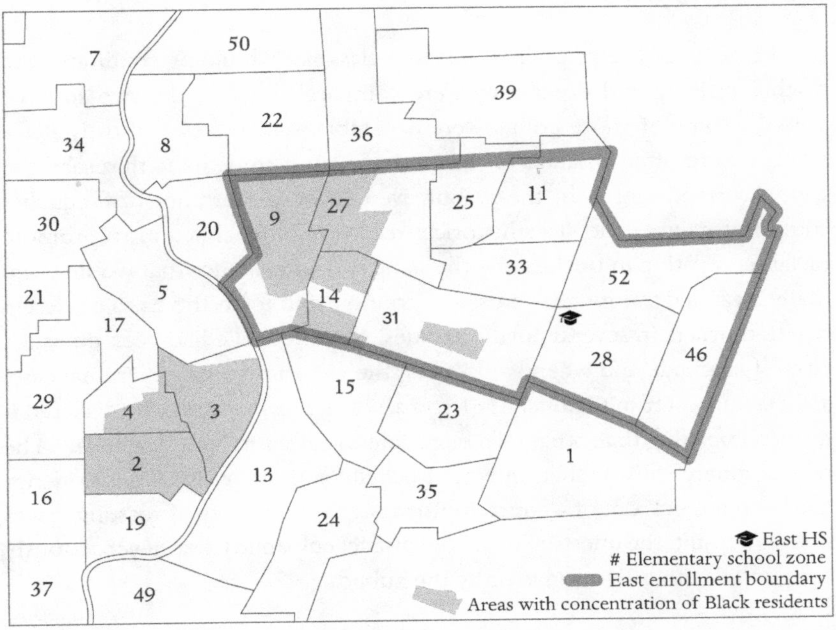


**FIGURE 3.3.** Attendance boundary for East High School before the construction of a new facility in 1959, with elementary school zones. Map by Alana Kornaker.

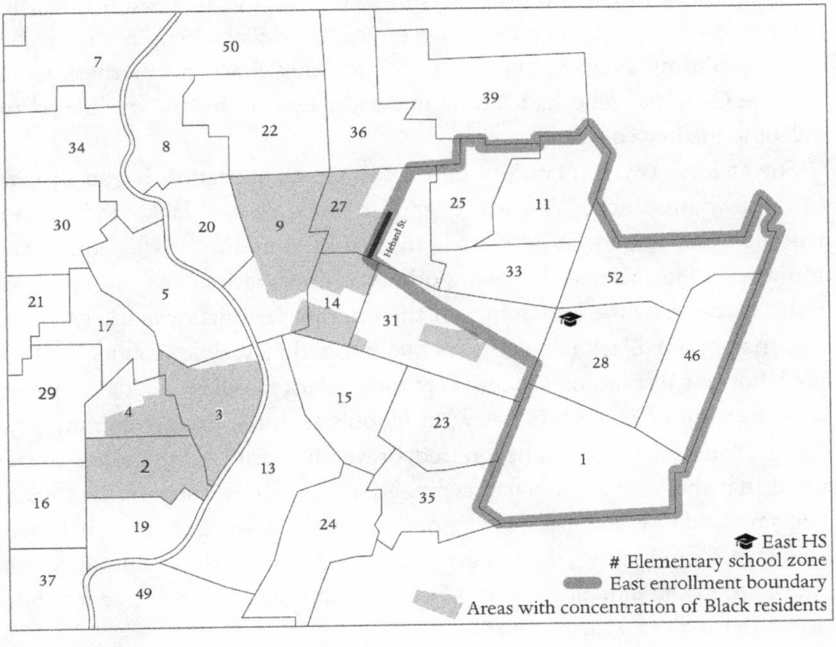


**FIGURE 3.4.** Attendance boundary for East High School after the construction of a new facility in 1959, with elementary school zones. Map by Alana Kornaker.

Department, Goldberg pointed out that class sizes, building condition, and teacher training and experience were comparable across the two sorts of schools. Some of those points were debatable—class sizes in mostly Black schools were often smaller, for instance, because students with disabilities were overrepresented in them. But even those protestations of equality could not gainsay the clear historical record of official action to promote racial segregation in Rochester—the same sort of evidence that would eventually sway federal judges across the country and form the basis of desegregation orders in several northern cities. New Rochelle had been one such city, for example, and when Paul Zuber, the victorious attorney in that case, visited Rochester in October 1961 and saw the Steepee study, he declared it more compelling than what he'd been able to gather in New Rochelle.[79] The crucial difference was that, in New Rochelle and other cities, the evidence had been put in front of a court. In Rochester, for a variety of reasons, it was not. As a result, the question of school district culpability was never seriously considered, either by a judge or by the public.

Shortly after World War I the Rochester *Post Express* ran a lengthy article under the headline: "Negro Exodus to This City Is Finished." The subheadlines shone with glee: "Many who came have gone back; experiment is a failure; homesickness and other factors keep them in the South now; no problem here." From the perspective of southern Black people, the article stated, white northerners were "unfriendly" and Black northerners were "Yankee C——ns" who had "come under the education law" and failed to welcome the newcomers.[80]

For at least two generations, since the Great Migration began in earnest elsewhere, Rochester's white (and, in some cases, Black) leaders had believed—had hoped, at any rate—that their community was somehow immune to the racial strife roiling other northern cities. They were aided in this delusion by the persistence of the migrant farm-labor market, which kept many poor Black farmworkers quarantined in Wayne County, and by harsh housing discrimination that kept those Black families who did arrive in Rochester out of respectable view. In schools as in the greater community, though, the issue could not be ignored forever. In April 1962 the *Times-Union* noted that the issue of de facto segregation in the city's schools had been "long avoided by the board." Two months later the *Aikens* suit made national headlines, "impugn[ing] the integrity and good faith of the community," as the *Democrat and Chronicle* saw it.[81] Now that the issue had received a public airing, there was no turning back.

## Chapter 4

# Six Rugged Years, All Uphill

In late May 1963, Rochester City School District Superintendent Robert Springer flew to Dallas for his brother-in-law's funeral. While staying at his sister's home, the fifty-one-year-old suffered a heart attack in his sleep and was rushed to the Baylor University Hospital. He died on June 19, a gallstone apparently having blocked his bile ducts and caused an infection. Herman Goldberg, the district's special education director, was appointed as interim superintendent after the school board's first choice turned down the assignment.[1]

The day before Springer's death, State Education Commissioner James Allen, had issued a directive that would come to define Herman Goldberg's legacy in Rochester. Specifically addressing Malverne, a small, segregated Long Island school district, Allen said that the district needed to redraw the attendance boundaries to create some approximate racial balance among its three schools. More generally, he wrote in an open letter to New York school leaders:

> The position of the department . . . is that the racial imbalance existing in a school in which the enrollment is wholly or predominantly Negro interferes with the achievement of equality of educational opportunity and therefore must be eliminated from the schools of New York State.

> If this is to be accomplished, there must be corrective action in each community where such imbalance exists. . . .
>
> It is recognized that in some communities residential patterns and other factors may present serious obstacles to the attainment of racially balanced schools. This does not, however, relieve the school authorities of their responsibility for doing everything in their power, consistent with the principles of sound education, to achieve an equitable balance.[2]

The legal victory in New Rochelle had encouraged potential litigants elsewhere in the state; Malverne's directive opened the floodgates for the next stage of the segregation struggle. In Rochester, the person standing shoulder-deep in those waters was Goldberg, a strapping forty-seven-year-old special education expert whose personal background suited him for the role. He was born in Brooklyn in 1915, part of a growing Jewish community in a mostly Catholic neighborhood. His mother was a teacher and his father owned a hardware store where tolerance across ethnic and religious lines was a requirement. "In the hardware store everyone needs nails and screws, hammers, lawnmowers—it doesn't matter what religion you are," he said. Goldberg attended Brooklyn College and played catcher on the baseball team. From there he was chosen for the US baseball team that put on an exhibition during the 1936 Berlin Olympics, making him one of the few Jewish athletes from the United States to venture into Nazi Germany for the games. He recalled seeing Adolph Hitler nearly every day during the Olympics, sitting just a few feet from him in the stands at swimming and wrestling matches.[3]

Goldberg reacted cautiously to Allen's desegregation directive. "We'll study the commissioner's statement very carefully; there will be no precipitous action," he said. Indeed, he spent the majority of his eight-year tenure as superintendent defending his deliberate pace of action from attacks on both sides. Nearly every desegregation action Goldberg proposed drew angry opposition, and sometimes court challenges, from aggrieved white parents; at the same time, the Rev. Franklin Florence, president of FIGHT, wrote him off as "timid and weak," offering "pablum instead of beef—public relations instead of programs—gimmicks instead of products."[4]

The six-year stretch from 1963, when Goldberg took office and Allen gave his first directive, until 1969, when a Goldberg-appointed committee proposed a vigorous reorganization just days before the decade turned over, was a time of great heat and no light in Rochester's schools. Despite a series of optimistic policy pronouncements, the overall picture of racial segregation did not improve—on the contrary, it worsened dramatically, with the number of elementary schools with more than 90 percent Black students doubling from three in 1962–63 to six in 1967–68.[5]

That happened largely because Goldberg and the district spent an enormous amount of energy and political capital pushing the concept of voluntary open enrollment even as they acknowledged, both publicly and privately, that purely voluntary changes could not turn the rising tide of segregation. This poorly designed, poorly executed push for progress not only failed in its stated objective but also poisoned the well for later, more ambitious efforts. Allies from across the pro-integration spectrum defected out of frustration and disgust. Some of them later emerged as Black separatist leaders, who could say quite accurately that the district had no track record of success in achieving quality integrated education. The uprising of July 1964 was a keystone event, proving the stakes for the community while also increasing the urgency with which many white Rochesterians either fled the city or dug in to fight.

The bedeviling thing is that Rochester, in some ways, had the most advantageous climate for successful integration of any northern city. As late as 1968–69, nearly half of its Black students were attending majority-white schools, more than three times the average among comparable cities.[6] Rochester had in Goldberg a leader committed to the cause. Desegregation had a broad base of support, comprising teachers, administrators, and organized labor as well as secular and religious organizations in both the Black and white communities. NAACP-backed litigation provided a potential vehicle for change and federal desegregation funding was available.

But, as a worn-out Goldberg said in January 1970, less than a year before leaving the district for a post in the US Department of Education: "It has been a period of six rugged years, all uphill."[7] His hopeful plans had been watered down or were insufficient from the start. The early pro-integration consensus on the school board and in the community had frayed, with school board president Louis Cerulli leading an increasingly emboldened opposition and Black groups reassessing their loyalties. As the tumultuous decade came to a close, the prospect of serious change in Rochester's schools was as dim as ever.

Allen's 1963 desegregation directive for the first time set a state threshold for racial imbalance: a school with more than 50 percent Black students. In Rochester seven schools in the Third and Seventh Wards met that standard, as would two others soon to open.[8] The district's official response to Allen later in the summer of 1963 contained the basic elements of the desegregation course it would chart over the next several years. In fact, some were already underway. The district had earlier decided to build junior high schools, replacing the K–7 and 8–12 configuration with a new set of middle schools that would alleviate overcrowding in elementary school buildings. The new buildings would have larger and more strategically drawn enrollment zones allowing for greater racial balance. In another proposal, known nationally as the Princeton Plan, two neighboring elementary schools, one mostly white and one mostly Black, would be combined into one enrollment zone. The two buildings would then split the collected students by grade level rather than geography, creating two perfectly desegregated schools in the place of two segregated ones. The most prominent new idea was "open enrollment," where students would be allowed to attend schools outside their neighborhoods, if space permitted and their parents agreed.[9]

Allen called Rochester's plan one of the best in the state, yet even at that early point, signs of trouble were visible. The school board, in accepting the plan, seemed to question its premise. "It has been observed that some pupils have not taken advantage of educational opportunities presently available to them," the board wrote. "Children without security, without a backlog of self-esteem . . . could conceivably be set further behind in their school and life experiences by the pressures of being integration pioneers." Goldberg collected feedback from his own administrative team and found several anonymous critics. "We must not overdo or we will cause an exodus from the community," one wrote.[10]

The first major organized opposition to desegregation efforts appeared in November after the board announced it would consider using the Princeton Plan with nine pairs of racially imbalanced schools, touching about 45 percent of the city's elementary school enrollment. More than a thousand mostly white parents swelled an informational forum on the idea, complaining of the increased distance their children would have to travel to school. Within two months opponents had gathered more than five thousand signatures on a petition asking for the idea to be put to a referendum. The plan was supported, meanwhile, by the NAACP, the Monroe County Human Relations Committee, and several faith groups. "I think it is plain personal dislike of Negroes," one proponent said. "This stuff about your children having to walk farther is just a smokescreen."[11]

The district bowed to the pressure and withdrew its Princeton Plan proposal in favor of two other initiatives. First, the school board announced it would send all fifth- and sixth-graders from 95 percent nonwhite School 3 to the all-white School 30 about two miles away. The goal, Goldberg said, was not integration but rather reducing overcrowding; School 3 was well over capacity, whereas School 30 was anticipated to have seven empty classrooms. School 30 parents nonetheless objected forcefully. "Don't ask us to do anything you wouldn't do yourselves," one parent told the board. The second initiative was a limited start to open enrollment, which many Princeton Plan opponents had said they would prefer. Goldberg sent a letter to families in six majority-Black schools, putting the offer in blunt terms: "There are many Negro children and only a few white children in your child's school. . . . We would like to know if you want your child to have a chance to attend a school where there are more white children." He and the district were expecting affirmative responses from about 2 percent of eligible children, based on precedent elsewhere in the country. Instead they received applications to transfer from 1,721 students, or 35 percent of those eligible, swamping available space in the receiving, mostly white schools.[12]

The transfer plan at schools 3 and 30 began in January 1964. It got off to a rough start when three quarters of the white fifth- and sixth-graders at School 30 were kept at home the first day the 118 Black children arrived on buses from School 3. Boycotts continued for the first week or so, even while the students who did attend reported a positive experience. "Aw, mister, that stuff about trouble is a lot of baloney," a twelve-year-old told a reporter. "I made five new friends today." The mostly Black children at School 3 regretted leaving their friends but mostly expressed optimism. "I would like to go to School 30 because I would like to ride the school bus every morning," one wrote. "I would be losing some of my best friends, but this is not very bad because I will be meeting new friends." On the other hand, because the Black children were a distinct minority, the burden of assimilation, both social and academic, fell on their shoulders. "You felt like you was living up to their expectations," one student later said. "You first had to be like them. So therefore, it took something away from who you were."[13]

Open enrollment, meanwhile, began in early February. About 640 were signed up to participate just days before the transfers began, but more than 100 reconsidered after what district officials described as a "campaign of terror" by white community members in Black neighborhoods over the preceding weekend. "My understanding is that individuals in cars drove through certain neighborhoods of our city and through whatever techniques they devised, indicated to children and parents and others in the area that it would be advisable for the children not to go on the buses," Goldberg said. Alice Young, the highest-ranking Black administrator in the district, agreed: "Many Negro parents were intimidated. . . . They feared something might happen to their children." Coming just a few months after the fatal bombing of a Black church in Birmingham, Alabama, the message was unmistakable.[14]

Opponents of both the School 3 to School 30 transfer and open enrollment also began more formal counterattacks in New York Supreme Court. A group of School 30 parents filed a lawsuit seeking an injunction against the transfer of School 3 children. The district was lying, they said, in claiming the action had nothing to do with desegregation. The parent leader Christopher Strippoli brought to court three aggrieved School 30 students who said they had become depressed "because they were unable to readily adjust to . . . being regrouped in the middle of the school year with children who were not their neighborhood playmates and with whom they had little in common." A parent association at mostly white School 40 issued a separate lawsuit over the presence of eleven Black children who previously had attended School 4. Goldberg's "whims and fancies," they argued, would destroy the neighborhood school concept all together.[15]

Local judges sided forcefully with the parents in both cases. State Supreme Court Justice William Easton saw in the School 3 transfer a threat to "the ethnic institutions within which Americans have organized their urban life." Both decisions, however, were overturned; the New York Court of Appeals decided unanimously that the opposing parents had not succeeded in establishing any constitutional violation. "If the complaint of these petitioners is that their children must now attend an integrated school, we call attention to *Brown v. Board of Education*," the court wrote in the *Strippoli* case.[16]

The complainants may have lost in the courtroom, but the anxious white parents they represented continued to vote with their feet. A census count showed there were now nine schools with more than 50 percent minority students, including for the first time a secondary school, Madison High School. At the same time thirty-seven elementary schools had fewer than 15 percent nonwhite students, a proportion the Citizens' Committee on School Integration called "grossly at variance with the overall composition of the school system," which then stood at 26 percent nonwhite students in the elementary schools and 11 percent in the high schools.[17]

The major Christian, Jewish, and ecumenical faith organizations in Rochester all came out early in support of the district's desegregation efforts, including submitting a friend-of-the-court brief in the open enrollment lawsuit. In February, though, just as the various transfer programs seemed to be progressing as planned, the *Jewish Ledger* threw cold water on optimism among proponents:

> We confess we cannot participate in the bubbling enthusiasm and joy expressed by many groups and individuals with the success of the open enrollment plan for Rochester's public schools. Frankly, our emotions

were sorrow and shame as we viewed these bewildered tots, identification tags dangling from their tiny necks, who rise early to shuttle across town to neighborhoods denied their parents. . . .

We were always led to believe that Rochester was a highly cultural city, enjoying excellent race relations—unless, of course, you wanted to buy a home, join a club or belong to a union. Let us not now be falsely lulled into believing we have opened our hearts by opening a few doors.[18]

In February 1964, the essay may have seemed unduly pessimistic. Five months later it proved prescient.

On the evening of July 24, 1964, a community organization called the Northeast Mothers Improvement Association held a dance on Joseph Avenue in the Seventh Ward. A twenty-year-old man got drunk and an organizer called the Rochester Police Department at about 11:25 p.m. to make a complaint. The police responded, as they often did in Black neighborhoods, with dogs. The tactic had long been controversial, reminiscent of more overt brutality in the South but also indicative of fraught community-police relations in Rochester. Police dogs were used in several instances of police misconduct in the early 1960s that served as an important galvanizing theme for nascent Black political organizing in the city. "In my entire upbringing the dogs were the number one subject that . . . most of the people thought about, talked about, wanted something to be done about, because that was a bad situation," a Seventh Ward resident, Trent Jackson, Jr., later said.[19]

Housing supply and conditions remained a dire problem, as did the city of Rochester's indifferent municipal services. Juan Padilla, an early Puerto Rican migrant, recalled that it was particularly unpleasant to walk down Joseph Avenue on a windy day in the early 1960s: "[The] streets were dirty, and when the winds would gust, it looked like a tornado with the swirling of papers and garbage." A 1967 confidential consultant report to Kodak on the city's Black neighborhoods noted they had been physically segregated "strategically" and showed "an alarming lack of municipal services," compounding the housing crisis: "The streets are littered and filthy, and the garbage stands open and uncollected. Rats are said to roam the streets at night. Traffic safety devices are lacking, there are fewer fire hydrants (though the buildings are the most flammable in the city), many of the sewer entrances are clogged, and trees have been allowed to grow and obscure street lights."[20]

This all served as kindling on that hot night in July 1964. As best as anyone could piece it together in the aftermath, the partygoers on Joseph Avenue became enraged by a fast-spreading rumor that a police dog had bitten a pregnant woman. That allegation was never verified, but within minutes a crowd had assembled, and the night filled with the sounds of breaking glass and blaring sirens. The violence spread on the second night from the Seventh Ward to the other Black neighborhood, the Third Ward. A white man was killed when he was hit in the head with a pipe, knocked into the street, and run over by a car. Three more people died when a helicopter crashed into a house on Clarissa Street. Only on the third night, after the National Guard had been called in, did calm return.

Nearly 900 people were arrested, 86 percent of them Black and Puerto Rican. Of the 720 Black people arrested, 92 percent had been born out of state, mostly in the South, a remarkable illustration of the growth of the local Black population. Black leaders threw their hands up, pointing out that they had been trying to call attention to the community's frustration and economic isolation for decades. To give one example, the State Commission against Discrimination described Rochester as "sitting on a pressure cooker whose relief valve has long been choked"—and that was in 1957. "The response to many warning reports, protests and discussions failed to activate an arrogant and complacent power structure," Walter Cooper wrote. "Their response to all legitimate complaints was to maintain the illusory policy of condescending paternalism." Franklin Florence, who was out of town the weekend of the violence, noted that the streets had filled with not only teenagers but also children, adults, and senior citizens. "There were grandmothers, fathers, mothers, aunties, young people," he said. "They didn't look at this as a riot. They looked at it as a rebellion."[21]

Predictably, the city government saw things differently. In a meeting with NAACP leaders the following Monday, Mayor Frank Lamb "referred constantly to, 'you people' and implied that all Negroes would have to suffer because of the acts of violence over the weekend," according to the Black leaders in attendance. In his official postmortem, City Manager Porter Homer characterized the violence as "an irrational orgy of lawlessness and disorder" perpetuated by "toughs and thugs," contained only through the admirable work of law enforcement. The community's efforts to help its Black residents had been unparalleled in the nation, he wrote—and, to the extent they had not resulted in significant improvements, the blame lay in large part with Black community leaders who had failed to communicate the good news to the masses. "Nothing the City government could have accomplished in the past few years would have so dramatically changed conditions for the Negro in the riot areas that his frustration and anger would have been eliminated," Homer concluded.[22]

As pivotal as those three July days were for Rochester, they were overshadowed on the national scale by a broader pattern of riots and uprisings in cities across the country, some much deadlier and more destructive. Locally and nationally, frustration and anger were channeled into a more confrontational, more impatient brand of Black leadership that eventually came to be known as Black Power. Followers of Stokely Carmichael, Malcolm X, and other Black Power leaders snorted at the essentially optimistic activism of Martin Luther King, Jr. and Thurgood Marshall. Facing what one historian called "the space between new rights and unclaimed freedoms," these more militant leaders demanded rather than pleaded, recoiled rather than reconciled.[23]

In Rochester, Black Power crystallized after July 1964 when a citywide group of Protestant clergy brought to town Saul Alinsky, the Jewish Chicago-based organizer and agitator. He described Rochester as "probably the most extreme example of benevolent paternalism in this country" and agreed to take on the city as a project—but only if invited by some representative group of the Black community. In 1965 that group, FIGHT, was formed, with the thirty-one-year-old Rev. Franklin Florence, pastor of the Reynolds Street Church of Christ, as president. "We have been guinea pigs in a prolonged experiment with paternalism—and we will stand it no more," Florence said at the inaugural FIGHT convention.[24]

FIGHT's primary concern was jobs, particularly for Black unskilled workers, and Florence sought them at the same place as everyone else in town—Kodak. The company was seen, not unreasonably, as the face of Rochester paternalism and the inevitable pressure point for social change. "Kodak's benevolent-father image is very strong in Rochester and has been fostered so assiduously and for such a long time that to some extent both the community and the company have become its captives," one researcher wrote. "Problems of minorities, militancy, and reallocation of power [do] not fit into Kodak's existing personnel makeup and decision-making process." Constance Mitchell, the first Black elected official in Monroe County, said it was "a [laughing] matter among the minority community that if you put your application in at Kodak, Bausch and Lomb or Xerox, any of the corporations, they'd put your application in File 13, which was the wastebasket."[25] A Kodak consultant, in a confidential 1967 report, observed that the company was, in the minds of Black residents, "the primary agent for thwarting the possibilities for human and social development in the ghetto . . . whose existence depends largely on Kodak's implicit or explicit approval." The consultant concluded: "The situation cannot become worse. The prime responsibility for reducing tension in Rochester must rest with Eastman Kodak."[26]

For two years Florence negotiated, threatened, and protested, jostling the venerable community institution in a way to which it was decidedly unaccustomed. "It's just like with Kennedy and Khrushchev," he said. "You can't have peace until you get the .45 on the table." After a labor war that garnered national headlines, FIGHT and Kodak eventually agreed to a somewhat anticlimactic pact that provided for training hundreds of Black employees. Although focusing most of its attention on jobs, FIGHT also took some early stands on education—namely, in strong support of integration along with other assistance for Black students. Florence in 1966 testified at a hearing of the US Commission on Civil Rights in Rochester, demanding integrated education. "To be black means, in America and in Rochester, inferior," he said. "So then it is impossible to get a quality education in an all-black school under the present system." The following year, FIGHT's education committee released a position paper on education, calling for integrated schools along with more Black teachers and administrators, Afro-centric curriculum, and more reading instruction.[27]

As FIGHT ascended, the NAACP and other more moderate groups faded. Florence derided nonmilitant Black activists—the same "Young Turks" who had so rattled earlier white and Black leaders just a few years earlier—as "Oreos and Uncle Toms." An anonymous flier circulated in the Third Ward with a cartoon of one such "Tom" carrying a suitcase labeled "Whitey's Bag of Tricks" in one hand and a satchel of cash in the other, hustling into a building marked "riot-proof." A national Committee on Racial Equality executive, on a visit to Rochester shortly after the riots, concluded: "We have in Rochester no real recognized leadership by the Negro community. . . . There has been nothing concrete done in terms of getting to the community, and I doubt whether or not [Black leaders] are really interested." A common wisecrack regarding nonmilitant Black activists was that PhD stood for "poor helpless dummy," longtime community activist Gloria Winston Al-Sarag recalled. "The intellectuals were told to go somewhere and sit down."[28]

More important than the NAACP's losses in the public eye was the fact that *Aikens*, the federal desegregation lawsuit it sponsored in 1962, was floundering. Indeed, the legal attack in that case had been disjointed from the beginning. Reuben Davis, the lead local attorney, had requested to be released from the case just two weeks before it was initially filed in May 1962, citing an unspecified concern "from a personal point of view." He ultimately remained part of the team. Then, in November 1962, the local NAACP learned it would be largely responsible for financing the lawsuit, an expense that it had not anticipated, and that Davis did not believe it could meet without significant outside assistance.[29]

Happily for the litigants, a group shortly formed to provide that assistance. The Citizens' Committee on School Integration, led by *Aikens* plaintiff Jerome Balter, intended to create and organize momentum for desegregation, whether court-ordered or otherwise, and to raise money for the cause. As the months and years went by, however, with *Aikens* no closer to resolution and the local NAACP experiencing a change in leadership, Balter grew frustrated. "As you know, there has been no action on this case for almost the entire period," he wrote in May 1964 to the national NAACP. "The local branch . . . has been conspicuous by its lack of activity on the question of school integration."[30] In the spring of 1965, the local chapter announced that it was dropping the case in favor of filing a petition for the state education department to intercede. Court rulings elsewhere in the state had led the NAACP legal team to believe such executive intercession was "obligatory" for court-ordered desegregation and would "offer the most expeditious route to the end which is involved." In the midst of the public debate over open enrollment and other strategies, the dismissal of *Aikens* caused hardly a ripple. Behind the scenes and among those who had volunteered as plaintiffs, though, the NAACP's apparently peremptory decision was disheartening. Balter reported it had been dropped "against the advice of the litigants." An NAACP effort to file a new lawsuit the following year was derailed "because of the bad handling of the original suit," a local representative conceded in an internal memo. "Many of the original litigants do not want to go along with us and refuse unless we give them a guarantee we will see this one through all the way."[31]

How would Rochester's schools have turned out differently if *Aikens* had led to a prompt judicial desegregation order? In other cases—New Rochelle, for example—judges ordered the merging of enrollment areas and the closure of schools, among other things. A progressive decision in Rochester might have implemented in full the Princeton Plan, creating pairs of racially balanced elementary schools across the city with only slightly increased transportation. Such a step would have capitalized on the comparatively broad consensus around desegregation—broad, compared to what it would become by 1970 after years of inaction. The Rochester lawsuit, with its interracial plaintiff group and its frank stance on the question of de facto segregation, had the potential to generate a landmark ruling. On the other hand, it is hard to imagine that a federal judge would have chosen Rochester to set an example. As paltry as the district's progress toward desegregation was, it nonetheless outpaced that of many other northern districts at the time. And though racial segregation in Rochester was worsening, it was still unremarkable compared with what could be found in other upstate New York cities.

In 1962–63 there were four elementary schools in the city with more than 80 percent minority students; in Buffalo, by comparison, there were fifteen such schools.[32] Given those mitigating factors and the courts' continuing reluctance to impose on northern districts while more overt opposition to desegregation was ongoing in the South, it seems unlikely *Aikens* would have resulted in a major edict.

One area where the NAACP and FIGHT agreed was the pressing need for more Black teachers. In 1963 there were just 96 Black teachers among a districtwide corps of 2,200, and many schools had none at all. Goldberg reported that the district was urgently seeking Black teachers but had been thwarted, in part, by housing discrimination, as newly arriving Black educators could not find a place to live. An ongoing commitment to recruitment, along with the continuing magnetism of the Great Migration, led to a significant increase in the number of nonwhite teachers in Rochester during the Civil Rights era, from 4 percent in 1963 to 20 percent in 1980. A parallel program brought a lesser number of Black teachers to suburban schools, where they often felt even more alien than they did in Rochester. "When I first arrived, the kids crowded around me to see if I was real," one teacher said of her experience at Greece Arcadia High School, just west of Rochester, in 1970. "I could tell they wanted to touch me." Nydia Padilla, a Latina, remembered arriving around the same time as a student teacher at an elementary school in the town of Webster and having children crowd around to touch her hair, excited to have "a real Indian in the school." One boy asked whether she was carrying a knife to stab people, like his parents said Puerto Ricans often did.[33]

The recruitment efforts were coordinated as part of a federally funded program known as Project UNIQUE (United Now for Integrated Quality Urban-Suburban Education). Its director was William Young, and two of the first teachers he succeeded in bringing to Rochester were his younger sisters. The Young family grew up on a farm in Daingerfield, Texas. Their parents had received hardly any education but saw five of their children become teachers—even if Lillie, the younger of the two sisters, wasn't originally interested in the profession. "They came home one summer and were telling me all about [teaching in Rochester] and asked if I wanted to try it," she said. "And I said, 'No, not really.' I already had four or five brothers and sisters who were teachers and I didn't want to do that." But when another recruit dropped out at the last moment and the federal funding for her brother's program came into jeopardy, she changed her mind and packed her bags.[34]

Lillie Young and other newly arriving Black teachers were to find in Rochester a delicate situation, as some of their white colleagues and supervisors were skeptical of their preparedness. "They were very strict on us," she said. "It was always: 'What are you doing? That can't work.'" Another Black recruit, Andrew Ray, would go on to become a well-regarded principal in the district after first arriving at Madison High School from Mississippi in 1969. In his first year he overheard a white teacher saying that the new Black teachers surely hadn't been properly trained in the South. He responded: "I'm here at the same level as you are, and you had a 300-year head start on me."[35]

The Black southern transplants, of course, had all attended strictly segregated schools, and therefore brought a different perspective on how to run a classroom from that of their northern counterparts. "We knew, when a teacher walked into a classroom in our schools: order," Ray said. "You automatically snapped to attention. . . . It was a famous saying among African-American parents in the South: 'Don't make me have to come to that school for you.'"[36] For many, that was part of a larger difference in expectations that allowed Black teachers to connect with their Black students in a way not every white teacher could. One former student, Bettina Love, remembered the lightning strike of entering third grade at School 19 and meeting her first Black teacher, a transplant from New Orleans: "I had never seen a woman, regardless of race, so powerful, so commanding, and so stern. . . . Mrs. Johnson did not just love her students, she fundamentally believed that we mattered. She made us believe that our lives were entangled with hers and that caring for us meant caring for herself. . . . I distinctly remember walking into class, looking up at Mrs. Johnson, and realizing my class-clown days were over. I was relieved. I was ready to get my voice back."[37]

Mrs. Johnson also made sure to connect with parents, Love wrote, learning about her charges as children and not just students—and instilling a healthy dose of fear in them as well. Another early Black teacher, Musette Castle, moved from Memphis, Tennessee, to Rochester in 1971 and stayed for a long career in RCSD, where she made a priority of connecting with—and respecting—her students' parents. "I make the assumption that a parent cares and wants their child to do well," she said. "Instead of [teachers] who just let him act simple and sleep and never contact the parent and let them know there's a problem—what kind of nuttiness is that?"[38]

At the same time that scores of minority teachers were arriving in Rochester classrooms, the district was also—for the first time but certainly not the last—looking to make its curriculum more inclusive. District reading lists and lesson plans had progressed little since the days of the Little Black Sambo controversy. The first dedicated districtwide effort culminated with

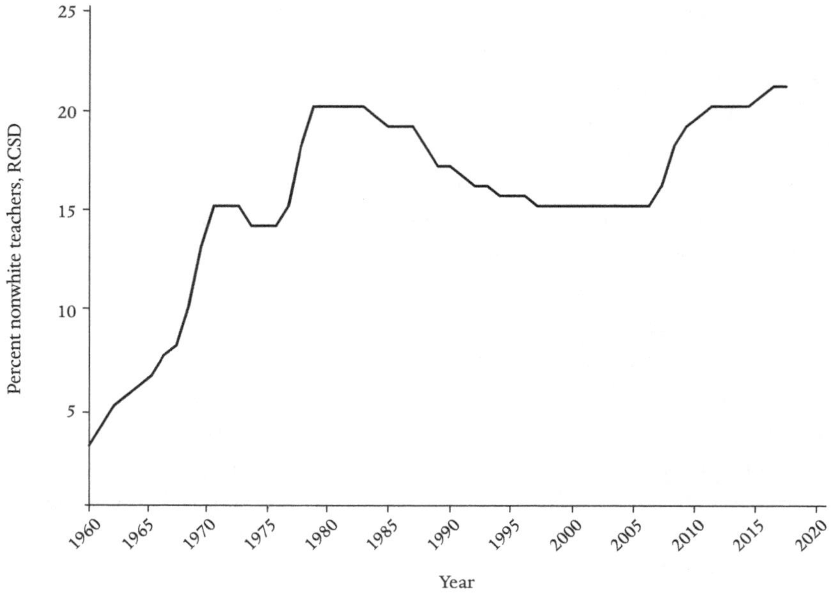


**FIGURE 4.1.** Percent nonwhite teachers, Rochester City School District, 1960 to 2020. Source: Compiled RCSD documents and news reports.

the publication in 1964 of "The Negro in American Life," a middle-school curriculum supplement meant to serve as a corrective for the "unrealistic and incomplete interpretation of our cultural heritage" that students had previously encountered. "No young person preparing to take part in his country's future can be considered educated without an understanding of the civil rights issue, its origins, and its by-products of fear, ignorance and prejudice," the introduction stated. Still, said Hannah Storrs, a Black teacher and the president of the local chapter of CORE (Congress of Racial Equality), in 1967: "Boys and girls in the inner-city and in other schools really believe that when we talk about our ancestors from Africa that they still swing around in trees." FIGHT called for teaching Swahili as well as for making "the contributions of Afro-American citizens to America's growth . . . an INTEGRAL part of the social studies and history curriculum."[39]

The introduction of Black teachers and culturally responsive curriculum, coinciding at the local and national levels with the rise of the Black Power movement, left many Black Rochester students with a sense of empowerment just as they were being placed on the front lines of a communitywide battle over desegregated schools. Black student unions (BSUs) sprang up at most city high schools; Charlotte residents looked on with trepidation as teenagers with Afros and dashikis got off the bus on Lake Avenue, James Baldwin paperbacks tucked in their back pockets. One of them was Idonia Owens, president of the Charlotte High School BSU and later a longtime RCSD administrator. "In high school, I was fully immersed in being Blacker than Black," she said. "I joined the local Black Panther group, I was active in the FIGHT organization, I read everything all the time by every Black author I could get my hands on."[40]

Another Black Charlotte student, Jonathan Perkins, recalled: "When we, the Black students, began to have meetings and our attire changed—Black and white dashiki, Black and white applejack hat, power fist—that sort of visible ornamentation allowed me to think of the necessity of expressing myself as not just a student, but an African-American student. I recognized there's a need for our voice to be heard, and even if I cannot articulate what I'm feeling, even just putting on this clothing is helpful to me."[41]

Nellie King recalled a trip to New York City in the early 1960s with the Junior NAACP and seeing modes of Black cultural expression she hadn't thought possible at West High School. That and protests over instances of police brutality served as gateways to greater pride in being Black. "That's how we learned about wearing our hair natural and other kinds of things we didn't have here," she said. "[Before], you didn't step out the door without your hair being very pressed. . . . Just to find that freedom to be who you are was a great experience to me." As another Black Charlotte student leader, James Beard, remarked: "My thought was, I have a right to be in this school if I want to be in this school."[42]

Participation in the open enrollment program grew from about 450 students in 1964–65 to about 700 in 1965–66. Others took advantage of another new avenue, called the Triad Plan, where students in some parts of the city could choose among three schools near their homes rather than just the one to which they traditionally would be assigned. All told, more than 1,200 students were participating in race-based transfer programs by the fall of 1966.[43] Even as participation in open enrollment grew, though, the basic problem of racial isolation in the schools was getting worse. In 1962–63, before the district had done anything to promote integration, there had been eight elementary schools with more than 50 percent Black students. Three years later, after intensive political and social activity, there were nine such schools, including five where the Black enrollment was greater than 95 percent.[44]

**FIGURE 4.2.** Kindergarteners at School 50 get to know one another after being placed in the same school through open enrollment in 1965. Photo courtesy of the *Democrat and Chronicle*.

It was assumed that, to the extent open enrollment resulted in desegregated schools, students would become more open-minded when it came to race. Yet though many children did experience such a transformation, it was far from universal. One extensive survey found that the introduction of a handful of Black transfer students had hardened, rather than eliminated, students' racial animus. For the white students, the researcher, Ralph Barber, attributed this largely to the influence of white Charlotte teachers, whose "open hostilities, . . . lack of tact and stereotyped, vituperative humor must certainly be communicated to students." Black students' antipathy, he wrote, was unsurprising when considering their rude welcome and distinct minority status: "Negro students at [Charlotte] have felt threatened, physically and emotionally, by the white community, generally, and by the white students specifically. White students at [Charlotte] have felt threatened by the appearance of Negroes in terms of social-class consciousness. This is also true of some white teachers. . . . The fear voiced most frequently by parents is that Negroes will cause [Charlotte] to lower its standards and thereby become a 'lower-class' school." Barber nonetheless concluded: "Synoptically viewed, desegregation at [Charlotte] has undergone all the labor pains of a difficult birth. It probably could not have been accomplished otherwise were it born now or ten years from now. Of greatest importance is its continuation."[45]

Academic results were more encouraging. Children who left segregated Black elementary schools for modestly desegregated ones saw appreciable increases in test scores, attendance, IQ test scores, sense of self-worth, and citizenship compared to those who stayed behind. Their report card marks were initially lower, but they mostly made up the difference within two years. Whatever mixed social and academic gains open enrollment produced, though, were limited to the small subset of students who had been prescreened by district officials looking for those most likely to succeed. "For every one child parachuted out of the ghetto, 12 stay behind in all-Black schools," Franklin Florence said. "A few benefit; the many are forgotten." Goldberg himself conceded in 1966: "I do not believe that open enrollment as it is now constituted can reduce racial imbalance in [all] schools."[46]

Nor could it improve overall academic achievement by minority students in the district, as gains among open enrollment participants were offset by poor marks at the most segregated schools. The district at that time did not systematically report academic data by race—it had not tracked student race at all until James Allen requested a racial census in 1961—but the available evidence showed that Black achievement overall lagged badly. Of the four schools in the district with remedial early elementary classes in 1965–66, three had at least 90 percent nonwhite students. The four schools with advanced programs, on the other hand, were all at majority-white schools. The Monroe County Human Relations Commission formally complained in July 1966 of "academic imbalance," and several Black parents wrote to tell Allen that their children in the city's segregated schools were "being slowly killed mentally."[47]

Those who sought a faster pace of desegregation were represented on the school board in the mid-1960s by Robert Bickal and Faust Rossi, who regularly joined forces on the losing side of 3–2 votes. In 1966 they managed to achieve a compromise, getting the full school board to request from Goldberg a fresh desegregation plan for the elementary schools. The urgency of the task was underscored when the 1966–67 school year began and about 150 white students at John Marshall High School protested the arrival of 110 Black students transferring in from Madison High School under open enrollment. Some held signs reading "Negroes go home" and "Keep Marshall clean."[48]

The proposal that Goldberg presented in February 1967 contained four different plans, from which he hoped the board would choose one.[49] Two of them captured the attention of the community and are worth discussing in detail. One plan called for the construction of seven "educational parks" that would replace nearly all the existing elementary school buildings with state-of-the-art campuses serving several thousand students each. They would be located mostly in public parks—Genesee Valley, Highland, Seneca, Cobbs Hill, and Maplewood would all get a campus—and offer amenities not available in smaller schools, such as science and language laboratories, auditoriums, and resource centers for teachers. This plan was discarded because of its fantastic cost but inspired a Greece school board member to put forth a similar concept for students of several school districts. His proposal will be discussed in chapter six.

The most practical of Goldberg's four plans was what he called the "Rochester plan"—in essence, a large-scale version of the Princeton Plan. It would split the primary years into grades K–3 and grades 4–6 buildings with greater demographic balance. The city would be divided into ten units, each comprising from three to six existing elementary schools, some of them clustered geographically and others not. Each unit would have a nonwhite enrollment from 28 to 37 percent, and the boundaries would be flexible to account for changes in neighborhood makeup.

Liberal and Black groups, including the Citizens' Committee on School Integration, the Rochester Teachers Association (RTA), CORE, and the NAACP, came out unanimously in support of the Rochester plan. FIGHT did as well, in its own way, demanding strict equity in the number of white and Black children required to ride buses and calling Louis Cerulli a bigot who "is going to have us gumming our way through the baby food Goldberg is feeding us."[50] Parent groups from majority-white schools, as well as those purporting to represent "taxpayers," submitted thousands of signatures opposing all of Goldberg's plans, saying they would cause "almost insurmountable financial problems" and destroy neighborhood schools.[51]

It was during the deliberations over Goldberg's 1967 proposal that Cerulli emerged as the unquestioned leader of the antibusing movement in the city, a position he would not relinquish until his death five years later. A West High School graduate and respected medical doctor in the city's Maplewood neighborhood, Cerulli won his first election to the school board in 1959 with a bland platform of fiscal restraint and putting children first. As late as 1964, an opponent of the Princeton Plan called for Cerulli to resign for inadequately defending the concept of neighborhood schools. "We don't need a man like him on the school board," the father taunted.[52]

Cerulli attended college in Louisiana and Alabama and often pointed to the strict racial segregation in place there as distinct from the developing imbalance in Rochester. Still, he never hid his reluctance about busing—or his skepticism about the value of racial integration in general. "The value to the education of an individual in an integrated or segregated school has never been proven satisfactorily to me," he wrote in 1966. "The education of an individual to me has always been the result of the individual's capabilities and effort together with motivation."[53]

It was largely in his last two years in office, starting in 1967, that Cerulli became not just an opponent of but an agitator against desegregation. At a meeting at all-white School 52, he encouraged hundreds of parents to "flood" legislators with letters against Goldberg's plans. He laid the blame for increasing segregation on Black southerners moving to Rochester: "I don't know why they're leaving [the South] . . . and get[ting] on the relief rolls right away." And, when asked whether busing could be of any conceivable value, he answered: "If you want to enhance the education of the underprivileged children, take them out to the zoo on the buses. We got the buses. We can use them on Sunday."[54]

**FIGURE 4.3.** Louis Cerulli, seen here in 1971, served on the Rochester school board from 1960 to 1969 and led the white opposition to desegregation. Photo courtesy of the *Democrat and Chronicle*.

Fellow board member Glenn Wiltsey was, like Cerulli, a strong opponent of progressive desegregation, and, as previously mentioned, Bickal and Rossi were strong proponents. This left the fifth board member, Frances Cooke, as the swing vote to find some way forward from Goldberg's four-part proposal. The board in March 1967 listened for six hours as more than one hundred speakers addressed them before the meeting formally began. It was after midnight when they acted. The board voted down all four of Goldberg's plans. None of them could have worked, Cerulli explained, "since they were built on assumptions of population trends and housing patterns not currently predictable." Instead, Cooke joined Cerulli and Wiltsey in approving a separate document called the 15-Point Plan that Goldberg, sensing defeat, had quietly provided to the board several days earlier.[55]

Of the fifteen points, eight were promises to continue programs already underway or vague pledges of support and cooperation. Two had to do with compensatory education in majority-Black elementary schools, including limiting class sizes and hiring additional reading teachers. Two others encouraged further study of regionalization, including a "voluntary cooperative federation of school districts in the region" and a state report on financial and legal barriers. Cerulli touted these last two points in particular as forceful steps toward desegregation, though integration proponents booed lustily as he spoke. The most substantive part of the plan concerned the development of a magnet program for gifted students at majority-Black School 2, together with a "reverse open enrollment" process whereby white students from the city's periphery could attend either that school or School 6, another brand-new building in a Black neighborhood.[56]

For liberals, the 15-Point Plan was an outrage. "There's not a damn thing in it," Bickal roared. Jerome Balter noted sarcastically the apparent "overwhelming consensus in favor of quality integrated schools . . . as long as nothing is done about it." Florence called it "a sellout to education on a straight racist line" and attacked Goldberg for sacrificing Black children "on the altar of political expediency."[57] For Cerulli and busing foes, though, the 15-Point Plan was the best possible outcome. It avoided compulsory busing and also did not exert any particular pressure toward a metropolitan solution extending beyond city limits. Instead it took another step in reframing the debate as about improving segregated schools rather than desegregating them.

For Goldberg, the 15-Point Plan was a capitulation. Despite his avowed opposition to racial segregation, the superintendent had for the second time buckled to the demands of recalcitrant white families in crafting a purported desegregation plan. The 15-Point Plan added little to the existing open enrollment framework that he admitted was inadequate. "[Goldberg] was very good at shooting down plans that were clearly going to be unpopular," Rossi said. "He was not a stupid guy by any means; he was very smart and politically astute." That political calculation was proven correct by the school board election of 1967, where voters showed a distinct lack of support for strong integration measures. Cerulli was re-elected and was joined by Michael Roche, a twenty-nine-year-old teacher who ran against busing just as vigorously, becoming the first Republican on the school board in six years. "People are getting away from extreme liberalism," Cerulli said. "People feel sick and tired of busing—moving kids around. They want the preservation of neighborhood schools."[58]

The 1967–68 school year began, then, with the district in essentially the same posture it had maintained since 1963. Even as racial isolation increased in a growing number of schools, RCSD continued to leave the execution of its desegregation plans in the hands of parents. For the first time, though, it now was offering an option to white families as well. The reverse open enrollment initiative, including the gifted program at School 2, represented Rochester's first experiment with magnet schools, a concept that would gain a great deal of currency in the generation to come. The idea was to use the gifted program (or MAP, for Major Achievement Program), as well as

*Table 2* Timeline of Rochester Desegregation Efforts, 1962 to 1972

| | |
|---|---|
| May 1962 | *Aikens v. Board of Education* filed, alleging segregation in Rochester; Alice Young appointed as first Black school principal |
| September 1963 | Herman Goldberg proposes series of desegregation measures in response to call from state education commissioner James Allen |
| February 1964 | Open enrollment begins; first formal desegregation effort in RCSD |
| September 1965 | Urban-Suburban program begins in West Irondequoit |
| March 1967 | School board rejects Goldberg's four desegregation proposals, adopts 15-Point Plan |
| September 1967 | World of Inquiry School opens; one thousand children skip first week of school in pro-desegregation boycott |
| December 1969 | Goldberg reorganization plan released |
| March 1970 | School board rejects Goldberg reorganization plan, then adopts a watered-down version after two-day teachers' strike and twenty thousand students boycotting in favor of desegregation; *Colquhoun v. Board of Education* filed, alleging segregation |
| February 1971 | Newly elected school board adopts Goldberg reorganization plan; massive antibusing protests |
| June 1971 | City council cuts district budget in attempt to stop busing; schools close early due to violence |
| September 1971 | Reorganized secondary schools open; some anti-reorganization parents withhold children and instead open five unlicensed block schools |
| February 1972 | School board rescinds reorganization plan |
| June 1972 | Regents exams canceled due to violence in schools |

the incentive of a brand-new facility, to lure white families into a neighborhood they otherwise would avoid. The problem with such initiatives—which create incentives to increase white enrollment at a mostly Black school—is that some artificial cap must be placed on Black neighborhood enrollment to ensure enough space for the targeted students. When the district sent canvassers out into the School 2 neighborhood seeking hundreds of Black families to volunteer to send their children somewhere other than the newly built, richly appointed school in their own backyard, it blundered into a hornet's nest.

"We strongly protest the use of 'integration' to pressure inner city students to accept busing away from a superior school program, in order to allow white children the obvious advantages available here," the School 2 Parent Association wrote to Goldberg. "We are confident that no child can benefit more from a superior education than our children." The situation provided fodder for antibusing advocates as well, including Roche, who called it "absurd . . . to [deny] children an excellent education in the convenience of their own neighborhood." The district responded that Black children transferring out of the neighborhood would receive supplemental programs at their new outer-city schools as well, including an after-school program. The 220 Black students who agreed to transfer to other schools faced one further indignity once school began, as the district failed to line up sufficient busing to get them to their new buildings.[59]

Numerically speaking, reverse open enrollment was a modest success in its first year. One hundred and eighty white students attended School 2, including about forty bound for the gifted program. They brought the school's white enrollment to 20 percent, up from 2 percent the year before, and both the district and the white parents touted the transfer program as a success. Year-end testing by the district showed positive effects for the Black students who were placed into desegregated classrooms at School 2. Notably, the desegregated classrooms at School 2 had a greater positive effect than greatly reduced class sizes at School 3, which remained deeply segregated. The district created a waiting list for the 1968–69 school year and announced a similar transfer program for School 6.[60]

Yet of the forty-eight students in the supposedly desegregated MAP program, forty-one were white. One of the other seven was Dana Miller, who had been in fifth grade at overwhelmingly Black School 4 when he was asked whether he would be interested in applying for the MAP program at School 2, within walking distance of his house. He agreed but was surprised on the first day of school to find that he and a friend were the only Black faces in a twenty-four-student class.[61] "We were a little surprised," he said. "We thought, 'integrated,' so [it would be] half-and-half maybe." Even more than race, he said, the difference was class based. Most of his classmates' parents were lawyers or doctors, whereas his father struggled working two jobs to pay the mortgage on the home he had purchased, through a white straw buyer, on Jefferson Terrace.[62]

With new desegregation activities strictly curtailed under the 15-Point Plan, the problem worsened across the district, and pro-integration community groups as well as teachers and administrators began to increase pressure on the district to act. Two men emerged as leaders: Reecy Davis, the fiery organizer of the newly formed United Federation of Inner-City Parents, and Laplois Ashford, the Urban League executive director who, in December 1967, became the city's first Black school board member when he was appointed to replace the departing Rossi. In August 1969 the federation disrupted several board meetings and announced that it would organize a boycott of the first two weeks of school in order to force a plan for integration. At the same time, Franklin Florence asked US Attorney General John Mitchell to withhold further federal desegregation funds from the district and launch an investigation, while the district's principals handed out fliers on downtown street corners and took out a full-page newspaper ad calling for immediate countywide desegregation. "Your children won't thank you for leaving them with the problem of separate societies," the advertisement read.[63]

Faced with louder calls for action, the school board in August 1969 resorted to a familiar tactic; it asked Herman Goldberg to study the problem. It requested yet another desegregation proposal from the superintendent, the third of his tenure. Specifically, it asked him to say what the district would do if the board were to order immediate desegregation and gave him four months to do so. Ashford blasted his colleagues for their inaction and called for immediate, compulsory busing of both white and nonwhite students. "What we need is not another study but a commitment," he said. "We can no longer sidestep our obligations. It would take an idiot not to understand the issue." Goldberg's due date was Dec. 31, the final day of the 1960s. When the school year began, more than a thousand students stayed home as part of the United Federation of Inner-City Parents boycott.[64]

In the meantime, the November 1969 elections triggered a major upheaval of the school board. The conservative Michael Roche left after winning election to City Council, part of a Republican sweep up and down the ballot. Laplois Ashford and Louis Cerulli, uncomfortable ballot mates on the Democratic ticket, were unsuccessful in their own runs for City Council, and both shortly announced their plans to depart from the school board.[65] All

**FIGURE 4.4.** From left: Superintendent Herman Goldberg, Richard Harrison, and Reecy Davis of the United Federation of Inner-City Parents. Photo ca. 1967 courtesy of the *Democrat and Chronicle*.

the school board candidates in November campaigned against the use of compulsory busing, leaving Goldberg in the unenviable position of rushing to finish a report for a new board that didn't seem interested in hearing it.

Indeed, Roche and Cerulli attempted to take decisive action before leaving office. With a third vote from Dorothy Phillips, on December 18 they passed a resolution banning the use of school buses for the purpose of racial balancing. It would have permanently spiked any feasible desegregation plan—and fulfilled all the victorious board candidates' campaign promises. Crucially, though, Phillips inserted an amendment conditioning the resolution on the ratification of the incoming board in January. The new board never took it up, so the resolution never took effect.[66]

The board's lame-duck stunt had the important effect of shaking some Black community leaders' last glimmer of confidence that the district was acting in good faith. Several members of Goldberg's advisory committee quit on the spot. "I'm finished with the council," Reecy Davis said. "I don't want any more to do with integration. White people won't permit integration." The Urban League of Rochester added in a statement: "We maintain our concern that the Board and this community are unwilling to totally integrate the schools and until such time, that the community is willing to approve some solution which will inevitably require the busing of white as well as black youth, the Urban League demands a strategy for real change and improvements in our inner-city schools." Goldberg's advisory council considered filing a lawsuit with the federal government, alleging that the board action constituted an affirmative step backward on desegregation.[67]

Undaunted by the antibusing resolution, Goldberg formally unveiled his third and most ambitious desegregation plan on December 29. It was, in essence, a variation on the controversial Princeton Plan of 1964. The elementary schools would be grouped into eleven "enlarged home zones" designed to include a racially balanced student body, and each building would become either a K–3 or 4–6 school. The secondary schools would likewise be split, with some current high schools—Charlotte, Douglass, Monroe, and West—converting to junior high schools and the remainder—East, Franklin, Jefferson, Madison, and Marshall—serving grades 10–12 (Edison Tech and World of Inquiry were not included). Some primary schools would still have more than 50 percent nonwhite students, but in buildings for grades 4–12 the proportions would be from 18 to 43 percent.[68] Goldberg estimated that 16,700 students, representing 36 percent of the student body, would take a bus to school under the new system, up from about 7,700 in 1969–70. The majority of them would be secondary students, versus just 9 percent of students in grades K–3. The plan would also provide for hot cafeteria lunches in every building; previously most students had walked home for lunch, so the service was unnecessary.[69]

Apart from the effects on transportation and racial imbalance, Goldberg's reorganization, as it came to be called, achieved some goals that the district had been pursuing for years. Chief among them was moving schools closer to "open classrooms." In this pedagogical design, similar to the Montessori model, students did not necessarily advance one grade level each year but rather could learn at their own pace within a cohort of peers about their age. At the secondary level, there was a wide consensus on the wisdom of splitting the seventh and eighth grades apart from older students. A recent study on increased fighting and misbehavior in city high schools had shown that younger students did a disproportionate share of troublemaking and urged shunting them into their own schools. Goldberg also called on suburban districts to join in long-range regional planning, including the cooperative use of federal Title I antipoverty funding. "Shall we have schools, and a nation, in turmoil?" he asked in conclusion. "Or shall we have schools free from racial and ethnic fears, where all children can learn well, each developing his special strengths and each participating in the building of a new and undoubtedly the best chapter in America's history?"[70]

Three days later, the calendar year turned over and a new school board was seated. Gordon DeHond was a conservative who immediately rejected Goldberg's proposal and sought final ratification of the antibusing amendment. The incumbent board president, Dorothy Phillips, and the newly elected Thomas Frey had also pledged to oppose compulsory busing while campaigning, though not as vociferously. David Branch, a liberal Democrat, was appointed to replace Cerulli, and Emilio Serrano, a moderate Republican whom Frey had defeated by only three votes in the November election, was appointed to replace Roche.[71] With the exception of DeHond, the board members kept their own counsel as they embarked on a series of informational meetings across the district. The stated purpose was to explain Goldberg's reorganization to parents at different schools and answer their questions. As it happened, the meetings served to incubate the increasingly riotous opposition to what one parent called "Goldberg's folly." Many meetings in elementary schools drew more than five hundred attendees, and those in secondary schools topped a thousand in the audience.[72]

Assistant Superintendent George Rentsch, a major figure in the district's desegregation efforts, gave a detailed account of one meeting in Charlotte that he said showed the pattern of dozens of others. "They wanted to question, to intimidate, and to threaten those of us who were making presentations," he said. Many of the troublemakers, Rentsch alleged, were "part of a 'flying squad' of persons who would go from meeting to meeting . . . in an attempt to disrupt the meeting as thoroughly and effectively as possible." As he left, two parents "threatened me with the fact that I would be 'gotten' if anything happened to their daughter." He continued:

> The pattern became predictable. Polite listening to some initial presentations; vociferous attacks on the premises on which the plan was based; and finally threats, cat calls, jeers, and other attempts to break up the meeting. At the end of these meetings, I would find that I was completely exhausted. My palms would be sweaty, my heart would be pounding. . . . Literally an irrational force, born of fear, was making them do something they did not necessarily wish to do.[73]

Major organizations supported and organized parents on both sides of the issue. More than two-thirds of Rochester teachers backed the plan, according to a February poll. Reecy Davis's United Federation of Inner-City Parents remained involved, though to a lesser degree than in 1969. FIGHT and the Ibero-American Action League, the latter representing the growing Puerto Rican population, gave tentative support while also demanding compensatory programs at the schools that would remain majority nonwhite. Those three groups joined together under the moniker Coalition of Concern and walked a fine line, backing an integration plan of the traditional liberal model while also staking out a position on community control of schools in mostly Black neighborhoods. The president of Xerox, Joseph Wilson, was among the business leaders to support the plan, calling it "a bold plan [that] should be tried." The countywide Teen-Agers' League for Responsible Citizenship called for its implementation, particularly the elements regarding metropolitan solutions. "We are the coming generation," a member wrote. "We do not want the problems inherent in a two-class society."[74]

In the opposing camp, the Rochester Neighborhood School Associations Council (RNSAC) emerged almost overnight as a major citywide force. Its president, forty-three-year-old Eastridge High School math teacher James Sims, Jr., made a name for himself by organizing about a thousand children and parents to march to the district office and City Hall in opposition to the Goldberg plan. Wilbur Gerst, the first Black RTA president, called Sims "Rochester's George Wallace." Louis Cerulli, less than a month after leaving office, told a crowd of supporters that city schools were full of drugs and "dirty people with long hair," and encouraged them to stand united in opposition to the Goldberg plan.[75]

Most observers believed the school board would pass a middle-ground measure, instituting greater busing but not to the extent that Goldberg

**FIGURE 4.5.** Parents demonstrating in favor of Herman Goldberg's reorganization plan in early 1970. Photo by Jim Laragy, courtesy of the *Democrat and Chronicle*.

**FIGURE 4.6.** Parents protesting against Herman Goldberg's reorganization plan in early 1970. Photo by Jim Laragy, courtesy of the *Democrat and Chronicle*.

proposed. Instead on February 25 it delivered the superintendent a shocking loss, defeating the plan 3–2 and instead approving the construction of two new junior high schools in the city. Frey and Branch, the two yes votes, accused the others of having bowed to explicit pressure from Republican leaders. Republicans conceded to having held a series of closed-door meeting with party bosses but insisted they were "exploratory and fact-finding in nature."[76]

The result, as a reporter summarized, "was like 1967 all over again. Now, as then, a sweeping desegregation proposal gave way to a much-diluted compromise." The Black groups in the Coalition of Concern organized a boycott of the federally funded World of Inquiry school, which they saw as a symbol of the community's half-hearted efforts. "Rochester can't afford to be smug in thinking that quality integrated education comes with one school with 130 kids," said Bernard Gifford, the president of FIGHT (World of Inquiry is discussed in chapter 6). The RTA went further, urging all teachers to attend an all-day emergency meeting at East High School on the Monday following the school board's vote, and Goldberg responded by canceling all classes for the day. On Tuesday and Wednesday as well, many schools were closed as about twenty thousand students stayed home from school, several thousand of them picketing and marching. Mostly lost in the hubbub was the filing of another federal lawsuit alleging the school district's failure to desegregate and requesting immediate intervention. It was filed as *Colquhoun v. Board of Education*, after the lead plaintiff, a parent named Lillian Colquhoun.[77]

Faced with such an uproar, Phillips, the board president and swing vote, wavered. On March 5, just eight days after defeating Goldberg's plan in its entirety, the board changed course slightly and approved a watered-down version to take effect in a small subset of schools. The resolution also created "community school advisory councils," a concession to the Coalition of Concern groups.[78] "Something was salvaged, I see," State Education Commissioner Ewald Nyquist wrote privately to Goldberg after the vote. "You have done heroic work. I wish the board would have matched your wisdom in full." Locally, though, the compromise satisfied no one. "The [Goldberg] plan itself was a compromise," Nancy Peck, the chairwoman of Goldberg's advisory committee, complained: "You cannot continue to dilute compromises endlessly." James Sims and RNSAC, meanwhile, were furious to see their victory overturned, even if only partially so. Sims called for yet another school boycott the following Monday. It was the third such disruption in five weeks, with about fifteen thousand students staying home. "I bet if I painted my face black you'd listen to me," Sims shouted at a meeting.

Another prominent busing opponent, Mary Nicolosi, charged the dais and school board member David Branch, yelling, "I'll get you, Branch," before being restrained.[79]

Another student boycott was planned for the opening of school in September. This time, in a twist, it was jointly endorsed by RNSAC's Sims and the former FIGHT president Franklin Florence, who otherwise were diametrically opposed. In this case, as Sims put it: "Neither of us is being listened to by the board. We're at different ends of the street, trying to be heard."[80] At the same time he was attempting to organize the first-day disruption, Sims was also running for a spot on the school board, which was having an off-year election to obtain elected representation for the seats to which Branch and Serrano had been appointed. Sims's seemingly strong electoral base toppled in September when Nicolosi and other RNSAC officers resigned, complaining that Sims had been ineffectual in stopping attacks on neighborhood schools. That archconservative splinter group shortly reconstituted as the United Schools Association, with Louis Cerulli serving as president.[81]

On the other side of the November ballot was Wyoma Best, a twenty-seven-year-old Urban League organizer seeking to become the first Black woman elected to the board. She ran a moderate campaign, attempting to straddle the line between the portion of the Black community supporting community control and that supporting integration. Perhaps for that reason, she emerged as the second-highest vote-getter in the November election. In a surprise, she was topped only by Branch, her fellow liberal Democrat, who had been considered an underdog to Serrano. One year after the communitywide Republican sweep, Best and Branch, with Frey, had wrested back control of the school board. Branch immediately announced that the new Democratic majority would reconsider the Goldberg Plan decision.[82]

Democratic party leaders viewed the victory with little enthusiasm. As a reporter wrote: "As far as the Monroe County Democratic and Republican positions stand on the school desegregation issue, there is virtually no difference. Both parties are based in conservatism." With a pro-desegregation majority in place at the end of 1970, both parties renewed the call for nonpartisan school board elections. For party leaders "based in conservatism," nonpartisan elections would have the virtue of removing their party labels from a school reorganization certain to infuriate much of the electorate. The state legislature in April 1971 passed legislation removing partisan labels and expanding the board from five members to seven, meaning that Best, Branch, and DeHond would need to run for new terms in November 1971, along with candidates running for the two newly created seats.[83]

Knowing its reign might be short, the new Democratic majority wasted no time. At the February 4, 1971, board meeting, Best, Branch, and Frey did something that never had happened before in Rochester—they introduced and passed a resolution implementing a districtwide reorganization, including compulsory busing of white students. It was essentially half of the Goldberg plan, involving secondary but not elementary students. Dorothy Phillips, the Republican board president, joined them in a 4–1 vote. As the outcome became clear, hundreds of white students at the five-hour-long board meeting rushed to the front of the auditorium, chanting, "Hell, no, we won't go," forcing police to escort the board members out of the room.[84]

There were some notable absences from Rochester liberals' subsequent celebration. Goldberg in late November 1970 had announced that he was leaving the district for a high-level post in the US Department of Health, Education, and Welfare's Office of Education. "I have heard the past eight years described as boiling and boisterous," he said in his farewell message. "I think of them rather as years that mattered; years with a message; mission years." He was replaced, first on an interim basis and then permanently, by John Franco, a Rochester native and the director of the district's compensatory programs for mostly minority students under the name Project Beacon.[85]

Also missing from the cheering were Reecy Davis, Bernard Gifford, and other key members of the Black and Puerto Rican constituency that had spent years pushing for just such a desegregation plan. The day before the board voted to enact part of the Goldberg plan, the Coalition of Concern groups announced that they no longer supported it, but instead wanted the district to further empower the community school councils that the board had created the previous year. The councils represented a turn away from the goal of desegregation and instead provided a means for the Black community to influence and support mostly Black schools. "This game of musical chairs that the board plays each year of chasing kids from one school to another has got to end," Gifford said. "We're not looking to build a separate black world for our children. All we're saying is that we're sick and tired of black children being used as pawns." Wyoma Best, who had helped conceive of the community school councils while working for the Urban League, became the primary lightning rod for Black critics in particular.[86]

Pushback to the secondary reorganization took a now familiar form. Hundreds of students stayed home from school and organized marches to district headquarters in the biting cold. Student leaders were suspended for organizing the boycott—but, as one of them noted: "They can't suspend 10,000 kids." The protests intensified in March after the Democrats on the school board approved Goldberg's elementary reorganization as well, to be phased in over several years. Increasingly the white anti-reorganization children and parents adopted the rhetoric of the civil rights protests of the previous decade. One white mother wrote about teenagers protesting against desegregation: "Daily they march. They shout, sing and freeze while doors slam in their faces. . . . Others in this nation probably laugh at their hair, beards, clothes, music and protests. I do not, for behind it all is a driving spirit that should be an inspiration to those who sit cozy and nonchalant at home while the political machine grinds them into dust and makes fools out of them daily."[87] More than two thousand people paid fifty cents admission each to an antibusing rally at the Rochester Community War Memorial arena in April, where Cerulli was the featured speaker. "I don't like to tell children to be violent . . . but I do believe in being militant," he said to a standing ovation. That same day, someone spray-painted "n—— eats shit and blows" in three-foot high letters on the front of Charlotte High School.[88]

Branch, Best, and Frey resisted the public outcry but were potentially vulnerable on another front. The reorganization depended on a $450,000 bond for building renovations. Because the district remained fiscally dependent on the city, the Republican-controlled city council had to give final approval on the borrowing request—and Michael Roche, the former school board member, quickly announced his determination not to do so. Only a last-minute defection from maverick Republican Robert Wood saved the bond issue. Although the council lacked line-item veto power of the schools budget, it also trimmed the overall school district budget request by $867,393, the exact amount projected for additional transportation under the reorganization. The Republican council members justified their action by citing a recent advisory report that had criticized the district for overspending and underperforming. The situation was further complicated by a similar political dynamic in Albany, where the legislature cut all desegregation funding from the state budget. Undaunted, the school board made cuts elsewhere in its spending plan to keep the reorganization intact.[89]

Until the beginning of the 1960s, Rochester's white leaders had mostly succeeded in ignoring the increasing segregation in the city's neighborhoods and schools. Again and again during the following decade, RCSD put forth proposals—some modest, some momentous—to reduce racial imbalance. They were occasioned by legal action, the threat of legal action, and the combined voices of the thousands of parents who spoke their mind at school board meetings and in the voting booth. Still, the problem grew worse. The thousands of Black children arriving in Rochester from Florida and South Carolina were funneled with uncanny precision into schools that were already filled to bursting with children who looked like them. In some cases, instances of desegregation yielded hopeful experiences of understanding across cultural and racial boundaries. In more cases, though, lines of demarcation were sharpened, not blurred, and ignorance and distrust allowed to fester.

Rochester figured prominently in a 1969 publication from the US Department of Health, Education, and Welfare with a title that surely set off alarm bells among those familiar with the fight for integration in Monroe County: "How Five School Systems Desegregated." The pamphlet listed Rochester as a community that "attest[ed] to the fact that desegregation can be accomplished, and that it can be accompanied by an increase in the quality of education available to all children, whatever their racial, cultural or economic backgrounds." It described with admiration the RCSD open enrollment and reverse open enrollment processes along with the various programs under the aegis of Project UNIQUE. "Rochester still has a long way to go before racial imbalance is totally corrected in its city schools," the researchers conceded. "[But the initial] effect on the whole metropolitan area is pronounced and growing."[90]

By then President Richard Nixon had made clear his opposition to ambitious desegregation programs, and federal education officials may have been eager to declare victory and move on. The political needle had moved right in Albany as well, but Education Commissioner James Allen's successor, Ewald Nyquist, maintained his policy in favor of dismantling segregated school systems. "'Busing' and 'neighborhood school' are emotional slogans, and I deplore the president's [position]," Nyquist told a conference of educators. A report he subsequently commissioned on Rochester and other cities belied the rosy picture in the federal pamphlet: "At present, it appears that our beginning [desegregation] efforts have been outrun by continued growth in the seriousness of the problem." The difference between the federal and state perspectives, issued just a few months apart, served to illustrate the yawning divide between a promising beginning and actual progress on the intractable problem.[91]

A Rochester reporter summarized the situation at the turn of the decade: "The old guard white liberals are frustrated, the city school officials are on the defensive, and the blacks are angry."[92] None of those groups, nor the white parents in determined opposition to integration, were soon to be placated. Goldberg's final, late-arriving proposal proved to be the foundation for a furious year of confrontation.

# Chapter 5

# From Charlotte to *Milliken*

One warm day near the end of the 1971–72 school year, a high-ranking RCSD administrator took a drive up to Charlotte Junior High School. It was one of the last days of a tumultuous year for the district's reorganization plan, which included, among other things, the transportation of students from various neighborhoods to racially desegregated secondary schools. The administrator saw the buses making their way up Lake Avenue and pulling into the school—but on one, he didn't see any passengers. It appeared to be empty except for the driver. Perplexed, he followed it into the bus loop, and there he finally saw the Black children passengers as they got up from the floor of the bus, dusted themselves off, and exited. They had been hiding, he realized, from people concealed in Holy Sepulchre and Riverside Cemeteries on Lake Avenue, waiting to throw rocks at the unwelcome visitors.[1]

For the weakened but remaining coalition of Black and white liberal activists pushing for racial integration in Rochester schools, the 1970s began with hope for meaningful action at last. There was a year of grueling political drama, with thousands of students, both Black and white, boycotting class and marching on the school board, where meetings lasted well past midnight. A fresh board majority eventually approved an ambitious, decade-long reorganization plan that would not only desegregate neighborhood schools but also revitalize teaching and learning at all levels. "Schoolmen and women of the Seventies must find ways to hasten needed change," Superintendent Herman Goldberg told teachers as the decade began. "[They] must see beyond the range of the crowd and must risk its anger if new ways of learning by students are to be accomplished by them with your help."[2]

As it turned out, though, these liberal crusaders were overwhelmed by an army of white opponents fighting a furious defensive battle on the home field of their neighborhood secondary schools—and the battle was literal as well as figurative. A yellow school bus, Charlotte-bound and filled with crouching, terrified twelve- and thirteen-year-olds, is as fitting an image as any. Rochester had looked on with horror at violent white opposition to desegregation in Arkansas and Alabama. Now, a generation later, white Charlotte residents were lined up on the east side of Lake Avenue, armed with bricks and rocks and chanting "n——s go home" over the heads of a police cordon at the teenagers leaving school across the street. They swarmed yellow buses and hanged a Black effigy from a tree. Black students in turn took to packing brass knuckles and chains along with their lunches and homework.

Bob Sagan began teaching English and theater at Charlotte High School in 1966. The students were well behaved to the point of torpidity, he said, and blissfully ignorant of anything happening south of Ridgeway Avenue and the Kodak plant where many of their fathers worked. He hoped to jolt them with art and teach them about the world. Instead, in 1971, Sagan found himself one day huddling in the library with his students after the building was locked down because of racial fights. Through the window he could look out at the front lawn and bus loop, where white Charlotte parents were speeding to collect their children. Nearly half a century later, Sagan could vividly recall one of them rushing into the school wearing a blood-drenched butcher's jacket. "The community, I think, was afraid of the outside coming in," he said. "I just remember when this integration was to take place, all hell broke loose."[3]

Black parents' desire for integration waned as their children began returning home from school bloodied and bandaged, and thus the progressive contingent splintered. Less than two months after the massive reorganizational plan was put into place, voters used an off-year election to rescind it, marking the third time in three dizzying years that a majority of the board had turned over. Even if integration proponents had been able to rally for another charge, developments at the federal level made it clear that the age of desegregation—at least as far as it concerned places like Rochester—was over.

Violence in schools, often based on race, had been a growing problem in Rochester for several years. By all accounts it peaked during the 1970–71 school year, even more so than in 1971–72 when the controversial reorganization was in place. "The number of student behavioral problems has increased markedly in the last two years in Rochester," the school board wrote in November 1970, announcing stricter disciplinary policies after a rash of incidents at Franklin and other high schools. Black student leaders responded by calling the heightened disciplinary actions "dehumanizing, unconstitutional and unjust," and accused the district of transferring Franklin's Black Student Union president to another school in an attempt to silence protests there. Charlotte closed early three times that year because of racial violence, including the last day of the year, when police separated Black and white students carrying tree limbs, tire irons, and baseball bats. A district official attributed the closing to "greater exuberance than usual."[4]

The violence was often instigated, directly or indirectly, by white parents or community members rather than white or Black students. "I've seen it in the halls—the kids will be great friends, then all of a sudden parents come down and you don't recognize the kids," a Jefferson school sentry said. An effigy of a Black student was hanged from a tree outside Charlotte High School with a sign on its chest reading "kill all n——s." Black Charlotte students also remembered the school bus being pelted with bricks and rocks as it made its way to and from the school. "They would hide in the graveyard, and there was a wall, and they'd come out from behind the wall and throw bricks, rocks, irons, anything they could find at the bus," James Beard, a Black Charlotte student leader, said. Marlene Caroselli, a Jefferson teacher, recalled the faculty forming a protective cordon to allow Black students off the buses and into the building, past the parents gathered outside. "I remember red faces as they screamed at the children," she said. "Sometimes they would use words that were enormously offensive. . . . Fear was in the air."[5] White community groups perpetrated or threatened violence away from schools as well. One integration advocate reported having a gun pulled on her outside of a meeting in northwest Rochester. Benjamin Richardson conducted dozens of interviews with white and Black community leaders on both sides of the question and concluded that white groups "accounted for all the reported instances of personal assaults and intimidation" in 1971.[6]

The malignant combination of fear, racism, and political expediency came together in a grotesque series of events on June 10, 1971, the Thursday before the school year ended. The day began with a tragedy, when an eight-year-old boy, playing on the sidewalk with his friends on the way home from School 8, fell into the street and was struck and killed by a truck. The accident had nothing to do with the reorganization plan; the boy attended his neighborhood school. Louis Cerulli, though, claimed that such deaths were "going to happen again and again" with increased student transportation.

He accused the district of neglecting to provide crossing guards—in fact, three had been on duty—and encouraged members of his United Schools Association to protest to take advantage of the moment. "If we fall flat on our faces, we'll never have this chance again," he said. "Even if it is a tragedy, we have to use it to get our message across."[7]

Cerulli's followers heeded his call. Late that night, about thirty of them stationed themselves in front of the home of David Branch, leader of the school board's liberal wing, some wearing white sheets. Cerulli was photographed with them as well, though he later said that he was seeking to calm them down. The United Schools Association vice president, Mary Nicolosi, who had threatened months earlier to "get" Branch, denied that the sheets had any significance. Instead, she explained, the protestors were using them to become "more visible at night on a very dark corner." Although the newspapers reported on just one night of protests, Branch later revealed that the white-sheeted demonstrators were there for eleven nights in a row, always coming after dark.[8]

Fighting at Charlotte on the last day of the school year triggered the early closure of secondary schools throughout the city. Thus did the 1970–71 school year mercifully come to an end. "Our children have become performers on a stage, acting out the hostility they sense in their parents' daily behavior," former RCSD assistant superintendent William Rock wrote. He continued: "The expressions on the students' faces at Charlotte are reminiscent of those seen thousands of times on the faces of their parents and others who have fought an eight-year battle to prevent integration of the city's schools, the city's housing and the city's employment rolls. The continuing disturbances in our city's high schools indicate that the children, segregated by the adults responsible for their education, have learned to mistrust, fear and even hate one another."[9]

The 1971–72 secondary reorganization had two main, related components. First, the eight schools that previously had served grades 7–12 were now split into two groups. East, Franklin, Jefferson, Madison, and Marshall became grades 9–12 high schools, while West, Monroe, and Charlotte were reserved for grades 7–8, joining the existing Frederick Douglass Junior High School. The second, more controversial part of the plan had to do with changes to the enrollment patterns at those schools. Rather than serving just the Charlotte community north of Ridgeway Avenue, for example, Charlotte Junior High School would now take in children from the mostly Black Joseph Avenue neighborhood as well. Jefferson, which had been overwhelmingly Italian, would get an influx of Black Third Ward children, while students from the all-white northwest quadrant would attend Madison Senior High School.

The school year started with no planned protests, and for the first three weeks relative calm prevailed. The major initial difficulties had to do with the enormous logistical operation that the reorganization entailed, such as renovating buildings and finalizing student assignments and bus routes. "I think parents worry more than we do," one Marshall student said. "But there hasn't been any trouble, so I guess they better stop worrying pretty soon." Reorganization opponents had spent the summer encouraging families to make their voices heard at the polls rather than picketing or boycotting. With the change happening smoothly, those opponents wondered whether they had misplayed their hand. "[People] are beginning to say, 'Why didn't we protest?'" Gordon DeHond said.[10]

By October, tensions began to flare. Large-scale fighting broke out at Franklin, where about two hundred white students met to form a White Student Union. When schools sent first quarter report cards home in the mail, an unusual number were returned to sender; it turned out students had falsified their addresses to remain in their neighborhood high schools. There was a rush on enrollment in the Russian language program at East High School, because students in such specialty programs were exempt from the normal enrollment rules.[11]

Each school faced different dynamics among its students, families, and communities as school buses crossed what had been sacrosanct boundary lines. West Junior High School, for example, had to reckon with the complex setting of the 19th Ward. On one hand, the 19th Ward Community Association had been an early and prominent supporter of integration efforts, something that continued even after 1972. The group represented "young people . . . who see the wasteland of the suburbs set against the wasteland of the ghetto, and who see that there has got to be something in-between," one leader said.[12] At the same time, Genesee Street, where West stood, was the city's most infamous racial dividing line. The gradual, pernicious effect of blockbusting had shifted that border farther west by 1971, but the West enrollment zone still included a great number of families who viewed school integration chiefly as a threat to their property values.

Ed Cavalier began teaching at West in 1968 and remained after the reorganization. By 1971 he was already considered a veteran teacher, in part because teachers with seniority by and large had declined assignments to the new middle schools, moving instead to the redesignated senior high schools. They were replaced by junior faculty and new hires, including many of the newly recruited Black teachers from the South. This skittish, unprepared faculty combined with a volatile new mix of students led predictably to a surge of disciplinary issues. Cavalier recalled finding a boy outside the school with a stab wound; he himself suffered a lasting back injury after falling down the stairs chasing after students. Incidents that might otherwise have been dismissed as middle school antics were often invested with much greater significance. "Any time there was a problem [between] a white kid and a Black kid, the white kid would probably be gone by the following Monday; his family would have moved to the suburbs," Cavalier said. "That's how everything was being solved in those days, was: 'We can't go to school with Black kids.'"[13]

At Charlotte, there were clear divisions by class as well as by race. As a federal judge would later put it, desegregation was "not a discontent of the well-to-do sector." Even before the reorganization, a researcher, Ralph Barber, had remarked on Charlotte's "social cleavage between upper-status Anglo-Saxons and lower-status Italian-Americans." The former called themselves the "Collegians," he said, and referred to the latter as "the Hoods." Many of those "Collegians" were the children of white-collar Kodak employees, comfortably swaddled in Rochester's socially conservative upper-middle class. "This insular condition," Barber continued, "breeds an intellectual lethargy and an immature and complacent social conscience. . . . The greatest, single frustration felt by teachers at [Charlotte] is generated by student apathy in all subject areas." Bob Sagan remembered plenty of dedication among his students, but said: "To those kids in Charlotte, the world began and ended at Ridge and Lake. . . . The community, I think, was afraid of the outside coming in."[14]

Large-scale racial fighting broke out at Charlotte in late September 1971, leading many Black parents to keep their children home from school. The perpetrators were largely "roughniks," as one student called them: "The ones that really wanted to start the trouble, that didn't go to school or class. It was a lot of outsiders who came to school to fight, too." FIGHT called for Black students to boycott Charlotte "until their safety [could] be guaranteed." A white community group, Charlotte Concerned Parents, demanded police officers on every floor of the school as well as the dismissal of two administrators whom they considered insufficiently sympathetic to the plight of the "intolerable situation" of white students at the school. Black parents reportedly were barred from meetings called by white Charlotte parents. Charlotte Concerned Parents organized its own boycott that brought attendance below 50 percent for several days and forced the school to close early at least once.[15]

The neighborhood around Jefferson Senior High School was as insular as Charlotte but owing to ethnicity more than geography or class. The school had been overwhelmingly Italian for several generations. "I remember kids saying they spent every Sunday afternoon listening to opera with their grandparents," said Sagan, who transferred there from Charlotte in 1971. "Now all of a sudden they felt their neighborhood was being invaded with Black people coming in. . . . They were working-class people and they feared Black people taking their jobs." The Italian students referred to Black students with the epithet *mulignan*, Italian for "eggplant," former teacher Bob Stevenson recalled.[16]

A roll call of some of the leading opponents of desegregation in the 1960s and 1970s is suggestive: Cerulli, Nicolosi, Di Sano, Strippoli, Bianchi, Ciaccia. In the Edgerton Park neighborhood around Jefferson as well as elsewhere in Rochester and indeed across the country, Italian Americans, both foreign- and native-born, served as what one national commentator called "the shock troops of anti-Negro politics." They were the last major immigrant group to arrive in the city prior to southern Black migrants and the next lowest in terms of economic prospects and educational attainment. Still, their prospects for advancement were much higher. Their social station was "a no-lid kettle," one academic wrote in 1970, "in that . . . the gates into the larger community are not closed nor are opportunities for alternate associations restricted." Newly arriving Black Rochesterians, on the other hand, "appear doubly bound to the 'kettle' . . . by the 'cooling' influences external to the Negro subcommunity and by the 'heating' generated from within it." Another researcher in Rochester concluded around the same time: "Since [the Italians] live in closest proximity to the ghettoes, are active in the illegal activities in which a large number of Negroes participate, and constitute a high percentage of the city's police force, there are numerous areas of tension between the two groups."[17]

For Cerulli and other board members who belonged to or counted on the Italian community, the politics of the school reorganization in particular were clear. Bob Stevenson, who later became close to Cerulli after marrying a Sicilian woman, said it plainly: Cerulli didn't support reorganization "because he was Italian. . . . The Italians and the African-Americans, they didn't get on." For lower-class, as-yet-unassimilated Italian Americans, reorganization presented a direct threat to their tenuous economic and social progress. "There was tremendous reactive fear [on the part of] Italian Catholics," one integration advocate said. "I had so many people say to me, 'You know, the church is changing, and all of a sudden the rules aren't the rules anymore. . . . And in the middle of all this, you're coming in and telling me you're going to take my kids and send them back into the inner city."[18]

The author Jerre Mangione, in his classic, lightly fictionalized memoir of Rochester's Italian community, described the same dynamic in his own family: "American morals bewildered my relatives. In Sicily their rules of conduct were well defined and though strict, fairly simple to follow, because the same rules had been used for many centuries and were known to everyone in the community, even those who broke them. Here there were many different kinds of people and, as far as they could make out, no rules that were taken seriously. In fact, everything seemed to conspire toward the breakdown of the rules they had brought with them."[19] Jasper Huffman had a vivid introduction to these social norms in the mid-1960s, when he was an underclassman at Franklin High School. He became friendly with an "attractive white Italian girl—gorgeous legs, nice smile." It was more a mutual flirtation than a true romantic relationship, he said. They'd talk in the halls, and he walked her home on occasion. One day he walked into school, he said, "and it was like Christ parting the waters. . . . I got to my locker and my buddy said, 'Hey man, her parents came to school this morning. You in trouble.'" Huffman was called to the main office, where he said a counselor cut right to the point: "White folks and Black folks—intermarriage—it doesn't work." Huffman was asked to come in once a week for "counseling." He declined, but also took care not to be seen with the girl again.[20]

Dana Miller did not know that context when, in tenth grade, he was assigned to ride a bus to Jefferson. Fifty years later, he vividly recalled a day when adults gathered outside the school as the bus pulled up along Bloss Street. He thought for a moment they were there as a welcoming party—until they began to smash the bus with baseball bats and bricks, breaking a window and setting it rocking before the students could escape into the school under police protection. He continued:

> When you saw those pictures [of violent protests] on TV, they were always, always Southern cities. Mississippi, Alabama. . . . My parents are from Kentucky. I always thought whenever we went down there it was like going backward in time. To see that happen in my hometown, where I'd grown up—it completely shocked me. . . .
>
> It's almost like time slowed down. It felt like it took an hour for the bus to get down the street, and seeing their faces and their anger. . . . Finally it kind of dawned on [me]: They're unhappy because *I'm* here. Not because the power went off, or the street flooded. As a 10th grader, that realization causes you to think: "Why? What did I do? I didn't even really want to be here." . . . That was a difficult thing to process.[21]

Nydia Padilla, her parents, and ten siblings were one of the early families to move from Puerto Rico to Rochester and one of the few in the Maple Street area, not far from Jefferson. Like many of their neighbors, the elder

Padillas worked long hours on their feet to make ends meet; Nydia recalled combing crumbs out of her weary mother's hair after her shift at the Schuler Potato Chip plant. Most of her neighbors and classmates at Jefferson were Italian and she made friends with them quickly. "They were Italian or Sicilian, but they were dark, and they faced a lot of discrimination just because of being dark, so we just hung out together," she said. "We had something in common." Spanish language classes weren't offered at Jefferson, so she took Italian instead, quickly gaining proficiency in the curse words her friends wielded so adeptly.

The 1971–72 school year, when reorganization took effect, was Padilla's senior year. If before her Puerto Rican ethnicity had marked her as a harmless oddity, she soon sensed that her Italian friends—former friends—now saw her as part of a nonwhite invasion. She was called a n——r and a s——c. A friend said Padilla couldn't visit her at home anymore because her parents wouldn't like having a Puerto Rican in the house. "It was like a disease that came out of nowhere," Padilla said. "With all the Italian students it was a sense of ownership and identity: 'We've got to keep this school the way it is.' . . . I felt like I'd been in this fantasy world, thinking we'd be able to get along and [race] shouldn't be such a big deal, but it started turning pretty ugly."[22]

Most white families adapted to reorganization as best they could, even if with reluctance. But hundreds of families pulled their children out of the district altogether in favor of a controversial new option. These were block schools: unaccredited, privately run "tutoring centers" that sprang up in the fall of 1971 to cater to parents who didn't want their children in the reorganized junior high schools.

The first block school opened just a few days after the school year began, with the help of the Cerulli-aligned United Schools Association. It enrolled about a hundred seventh- and eighth-grade students in classes held at the Italian-American Sports Club on Emerson Street beginning September 14. Over the next two months four block schools more opened, enrolling about five hundred students combined at their peak. Children and their parents said that they had abandoned RCSD schools after violence or threats of violence at the beginning of the school year, or because of an unwillingness to take a bus to school. Students attended class in shifts for two hours a day; their parents paid $5 a week in tuition and claimed their children were learning more in the short session than they would in a full day in district schools. Many of the teachers and administrators were either retired from RCSD or unable to find a teaching job elsewhere, and books were hand-me-downs donated from unknown sources. A windfall came in October, when the Holley Central School District provided several hundred surplus textbooks, thinking they were going to "Black schools," not block schools. "I feel terrible," the district superintendent said. "It was a difference of an 'o' or an 'a.'"[23]

United Schools Association president Frank Bower and the rest of the block school leaders quickly came to find out that many state regulations are involved in opening a school. Among other things, they needed to provide five and a half hours of instruction each day, covering all required topics, and the buildings—most of them in commercial space or churches—had to meet rigid standards for educational facilities. The block schools argued that they were "tutoring services," not schools, and therefore had to meet lower standards. "There's no such thing as setting up a tutoring service," Superintendent John Franco responded. He declared the block schools illegal and their students truant. "These parents deprived their children of an adequate [educational] program but taught them a meaningful lesson in racism," former assistant superintendent William Rock wrote. School Board member David Branch likened them to the "segregation academies" in Prince Edward County, Virginia, and other southern communities where white parents had withdrawn their children from newly desegregated public schools and entered them instead into hastily formed private academies, usually with the use of public tax dollars.[24]

In March the block schools remained open, and state education commissioner Ewald Nyquist chided Franco for not acting sooner to resolve the situation. "At the rate you're going, some kids will have lost a whole year . . . in below-standard schools," he said. In May, the district formally brought child neglect charges against the parents of more than 250 children who remained in the block schools. The charges ultimately were dropped, but not before the parents and their children paraded triumphantly to the courthouse to defend themselves. Three of the five block schools continued operating until the end of the school year, and the grades they handed out were recognized by the district the following year.[25]

The block schools provided yet another rallying cry for reorganization opponents in the weeks leading up to the momentous November 2 election, when five out of seven school board seats would be decided. The conservative United Council on Education and Taxation put forth a five-person slate, headed by DeHond, who pledged to overturn the reorganization plan in its entirety. They faced off against Branch, Best, and two pro-reorganization newcomers, Ann Camelio and Dean Miller. Complex issues of racial justice, fiscal responsibility, pedagogy, and organization ultimately boiled down in voters' minds to one question for the candidates: Will you maintain the reorganization plan, or won't you?

DeHond's anti-reorganization slate included one unlikely candidate: twenty-four-year-old Frank Ciaccia, a 1965 private school graduate with no children in the district, still living with his parents on Maplewood Drive. DeHond had been his social studies teacher at Aquinas Institute and, though they hadn't spoken since then, called to recruit him to run for the school board. The campaign, Ciaccia said, was a simple one: a return to neighborhood schools, full stop, and an end to race-based policies of any kind. "We felt the main point of a school board is not to solve social issues or housing patterns; it's to educate the students," Ciaccia said. "Anything that interferes with that, get rid of it."[26]

In describing the campaign, Ciaccia also proposed a much narrower definition of racial segregation than New York, or indeed the country, recognized at the time. He recalled watching with anger on television when Arkansas governor Orval Faubus barred Black students from integrating the schools in Little Rock and, following Cerulli, drew a stark distinction between that and the situation in Rochester. "We never had segregated schools," he said. "I wouldn't be part of a segregated school system. . . . Yes, some schools were majority-populated white or Black, but they were integrated." The only all-white schools in the city in the fall of 1971 were the block schools.[27] Ciaccia also described receiving significant support from Black voters as well as white ones: "I would campaign in Black wards and they'd say, 'Why is my kid being put on a bus and taken to the other part of the city?'" This, to him and the others on his slate, was proof that their position was based on common sense, not racism. They ignored the fact that Black families and community leaders abandoned the push for integration only after becoming convinced that white racism represented an insurmountable barrier. As Reecy Davis said in 1969 after the school board (unsuccessfully) attempted to implement a total ban on busing for desegregation: "After a move like this I have no alternative but to give up the fight for integration. But I'm not going to say we worked in vain. We've helped show black people like myself that no matter how hard we work, white people don't want integration."[28]

The anti-reorganization slate and its supporters were in general fiscally, culturally, and pedagogically conservative. They campaigned on rescinding reorganization and trimming the budget, but also on the breakdown of school discipline and the harmful potential effects of sex education. They "tended to look with skepticism [at] anything that dealt with flexibility or openness or humanness," a central office administrator later observed. As Cerulli put it at a February 1970 rally: "If you don't know enough to stay away from dirty people with long hair, then you don't deserve an education." Anti-reorganization supporters advocated for a minimal educational program featuring little more than basic literacy and numeracy. "I don't mind if there is a lack of, you know, special teachers," one anti-reorganization organizer said. "I don't believe that the majority of the kids in the school system are going to turn out to be artists or musicians."[29]

The result of the election could not have been clearer. DeHond's five-person anti-reorganization slate swept all five seats on the school board, with more than 6,000 votes separating them from the rest of the field. They lost only six of the city's twenty-four wards, including the Third and Seventh Wards, where the largest nonwhite population was concentrated. Immediately they pledged an end to "forced busing," beginning in the 1972–73 school year. "This is the referendum that the people of Rochester waited so long for," Elizabeth Farley, one of the victors, crowed from the victory party at a downtown steakhouse. "The idea that you can't have quality education without busing children didn't snow them at all."[30]

Why did voters overwhelming reject the reorganization plan just a year after having voted, in a similar referendum-style election, to enact it? The anti-reorganization slate in 1971 ran a better organized and more vigorous campaign in comparison to both their current opponents and their predecessors in 1970. The support of the United Council on Education and Taxation proved significant, providing the manpower and funding to "campaign them to death," as Lewis Bianchi put it. "Everything [we] printed, was done in the tens of thousands. We covered the areas again and again."[31]

Branch and Best had approached Election Day with confidence. Ed Cavalier remembered sitting with them in a hotel room at Midtown Plaza, watching Branch shake his head as the results came in. "We were all positive they were going to win," he said. "They all thought they were doing what this community was asking for." Yet the definition of "this community," as always, had shifted. The splintering of the pro-integration coalition cut into voter enthusiasm and hindered campaign coordination. Reports of violence in the schools over the first few months of 1971 had left parents feeling skittish, while the ways that integration benefited children were hard to demonstrate. "A basic problem was defining the educational advantages of reorganization for the children to the parents," Best said. "It was the emotional level of the people. They felt a bit threatened."[32]

In a letter shortly after the election, Nyquist held out hope that the new board, once seated and "responsible in a different way for their words and actions," might have a change of heart.[33] This was certainly overoptimistic. Rescinding the reorganization plan, however, proved more difficult than they anticipated.

Asked to describe her mother, Sereena (Brown) Martin pursed her lips and began with what she wasn't: mean.

"She was strict, but she wasn't mean," she said. "We had a voice within limits. But there's a line you don't cross, and we never did."

Lillian Colquhoun grew up in New York City after her parents moved up from Savannah, Georgia, searching for a better opportunity. Lillian, in turn, moved farther north to Rochester, hoping for better wages and accommodations and "something slower for the kids," Martin said. She and her four daughters landed in the Hanover Houses, which by then were already well advanced on their descent into chaos and eventual demolition. The conditions offended Colquhoun; for instance, that residents paid rent but could not control the temperature in their own apartments. So, along with FIGHT president Raymond Scott, Sister Grace Miller, and others, she began to organize the tenants to protest for greater rights. In March 1970, after the Rochester school board rejected Herman Goldberg's ambitious plan to reorganize the schools in the interest of better education as well as racial integration, Colquhoun did not hesitate to put her name on a federal lawsuit accusing the district of failing to address segregation.[34]

Colquhoun was one of three Black mothers in the district to serve as plaintiffs, accusing the district of intentionally allowing segregated schools to persist and demanding a comprehensive desegregation plan by May 1971. The case landed in the court of John Henderson, the top judge in the Western District. Oral arguments were not held until September 1971 and by then the local situation had changed dramatically—the Goldberg plan had been enacted, and secondary students already attended reorganized schools. The district asked Henderson to dismiss the case for that reason, but the plaintiff's lawyers sought to proceed, arguing that a future board could undo the plan—as, in fact, happened.[35]

The relevant federal case law was moving fast. In particular, court watchers in Rochester were paying close attention to a similar case in Denver (*Keyes v. School District No. 1, Denver*). Voters there in 1969 had chosen an antibusing board, which rescinded a previously implemented desegregation plan. A federal judge ruled, in response to a subsequent lawsuit, that the new board's actions were a deliberate step backward for the purposes of integration and thus represented the sort of de jure segregation that had been disallowed by *Brown v. Board of Education*. The upshot in November 1971 was that, as slowly

**FIGURE 5.1.** Lillian Colquhoun and her daughter, Sereena Brown, in 1971. Colquhoun was the lead plaintiff in a 1970 desegregation case. Photo courtesy of the *Democrat and Chronicle*.

as a northern school district might move in addressing racial imbalance in its schools, it would be courting trouble if it took decisive action and then walked it back—exactly what the new Rochester school board members had promised to do. "My colleagues who were elected with me are finding out rescinding reorganization isn't so easy," Joseph Farbo said. "We have a tiger by the tail. . . . And if we wind up with a high school that is 90 percent Black, we are in trouble." The *Colquhoun* plaintiffs' lawyer dared the school board to rescind the plan, predicting that a judge immediately would force desegregation to occur even faster than originally had been expected. Frey and Phillips, the school board holdovers, said that a repeal had "no chance" of passing judicial review, especially given that Nyquist just that month had ordered the Buffalo school board to draw a desegregation plan with nonwhite students spread more or less evenly across the district. In Rochester, that would mean nonminority enrollment of about 40 percent in every school.[36]

Such legal quibbles, though, meant nothing to the tens of thousands of voters who had cast a ballot to rescind the reorganization plan. Rather than consider its options further, the new board opted for immediate action. On February 1, 1972, with central-office staff still feverishly at work on redrawing neighborhood zones, the board announced that it would repeal the secondary reorganization beginning in the fall. "If we have to fight in court, we might as well get it over with now before the staff has done all the work," Elizabeth Farley said.[37]

The reorganization repeal plan restored all the junior and senior high schools as 7–12 schools, with the notable exceptions of Madison and West, and gave all students the right to attend their neighborhood high school. In practice, though, the repeal plan depended on Black students at Madison and West applying for transfers to mostly white schools. Madison, for instance, would be over capacity by 625 students if none of them transferred elsewhere instead. Nonwhite parents and community leaders saw the gambit as coercive and a return to one-way busing. They also did not detect in the new plan any increase in local control over schools in minority neighborhoods. "I voted for you because you said you liked the idea of community schools," the Community School Council chairman, Cero Sepulzeda, said. "If the devil or God gives me justice, I'll take it from either one. But you haven't said you will give us control of the money and hiring in our schools. What you have planned is one-way busing of black and Puerto Rican children." Joseph Farbo responded: "Sure, it's one-way busing, but . . . I haven't heard anyone say that anyone who attends an all-white school doesn't get a good education."[38]

The school board next voted to rescind the elementary portion of the reorganization, and there too it faced opposition. School 14 on University Avenue had been the only elementary school affected by the 1971–72 reorganization, changing to grades 4–6 from K—6 and decreasing its nonwhite enrollment from 96 percent to 39 percent. Just a few months into the school year, white parents who at first had objected to their children's new assignment now fought to preserve it. They, along with the teachers and principal Warren Heiligman, protested the reversal. The faculty wrote directly to Ewald Nyquist, asking that he do "everything in [his] power to prevent . . . a blatant move to resegregate our school." The school board threatened to fire Heiligman or remove him from the school, but ultimately did neither.[39]

The elementary reorganization repeal vote took place on March 11, a week before a scheduled hearing in the *Colquhoun* case. As anticipated, the plaintiffs had asked Henderson to stop the board from rolling back the reorganization plan. District administrators, dreading the logistics of a second massive citywide restructuring in two years, pleaded for a decision from the judge that would allow them to proceed one way or another. At the national level, though, the backdrop for the case was very much in flux in all three branches of government, and Henderson was loathe to make a misstep. The Supreme Court had not yet ruled on the Denver case, which had the potential to govern the situation in Rochester. Meanwhile the idea of desegregation was coming under increasing attack from Congress and President Richard Nixon.

Indeed, the 1971 Rochester school board election and the subsequent battle over rescinding Goldberg's reorganization plan were part of a nearly universal rightward swing in the national politics around segregation. The Supreme Court's momentous 1971 decision in *Swann v. Charlotte-Mecklenberg Board of Education* made it clear that compulsory busing was, in at least some cases, a constitutionally acceptable remedy for segregation. That, along with a political clash over federal funding in Chicago and a looming metropolitan solution in Detroit, had brought many northern legislators into an awkward but sturdy coalition with southern avowed segregationists. Both feared the effects of the courts' "mania for busing" for their constituents and for their own re-election prospects.[40]

The same week that the Rochester school board rescinded the elementary school reorganization, Nixon gave a televised address introducing legislation that would put a national moratorium on busing orders. Yellow school buses, he said, had become "a symbol of helplessness, frustration and outrage—of a wrenching of children away from their families." National polls demonstrated again and again an overwhelming antipathy for desegregation actions, and Congress took note. The House of Representatives passed a slew of antibusing bills and amendments in the late 1960s and early 1970s, and a Long Island conservative introduced an antibusing constitutional amendment.[41]

Henderson, then, had reason to tread carefully in *Colquhoun*. He signaled in March that he was not ready to decide. District administrators moved forward with crafting the repeal plan, including an option added later in March allowing most white secondary students to stay in their current, comparatively desegregated high schools in 1972–73 if they wished. While any potential judicial consequences to overturning reorganization were delayed, however, the district's significant federal desegregation funding fell into jeopardy. US Office of Education officials visited Rochester in February to understand how a $137,000 desegregation grant would be used after the district's flagship desegregation program was ended. "Rochester now has people federally funded to work on problems of desegregation and others locally funded working in exactly the opposite direction," a state education official observed. In April, federal officials pulled the money.[42]

In June Henderson denied the plaintiffs' request for an injunction in the *Colquhoun* case, a step that would have stopped the repeal from proceeding in the fall. "The resolution rescinding the reorganization plan is not, on its face, based upon a classification of race," he wrote. "[There] are material questions of fact . . . which preclude the granting of summary judgment at this stage. Although Henderson called for a trial, he did not schedule one, and in fact none ever took place.[43]

Desegregation advocates waged one final, unsuccessful campaign with the board that spring. The 19th Ward was one of the two areas of the city where Goldberg's recommended "home zones" had been permitted to go into effect in 1970–71, chiefly because families there were supportive and no busing was required. Now, the 19th Ward Community Association urged the school board to leave reorganization in place there. A parent survey showed that 80 percent were in favor of keeping the nongraded, reorganized structure. It would be especially appropriate, they said, given that nearby West and Madison were the only secondary schools not being returned to grades 7–12. "What we can't get through [their] heads is that having children of all one age group in this school has meant we can provide music, art and physical education specialists without increasing costs because all the children in the school can be grouped together at times," School 44 Principal Mildred Ness said.[44]

In the original vote to rescind the elementary school reorganization in March, Gordon DeHond had indicated that he would spare the 19th Ward, if that was what people there wanted. When an amendment came up in early May to do just that, however, he opposed it, instead casting the crucial fourth vote to defeat it. His change of heart came, he said, after a "two-day mental retreat." Others took note of the fact that DeHond had announced a primary campaign for the state senate. The campaign would rely heavily on the support of the United Council on Education and Taxation, which opposed any carve-outs to a full repeal. The 19th Ward Community Association, led by president Conrad Istock, went further, appealing directly to Nyquist to intercede where Henderson had not and block the repeal altogether. Nyquist declined, just as James Allen had done before him.[45]

A school year of threatened and actual violence came to a fitting conclusion in June 1972. On the final Friday of the year, June 16, Charlotte community members pelted the Black students' school bus with rocks as it departed, while a mob of white parents gathered outside Jefferson after hearing a rumor that a white student had been assaulted the day before. The ensuing fighting, a Jefferson school sentry said, was begun by "irate parents who took off half-cocked without getting all the information." Both white and Black students then spent the weekend preparing for violence on Monday. Dozens came to school with bricks, bats, rocks, and other weapons. "The black kids came to school as usual Friday, but some white kids brought clubs, threw rocks and taunted them," Charlotte principal Santo Patti said on Monday. "A number of black kids came prepared today to get revenge. They were tired of being called names." At West, similarly, teacher Ed Cavalier recalled: "Toward the end of the year, it was very much the Black kids feeling like: 'You don't want me? I know how to handle you.' And we were holding on by our fingertips."[46]

What followed was the single most violent and chaotic day in the history of the city's schools. Dozens of students and several teachers were taken to the hospital with injuries ranging from lacerations to a broken back. A thirteen-year-old girl at Charlotte broke her arm after falling, or being pushed, from a second-story window. Nearly a hundred windows were broken, among other property damage. A white Charlotte teacher said that forty Black students broke into his locked classroom and assaulted him, and Black students said that a white police officer threw a Black school counselor to the floor, then beat students who tried to come to her aid. At Franklin High School, teacher Dorothy Pecoraro remembered walking down the hall with a fellow female teacher who had just given birth and seeing students running out of the cafeteria brandishing broken-off table legs. "She said, 'Oh my God, I'll never see my baby again,'" Pecoraro recalled.[47]

White parents gathered outside by the hundreds, opposing the Black students exiting the schools as well as about a dozen Black parents and community leaders. "There were parents—perfectly nice, decent, good people—throwing rocks at school buses," Jefferson teacher Marlene Caroselli recalled. "It was horrifying. . . . It wasn't the Jefferson I knew, the Rochester I knew." Idonia Owens, one of the few Black students who lived in Charlotte, said: "It is amazing I have my life, honestly. These same parents I had seen, had grown up with their kids, knew who I was, were standing on the street saying: 'N——s go home, we don't want you here,' throwing bottles, all kinds of stuff at us. It was absolutely horrible." At the urging of the police commissioner and with the consent of the state's education department, the district canceled the rest of the school year, including statewide Regents tests and local final exams.[48]

Later, in testimony for a school board investigation, several teachers and Black students and parents highlighted the harm that police had done—not just in failing to break up the rioting but also in taking the side of the white people. Josh Lofton, a district administrator, was among several to say that he heard police using racial slurs. Police aggressively frisked Black students but mostly let white students through, according to several teachers and Black students and parents. Though the white parents outside Charlotte and Jefferson greatly outnumbered the Black ones, police reportedly focused their energy on the Black side. James Beard said that the same thing had happened in June 1971, when he graduated: "I remember one riot we had where they called the cops in and they were facing us. . . . "The guys across the street are yelling, 'N——s' this, 'n——s' that, throwing shit. I said, 'Wait a minute, they're throwing shit! Why's your back turned?'" A sixteen-year-old girl at Jefferson told the school board that she was hit by a rock while leaving school. When she turned to see where it came from, she said, she saw "nothing but white people . . . [and] a policeman with his arms folded." The police chief, John Mastrella, defended officers for not acting more aggressively against the white contingent, saying that if they had done so, "it's very possible some serious injuries would have resulted."[49]

One seventeen-year-old Black Jefferson student, Perry Lang, was charged with reckless endangerment for throwing a rock. He, in turn, succeeded in having criminal harassment charges brought against a police officer, David Cona, who he and others said struck him with a club for no reason. At trial, Cona's attorney had a different police officer wear Cona's uniform and badge and sit at the defense table. Lang correctly remembered the badge number but mistakenly identified another person in the audience as Cona. The judge called the tactic "shrewd" and dismissed the charge against Cona for a lack of proper identification.[50]

Absent from these incidents was Louis Cerulli. In January 1972 he stepped down from leadership of the United Schools Association because of worsening lung cancer. He died in the hospital on March 13 at age sixty-one, two days after the DeHond board formally rescinded the reorganization plan. The newspapers and Cerulli's admirers highlighted his long medical career and framed his time on the school board as part of a life of integrity and courage. "He had what most political men don't have—the courage to stand up for what he felt was right," one ally wrote. Two years later, the school board voted to rename School 34 on Lexington Avenue after him, an honor pushed by the Italian-American Civil Rights League. There was no public criticism of the move then or later, but, as Ed Cavalier said: "I wouldn't be surprised if at some point someone brought up changing his school name. . . . There's other problems the district has to figure out, but he was a segregationist."[51]

The 1972–73 school year was supposed to represent a return to normalcy, at least for parents who had supported maintaining neighborhood schools rather than reorganizing to desegregate. Because the school boundaries were not exactly the same as they had been previously, however, the district was inundated with enrollment complaints nonetheless—the same number of them as in 1971–72, in fact. "We have former East High students who don't want to go back to East from Franklin and East High students who don't want to go back to Monroe and Frederick Douglass students who don't want to go to East," secondary schools director Herbert Norton said. Several schools saw dramatic resegregation. Madison, for instance, went from 59 percent to 79 percent nonwhite, and Charlotte went from 32 percent to 10 percent. School 4, with an enrollment of 638, became the first school in the district without a single white child.[52]

The number of students riding buses decreased, from 12,100 in 1971–72 to 9,700 in 1972–73, but not as sharply as the district had anticipated and still well above the pre-reorganization mark. This shortcoming was not held against the purportedly antibusing school board—proof, to Black families, that all the "emotionalism of busing" was never about transportation. "Is busing the real concern of those parents who threaten to move out to the suburbs where there is no doubt that their children will be bused during their entire school career?" Jerome Balter asked. In his book *Why Busing Failed*, the historian Matthew Delmont used the word "busing" in quotation marks throughout to acknowledge its added semantic cargo: "With 'busing,' northerners found a palatable way to oppose desegregation without appealing to the explicitly racist sentiments they preferred to associate with southerners." Noting that transportation on school buses was commonplace throughout the country by the early 1970s, Delmont concluded: "School buses were fine for the majority of white families; 'busing' was not." Or, as the NAACP Legal Defense Fund put it: 'It's not the distance, it's the n——s.'"[53]

The *Colquhoun* lawsuit—seen as recently as March 1972 as a powerful potential bulwark against a retreat on desegregation—died quietly, as the *Aikens* case had before it. Like *Aikens*, it had been poorly funded and, as a result, timidly litigated. Just three months after it was first filed, in June 1970, its organizers were soliciting for "tangible evidence of support by the community for this effort in the form of a fund to meet certain expenses." The national NAACP declined to support it despite entreaties from local leaders as well as national advisors, including J. Harold Flannery, who was deputy director of the Harvard University Center for Law and Education at the time. "To dismantle for racial reasons an education-based plan . . . must be a new world's record," Flannery observed. The case was dismissed for good in February 1976, any momentum for an appeal having been thoroughly squandered.[54]

Conrad Istock of the 19th Ward Community Association, one of the most active proponents of desegregation in the final years that the city wrestled with the question, wrote to Nyquist in September 1972. He acknowledged the broader defeat and conceded that little remained beyond "this rather esoteric writing up of the denouement." He continued:

> The entire indigenous education-reform movement in Rochester has been defeated and largely destroyed. . . . We had throughout hoped we could rely on swift action by state and federal judicial authorities once this critical juncture [i.e., backlash to reorganization] was reached. Thereafter, we expected palpable educational advances to steadily increase popular support. . . .
>
> The momentum in Rochester . . . has been broken and it now seems likely that no court decision can come in time to repair that damage and remove the losses in educational opportunities for thousands of children which we must now bear.[55]

The journalist Jerome Zukosky reached the same conclusion in an article about Rochester in *Time* magazine. Its title was "Giving Up on Integration." The city, Zukosky wrote, had seemed "an inspirational example of what can be done by local initiative and quiet leadership . . . without court order or significant special help." Instead, he wrote: "Rochester didn't make it. . . . The school board was controlled by mean-spirited 'antis' determined to return to the old days when Rochester's 'happy blacks' kept their problems and their children to themselves. A mood of acceptance has settled on the city: it is as if an era has passed."[56]

Rochester's experiment with reorganization lasted, in effect, from the first day of school in September 1971 until the decisive school board election fifty-four days later. It was marked by protests, violence, and logistical mayhem. For most students, it was the first time they had ever boarded a school bus and been dropped off in another part of town. It was also the first time that most of the city's secondary teachers had been tasked with working in classrooms with rough racial balance.

Perhaps the most remarkable aspect of the entire episode, then, is that so many students and educators viewed reorganization as a success, no matter how short-lived. Teachers stressed the stimulating effect of diversity in classrooms. Marlene Caroselli recalled introducing Black literature into her English classes at Jefferson for the first time. One militant Black student wore a scowl in her classroom throughout the entire semester—"but his poetry was marvelous." She entered one of his poems into a regional contest, where it won the fifty-dollar first-place prize. Teachers and administrators advocated strongly for the ungraded "open classrooms" and the increased peer training time and professional development that came with them. "We're going to find more and more teachers who are going to look [back on] 1971–72 as a high mark in terms of the schools we had," one community leader told Benjamin Richardson. "I think we are going to be more strongly in favor of it when we begin to live with the alternatives."[57]

Students—even those who vividly recalled their lives being threatened—said the brief experience of a significantly desegregated school building had changed them for the better. White students at Madison, now a distinct minority after relative parity in 1971–72, responded to a spate of violent incidents at the start of the 1972–73 school year by creating a "unity group" with Black students and petitioning the school board to better balance enrollment. In a meeting with Franco, they expressed a desire that "relationships in the school could be like last year when black and white students got along well together."[58]

James Beard, a Black Charlotte student, said:

> When you're young and you're Black and you come from a totally Black environment and community, you learn something when you're immersed into a white culture and community . . . in a way that's almost organic. I am so grateful, regardless of all that happened at Charlotte—all the tears, all the fighting, all the blood, everything—I am so grateful that I got the opportunity to meet people whether they were Black [or] white. . . . Because I didn't have any white friends. There were no white people in my community.
>
> When I started to develop friendships with those young white guys, I had a consciousness shift, and my revolutionary [attitude] of, "All white people need to just die"—regardless of what was going on at Charlotte, I then knew—"Wait a minute, all white people aren't like that. I actually love some of these people." And I know that sounds crazy, but I'm grateful for that.[59]

*Keyes v. School District No. 1* was finally decided in 1973 in a difficult-to-parse Supreme Court ruling, the first since *Brown* in 1954 not to command unanimity among the justices. The court found clear evidence of intentional segregation but declined to spell out the standard by which it had done so. It declined as well to address head-on the burning question in northern cities: whether so-called de facto segregation, of the sort seen in Rochester, would be subjected to the same strong medicine as southern-style de jure segregation. For the purposes of Lillian Colquhoun and the Rochester plaintiffs,

Denver ended up being much less useful a guidepost than Judge Henderson or other observers had anticipated.[60]

Meanwhile, continuing demographic shifts in the Rochester area were beginning to make the matter of intracity desegregation obsolete. When the district first tallied its nonwhite students in 1963, they made up 20 percent of the student body. A decade later that proportion had more than doubled. That occurred largely because of in-migration; US Census data showed that the city had a net increase of more than 44,000 nonwhite residents from 1950 to 1970. Equally important, though, was a loss of 80,000 white residents, or one in four, over the same time. They had left the city for the Monroe County suburbs, which registered a net gain of 224,000 residents in that twenty-year stretch. None of those trends—the growth of the nonwhite population, the decline of the white city population, and the shifting of the county's population base from the city to the suburbs—were to relent anytime soon. For that reason, even before *Keyes* was decided, education officials and advocates in Rochester had shifted their attention to litigation in Detroit.[61]

In the broadest sense, racial segregation of housing and schools in Detroit followed the same pattern as in Rochester. Detroit was an early organizing point for the Black Power movement, and its schools proved to be an important battleground. From 1969 to 1971, Detroit Public Schools suffered waves of violence that made Charlotte Junior High School in June 1972 look like a nursery school picnic. "Literally hundreds of incidents, including shootings, stabbings, rapes, student rampages [and] gang fights . . . occurred in the schools or school property," one historian wrote.[62]

In the middle of a complicated, multiyear fight over community control and desegregation, the NAACP in 1970 filed a lawsuit on behalf of Ronald Bradley and other Black Detroit schoolchildren. Hoping to restore an earlier intracity desegregation plan, it presented evidence to the court of segregative actions not only by Detroit school officials but also by the state of Michigan. The federal court trial judge, Stephen Roth, accepted the plaintiffs' argument and—following the recent Supreme Court guidance in *Green v. County School Board* to find a remedy that "promise[s] realistically to work now and hereafter to produce maximum actual desegregation"—rejected proposed Detroit-only desegregation plans, instead issuing an order that would include more than fifty suburban school districts in three surrounding counties. "The higher courts . . . say when you find segregation you have to go about desegregating," Roth explained. The state and the outlying districts, which had not been given the opportunity to defend themselves at trial, promptly appealed, but an appellate court upheld Roth's order.

The next stop for the case, *Milliken v. Bradley*, was a highly anticipated hearing before the US Supreme Court.[63]

The question before the court was a simple one: When a constitutional remedy ran up against a locally drawn school district boundary, which must yield? The NAACP warned against a legally sanctioned "containment" mechanism: "If that dividing line is permitted to stand without breach to perpetuate the basic dual structure, the intentional confinement of black children in schools separate from whites will continue for the foreseeable future," it wrote. US Solicitor General Robert Bork, whom Nixon had instructed to intervene, pointed instead to the admonition in *Swann v. Charlotte-Mecklenberg* that "the nature of the violation determines the scope of the remedy." Because no evidence had been presented at trial of the outlying districts' segregative actions, he argued, they should not be implicated in the solution.[64]

The *Milliken* decision was the exact moment Richard Nixon had been preparing for since taking office. In choosing his nominees for the Supreme Court, he had said: "I don't care if he's a Democrat or a Republican, [but] . . . I have to have an absolute commitment from him on busing and integration." At the critical moment, his men kept their commitment. The four Nixon appointees, along with Potter Stewart, held in a 5–4 decision that Judge Roth's metropolitan plan was unconstitutional. "Without an inter-district violation and an inter-district effect, there is no constitutional wrong calling for an inter-district remedy," Chief Justice Warren Burger wrote in the majority opinion. The question, he said, was not whether the plaintiffs achieved "the racial balance which they perceived as desirable," but whether Black students in Detroit were treated equitably.[65]

To desegregation proponents who see *Milliken* as a fatal blow, the eloquent dissent of Thurgood Marshall has come to serve as a eulogy. Marshall, who twenty years earlier had helped lead the victorious NAACP legal team in *Brown v. Board of Education*, accused the majority of "conjur[ing] up a largely fictional account" of the facts of the case, including the possibility of intra-district desegregation, and of bowing to political pressure:

> Desegregation is not and was never expected to be an easy task. Racial attitudes ingrained in our Nation's childhood and adolescence are not quickly thrown aside in its middle years. . . .
>
> Today's holding, I fear, is more a reflection of a perceived public mood that we have gone far enough in enforcing the Constitution's guarantee of equal justice than it is the product of neutral principles of law. In the short run, it may seem to be the easier course to allow our great metropolitan areas to be divided up each into two cities—one

white, the other black—but it is a course, I predict, our people will ultimately regret.[66]

The importance of this ruling is hard to overstate. If *Brown v. Board of Education* can be seen as the dawn of the Civil Rights era, *Milliken* was its sunset. It marked the first time that the Supreme Court voted to overturn a locally developed desegregation policy. By leaving a clear escape hatch for worried white families, one scholar wrote, it "calcified the lines of racial and social class inequities between urban school districts of color and wealthy, white suburban districts." The harm was compounded by the Supreme Court's decision the previous year in *San Antonio Independent School District v. Rodriguez*, which held that unequal school funding did not imply a lack of equal protection under the Constitution. "Today's decision, given *Rodriguez*, means that there is no violation of the Equal Protection Clause though schools are segregated by race and though the black schools are not only 'separate' but inferior," Justice William Douglas wrote in his *Milliken* dissent.[67]

In Rochester, the *Milliken* decision was mostly an afterthought. Frank Ciaccia, now the school board president, said that it settled "once and for all Rochester's right to maintain neighborhood schools without any court interference." Reporters sought no comment from desegregation advocates; perhaps they did not know whom to call. Goldberg's reorganization, by now, felt like a lifetime ago.[68]

"Our efforts may have resulted in setting back integration in Rochester several years," one frustrated former district official wrote. "The black community knows even more concretely what it has always known before: the white community will not have integration. Can they be blamed then if the only hope they see is to establish black schools, run by black staff, for black children? And if this occurs, the integration movement will have gone full circle."[69]

# Chapter 6

# Considering the Metropolis

Even as debate over the contours of desegregation raged in the Rochester City School District in the 1960s and 1970s, it was becoming increasingly clear that the solution to racial isolation and inequality could not be contained within city lines. Every year the white population—and with it, the tax base—was shifting to the suburbs. In 1940, 74 percent of white Monroe County residents lived in the city of Rochester. In 1970, only 37 percent of them did. By 2010 it was down to 16 percent. Many of these suburban residents were glad to have escaped the social, educational, and financial crises of Rochester and staunchly resisted efforts they believed would draw them back in. "We are in the business of education, and any extension beyond this is not the business of boards of education," Greece school board vice president Wilho Salminen wrote in 1966 in opposing joining Urban-Suburban. "[The] Greece Central School District is beset with too many problems of its own to become physically involved in racial problems."[1]

Others, though, considered it a moral obligation for the suburbs to share in the city's deepening woes, or otherwise saw the looming workforce shortage as a regional economic dilemma. Opinions varied considerably as to the proper scope of involvement, ranging from one-time "cultural exchanges" to forming a single, unified countywide school district. "The basic solution, to indulge in a bit of oversimplification, is a metropolitan form of government where all residents of the county can participate equally in some of the problems peculiar to the City of Rochester," the developer James Wilmot wrote to Xerox CEO Joseph C. Wilson in 1966. "The biggest obstacle seems to be just plain human nature." This idea had a long history, dating to before the Great Migration, when towns saw a potential marriage with the city as a boon and not an act of altruism. In the suburbs as in the city, though, "human nature" surfaced repeatedly in the form of packed public meetings, angry letters to the editor, and resounding electoral rejections, opposing even voluntary desegregation efforts that crossed district boundaries. "If I wanted a racially balanced school district I would have moved into one," an Irondequoit man said when Urban-Suburban was first developed. In other cases, this level of excitement was not necessary—a school board's lukewarm pledge to take a desegregation proposal into consideration, rather than a positive vote to act on it, had the same effect.[2]

A number of small desegregation programs did take place. They were voluntary pilot programs, intended to build goodwill and demonstrate success on the way to further, unspecified advances in desegregation. And they did have success—great success, in some cases, illustrated by long wait lists for enrollment and strong academic achievement for white and nonwhite students. What they did not have was stable funding to sustain them. Local dollars are guarded jealously and state and federal funding is inconstant, ebbing and flowing according to shifting politics. From the creation of Urban-Suburban in 1965 to the Great Schools for All initiative starting in 2013, desegregation initiatives crossing district lines have all run into the same problem: In a system where all education funding runs through individual school districts, how can interdistrict partnerships be sustained? Only Urban-Suburban, which will be discussed separately in chapter 7, has managed a permanent solution. Other programs, no matter how promising, have either run aground or failed to launch all together. This failure to thrive has left proponents dejected and contributed greatly to the community's learned helplessness when it comes to addressing racial and socioeconomic injustice.

Today the concept of a metropolitan school district covering all of Monroe County is discussed chiefly as a means to achieve racial desegregation. In the years before the Civil Rights era—or, perhaps more significantly, the years before the Great Migration hit Rochester—the same idea was thoroughly aired for a different set of reasons. In 1941, RCSD assistant superintendent Harold Akerly called for countywide schools as the most efficient way of spending taxpayer dollars. "Equality of opportunity in education cannot be afforded to all children in a natural community or metropolitan district so long as it is broken up into one larger and several small administrative units," he wrote.[3] The local Council on Post-War Problems in 1945 likewise gave its full endorsement to a metropolitan school district. Among the benefits it listed was a final severing of the fiscal relationship between the city of Rochester and its coterminous school district. Then as now, the former was responsible for education taxation and the latter for education spending. "However well disposed and statesmanlike may be school authorities and city officials, this dual responsibility has been and will continue to be a source of friction for all concerned," the committee wrote.[4]

Of equal importance were the highly dynamic and closely related issues of student enrollment and school buildings in different parts of the county. The swelling suburbs had a surplus of students and a shortage of facilities; the city had gleaming new schools but not enough children to fill them. Rochester school board member Rachel Lee wrote in 1947: "People with children move out of cities, leaving half empty school buildings. Just over the lines they immediately start assembling bricks, stones and flags for more buildings. That is not the solution. The solution is to remove the lines, utilize the existing buildings, reduce the disproportionate investment in building materials and put the money into . . . a richer, fuller and more attractive educational program for all the children of the larger community."[5]

If school officials seemed unusually open-minded, it was because a major political upheaval was already under way. Before World War II, a "school district" most often referred to the enrollment and taxation area of a single, independently administered school building. As the regional population grew, academic standards rose, and transportation options improved, those districts came under increasing pressure to expand their tax bases by joining together into larger amalgamated districts where relatively distant elementary schools could all feed into a single secondary school. The central school districts now ubiquitous throughout the country are the result of this process. The first in the Rochester area was the Brockport Central School District, approved by voters in 1927. From 1932 to the early 1970s, the number of school districts in the United States fell from about 128,000 to about 20,000.[6]

Occupying a middle ground between the rural and urban districts were several free school districts in new parts of the city, the bane of several generations of city and RCSD leaders. From 1901 to 1926 the city annexed parts of the outlying towns of Brighton, Gates, and Greece, adding substantially to its physical and economic footprint. Because the annexations could only proceed with an affirmative vote from the residents in question, the city was obligated to offer various enticements. One was a promise that those residents' children would be able to attend city schools without paying taxes, hence the term free school districts. The city rued the deal almost before the ink was dry. Areas that had been semirural and sparsely populated were shortly bristling with development, and with that development came hundreds of school-age children entitled by law to a no-cost education. A 1931 report called the annexed tracts "parasite districts" and stated that they were costing RCSD $113,000 a year. The towns in question said the city should keep up its end of the bargain; the city complained that the value of the land taken had long since been paid back in free education. The city tried amending its charter and filing legal challenges, but it was to no avail. By the time the state legislature finally rescinded the annexed districts' tax-free status in 1975, the annual cost to the city had risen to about $800,000 a year for 1,700 students.[7]

The desire to shed this financial burden was a main impetus for city political leaders' fervent wish to separate RCSD from the city and instead grant it financial independence. Rochester-area assemblyman Homer Dick repeatedly introduced legislation to that effect in the 1920s. Crucially, it would have amended the state law declaring the city school district boundaries to be identical to the city line. The director of the Bureau of Municipal Research, Earl Weller, helped draft a similar bill in 1929, but neither the Dick legislation nor the Weller legislation was ever seriously considered in Albany. School districts in cities with fewer than 125,000 residents got autonomy in 1950, but the state legislature did not extend the same rights to larger cities like Rochester despite the urging of then-City Manager Robert Aex and Deputy Commissioner of Education James Allen, among others.[8]

As late as the early 1960s, when suburban centralization was not yet complete and most of the county population was still living within city limits, RCSD was the unquestioned educational gold standard. RCSD at that time allowed suburban students to pay tuition to attend its schools, and in 1956 more than 1,800 students did so. One of its most compelling attractions was Edison Technical and Industrial High School, which offered an array of cutting-edge technical training programs even while stuck in an aging facility. Throughout the postwar years the majority of the school's students came from outside the city or from parochial schools rather than from RCSD. Superintendent Howard Seymour in 1958 proposed granting Edison autonomous status with its own power of taxation, a way to expand its financial base and more seamlessly recruit suburban students. A committee studied the question and concluded that the state law on school boundaries would not allow it. Instead Edison changed its admission standards, allowing female students for the first time and revising the entrance requirements in a way that desegregation advocates argued was intentionally discriminatory against Black prospective students.[9]

At about the same time, students from some city-adjacent areas of what is now the East Irondequoit Central School District still attended Franklin High School. RCSD warned that it would soon run out of space for the nonresident students and urged Irondequoiters not to delay in centralizing and building their own high school. The *Times-Union*, on the other hand, urged consideration of a joint arrangement between Irondequoit and RCSD that would accommodate students across the city line. "This is a situation ideally suited to taking the first steps toward handling our joint problems on a metropolitan scale," the editors wrote in 1952. "City and town boundary lines are the root of endless troubles and frustrations. The place to begin obliterating them is here." But though the East Irondequoit parents recognized that centralization was likely inevitable, they found their current arrangement at Franklin too good to relinquish. "We realize that a city high school—and this has been proven time and time again—can give our children a far better education than a small town one can," one leading opponent of East Irondequoit centralization wrote. "Also, Rochester schools have the highest standards."[10]

A referendum on building a new high school in East Irondequoit was defeated by twenty percentage points. That vote took place in early June 1954, after years of debate and less than a month after *Brown v. Board of Education* was decided. At about the same time, word continued to spread in the Black communities of Sanford, Florida, and Greenville, South Carolina, about the factory town on the shore of Lake Ontario where a better life could be had. East Irondequoit residents shortly reconsidered their stance and Eastridge High School opened its doors in 1958. It ended up as one of the last major events of the school district consolidation movement that swept Monroe County and the rest of New York in the twentieth century, with only large cities such as Rochester excluded.[11]

It is interesting to contemplate how the course of public education in Rochester would have been different if a version of the Dick or Weller legislation had passed, breaking the bond between district and city lines and throwing the city school district into the mix during the dynamic period of centralization. From the perspective of Monroe County's single-building districts, RCSD was a model of efficiency and scale and would have been an ideal nucleus for centralization. In hindsight, the failure of the Dick and Weller bills represents an incredible missed opportunity. The two major obstacles to Rochester-area metropolitan schools in the twenty-first century are racism directed at Black and Hispanic families living in the city of Rochester and—even if that could be overcome—the need to negotiate simultaneously with eighteen independent school districts. If RCSD had been emancipated from the legal restriction on its borders in the 1920s, it could have been a dominant force in the wave of school district mergers, potentially creating a single district that included inner-ring suburbs or even the entire county. In such a scenario, assimilating the Black students entering school during and after the Great Migration would have been the collective responsibility of the wider community, not just the city. Cooperation and centralization in education could have led to breakthroughs in other areas as well, chiefly housing and transportation.

There was, in the years before the Great Migration, a growing conviction that the Rochester city limits could no longer serve as the horizon line for community planning. This included not just schools but also housing and transportation policy, sewer lines, water supply, and public safety. Greater regional cooperation, though frightening for many, seemed inevitable. "The automobile has made it possible for [residents] to live in the suburbs, but to earn, and to spend, their money in the city," the *Democrat and Chronicle* wrote in 1940. "It is high time the government of the area was extended to fit the area's actual scope." In fact, the morning newspaper was a standard-bearer for the idea of tearing down the lines that divided. The growing wealth in the suburbs, it argued, had been subsidized by city residents in many ways:

> They could not enjoy their prosperity if they did not live close to the city; and most of them do everything but pay direct taxes in the city. . . . In return for what they have drained out of the city in tax funds to build up their own facilities, they now, as part of [a metropolitan school] district, should contribute their share in tax money to . . . the poorer city districts. This suggestion and these arguments may shock some of our suburban residents. Both are based on facts, however, and simple justice. . . .
>
> Some day the government of the county and that of the city will be merged. Until then, the metropolitan area should adjust its governing and tax support for specific functions to its actual condition.
>
> A metropolitan school district is an immediately necessary step.[12]

The social dynamic between the city and suburbs had shifted considerably by the mid-1960s, when RCSD for the first time was giving serious consideration to racial segregation. Still, those who debated Herman Goldberg's proposed desegregation measures remembered the postwar faith in metropolitan solutions. Both proponents and opponents of desegregation used the idea for their own purposes.

When Goldberg released his suite of desegregation plans in 1967, he was also looking further into the future—and farther into the county. "It has become clear that the adoption of any plan must be accompanied by increased participation by all school districts in the Rochester metropolitan area," he wrote. He included a map showing that nearly the entire county was within a fifteen-mile radius of downtown Rochester. Goldberg ultimately did not suggest a metropolitan solution, he later explained, because to have "offered a plan that included immediately projected full involvement of all the suburbs would have bordered on affrontery [*sic*]. . . . Just precisely because we did not demand suburban involvement, we may feel the people in the suburbs, through their school boards, will participate reasonably in the future."[13]

This hope for reasonable participation was misplaced. A 1966 survey showed strong opposition to a metropolitan school system among what researchers called the "contented" majority in the suburbs, who would oppose such consolidation even if it lowered their taxes—despite the fact that the majority of them could not name their own school district's superintendent or school board president. Nonetheless the Rochester school board, in receiving Goldberg's plans, seconded him: "The board realizes that the desegregation of the public schools is not a problem of the city alone and ultimately should involve metropolitan or suburban school districts." They were echoing, in part, state education commissioner James Allen, who had been at Gates Chili High School a few weeks earlier for a speaking engagement. There, he had said that legislation allowing large urban districts to merge with neighboring suburban districts was a necessary step toward solving school segregation.[14]

The *Democrat and Chronicle*, though sympathizing with the objective, called a metropolitan district "the most astronomically remote of all possible plans, [requiring] state legislating, county concurrence and years of red tape."[15] That analysis from the typically conservative editorial board gives a clue to the reason for the otherwise paradoxical popularity of a metropolitan school district among desegregation opponents, in particular School Board president Louis Cerulli and his allies. On one hand, a countywide school district would certainly provide the greatest degree of integration. On the other hand, the *Democrat and Chronicle* and Cerulli correctly gauged that, even before white flight had fully taken effect, the logistics of creating such a district would prove nearly insurmountable. "If this [Goldberg] plan is so necessary for all of us to live together as a black and white community, then we suggest an absolute 'must' is a metropolitan school system, so our friends from the lily white suburbs can share alike with us city dwellers in quality integrated education," one skeptical white city parent wrote in a 1971 letter to the editor. Indeed, Cerulli went even further than Goldberg, saying that he would have preferred a plan for a full metropolitan system. As Jerome Balter observed at a school board meeting: "Dr. Cerulli says the way to eliminate imbalance in the schools is by adopting a Metropolitan School Plan which would involve the entire county, but that he is unequivocally opposed to involuntary busing. Could it be that Dr. Cerulli has some super-secret method of transporting students which he would approve for the larger geographical area of the Metropolitan Plan? Or is the Metropolitan Plan merely a smokescreen for avoiding his responsibility?"[16]

If it was a smokescreen, it worked. Those who opposed busing in Rochester were never put to the test on their purported support for a larger countywide district. Indeed, after the opportunity to institute significant desegregation measures in RCSD passed by—and as many of the more conservative white parents relocated to the suburbs—enthusiasm for countywide schools fell off markedly. Cerulli's promotion of a metropolitan solution did have one significant impact, though. The 15-Point Plan that the school board adopted in 1967 contained little of consequence in terms of forcing desegregation but did discuss the establishment of a "voluntary cooperative federation of school districts in the region to discuss and plan ways of reducing racial isolation in Monroe County as well as other matters of mutual concern." This resulted, eventually, in the creation of the Monroe County Educational Planning Committee in 1970 and the publication of a major proposal in 1971.[17]

The concept of metropolitan planning for education already had many local antecedents. Most immediately, the Bureau of Municipal Research in 1969 decried the lack of effective metropolitan planning and governance structure and argued that Rochester-area students were being shortchanged as a result. Money was disbursed and spent haphazardly and without reference to either student need or the ability to pay; students in urban and rural schools had significantly less access to high-quality education than did their suburban counterparts; and regional planning was piecemeal and inefficient. "It is now generally realized that the tendency to relate urban problems and solutions exclusively to older jurisdictional boundaries is at the heart of our inability to take effective action to combat them," the authors wrote.[18]

This research served as a foundation for the 1971 Monroe County Educational Planning Committee report. Importantly, though, the report dismissed out of hand the idea of a true countywide school district. "The practical headaches of administratively effecting such a merger in Monroe County, when added to the vehement arguments against the loss of local control which would result, ruled merger or consolidation out as a viable alternative," the Educational Planning Committee wrote in 1971. At the same time, the committee concluded that some degree of centralized decision-making and authority was necessary. It thus proposed the concept of a federation, using as a model metropolitan Toronto as well as the Twin Cities in Minnesota. That meant "decentralized districts for educational functions relating to neighborhoods and districts and a community-wide educational agency for central functions, including financing," as the 1969 report put it. This community-wide agency would be a new, combined version of the existing Board of Cooperative Educational Services (BOCES), a regional educational planning unit prescribed in state law but excluding Rochester and other large urban districts. There are two BOCES in Monroe County, one on the east side and one on the west side. They provide certain special education and career education programs as well as professional development and other services districts might find too costly to offer on their own. The proposal would have combined the east- and west-side BOCES and, crucially, would have included the city of Rochester after an amendment to the state law barring its participation.[19]

The federation model would have gathered every Monroe County district into a single, strengthened BOCES-like entity known as the Educational Council, a twenty-seven-person decision-making body with proportionate representation from all area school districts. Second, rather than permitting districts to contract with the council for services as they pleased, the model would put the council in charge of financing and providing all special and vocational education, transportation, and capital planning, along with some other programs, to all schools in Monroe County. The use of the council's special education program and other BOCES-style services, in other words, would become mandatory rather than supplemental. For the proposed council to have true authority, it would need to control its own budget. The model proposed funding its operation by having the state direct specific categories of aid to the federation rather than to its component districts, and also by a countywide educational income tax of about three-tenths of 1 percent.[20]

Don Pryor had just been hired by the Bureau of Municipal Research, and the 1971 plan was one of his first assignments. "We really thought we had something," he said fifty years later. "We all felt we had come up with something that had a chance to significantly change the way educational issues got addressed in this community, and also something that was politically feasible with a real chance to be implemented." The committee that created the plan included representatives from RCSD as well as several suburban school districts, the Monroe County School Boards Association, the University of Rochester, the Catholic diocesan schools, and the state government.

It would require, among other things, state legislation changing the structure of BOCES and permitting a redirection of state aid.[21]

Some desegregation plans in Rochester have faltered under a hailstorm of opposition. The federation plan, by contrast, "just kind of died a sad but natural death," Pryor said. After it was published in August 1971, it never received any further attention in the newspapers. No rallies or public forums were held, and legislation was never introduced in Albany. "I think a lot of the participants tried to rally support in their own spheres of influence, and I think a fair amount of that happened," Pryor said. "[But] the kinds of things that would have been necessary to build a fire under this really didn't happen. . . . It just kind of died." Half a century later, the 1971 plan remains the closest thing Rochester has seen to a fully developed concept for metropolitan educational planning.[22]

A less considered metropolitan proposal came in May 1983, when RCSD was facing a particularly painful $6.1 million budget gap. Rather than find more cuts to close it, the school board approved the unbalanced budget and forwarded it to the city council. Superintendent Laval Wilson supported the board and said that rather than suggesting further cuts he would petition the courts to dissolve the city school district altogether, leaving the surrounding suburban districts to take up the task of educating Rochester children. "There is no purpose in having a school district if you lose all those programs," he said. It was essentially a political ploy for additional funding; Wilson admitted he had given no thought to the specifics of the notion. But just mentioning the concept led to anxiety around Monroe County. "It's an expression of the very deep, obvious concern and frustration they are feeling," Greece superintendent David Robinson said. "There is going to have to be some kind of redistribution of resources so that all students can benefit equally. . . . [But] local communities are very jealous. They identify very closely with their schools." The *Democrat and Chronicle* editorial board dismissed Wilson's idea as "last-ditch, last-resort thinking" but nonetheless affirmed the essential inequity in question. "The folding of the city school district into the suburban districts is, of course, something that should have happened long ago," the editors wrote. "It simply isn't fair or equitable to saddle the city children with an inferior education, which is exactly where Rochester is headed."[23]

The uprising in July 1964 in the Third and Seventh Wards came just as the Rochester City School District was beginning to take its first, tentative steps toward intradistrict desegregation. That progress set off a battle that continued into the 1964–65 school year and beyond. The most immediate impact of the riots on education in the city, though, began shortly after the violence subsided. Herman Goldberg met with Dean William Fullager of the UR College of Education as well as professor Dean Corrigan, a staunch advocate of integrated schools, to consider the educational roots of the uprising and "design programs relevant to the needs of the city schools." Corrigan was named an official liaison between the district and the university and helped establish a task force that eventually morphed into a wide-ranging initiative and funding mechanism called Project UNIQUE.[24] "We believe that our responsibility in Project UNIQUE is to show that children from different educational, cultural, racial, and ethnic backgrounds can learn effectively together," Director William Young said. "Our major responsibility then is to show what changes in schools are needed, and what minimum staff is needed, to make quality integrated education a viable reality."[25]

During the short period in the late 1960s when the federal government was substantially investing in desegregation, Project UNIQUE was Rochester's main funding vehicle. In May 1967, it received $1.7 million in federal Title III funding for a slate of nine programs. Several of them took aim at the teaching profession, such as the creation of an urban education major at UR and a program intended to help Black paraprofessionals and other partly trained people gain their teaching credentials. Others sought to strengthen school-community relations, including via paid outreach positions at city schools and a "community resources council." The idea that got the most attention at the time was a demonstration classroom on the fourth floor of the downtown Sibley's department store, where shoppers could peer into lessons through a one-way mirror. Georgianna Sibley, the grand dame of Rochester's industrialist-philanthropic class, invited the children up to her top-floor executive suite and took them onto her lap as she explained how a department store runs.[26]

The grant also included money to greatly expand the number of students attending suburban schools through Urban-Suburban. Indeed, at the outset, Urban-Suburban was seen as an extension of RCSD's experiment with open enrollment, not as a categorically different initiative. It was run through the same administrative department, and early media coverage did not always differentiate the two programs. And though Urban-Suburban was not originally envisioned as two-way, it did face pressure at different times to enroll suburban students in the city. In 1979 the state education department made $50,000 in needed funding contingent on the acceptance of a small number of white suburban children in city schools. For the program to continue to accept only outbound minority students, one state official said, would "result in something like a 'raid' on the Rochester School System."[27]

Many of the Project UNIQUE initiatives went by the wayside after federal funding expired a few years later; others hardly managed to launch. The most important of them, and the longest lasting, was the creation of the World of Inquiry School in September 1967. Housed at first in the eighty-year-old School 58 building off West Main Street, it was designed as a "laboratory," with students of different ages grouped together as "families" and learning through hands-on projects and individualized instruction. The school had no report cards and no assigned textbooks, but rather frequent parent conferences and books on a variety of subjects from which students could choose freely. "There will be a great deal of flexibility," Principal William Pugh said. "A child learns by inquiring into the world around him, not by sitting in a chair in a straight row and having a teacher tell him something."[28]

The school was the city's first formal attempt at a magnet school, intended to draw middle-class families from both the city and the suburbs. "The school's neighborhood is metropolitan Rochester, but it is located in the inner city," Project UNIQUE officials wrote. The desegregation pitch worked. Interest for the inaugural 1967–68 school year exceeded school capacity by May 1967, before the district even began soliciting applications. The initial racial composition was about 60 percent white and 40 percent nonwhite, roughly equivalent to the district-wide demographics. About twenty suburban children enrolled and another fifty or so went onto a waiting list.[29]

There were only around 125 students at World of Inquiry in its first year, about a quarter of the planned final enrollment. Expansion proved elusive, though, as federal funding lapsed and other district priorities pressed for attention. The teachers union protested a proposal for constructing a new home for the school with room for 800 students, saying it would be "an affront to an already aroused black community," unfairly leapfrogging larger, majority-Black schools for badly needed renovations.[30] Indeed, the school's small size made it a target for criticism as larger-scale desegregation efforts foundered. After the school board rejected Herman Goldberg's reorganization plan in 1970, FIGHT president Bernard Gifford called for a picket in front of World of Inquiry until it could be closed altogether. "[World of Inquiry] at one time symbolized hope of things to come, and now it only symbolizes a gigantic fraud and a big lie," he wrote. The school managed to stay open through the turmoil of open enrollment, reorganization, and white flight, but it remained in what were expected to be temporary quarters for more than a decade after it launched.[31]

"There was stuff falling apart—it was a somewhat decrepit building," said Thomas Warfield, who began at World of Inquiry in third grade in 1969. Warfield was born into a prominent musical family, and it was no surprise that he found a home at the experimental school. He credited his music teacher there, Geraldine McFadden, with pushing him to become a professional singer. He wrote a play about Daniel Hale Williams, a pioneering Black heart surgeon. He remembered learning about political systems by having an "anarchy day"—students built forts with their desks—followed by "dictatorship day." "I felt like the teachers there, the nurturing they did—it wasn't just about teaching us stuff," he said. "It just taught me about being part of humanity. . . . We really were being prepared for an integrated world."[32]

Well into the 1980s, World of Inquiry was one of the few RCSD schools that appealed to suburban families. Patricia and James DeCaro moved to the Rochester area from England in 1980 and landed in Pittsford because they wanted a big house with a garden. But, Patricia DeCaro recalled: "We had overheard young school kids talking about what kind of special car their mom or dad had, and what kind of special clothes they had, and that's not what we wanted our kids to be a part of, frankly." Instead, they heard through a friend about World of Inquiry and enrolled their son and then their daughter there. "[My parents] knew that if the academics were lacking in any way . . . they were able to make up for some of that at home," their daughter, Tate DeCaro, said. "But the thing they couldn't make up for at home was being around different kinds of people."[33]

World of Inquiry students in the mid-1970s were consistently above district, county, and national norms in reading and math; maintained above-average attendance; and "indicated a more positive attitude toward school and learning in general . . . and were more accepting of others with diverse backgrounds." As a result the school had about a thousand children on its annual waiting list, almost half of them from the suburbs. When federal desegregation funding vanished in the 1980s, RCSD took World of Inquiry into its own budget. The district stopped enrolling suburban students, not wanting to eliminate spots for city families in one of its most popular programs. By 1995 there were around 30 suburban students in city schools, down from about 150 at the peak of the magnet school experiment. Beginning in 2008–09, the school was grown out from an elementary school into a K–12 program; the first cohort of twelfth graders, in 2014, had the highest graduation rate in the district. Its waiting list in 2021 was more than twice as long as that of any other school, both for primary and secondary placement. And yet, though World of Inquiry is less racially homogenous than the majority of RCSD schools, it no longer stands apart from the district either in terms of funding or as a magnet to suburban families.[34]

As programs persisting largely on federal funding, World of Inquiry and Urban-Suburban were at perpetual risk of closure throughout the 1970s, when spending on school desegregation was hardly a priority. They both held on long enough, though, to transition over to more stable local funding sources, and both still exist today, though in somewhat different forms. Two other notable interdistrict programs were not as lucky: the Brockport Center for Innovation in Education and the Metropolitan World of Inquiry School. Both grew out of earlier, successful models, showed promising results, and then went under because of the vagaries of state and federal funding streams. Both provide valuable evidence in favor of intentionally integrated, cross-district schools—and a warning that popularity and academic success alone do not guarantee that programs will continue.

The Brockport Campus School opened in 1867 as one of New York's four "demonstration schools," where teachers in training could try out the latest in instructional innovation under the watchful eyes of their professors. The students did not belong to a traditional school district but rather attended by choice, a factor that later would become critical. In the early 1960s, the school, under the leadership of Principal Andrew Virgilio, developed a satellite campus in the city of Rochester, where students lived, student-taught at RCSD schools, and received their own instruction from both SUNY Brockport professors and RCSD educators.[35] That existing relationship became important in 1965, when Herman Goldberg was looking for partners outside the city to help slow galloping racial segregation. At the same time, the Campus School—renamed the Center for Innovation in Education—had just opened a gleaming new facility and SUNY Brockport had a new, forward-looking president in Albert Brown. A trial summer program in 1966 was a success, and the two sides agreed to continue during the 1966–67 school year with about 35 students from Rochester's School 20. City enrollment at the Brockport Center for Innovation in Education rose to about 120, more than half the total student body, by the end of the school's fifteen-year experiment with desegregation.[36]

Gian Carlo and Maria Cervone's father worked at the college, so they both attended the school starting in kindergarten. They recalled classmates from the city bringing in Jackson 5 records to play during lunchtime. "Those were just my classmates and we just grew up together," Gian Carlo Cervone said. "We did not grow up really even knowing there was any kind of racial problem. . . . It wasn't until I left the campus school in sixth grade [that] suddenly all this sort of ugliness came into the picture that really had not been part of our world." There were significant numbers of students whose parents were migrant farmworkers—both African Americans and, increasingly, people from Mexico and Central America—and also refugees from Vietnam and Southeast Asia. "I view it as a beacon in the western part of the county, showing what you can do with integrated education," said Norman Gross, the director of Urban-Suburban.[37]

An important feature of the Center for Innovation in Education was a teaching corps that was dedicated to integrated education and trained to implement it. The school was a site for observation and hands-on training for both student teachers and veterans from the Rochester City School District. "A teacher who would choose to be in this type of school had to be different to begin with," Jeannette Banker, a longtime teacher and administrator at the school, said. "They had to be past the stage where they wanted to stand in front of the class and have the kids say 'yes' and 'no.'"[38]

Terry Carbone graduated from the teaching program at Brockport in 1969 then taught at the Center for Innovation in Education from 1973 to its closure in 1981. She grew up in the rural area between Rochester and Buffalo but drew inspiration from her grandmother—perhaps the only subscriber for miles around to *Ebony* magazine. "I want my grandkids to know there's different people than just white farmers," Carbone recalled her telling incredulous family members. If the predominant mode of teaching diversity in those days was "multicultural education"—lessons focusing on easy-to-grasp aspects of nonwhite cultures without plumbing the harder questions of racism and differing perspectives—the Center for Innovation in Education embraced difference. "That's not to say that things didn't happen," Carbone said. "[But] we were a family that got along; we were a problem-solving classroom. . . . There's a philosophical mindset difference that has to occur, and it's much deeper than, 'Let's just get all the kids together.'"[39]

In 1976 New York state decided to close all eight of its campus schools, seeking to direct higher education funding away from the K–12 programs. The Brockport school escaped closure when Gross succeeded in obtaining federal funding. That lasted until 1981, when Urban-Suburban saw its grant cut by $1 million, leaving it unable to maintain support. The news came in late August, just a week before the 220 students and thirteen teachers were set to return. "It was a death," Carbone said. "I remember literally throwing files from our research into a garbage pail. We had to clear out the building, clear out the kids. It was as if we didn't exist."[40]

On the other side of Monroe County, a similar program met the same fate. The Metropolitan World of Inquiry School, funded through Urban-Suburban's federal grant and operated by the east-side BOCES, opened its doors in September 1973 in rented space in Webster's Schlegel Road School. It had only secured the needed funding and state approval to open in August, less than a month before the first day of school, yet still managed to enroll nearly three hundred students in its first year, mostly from Rochester, Webster, Penfield, and West Irondequoit. The academic program was patterned on the original World of Inquiry school in the city. By the terms of the grant, both the student body and the faculty were 40 percent minority.[41]

"We're demonstrating that a quality educational program in an integrated school is a feasible project coupled with the open classroom concept—and it's a more effective way of educating people," Principal W. McGregor Deller said during the first year. That echoed the experience of people involved in the city World of Inquiry school, as well in as the elementary schools in the 19th Ward during the short-lived implementation of open classrooms there from 1970 to 1972. Parents reported that their children were taking more interest in school than they had before. "The situation is real at this school," a teacher said. "When it's successful we all vibrate and when it goes wrong we all care deeply." Federal policymakers, though, were unmoved. New funding guidelines prohibiting transportation for desegregation threatened the school's federal Urban-Suburban funding stream after its first year, then ended it completely in 1975. "There's so much bull to it," Norman Gross complained. "Proven successful programs are disqualified while questionable ones are funded."[42]

The school lasted for a third year on last-minute, bare-bones funding from the state legislature. It was moved from Webster to the Karlan School in West Irondequoit and its enrollment was cut dramatically, from three hundred students to fifty. Then the state funding dried up as well, and after a failed last-ditch effort to merge the Metropolitan World of Inquiry with the temporarily revived Center for Innovation in Education in Brockport, it closed its doors for good. Gross blamed Congress, the Nixon and Ford administrations, and "opportunists who make political capital of the emotional term 'busing,'" while the *Times-Union* noted the lack of local and state money. "Racial integration is not a popular topic these days," the editorial board wrote. "But bridges must be built. . . . The urban-suburban transfer program and the suburban World of Inquiry are small voluntary efforts which threaten no one. They should be encouraged and expanded, not cut back or eliminated."[43]

World of Inquiry in its original form, the Center for Innovation in Education in Brockport, and the Metropolitan World of Inquiry represent the only three experiments in Rochester with intentionally integrated schools drawing students from across district lines. None of them lasted. World of Inquiry exists today without the metropolitan component; the others thrived briefly before closing. That common fate illustrates the challenge of obtaining reliable annual revenue outside the traditional school district funding mechanisms of local property taxes and regular state aid. But the three programs had much in common from a programmatic and structural viewpoint, as well. Perhaps most significant was the development of innovative pedagogy. In this, they are similar to the 19th Ward elementary schools that were reorganized from 1970 to 1972 according to Goldberg's plan. All the schools used open, ungraded classrooms, where students could advance at their own pace and teachers could focus closely on a certain developmental stage. All of them stressed experiential learning as opposed to traditional recitation of lessons. "It wasn't one-curriculum-fits-all; far from it," Terry Carbone said of the Brockport school. "You started with a topic and kids dove into it with their style of learning and interests."[44]

Although the three programs were noteworthy for their commitment to racial integration, students and educators there did not recall explicit attention in the classroom to race per se. "There wasn't really talk about Black and white," Thomas Warfield said of World of Inquiry. "I don't remember any discussion or anything to do with race. . . . It was sort of like everyone was the same." At Brockport, Carbone said: "We actively downsized the multicultural approach of, 'Let's talk about Hispanic kids; let's talk about Asian kids.' . . . [That] was too shallow. It goes really to your soul, to believe that difference was OK." The cause was aided, of course, by the fact that every student and adult in the buildings had actively signed up for a racially integrated experience. "The ones who were there were the ones whose parents wanted them to have a broader experience," Jeannette Banker said.[45]

Two other projects from the period are worth mentioning, though neither got off the ground. The first grew from one of Herman Goldberg's 1967 desegregation plans—the idea of creating "educational parks" in existing city and county parks. The board never seriously considered the idea because of the tremendous cost involved in building seven brand-new school campuses. The plan did, however, plant the seed for a different cross-district initiative proposed by Greece school board president John Woods. Whereas Goldberg had sought to create seven educational parks within city limits, Woods wanted to build just one, in Genesee Valley Park, that would pull students from not only the city but also the suburbs. It would be run by RCSD with heavy involvement from suburban school districts, the University of Rochester, and local industry, and would serve as a "regional educational research laboratory," with teachers from all over Monroe County rotating through it. "Lest we forget it, Rochester *is* our city," Woods wrote. "This can be accomplished by proving . . . that one large superior educational center is workable and a natural solution to de facto segregation."[46]

Woods embarked on a tour of the suburban school districts seeking their support—as well as a financial ante. Part of his idea for funding the park was for all the districts, including RCSD, to pool their federal Title I money, intended to fight poverty. "I didn't feel Greece deserved to have the Title I money," he said in a 2019 interview. "I didn't feel we had the underprivileged people who deserved it, but it came to us anyway because of the way it went." Other towns felt similar pangs of conscience, including Brighton, which spent its $23,000 allotment in 1966–67 on a remedial reading program. "Actually we have felt guilt spending it on this program," school board member William Dieck said, "because many of the participants are not, strictly speaking, 'underprivileged.'" The following month Greece took the first step, with its school board setting aside $50,000 of its own Title I funds for Woods's plan. Other districts gave bland statements of interest but said their federal funding was already committed elsewhere.[47]

Apart from that tepid buy-in, Woods faced serious obstacles on two fronts. First, Greece in February 1967 had voted against joining Urban-Suburban after 2,500 residents attended a school board meeting to protest the idea. The board repeated its 'no' votes the following two years, each time hearing massive opposition. "[The opponents], by their howling, vulgar cat calls and general offensive behavior, showed the rest of Greece and the world what bigotry and white racism is all about," one aggrieved resident wrote. "You couldn't help but get the uneasy feeling these people would have been more at home in the Roman Colosseum, cheering as the lions chewed up the Christians." Any further hint of busing or cooperation with the city, then, was sure to set off alarm bells, and Woods's proposal did just that. The school board had voted to set aside the $50,000 in Title I money only with the understanding that it could be retrieved later for another use if the park did not come to fruition.[48]

An even greater roadblock was the Rochester school board, which needed not only to set its Title I money aside but also to assume the massive obligation of designing and operating the educational park. Herman Goldberg called Woods's idea "most commendable," but the board's conservative majority did not share his assessment. "Let him propose what he wants to; he's not going to tell us how to solve our problems," Louis Cerulli said. Faust Rossi was the only board member to endorse the plan, but added: "If the federal government were to say that it would build an educational park at no cost to the city, there still would be three members of the board who would not agree to it." Indeed, the proposal languished until April 1968, when Greece redirected its $50,000 to a regional summer school program. RCSD's elected leaders had squandered "an opportunity undoubtedly they will never receive again," Woods said. "All that was asked of them was vision and leadership and cooperation. They could not supply one of these."[49]

The Woods Plan was hotly debated at the time and amply covered in the newspapers. By contrast, another potentially momentous idea was never made public. Evidence of it exists in the papers of state education commissioner Ewald Nyquist in the New York State Archives in Albany. In February 1970, just as the Rochester school board was rejecting Herman Goldberg's most ambitious reorganization plan, the superintendent was having separate discussions with Brighton school superintendent John Bennion, the chairman of the Monroe County Educational Planning Committee Task Force on Reducing Racial Isolation. Goldberg reported on those discussions to Nyquist: "This letter will confirm the discussion which we had several weeks ago . . . concerning the possibilities of building a new school to be operated jointly by the [Rochester and Brighton] school districts." He asked the commissioner's staff to "explore ways in which the legal and financial hurdles to such a joint venture might be eliminated," and to help secure full state funding. Nyquist responded three weeks later, telling Goldberg that his staff had held "a series of meetings to evaluate your proposal" and inviting him and Bennion to Albany for further talks. "While there are many obstacles which would have to be overcome, discussions of the possibilities would certainly be in order," he wrote. "Certainly we will do everything we can to assist you."[50]

There the correspondence ends. No further detail exists as far as the proposed structure or governance of the jointly operated school. Goldberg apparently was counting on significant state funding, which certainly would have been a hurdle in the conservative-leaning legislature. At any rate, the idea never saw the light of day. The only possible hint comes from Bennion, writing a year later in a report on his task force's activities. He described at length a potential "regional demonstration school project" which, he said, "would be a model ethnic mixture of the children of Monroe County and provide a facility where new educational concepts could be refined and demonstrated." It had been developed in 1970 by a committee including Brighton school board president Herbert Elins but had floundered, partly due to "a lack of general interest among the school districts of the county, and partly to the lack of facilities and funding." Brighton High School student Peter Essley may have been referring to the same thing when he wrote in April 1970: "We hope our parents will support steps toward cooperation which may eventually lead to the construction of a joint school somewhere near the city line." In his May 1971 report, Bennion suggested attempting to graft the concept onto the Brockport Center for Innovation in Education. That, perhaps, was a fallback plan after the joint venture with RCSD collapsed.[51]

It is, of course, impossible to assess what the impact of the Brighton-Rochester school might have been. Goldberg asked Nyquist to keep the idea secret because of the "very delicate situation"; had it become public, that delicacy would surely have been on full display. As the Brighton Teachers Association wrote in 1970, though, in a statement of support for integration: "We can think of no community in a better position to exercise leadership in such a situation. We are a residential area dependent on the well-being of the city; we have a liberal community in Brighton of some size; and we have a school board that has in the past been sympathetic and sensitive to the problems of the city and its schools." There would have been daunting political obstacles in Brighton but also in Rochester when the anti-reorganization board took office. More important than the school itself, though, would have been the funding mechanism that the two parties and the state agreed on. That problem has vexed every single interdistrict program contemplated in the Rochester area. Indeed, with the exception of Urban-Suburban, it has never been solved.[52]

Rochester during the 1980s and 1990s flung itself into the burgeoning education reform movement, which will be discussed in detail in chapter 8. Concomitant with this trend was a broad retreat from the concept of integration as a goal and from federal funding to support it. For that reason there was little discussion of interdistrict cooperation in the two decades after the Brockport Center for Innovation in Education closed in 1981. The lessons of the various metropolitan programs had largely been forgotten by 2005, when Tom Frey and Bryan Hetherington paid a visit to Fairport superintendent William Cala.

Frey's belief in the importance of integrated education had not waned since his time on the Rochester school board. Since then, he had been a state assemblyman, the Monroe County executive, and a member of the state Board of Regents. Hetherington, a lawyer with the nonprofit Empire Justice Center, had just finished work on an unsuccessful legal challenge to socioeconomic segregation in Monroe County in the case *Paynter v. New York* (discussed in chapter 8). They wanted to propose a new project with Cala, who in 2003 had made Fairport the first new district to join Urban-Suburban in thirty-five years.

That project came to be known as the Regional Academy. Its design was similar to that of the Metropolitan World of Inquiry, but on a grander scale: a fifty-fifty mix of urban and suburban students in a school that eventually would serve grades PK–12 on two campuses. The elementary school would be in the city, possibly at the Strong Museum of Play, while the secondary school would be on the Nazareth College campus. Students would be chosen through a blind lottery, including students with disabilities and those not speaking English as a first language, and no more than 40 percent would be living in poverty. It would be a nonpublic school, technically speaking, "operated under the direction of Nazareth College," and students would not take Regents exams.[53]

"It was setting up a voluntary program—it's pretty hard to argue against a voluntary program," Cala said. He retired as Fairport superintendent in June 2006, then served a year as the interim superintendent in Rochester after Manuel Rivera departed. Beginning in 2008 Cala took a faculty position at Nazareth and began to spend the majority of his time on the Regional Academy proposal. There were thirteen working groups with more than 150 participants, including several suburban superintendents as well as Rochester superintendent Jean-Claude Brizard.

It was an impressive showing of support. Behind the scenes, though, progress was minimal. "It seemed to make some people in the suburbs upset, because they define themselves on the quality of the schools. That's why you live there and pay taxes there," Hetherington said. "There was some personal buy-in from suburban superintendents, but at the end of the day it was always: 'I don't know how I'm going to get this by my board.'" Cala recalled more overt opposition. After months of attempts, he, Hetherington, and Frey were invited to present the idea at the suburban superintendents' regular business meeting. But several of the school leaders walked out of the room before the presentation began, Cala said, and none were willing to sign a letter in support of the concept.[54]

As always, funding was an issue. Cala held out hope for a separate stream of state money but never made any progress toward achieving it. Draft state legislation for the academy provided for state and federal aid following students from their home districts, as at charter schools. The suburban districts were dubious and unwilling to sacrifice their own budgets. "It wasn't enough that it was just no big drain on their resources; some of the suburban superintendents felt we had to figure out a way for absolute fiscal neutrality," Hetherington said. "From a financing perspective, that became really challenging."[55]

The Regional Academy also required enabling legislation, with Assemblyman Joseph Morelle as the point person in Albany. Morelle's office drafted the bill and had been helpful in building local support, but the legislation never reached the Assembly floor. As Cala tells it, Morelle spiked the plan out of spite in response to implicit criticism in an essay Cala published around the same time. According to Morelle, important legal points about funding and control were never fleshed out fully enough to merit introducing the bill.

He said that Cala was overambitious in insisting that the school would operate outside the traditional state assessment system rather than simply focusing on diversity. "Frankly, I didn't want to take on *everyone* in the world," he said in 2020. "I wasn't interested in being the poster child of making an academy that brings everyone together, and also let's tell the state that all their positions on assessments are wrong." Hetherington also recalled that Cala's firm stance against most forms of standardized testing "ended up alienating some of the people who needed to be involved."[56]

Morelle, who in 2018 was elected to serve the Rochester area in Congress, was correct about remaining fundamental questions, including how an independent school would accept state funding from public school districts, and what governance role Nazareth would play. In any case, by the time Frey died in 2017 the Regional Academy was no closer to accepting students than when they first discussed the idea twelve years earlier. Like many other such concepts, the Regional Academy died quietly. "Poor Cala—he tried everything," said Malik Evans, the Rochester school board president at the time and a supporter of the project. "But if you ask me whatever happened to it—I don't know. It just went away."[57]

In another sense, the Regional Academy idea lived on indirectly. In September 2011, Cala gave a talk at Third Presbyterian Church, a congregation with a history of commitment to social justice in education. At about the same time, the church book club read *Hope and Despair in the American City* by Syracuse University professor Gerald Grant. It compared the public schools in Syracuse, New York, and Raleigh, North Carolina, which has a countywide school district, and concluded that the same solution was needed in northern urban areas. Energized, the church organized a group called Great Schools for All and received grant funding for a three-day, eleven-person visit to Raleigh and Wake County, where Raleigh is located, in 2014. Mark Hare, a former *Democrat and Chronicle* columnist and one of the main Great Schools for All boosters, summarized the group's findings: "Integration has dramatically improved results in Raleigh, and helped build a community consensus that public schools are one of the county's best assets, not its chief liability." Raleigh was not perfect, he conceded; teacher pay was too low and achievement gaps persisted. Still, he concluded: "Wake County is struggling forward, while Rochester is just struggling."[58]

Impressive as it found the metropolitan system in Wake County, Great Schools for All did not advocate for the same thing in Rochester. "I think most of us around the table would jump at the countywide option if we felt there was any opportunity to make that happen," said Don Pryor, one of the group's leaders. "But with the politics, we didn't want to waste time on that. We felt it was just a sinkhole and we didn't want to go down it." Instead, the group pushed for the creation of a network of interdistrict magnet schools, each with a limit of 50 percent of students in poverty. Like the magnet schools in Wake County, each school would have a particular curricular focus, such as the arts, language immersion, or science and technology. Each of them would be jointly administered by two or more school districts and would have diverse faculty and staff.[59]

Like the Regional Academy, the Great Schools for All plan attracted a great deal of interest, at least conceptually. In a May 2016 scientific survey, 81 percent of urban parents and 66 percent of suburban parents said that they would consider sending their children to a socioeconomically diverse magnet school outside their current school district. A majority also said they would consider a school where their children would be in the racial minority. On the other hand, 93 percent of suburban parents said they were satisfied with their child's current school, and about two-thirds thought that their current school was already diverse enough. Several suburban superintendents expressed interest but wanted RCSD to take the lead, Pryor said.[60]

After seven years without tangible progress, the Great Schools for All organizers cast themselves increasingly as "connectors, to bring people together to understand the value of integrated schools," rather than as school architects, as co-convener Lynette Sparks put it. Notably, they did not attempt to draft, or even fully think through, enabling state legislation, including details of governance and funding. "Over time it became clearer and clearer that . . . there would be no impetus on the legislative side to take action until school districts bring a proposal forward," Pryor said.[61]

In other words, the legislature was waiting to hear from school districts—at least several of them, if not all of them—while the suburban districts in turn were waiting for RCSD to lead. And though the Rochester school board did pass a resolution in favor of Great Schools for All in June 2017, its administration and elected leaders have not made the project a priority. That is in part because those leaders keep changing. In 2018, for instance, RCSD superintendent Barbara Deane-Williams floated the idea of a downtown elementary school drawing half of its enrollment from suburban students whose parents were commuting into the city anyway. It was never discussed in public again, and nine months later Deane-Williams resigned. As Cala said about the Regional Academy: "Every time [we] would meet at district office, they'd have a new administrative team. . . . Every time we showed up we had to start from ground zero."[62]

The Great Schools for All leaders never quite gave up. In 2017 they attracted more than six hundred people to a talk by the investigative journalist and desegregation advocate Nikole Hannah-Jones. The organization is part of the umbrella children's advocacy group ROC the Future and attempts to nudge it toward considering racial and economic segregation. But, Sparks said: "They told us in Raleigh, 'You're embarking on a 20-year project,' and they were right. . . . People in Rochester, in my experience, have a hard time even imagining an integrated setting." Indeed, the Regional Academy and Great Schools for All both received significant, favorable media attention and community support, but neither has approached even the short-lived success of the Brockport Center for Innovation in Education or the Metropolitan World of Inquiry.[63]

"You can't even mention the words 'metro' or 'regional' without the hair on the back of the necks of suburban people going berserk," William Cala said. One case above all illustrates his point: the 2003 Monroe County executive race between Bill Johnson and Maggie Brooks.

It was the first election for the office without an incumbent. Either Johnson, the three-term Democratic Rochester mayor, would become the first Black person ever elected as executive, or Brooks, the Republican county clerk and a former television reporter, would be the first woman. Each spent more than $500,000 on advertising, making it the costliest county executive race to date. Johnson campaigned on a promise of fiscal reform and said that it was unrealistic to suggest that the county could continue to balance its budget without increasing tax revenues. Brooks countered with a narrow conservative platform of keeping taxes flat and streamlining government—but also succeeded in refocusing attention on a point Johnson had made the previous year in his 2002 State of the City address.

Pointing to low student achievement in the city schools and fiscal crises at several levels of local government, Johnson in March 2002 elaborated on an idea he often had touted in the past: consolidating levels of government, up to the point of a full metropolitan government. "Can we afford the luxury of maintaining thirty local municipalities and eighteen school districts in a compact, urbanized county?" he asked. "Yes, school and municipal consolidation carries intense—often painful—emotions. But the pain of fact-finding and reasoned discourse is negligible compared to the pain of non-competitiveness and stagnation."[64]

The possibility of a metropolitan school system in particular had been discussed in a series of hearings sponsored by Monroe County legislator Christopher Wilmot in 1996. More generally, metro government was a sore spot between Johnson and county executive Jack Doyle, who opposed it. After Johnson's speech, Doyle convened a series of public hearings on the idea—and advertised them as discussions of a proposal by Johnson for "the elimination of all towns, villages and suburban school districts and their replacement by a single, giant, city government." Johnson had not in fact made any specific proposal or stated that eliminating all lower levels of government would be required. He boycotted the forums, accusing Doyle of seeking political gain from stoking fears and "trying to shut down any open dialogue of what consolidation could bring to this area." Furthermore, as he later said about school districts in particular: "The county executive has no power to bring about consolidation. If I'd been elected, almost invariably we would have had a Republican-controlled Legislature. And even if somehow I'd gotten around that and got a bill to Albany, there was a Republican-controlled Senate and a Republican governor. And even if I had some magical powers and I could overwhelm all the Republicans, it was a permissive referendum that had to come back, and any one of the 18 towns could have killed it."[65]

No matter how hard Johnson tried to center his county executive campaign on fiscal reform, he could not escape questions about his metropolitan designs. "I said: 'Look, it's never going to happen,'" he said. "Then [people] would say: 'I hear what you're saying—but if you could, would you?'" After he released a television ad stating that he was "not talking about consolidating schools or eliminating towns and villages," local Republican leaders held a press conference to say he was being disingenuous. Two weeks before the election, the Republican party released a television ad that caused a sensation and would later serve to define the campaign. It showed a Pac-man character roaming through Monroe County, gobbling up towns, villages, and school districts and stating that Johnson would seek to create a single school district and municipality.[66]

For observers in the city, the fixation on possible political "amalgamation" had an unmistakable racial underpinning. They pointed as well to Doyle's comment that the city would be in much better condition if it had "a mayor that looked like me." Their conviction was only sharpened in September 2003, two months before the election, when right-wing radio host Bob Lonsberry was fired after referring to Johnson as a "monkey" and an "orangutan" on the air. "He would have never said that kind of stuff if he didn't think there was an audience for it," Johnson said at the time. He also recounted party leaders urging him to drop out of the race, saying that a Black man could never win a countywide election.[67]

Whatever role race and metro government–related fears played in the election, the final result was a blowout. Brooks beat Johnson by thirty points, including winning in every suburb except Brighton. "I guess tonight says it clearly," county Republican chairman Stephen Minarik said on election night. "Bye-bye metro government; bye-bye one school district; bye-bye Bill Johnson." It was Minarik who thought up the Pac-man ad, which won him a national award from the American Association of Political Consultants. *Rochester City* newspaper editor Mary Anna Towler—a veteran of the desegregation campaign of the late 1960s—called it an "anti-city vote based not only on Johnson's skin color but the fear of hordes of black and brown school children and welfare recipients crossing into the towns."

"That sentiment will be hard to overcome," Towler wrote. "It's emotional and it isn't easily influenced by facts. And in the time it takes to overcome it, the community will become more polarized and more segregated, and the city will become poorer." A generation later, it is still common in Rochester to hear mention of Bill Johnson's plan for a countywide school district—the desegregation plan that never was.[68]

In reviewing the various cross-district schools and programs over the last fifty years, one thing is clear; students, parents, and educators loved them. The Brockport Center for Innovation in Education and the two World of Inquiry schools were consistently oversubscribed and energized the teachers who led them. Indeed, even projects that failed to launch, like the Regional Academy and Great Schools for All, nonetheless generated a great deal of preliminary interest before petering out. Their failure, then, had nothing to do with their appeal to parents or their likelihood of academic and social success, but rather stemmed from the hostility of the state education law to any model outside the established funding paradigm. Who will run it, and who will pay for it? In the absence of generous federal funding, the questions have proven insuperable—except for one instance. That is Urban-Suburban, whose greatest achievement over more than fifty years may be its very survival.

## CHAPTER 7

# The Urban-Suburban Program

In the Black Third Ward of 1965, six-year-old Kirk Holmes was part of Rochester royalty.

His maternal grandparents, Stanley and Dolores Thomas, were co-owners of the Pythodd Club, a legendary jazz venue that hosted musicians like Miles Davis, George Benson, and Wes Montgomery. Stanley was a leader of the local Elks and Masons and had been the first Black person to work as a department manager in city government. Kirk's great-grandfather was one of the first Black students at Cornell University. A child could hardly have been better suited to succeed in the neighborhood school, School 19, just a few blocks from the Holmes house. Kirk's mother, though, had other ideas. "I think she'd already seen there was a decline in the school system from when she was a child," he said. "She was very interested in us having a better experience." That is how Holmes, on the first day of first grade in 1965, found himself on an unfamiliar bus ride to Briarwood School in West Irondequoit, one of twenty-five pioneers in a momentous experiment in education called the Urban-Suburban Interdistrict Transfer Program.[1]

State education commissioner James Allen's 1963 letter asking about desegregation efforts had created a stir in the Rochester City School District. By contrast, suburban Monroe County school districts, including West Irondequoit, mostly ignored it. Race relations were fine, they responded, because there were hardly any minority students with whom their white students might quarrel. But "on more careful consideration, it became apparent to several sensitive [West Irondequoit] board members that there was indeed a problem of racial isolation in reverse in Irondequoit." At the time there were 2 Black students out of 5,800 in the district.[2]

A series of community conversations and closed-door school board meetings culminated in March 1965 with a unanimous board resolution recognizing that the racial makeup of the town "[did] not provide the environment in which . . . intercultural experience can take place" and accepting the school district's obligation to solve that problem. A much-publicized set of cross-district conferences the previous year and RCSD's ongoing experiment with open enrollment pointed the way toward the solution, which was announced the following month. The district said that it would accept eighty Rochester first-graders as part of the open enrollment process, a figure that was later revised downward to twenty-five. It also pledged to develop "curriculum materials dealing with minority group problems." Walter Crewson, the associate state education commissioner, called the plan a "major breakthrough," unprecedented in the nation.[3]

This was the beginning of Urban-Suburban, then and now the most prominent plank in Monroe County's meager desegregation platform. Its legacy is decidedly mixed. Through it, generations of minority children have found an alternative to RCSD, even as the vast majority of applicants have been turned away. The program earned high praise as a national innovation in the late 1960s but has since been bypassed by more comprehensive efforts, voluntary or otherwise, in cities in every region of the country. An evolving state funding mechanism has turned it into a budget hustle for suburban districts with declining enrollment. Standing in the way of change or expansion is the same prejudice it was intended to address more than half a century ago when Holmes, age six, first stepped off the bus in Irondequoit. "I remember being kind of nervous and scared of walking into a strange environment. It was fairly intimidating," he said. "I don't think I had a real understanding of why, but I knew I stood out and I felt very self-conscious and nervous about being the oddball."[4]

The program grew out of a number of fledgling voluntary desegregation efforts in both the city and the suburbs. Among the first was a series of cross-town field trips within the city school district, bringing together students from majority-Black Madison High School with those from schools that were exclusively white or nearly so. The first such conference took place in November 1963 at Madison, with twelfth graders visiting from John Marshall High School, which had 1 Black student in a student body of more than 1,500;

another followed several months later with students from Charlotte High School. The idea then crossed into the suburbs, with Madison students joining peers from Brighton and East Irondequoit to talk in general terms about racism. One Madison student felt obliged to declare that intermarriage was not his aim.[5]

The common denominator was Norman Gross, the strong-minded, sharp-tongued head of the social studies department at Madison. Born in Rochester in 1923, Gross received his PhD from the University of Rochester and took a teaching job in the city, quickly rising through the ranks to become president of the Rochester Teachers Union in 1956 at age thirty-three. He was also active in the NAACP and, along with a Black science teacher named Regina Brown, started the first Black history course in the district.[6] His daughter, Deborah Gitomer, said that growing up Jewish during World War II, as well as seeing his parents divorce at a time when that was uncommon, gave Gross empathy with marginalized groups and a penchant for combat. "He was just one to fight back—physically at first, but then he got into these causes," she said. "He was always a champion of the underdog. . . . He was more accepting of people with different ideas and was willing to defend that."[7]

Gross believed strongly that Black students' isolation would create an even greater social chasm in future generations. "The next generation of adult Blacks are becoming very embittered toward white society," he warned a suburban audience in 1968. "This problem is not just the city's; it's the county's, too. We are all in this together whether we like it or not."[8] His outlook, experience, and willingness to scrap made him an ideal partner for West Irondequoit, where Superintendent Earle Helmer and the school board were committed to a change themselves. "We had sort of a segregated society, and we thought it would be good for our kids to mix with other kids," one board member, James Littwitz, said forty-nine years after Urban-Suburban began. "It turns out they get along fine if you leave them alone."[9]

They were not, in fact, left alone—at least not at first. Before Rochester children even arrived in Irondequoit three town residents sued to stop the program, arguing that the district had pushed it through without public involvement and that it was racially discriminatory against white Irondequoit children. The main plaintiff, Doyle O. Etter, said that the district should not be occupying itself with a "purely social matter" like racial segregation. The plaintiffs' request for an injunction was rejected the day before school began and the case was eventually dismissed after a series of unsuccessful appeals. James Allen also rejected an administrative objection, writing that it was "too late in the day to maintain any such position." Inside the schools,

**FIGURE 7.1.** Norman Gross, founding director of the Urban-Suburban Interdistrict Transfer Program, seen in 1982. Photo by David Cook, courtesy of the *Democrat and Chronicle*.

meanwhile, some teachers harbored biases of their own. In a survey distributed before the program began, the eight participating first-grade teachers in West Irondequoit unanimously said that they "would not be willing to admit Negroes to close kinship by marriage."[10]

Critics of the program in Irondequoit eventually shifted their activity to school board campaigns. An antibusing candidate named Stephen Rounds overwhelmingly won a seat in the summer of 1965, just two months after the program was announced, trouncing his more moderate opponent by twenty points in an election featuring the highest voter turnout in years. He was joined on the board by fellow program critics Rebecca Herdle (in 1966) and Marilynne Anderson (in 1967). District residents also turned down a bond proposition and the 1967 district budget. Gross dismissed these opponents as the town's "resident bigots."[11]

Early participants in Urban-Suburban reported a mostly positive experience, at least during their elementary school years. Some racial incidents were born of curiosity; one researcher noticed many instances of children questioningly touching the skin or hair of a child of the other race. Mary Halpin, one of Kirk Holmes's teachers at Briarwood, recalled a white girl asking a Black boy who was sucking his thumb whether it was chocolate or vanilla. "I think they were a little unsure, but on the other hand, I wonder if they really saw color," she said. "They must have . . . but I didn't sense any unfriendliness. They played with each other."[12]

Middle school and high school were where many Urban-Suburban students first ran up against explicit racism in their suburban settings. Holmes recalled a middle school teacher who wouldn't recommend him for advanced mathematics despite his high grades in her class, informing him that Black people lacked the "intellectual capacity" for math. He got his hands on the advanced textbook and tested into the class the following year. He later achieved a nearly perfect score on the math portion of the SATs and eventually got engineering and business degrees from Massachusetts Institute of Technology and Stanford University. "Some teachers I'll be indebted to forever and think fondly of," he said. "I had others who did everything they could to hold me down and put me down." The logistics of the program grew trickier (and still do) in high school, when sports practice and other after-school events ran late into the evening. Some suburban parents assumed the role of proxy parents, driving Urban-Suburban students back to the city in the evening or letting them sleep over. "We never, ever missed out on anything," one early Brighton enrollee, Yvette Singletary, said.[13]

In 1967 West Irondequoit commissioned a review of the program, interviewing teachers, administrators, and other school staff about their experiences. Their responses revealed both implicit and blatant racism that the Black children may have overlooked or chosen to ignore. "At the beginning, 'you dirty n——' was a recurrent comment by the Irondequoit children," one teacher wrote. Another reported: "When we found the word 'Black' standing for 'bad' in the literature, one child said [to a Black girl], in a derogatory tone, 'Just like you.' The child's parent is actively opposed to the program."

Indeed, the teachers' overall conclusion had more to do with the paucity of the Irondequoit students' cultural understanding than with the progress of the Black children. "The students here are so much alike in their thinking. So many of them are from Kodak families," one wrote. "[They] don't have any interest in anything but themselves and their neighborhood. . . . They know plenty of bigoted comments, however, that they use whenever we discuss current events dealing with race." Another said: "I have a sophomore who hasn't been downtown in four years. Most are so sheltered that the existence of different cultural viewpoints is meaningless."

Many teachers complained about the lack of curricular materials that represented Black people fairly, or at all. One teacher said that during a geography lesson she decided to skip the section on city living because it contained only pictures of slums. The mere fact of a diverse classroom, though, was a powerful teaching tool, for Black children but especially for white children: "The Negro [in the classroom] was clearly the prime stimulant of serious thinking. In that class the students brought in and knowledgeably discussed a greater diversity of ideas than appeared to have been absorbed from the readings, which had been selected for diversity. . . . Students also observed the decrease in their own use of stereotypes about Negroes, other societies and in their own society as they found that they simply didn't fit their observations."[14]

Other suburban districts were watching the West Irondequoit experiment closely and taking tentative steps of their own. In the summer of 1964, Brighton had accepted twenty-five children from School 19 into its summer school program. The experiment was organized and largely funded by the parent-teacher organizations at both schools and, it was concluded, allowed the children to "experience a break in their usual patterns of separateness." It continued for two more years before Brighton decided to take Rochester children during the school year as well. Brighton was joined in 1966 by the Harley School, a private school, as well as by Brockport, where another desegregated summer school program had been running on the SUNY Brockport campus. Two years later Penfield, Pittsford, and Wheatland-Chili joined, along with several other private and parochial schools; by 1969, more than three thousand city students were participating. As Project UNIQUE noted hopefully a few years into the program: "References to 'your children' and 'our children' are diminishing and comments about 'children' are becoming increasingly common."[15]

The decision to take part in the program drew opposition in other districts just as it had in West Irondequoit. The leading antibusing advocate in Brighton, real estate agent David Cromwell, said: "We do not object to Negroes living in Brighton, but we pay a premium to live here and associate with certain kinds of people. I don't want to sound snobbish, but this is a fact." A newspaper survey in Brighton and Pittsford showed stark differences in opinion. Some parents were in favor; others agreed with one mother who said: "It would be very cruel to inner-city children to expect them to compete socially with Pittsford children. I feel sure they wouldn't be able to make real friends."[16] Nor did this opposition end once the program had been adopted. As late as 1972, a poll showed that 60 percent of suburban parents wished that their districts would stop accepting Black students through Urban-Suburban.[17]

Other districts avoided the controversy altogether by opting against participation. The Hilton superintendent polled administrators and teachers in 1967 and found that though the majority believed that the district bore some responsibility in "equalizing educational opportunity" with the city, only three of thirty-two were in favor of joining Urban-Suburban.[18] The topic brought opposing residents to school board meetings in huge numbers. An East Rochester crowd told Norman Gross that they opposed the program because of fears of violence and interracial marriage. In some cases, opposition organizations formed. "The Black community is sick of the 'general assembly' suburban school board meetings where 600 white people turn up to decide if twenty-five little Black children can go to school in their district," Gross complained. Nonetheless, he was traveling through the county well into the 1970s haranguing suburban districts to join the program, to no avail. Webster studied the question on and off for ten years before ultimately voting against participation in March 1978. Board members said that they were interested in pursuing other avenues toward integration. Gross didn't buy it. "The people in Webster just seem not to want minority kids out there, unless they just happen to move out there and they [the residents] can't help it," he said. A poll of residents released by the district the previous month showed 75 percent opposition.[19]

In an essay submitted to the Black magazine *about . . . time*, Gross chided suburban residents for shedding "crocodile tears" over the fate of Black city residents and dispensed with their purported reasons not to participate in

Urban-Suburban. "Unfortunately, even if we distill all the arguments and rationalizations opposing the program, we are left with one impurity—*a racist attitude*," he wrote. "If only people would come to grips with the sad reality of their attitudes, perhaps, they would try to make some accommodations for it."[20]

At the same time, the program was struggling to stay afloat financially. It received most of its initial funding from the US Department of Education, in particular the Title I program for educating children in poverty. In 1974 a law was passed prohibiting the use of Title I or other federal funds to bus children for the purpose of racial desegregation. The state then took over most of the transportation costs and the program became dependent on irregular grant funding from public and private sources. Gross waged annual battles with state and federal officials, begging for additional funding and shrinking the program when he didn't receive it; Rochester parents filed a federal lawsuit in 1974 to keep it operational. Because the state busing funding did not cover all costs, the city and suburban districts swapped students like hostage negotiators in an attempt to even out their costs. "It's become a nightmare of red tape and contradiction," Gross said in 1975. "Their [federal officials'] positions are so idiotic, it's unbelievable." The program's enrollment dipped by several hundred students until 1982, when the east-side BOCES assumed the role of fiscal sponsor and the districts agreed to pay for it out of their own per-pupil funding.[21]

The program found its financial footing just as two important changes were happening; both had the effect of greatly reducing the program's public profile for several decades to come. First Gross, its founding director and most public advocate, retired in 1982.With him went much of the energy and most of the institutional knowledge behind the push for expansion. More important was a noticeable shift in the national discussion about racial equity in education. By the mid-1980s most communities had either gone through their reckoning with court-ordered segregation or, like Rochester, managed to escape it. The integrationist fervor of the Civil Rights era was replaced by a trust in technical rather than social fixes. The age of accountability was beginning, and Urban-Suburban found itself on an island. Enrollment fell from 1,100 in 1980 to fewer than 400 in 2003. The program administrators turned their priority from recruitment of new suburban districts to the support of the students already participating.[22]

"It was like this secretive thing," former Fairport superintendent William Cala said. "[All the county superintendents] would meet monthly and there would be an Urban-Suburban report and I didn't even know what it was. . . . Absolutely fear is what drove the whole thing underground, and it drove the spirit of not talking about it."[23]

Under Cala's direction, Fairport in 2003 became the seventh participating suburban district. The motivation to join came after a series of "mini racial conflicts" in the middle school and high school. To address the problem, Cala invited a local speaker on diversity to present at the high school. Afterward the speaker, a Black man, told Cala that a student had yelled a racial epithet at him as he walked into the building. "That was it for me," he said. "It fortified my thought I had to do something. . . . I told the board: 'I believe the only thing that will change the attitude is to have more kids of color in the school, period.'" The board was supportive of the idea of joining Urban-Suburban and a series of public hearings and information sessions did not bring about the level of vitriol Cala had been expecting. The resolution to join passed unanimously and Fairport quickly became one of the program's most active participants.[24]

In 1965 West Irondequoit's action prompted several other schools and school districts to join as well. Fairport's decision, on the other hand, did not prove catalytic. The Honeoye Falls-Lima, Hilton, and Churchville-Chili school districts all considered the program from 2006 to 2011 and ultimately decided against participating. Churchville-Chili's school board determined that the program "did not match the district's core beliefs" and instead announced that it would "increase dialogue on the topic."[25]

"I thought it would be a baptism of fire getting the program into another district after 38 years, and then the rest of them would just fall into place because they'd see it wasn't so difficult," Cala said. "That movement didn't come until later. . . . The kind of response you got from other boards and superintendents was frightening, and if they don't want to hear it, you're not going to get very far."[26] The opposition that Cala described was, for the moment, limited to private conversations among district leaders. That remained the case until 2014, when the outcry that program administrators had long feared came boiling to the surface in the west-side district of Spencerport.

The Urban-Suburban debate in Spencerport began innocuously enough in October 2014 with a presentation from Superintendent Michael Crumb to the school board. He repeated the talking points provided by the program. Principals are allowed to choose the students they take in, with parental involvement a key consideration. Transportation and all other costs are covered. Nearly all students persist and graduate from the district they're placed in. A community forum was scheduled for early December in advance of a vote on joining for the 2015–16 school year.[27]

The district had prepared responses to the questions it thought residents might have. Instead they heard racist arguments of the kind honed during the fights over busing in Rochester in the late 1960s. What if, some asked, the city children took all the spots on the basketball team? What if their properties values went down? Why didn't the families who wanted to attend Spencerport schools just buy houses in town? One man insisted that he'd stop paying property taxes if the vote went through; a recent alumna said she'd never send her children to Spencerport schools if the city children were there as well. "Personally I feel we're sending the wrong message in this program," one resident said. "We're saying that working hard and doing what's necessary for your family is not necessary because someone else will pick up the tab. . . . People should learn a work ethic to get something they want in this world." The crowd of hundreds, a clear majority, shouted its approval.[28]

Sitting near the front of the auditorium were Jeremy and Rachel Ouimet. He is white and she is Black; some of their six children, three from previous marriages and three they'd had together, were part of the district's 13 percent nonwhite enrollment. As neighbor after neighbor took the podium to warn about "those kids," they heard very clearly a reference to their own family. "When we found out Spencerport was considering this, we were excited," Rachel Ouimet said. "We didn't think there'd be any pushback whatsoever. . . . This may be ignorant, but I thought the community had gotten past that. But when you hear the racism, you realize how segregated our schools really are."[29]

Supporters of the program, including the teachers association and several Spencerport residents who taught in participating districts, came out in greater numbers at a second public forum to voice their opinions. The district cut the number of Rochester students it intended to take by half in an effort to appease the detractors, and the board ultimately approved the measure by a unanimous vote at the end of February. "We're not talking about social engineering or any other nonsense that's come out of this discourse," board member Gary Bracken said. "We're talking about a small group of kids that wants a chance for a better education."[30]

Spencerport was the first site of Urban-Suburban's second great burst of energy, from 2014 to 2017, coinciding with its fiftieth anniversary. In the fall of 2014 the director, Theresa Woodson, and West Irondequoit superintendent Jeff Crane, the chairman of the program's board of directors, undertook a tour of the outstanding districts to ask what was keeping them from joining. They proved more persuasive than Gross ever had, cajoling another seven districts to participate. They were helped along the way by a wrinkle in the state's school finance formula, a tweak in the eligibility rules and, perhaps, the heat emanating from the conflagration in Spencerport, where the two forums became touchstone moments in an otherwise languid countywide investigation into racism and privilege.

Even in defeat, the Spencerport opposition ultimately succeeded in reintroducing an issue that most thought had already been settled. It is the definition of racism, opponents said, for the program to disallow Rochester's white students based solely on the color of their skin. That is the same point that the parents of a nine-year-old girl in Irondequoit had raised sixteen years earlier.

According to the original Urban-Suburban charter, the purpose was "the reduction of minority group isolation." Nevertheless, a few white Rochester students gained admission to suburban schools, including at least one in the inaugural 1965 class, which an RCSD official said had been "chosen without regard for race." Norman Gross dismissed these as aberrations and called them instances of parental "subterfuge" rather than policy. "It was well understood [at the beginning] that white children were not eligible for transfer from Rochester to suburban schools," he wrote in 1998. "Obviously, the transfer of white students to suburban schools would not reduce minority group isolation."[31]

His comments came in response to the most significant challenge to Urban-Suburban since its funding crisis was resolved. That challenge came in the person of Jessica Haak, a white city resident whose parents had managed to enroll her in West Irondequoit's Iroquois Middle School. Haak's mother, Laurie Brewer, said no one ever told her about the minority-only rule, even when the family had a face-to-face meeting with an assistant principal before the school year began. Nonetheless, program administrators realized that Haak was white the first week of the 1998 school year and ejected her from the program. Her enrollment, they said, would "breach the integrity" of the program and could jeopardize its funding, which required faithful adherence to its charter mission. Instead Haak returned to School 39 in RCSD while her parents retained an attorney.[32] They filed suit and, in January 1999, obtained an injunction from US District Court Judge David Larimer holding that the use of racial admissions criteria was unconstitutional. Haak packed her backpack up again and returned to Iroquois while BOCES put new admissions to Urban-Suburban on hold.[33]

For eighteen months the future of the program and its six hundred students was very much in doubt. As program advocates pointed out, the entire premise of Urban-Suburban was the shuffling of students to equalize the racial balance, at least in suburban schools. A prohibition on racial selection criteria would not only frustrate that effort but also run afoul of the program's enabling legislation. The case was sent on to the US Second Circuit Court of Appeals, which in May 2000 reversed Larimer's ruling—in particular, his decision to grant an injunction allowing Haak to attend Iroquois Elementary School immediately rather than allowing the case to proceed through the courts. In his majority opinion, Judge Chester Straub ruled that the injunction was premature. He then proceeded to the meatier question of whether reducing racial isolation could be considered a "compelling governmental interest." The law on that point was far from settled. Haak's attorneys and Larimer relied on the recently set precedent of *Hopwood v. Texas*. There, four white applicants to the University of Texas at Austin's School of Law sued over their rejection, saying that it occurred because of the university's affirmative action plan. The US Fifth Circuit Court of Appeals in 1996 upheld their case, ruling that the consideration of students' race in admissions was unconstitutional.[34]

*Hopwood* became binding precedent in the Fifth Circuit after the US Supreme Court declined to hear an appeal. That did not, however, make it the law elsewhere in the country. As Straub wrote, "This Circuit has not previously taken the position that diversity, or other non-remedial state interests, can never be compelling in the educational setting." He instead based his decision largely on an earlier precedent from the Second Circuit having to do with a voluntary desegregation plan in Queens's Andrew Jackson High School. That plan from the 1970s allowed both white and minority students to transfer within the district, but only to schools where they would join a demographic minority—white students to mostly Black schools or vice versa. The plan was struck down as a court-ordered desegregation plan, but the underlying logic was affirmed: "The state has a compelling interest in ensuring . . . the continuation of relatively integrated schools for the maximum number of students." Based on the precedent of *Parent Ass'n of Andrew Jackson High Sch. v. Ambach*, Straub wrote: "We conclude that we are bound [to rule] that a compelling interest can be found in a program that has as its object the reduction of racial isolation and what appears to be de facto segregation."[35]

Coming on the heels of *Hopwood*, the court's 2–1 ruling raised eyebrows. "I would be very surprised if this is going to hold up," one expert said. Yet hold up it did. Rather than appealing the ruling, Haak's family came to a settlement with the program. She was allowed to stay in West Irondequoit with the understanding that it did not create a precedent for the program. In June 2000 Urban-Suburban reopened its application process.[36]

The immediate crisis had passed but the feeling of uncertainty lingered. Program leaders knew that their standing remained susceptible to a more finely honed challenge in front of a different bench of judges. This instability only increased in 2007 when the US Supreme Court issued perhaps its most significant ruling on the question of school segregation since *Milliken v. Bradley*. The ruling addressed student placement plans in place in Seattle and Louisville, Kentucky, that used students' race as a criterion in assigning them to schools. In a 5–4 ruling, Chief Justice John Roberts declared such an assignment protocol inadmissible under the logic of *Brown v. Board of Education:* "The way to stop discrimination on the basis of race is to stop discriminating on the basis of race." The only saving grace from the districts' perspective was a tempering concurrence by Justice Anthony Kennedy, the swing vote: "A district may consider it a compelling interest to achieve a diverse student population," he wrote. "Race may be one component of that diversity, but other demographic factors, plus special talents and needs, should also be considered." The case opened Urban-Suburban and similar plans across the country to broad challenge in the courts. In Rochester, however, the ruling had no effect. Cala, by then the RCSD interim superintendent, met with the six other participating suburban superintendents to discuss the development. "I said, 'Here's the deal, guys: You can't go on selecting kids the way you're selecting kids,'" Cala said. "And they didn't do anything. They just kept on doing it the way they were doing it."[37]

Roberts's admonition may not have led to changes in the program in 2007, but it was very much in the minds of Urban-Suburban leaders in the winter of 2014–15 as Spencerport boiled over. Other districts joined the program with less public outcry—East Irondequoit, East Rochester, and Hilton in March, Kendall in April—but there, too, school board members and residents said that they'd prefer to see white students in Rochester included. Rush-Henrietta went further, saying that it would not participate unless the program governance board changed the fifty-year-old mission statement to put an "emphasis on increasing opportunities for economically disadvantaged city students rather than emphasizing race or ethnicity."[38]

In June the board did just that. To the program's original purpose of "voluntarily decreas[ing] racial isolation" the board added that it should "deconcentrate poverty and enhance opportunities for students in the Rochester City School District and in the suburban districts of the Greater Rochester Area." That change in emphasis opened the way for poor white students from Rochester to apply to suburban schools. The following year three white children were chosen to attend such schools. "Hopefully, at least around the [governance board] table, we felt we were becoming even more inclusive and creating more opportunities for kids," Crane said. "We'd been talking about the kids in the city who were not of color being part of the process and the Spencerport experience actually helped our decision-making by making it more urgent."[39]

The following three years saw Honeoye Falls-Lima, Rush-Henrietta, and Webster join the program as well.[40] All eight joining districts professed a strong interest in providing an option for Rochester students as well as exposing their own students to greater diversity. When explaining the program to their own board members and residents, though, they all added another important consideration: the opportunity to prop up sagging enrollment and make money in the process.

When students leave RCSD for another public option, including a suburban district or a charter school, they bring along their allotment of state education dollars, known as per-pupil funding. The New York State Education Department uses a variety of factors to determine the per-pupil figure for each district, and that figure can vary widely from one district to another. Rochester's per-pupil figure is by far the highest in Monroe County, in recognition of the increased challenges many of its students face. When its students go to suburban schools with significantly lower per-pupil figures, those receiving districts pocket the difference in state funding. Multiplied by dozens or scores of students, the net impact for a suburban district can be substantial. The three districts with the highest Urban-Suburban enrollment in 2017–18—West Irondequoit, Pittsford, and Brighton—all took in more than $1 million in incremental state funding, an average of more than $9,000 per student. Overall, suburban districts generated a net revenue of $7.1 million from 807 Urban-Suburban students, or 0.8 percent of their total operating budgets that year.[41]

At the same time, nearly every Monroe County school district faced declining enrollment, jeopardizing their ability to offer some specialized classes or fill regular classes to capacity. In the wave of Urban-Suburban entrances from 2014 to 2017, every suburban district to join noted the benefit in terms of maintaining programs for its own students. "If you look at it from a sustainability standpoint, it starts to make sense for some districts," East Rochester interim superintendent Richard Stutzman said in January 2015, a month before that district joined the program. "If people really took a hard look at our numbers and what we stand to gain out of this, most rational people would say it's worth a shot."[42] A task force in Honeoye Falls-Lima (HFL) noted it had lost an average of forty-four students per year over the preceding five years. "The Urban-Suburban Program provides a mechanism for selectively increasing enrollment to maintain HFL's current program offerings," it wrote. "In addition, boosting enrollment through this program provides more incremental revenue to the district than if the increased enrollment occurred through families moving into the school district."[43]

School officials in Rochester observed the same trend with less enthusiasm. After all, the reason the city has a higher per-pupil rate is its substantially higher proportion of students with disabilities or other special needs, none of whom were being selected to attend school in the suburbs. It is also responsible for busing the students to and from their suburban schools every day, an expense that totaled $1.8 million in 2014–15. "Suburban districts have asserted that the incoming state aid has proven to be a consistent revenue stream, which significantly more than offsets the expense," the RCSD budget office observed in an internal memo. As one mother put it, shortly after pulling her son from Spencerport over what she believed was a racist incident: "It's just like with the jail and prison system. Every person is a dollar amount." Crane, Urban-Suburban's most prominent backer until his retirement in 2018, acknowledged the issue but said that he considered the funding differential an admittedly unsavory means to a greater end. "I think most of the school districts are in there for the right reasons," he said. "I think maybe there's a couple that joined for the wrong reasons, but I'm hoping that once they see the good it does for all kids, their priorities will change."[44]

The Jessica Haak case was decided by a narrow 2–1 opinion in the US Court of Appeals, with the second vote coming from Judge Fred I. Parker. In his brief concurring opinion, Parker pointed out that racial isolation—the social ill that Urban-Suburban purportedly addresses—had worsened markedly since 1965, with the proportion of minority students in RCSD more than tripling to 80 percent:

> It is important to note that this program has been in existence for 35 years. The program's goal, as acknowledged in the majority opinion, is reduction of racial isolation. . . . It is extremely difficult to see how this program has had any meaningful impact upon the existence of schools or school districts with "a predominant number or percentage of students of a particular racial/ethnic group."
>
> Therefore, even though the defendants may have had a sufficiently compelling interest to justify the program at its inception, it is difficult to see how the interest continues, given the program's limited impact. If a compelling interest no longer exists, it seems to me that the entire program may fail as being unconstitutional, and the plaintiffs would have no remedy.[45]

The question, in other words, was not just whether the program was appropriately tailored to the governmental interest in question but also whether, after several generations, Urban-Suburban could still claim to be serving any relevant purpose.

Parker's criticism touched a point that has been controversial since the first cohort of second graders from School 19 boarded an Irondequoit-bound bus in September 1965. The program's advocates point to the academic opportunities that Rochester children have gained from participation, and the greater, if anecdotal, benefits to all children from racial integration. The initial mission statement, though, does not concern itself with providing benefits to the specific, fortunate children chosen to participate; it promises a community-wide reduction of racial isolation. As Norman Gross wrote: "The Urban-Suburban Transfer program is not a statistical exercise in which students become numbers and groups become totals. Our hope is to alter the current trend toward racial polarization by reducing racial imbalance in the schools."[46]

Has such a reduction taken place? The answer, of course, is no. As early as 1967, a West Irondequoit teacher conceded: "What we have is two hand-picked Negroes in the class."[47] Greater Rochester, like many similar metro areas, is more segregated by race today than it ever has been. Was Parker right, then, to observe that the program "has [not] had any meaningful impact" on the relationship of minority and white students in Monroe County? Does Urban-Suburban do any good?

After some early, mostly qualitative indications of success in the late 1960s, Urban-Suburban has received relatively little scrutiny from either researchers or participating school districts. Then and now, media accounts of the program have focused on anecdotes of satisfied minority students and, ideally, their white suburban friends. Suburban districts have either committed to it or not; no one found an examination of its greater purpose and efficacy particularly convenient. One exception came in 1979, when researchers noted that high-achieving students were much more likely than others to leave city schools via Urban-Suburban. "One is to seriously question what impact the Urban-Suburban program is having on the district and those Black and Hispanic students left behind and not in the program," they concluded.[48] As the city school district slid, though, both in fact and reputation, its leverage in advocating for outside change declined. The scope and urgency with which Urban-Suburban was hatched came to be ignored.

The most comprehensive research into the program was conducted by Kara Finnigan, a professor at the University of Rochester's Warner School of Education. She and her students obtained and meticulously compiled enrollment records from 1965 through the 1990s and conducted two dozen interviews with past and present program administrators, including suburban principals responsible for selecting students for their schools. Finnigan and fellow researchers have also placed Urban-Suburban into the larger national context of interdistrict exchange programs. Their conclusions—at least for those who defend the program as a meaningful countervailing force against school segregation—are discouraging.[49]

The selective enrollment standard for Urban-Suburban was established at the beginning, when West Irondequoit residents were assured that Rochester students in the inaugural class "would be chosen carefully for the ability and achievement qualifications which would enable [them] to fit easily into our class situations."[50] This care in selection was enforced in the administration of the program through a feedback loop from students and teachers. One early researcher in West Irondequoit noted:

> As long as the city sent pupils to West Irondequoit who were average or better in ability and social adjustment, restraints seemed to be minimal. Those pupils who fell below these standards, however, seemed to create more problems for teachers than did similar white pupils. While no cause and effect relationship was identified, white pupils appeared to more readily reject Negro pupils who were unable to keep up or who became behavior problems. City and suburban administrators, through orientation activities and other information, encouraged the average ability, well-adjusted expectations of teachers.[51]

If anything, the choosing has become even more careful after fifty years. Like National Football League general managers scouting quarterback prospects, suburban administrators have full access to applicants' academic records and conduct careful interviews with prospective students and their families. Enrollment at each school is capped to ensure that city students are only taking vacant seats in classrooms and not leading to additional costs. This aspect of Urban-Suburban—having a draft rather than a lottery—is unique among the handful of similar programs nationwide. Interdistrict choice programs in St. Louis, Hartford, Minneapolis, East Palo Alto, Boston, Omaha, and Milwaukee all use some sort of random lottery to place students in suburban districts.[52]

Through her database of enrollment and transportation records, Finnigan was able to determine the zip codes of participating Rochester students over time. She found some evidence that in the decades since the program began, an increasing proportion of participating students have come from the city's comparatively wealthier neighborhoods rather than the poorest ones. The zip code including the former Seventh Ward, for instance, contributed 7 percent of Urban-Suburban students in the 2000s compared to 26 percent in the 1960s. This may have been, in part, an artifact of informal information-sharing networks—the program since the 1980s has done very little marketing to Rochester families—as well as a reflection of a teacher referral program, since discontinued, that kept some children's names out of the application pool, the first step in a stringent screening process.[53]

In the wave of conversations from 2014 to 2017, a constant theme at suburban school board meetings was the academic and moral quality of the students who would be participating. Rush-Henrietta assured residents that the students would not bring "city issues" into the district. Another administrator said, "The students we bring out here couldn't be better behaved, to be honest with you . . . because they've been so diligently selected to come here." This tale of the talented tenth proved an important selling point for suburban residents most interested in their own children's education. From a wider perspective, though, it represents an inequity that even the program's staunchest supporters find uncomfortable. If suburban schools ever choose students with disabilities, or those with unstable family backgrounds, or those who don't speak English well, it is unintentional. As the Honeoye Falls-Lima task force wrote, "The selection process gives the district significant latitude to select students who can enter HFL with minimal transition needs and supports. . . . The intent is to enroll general education students without materially increasing costs."[54]

Suburban administrators were even more frank when Finnigan allowed them to speak anonymously. Besides high academic marks, the criteria they mentioned included an intact two-parent household and a clean disciplinary record. One admitted to rejecting an applicant after the parents asked what support systems the district had in place for Black children. Above all, administrators were unanimous in screening out city children with disabilities that might require costly interventions. As one said: "It's a philosophical understanding that we will co-exist with Urban-Suburban as long as it can benefit us with our cultural diversity as well as our fiscal responsibility to the taxpayer here." Another said it was important to avoid children who might end up "soaking up all our resources."[55]

Students accepted into the program count toward their suburban district's statistics and are treated as if they lived in that district. But they can be removed at any time and sent back to RCSD. Although administrators downplay the frequency of such expulsions, Finnigan found that the program had a high level of attrition, with nearly half of all accepted students participating for fewer than two years. Many of those students withdrew because they moved to the suburbs or out of town, but in one year nearly a third voluntarily left for either RCSD or a private school and 10 percent were made to leave.[56]

Administrators told Finnigan that students are asked to leave because of either disciplinary or academic shortcomings. In at least one case, though, a family accused a suburban district of retaliating against their daughter's need for special education services. In 2004 a woman named Lorie Dennis sued the Pittsford Central School District in federal court after her seven-year-old daughter was removed from Urban-Suburban there. The district evidently had not realized when it accepted the girl that she had received some special education services in prekindergarten. When she began to struggle academically in school her mother pressed for another evaluation, at which it was determined that the girl had some developmental delays. According to the lawsuit, the district then asked the mother to withdraw her request for special education services; when she did not, it notified her that her daughter was not welcome to return in the fall. The lawsuit, for discrimination and retaliation, was settled out of court.[57]

An even clearer illustration came in 1994 when Penfield, one of the longest-standing districts in the program, announced it would pull out unless the city school district covered the cost of any supplemental help participating students needed, including special education or tutoring. "We're continuing the ownership, but feel the sending school district has to accept its financial responsibilities," Superintendent Richard Mace said. The particular case he had in mind was that of a female Urban-Suburban student who became pregnant. After her son was born, Penfield objected to paying the cost of the girl's home tutoring and Urban-Suburban director Evelyn Scott told her she had to return to RCSD. "I feel that when an Urban-Suburban girl gets pregnant, that's not exactly a good role model for other Urban-Suburban girls coming up," Scott said. The student appealed the decision with help from the Legal Aid Society and was allowed to remain. "Out in Penfield, there are a lot of white girls that get pregnant, [and] most of them stay right there," she said.[58]

Students who stayed and graduated from their adoptive districts have said, almost uniformly, that they were thankful for the experience and would do it again. "It was the best experience of my life," stated Jessica Lewis, a 2003 West Irondequoit graduate who later worked for Urban-Suburban at BOCES. "It's just an incredible opportunity I'm very grateful for." Wayne Johnson, a member of the first class in Irondequoit, recalled how his classmates' parents created an informal network to drive him home after sports or other activities when the bus wasn't available.[59] The Urban-Suburban Alumni Association boasts of a number of members in impressive professional fields. Almost without exception, though, alumni also report having learned early to navigate various forms of prejudice, explicit or otherwise. A third grader in Brighton was enlisted to play the part of an enslaved person in a role-playing activity. Lewis recalled a secretary who objected to giving her a parking pass as a senior, saying they were only for "tax-paying residents." Many also mentioned a sense of isolation from other Black students, particularly if they attended schools with very few minorities. Urban-Suburban students are touted in the suburbs as the agents of cultural exchange, a role that can be wearying in practice. "It definitely can get tiring," one Urban-Suburban student said. "Some days I just don't feel—not that I don't want to have to be the representative [for my race], but I feel sometimes I shouldn't have to be."[60]

Amending Urban-Suburban to make it more equitable would not be complicated. First, institute either a true lottery or a requirement that suburban districts accept cohorts that are roughly representative of the RCSD student body. Second, bar districts from "exiting" students based on behavior, grades, or special education needs. Third, add supports to help students and their families become better integrated into the school community. These changes, laid out in the conclusion, would bring the program more into line with what exists in other communities and would go some way toward alleviating the strain on the city school district.

What stands in the way of such changes is district leaders' vivid fear of backlash from their residents. Many school administrators told Finnigan about how changes in the direction of greater equity—changes they themselves believed in—would not be "viable" in their districts. "It's a dicey topic and it brings out the ugliness in people," one said.[61] Crane was acutely aware of lurking racism in his own and other suburban communities. On the one hand, he said it was the responsibility of leaders not to bow before that pressure; on the other hand, he conceded the many ways in which even the prospect of dissent has been a hindrance to change. "We've talked more about how to get it more like a lottery without opening ourselves up to people trying to force us to lose the program," he said. "Now, compare (our) interview process to the other seven inter-district transfer programs in the country, and they're like, 'What?! It's not a lottery?'" As Webster Board of Education president Mike Suffoletto said in January 2015, "You don't want to create a situation like Spencerport is going through right now."[62]

In the absence of structural changes to the program, dogged faith in its premise continues to maintain it. Crane graduated from Fairport High School in 1970 and went off to Athens College in northern Alabama, where one night he and some classmates went out to a bar. On his way to the restroom, Crane saw a back room he hadn't noticed before with a solitary Black customer inside. The man gave his order to the Black bartender, who relayed it to the white bartender, who made the drink and passed it back to the Black bartender and, ultimately, the Black customer. The man's money took the same circuitous route in reverse. It shocked him, he said, and put him on a life course he believed to be "more relevant."[63] That included transferring back to SUNY Brockport to earn a teaching degree and, ultimately, leading one of Monroe County's more diverse suburban school districts for nearly twenty years.

His belief in the efficacy of Urban-Suburban can be traced to that chance encounter in a dive bar in Alabama in 1971 and the lesson he drew from it—that a single personal interaction across racial or cultural lines has the potential to unsettle the assumptions of a person or even a community. That sentiment has always been the hope behind the program and the defense against its critics. "We've been accused of being a token—well, we certainly are," Norman Gross said when retiring in 1982. "But we're better than no program at all."[64]

Or, as Crane said on his own retirement thirty-six years later: "You take somewhere between 400 and 900 kids every year for 50 years, then you add in the thousands of kids that those kids have met—that's important. That's a worthwhile effort, and one we've worked hard to protect even though it's got its flaws."[65]

More than half a century after the program's founding, it is important to remember the different political context that prevailed in 1965. White Monroe County residents then could read in the newspaper nearly every day about the federal government taking action against school segregation, mainly in the South but also, ominously, in the North. The local NAACP had filed a lawsuit against the Rochester City School District, where open enrollment was already underway. There was little reason to believe then that the community would emerge with its racial status quo unmoved—it was just a matter of how momentous the change would be, and whether the local white community would manage to exercise any control over its direction.

For this reason, the prospect of gradual, voluntary, small-scale desegregation efforts such as the transurban student conferences and, later, Urban-Suburban, was immediately appealing. Here was a way to get out in front of the problem in a resolutely incremental way. It allowed white school leaders in both the city and suburbs to trumpet the community's measured progress while staving off a judicial intervention that surely would prove more disruptive. The federal government in 1969 chose Rochester as a national exemplar in desegregation. "We have done more or as much as any other city [in addressing racial imbalance]," Rochester Board of Education president and staunch busing opponent Louis Cerulli said in 1966.[66]

At the same time, the program was never envisioned as a full solution. Throughout its first decade, discussions about Urban-Suburban regularly veered into speculation on topics later deemed verboten, including cross-district magnet schools and a metropolitan school system. "It was always our idea that you eventually would have a metropolitan school district," said Walter Cooper, who was part of the discussions around the program's founding and helped launch it in Penfield. "Experience with students in Urban-Suburban would at least give . . . the idea that it was a situation that was good for everybody. But it was never really pushed."[67]

White liberals early on adopted the program as a key component of a communitywide vision of education and spent more than a decade fighting for sustained funding to keep it alive. By the time that battle was won in the early 1980s, though, Urban-Suburban was the only local desegregation effort remaining and the politics of school improvement had shifted. Other northern cities, including Buffalo and Boston, had been forced into desegregation efforts via court order while Rochester waited patiently for the returns of Urban-Suburban to come in. When those returns failed to materialize no energy remained to renew the desegregation effort—or even to diagnose its failure. The initial focus on countywide desegregation had narrowed to a tallying of individual success stories from a carefully curated group of high-performing students. Initially hailed as a lighthouse in the national striving for educational equality, Urban-Suburban instead became more like a safe harbor for Monroe County to wait out the storm of the Civil Rights movement.

## Chapter 8

# The Age of Accountability

There was widespread agreement during the Civil Rights era in Rochester that Black children were not receiving fair access to education. The question was the form of the remedy. Should the school district integrate Black children with white children, abolishing the distinction between the two classes of schools, or should it direct additional resources into the majority-Black schools so they could improve without the need to move students? Most plans included elements of both approaches. Broadly speaking, and especially before the Rochester school board scotched Superintendent Herman Goldberg's desegregation proposals in 1967, the idea of repairing Black students' access to education without a significant desegregation component was a conservative, even reactionary position. "Being for school integration but against compulsory busing is like saying, 'I'm for the abolition of slavery, but it must be voluntary,'" one integration proponent, Alfred Sette, said in 1969.[1]

The last half century has seen a massive swing in orthodoxy in this regard. The fundamental question of whether to integrate schools or to fix them in place has been settled decisively. Every new current in education reform—magnet schools, charter schools, standardized testing, governance changes—falls into the latter paradigm. In the city of Rochester and elsewhere this has led to a dizzying series of reconfigurations, reorganizations, and reforms that has continued uninterrupted to the present. Desegregation, when mentioned at all, is considered only if done on a piece-meal, voluntary basis. In March 2019 Mayor Lovely Warren stood with fellow elected officials and leaders from nearly all of Rochester's educational nonprofits to call for "comprehensive, evidence-based and transformational responses to the needs of our children," adding up to nothing less than a "complete overhaul of the entire school system." The idea of tackling racial segregation as part of that effort, however, was dismissed out of hand. The mayor said that she was "not interested" in trying to get the suburbs on board, while County Executive Cheryl Dinolfo cautioned against "taking what's broken and injecting it into other systems." The logic of *Brown* is forgotten; a disavowal of desegregation is implicit in local, state, and federal education policy.[2]

This philosophical shift is based in part on demographic and geographical reality. When the movement for desegregation in Rochester failed in 1971, white students made up about 60 percent of the district enrollment and 45 percent of Monroe County's white population still lived within city limits. The political will to desegregate may have been lacking, but the possibility was there from a numerical perspective. As white flight into the suburbs continued over the next several decades, that possibility disappeared. By 2010 the city school district's white enrollment was about 10 percent, and just 16 percent of white county residents lived in the city. The challenge of reforming an existing system to create better racial balance was replaced with the exponentially more difficult job of dismantling district lines and state laws to engineer something that has never existed before, against the wishes of many. Faced with this task, educators and community leaders chose instead to focus their attention elsewhere.[3]

During the 1950s the city of Rochester began to swell with new Black residents, mostly transplants from the South—but these were not the only arrivals. The early 1950s also saw the beginning of Rochester's Puerto Rican community, which grew from two dozen in 1950 to perhaps 4,000 people by 1955. They settled first on the northeast periphery of downtown and accepted low-end jobs in food and clothing production—though even those were available only sparingly. "Neither Kodak, General Dynamics, Stromberg Carlson nor Xerox were hiring Puerto Ricans," said Ramon Padilla, an early community leader who arrived in 1947. "Many whites would say Puerto Ricans were lazy, could not speak English, and did not belong here. . . . If 25 [Puerto Ricans] would show up, maybe one person would be hired, as a test."[4] As the Puerto Rican community grew—9,400 people in the city in the 1960 census, then 13,000 in 1970—the Rochester City School District spearheaded early efforts to create English language classes for children and adults, including a federally funded bilingual education program called Adelante, or "forward." Well into the 1980s, though, the district's best method of classifying students as Latino was eyeballing their last names, and the fate of Puerto Rican children in the reorganization plan of 1971–72 was an afterthought.[5]

The city's diversity began to gain yet another aspect in the mid-1970s. After the end of the Vietnam War in 1975, people from South Vietnam, Cambodia, Laos, and other affected countries in Southeast Asia began to arrive in the United States as refugees. Rochester and other northeastern cities had welcomed refugees for centuries, of course, but this was the first time they came from outside Europe in significant numbers. The Southeast Asian refugees were gradually supplanted by those from other troubled parts of the world: Somalia, Sudan, and Congo; Iraq and Syria and Bhutan; again from Southeast Asia. Non-European refugees became a significant population driver as a generation of Kodak and Xerox employees moved to the suburbs, left the state, or died. As it had with the Puerto Ricans, RCSD undertook the initial task of teaching the refugees and their children English and providing some basic job skills. In 2011 the district created a newcomer program for refugee children, the Rochester International Academy.[6]

The influx of Black people in the Great Migration broke the pattern in Rochester and other northern cities as far as welcoming newcomers into the native population. After 150 years of a simple Black-and-white racial paradigm, Rochesterians were initially slow to understand where the new Latino and Asian arrivals fit into an increasingly stratified society, and the sophisticated system of physical segregation designed for the containment of Black people ended up ensnaring subsequent groups as well. Puerto Ricans and Southeast Asians, too, found it difficult to escape low-income neighborhoods that were adversely affected by urban renewal and served by increasingly segregated schools. Puerto Ricans in Rochester were often bewildered by the demand for neat racial classification. Nydia Padilla-Rodriguez had ten brothers and sisters with skin colors ranging from light to dark. She recalled that her next-door neighbor would let the lighter-skinned siblings play in her yard, but not the darker ones. "It just didn't make sense, but you knew you had to deal with it because it's part of what happens when you walk out of your home," she said.[7]

By 2020, one in three RCSD students was Latino or Asian. The academic achievement of Latino students in RCSD now mirrors that of Black students. Asian students fare better, but a significant divide exists between refugee students from Southeast Asia and the children of highly skilled immigrants from China and South Korea who come to the area for college or jobs.[8]

The proportion of Latino and Asian students grew not only through in-migration to Rochester but also because African Americans began in the 1970s to disperse more broadly outside the city of Rochester. Between the passage of the Fair Housing Act in 1968 and the maturation of a professional class of Black employees at Kodak, Xerox, and other large employers, Black families with means increasingly chose the newly open path of homeownership in the suburbs. From 1970 to 2000 the number of Black adults who had attended college grew by a factor of twelve in the Monroe County suburbs, far outpacing the rate in the city. "I wasn't moving [to the suburbs] because I was running from something," said Musette Castle, an RCSD teacher who moved to Pittsford around 1980. "I was doing what most people who work do: looking for a phenomenal home, the best I could have, in the best neighborhood I could have." "The best," of course, included the school system. Middle-class Black families often regarded the city school district with the same alarm as their white peers. "In the city, kids could be out of school for weeks before their parents are called," said Gloria Winston Al-Sarag, who moved to Henrietta with her children in 1990. "In Rush-Henrietta, if my kid missed homeroom, I got a call: 'Is Michael home sick today?'"[9]

At the same time, housing discrimination in Rochester became less overt but remained pernicious. The Urban League of Rochester conducted a series of housing audits in the mid-1970s in which white and Black couples approached real estate agents with the same cover story. In case after case,

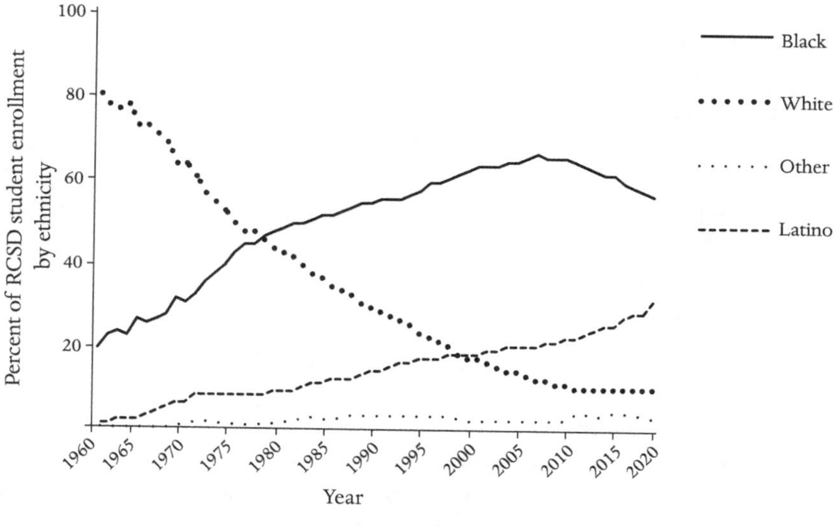


**FIGURE 8.1.** Students by race and ethnicity, Rochester City School District, 1961 to 2020. Source: RCSD and New York State Education Department data, available at data.nysed.gov.

the white couples were steered toward well-maintained houses at the top of their price range and assured that financing could be secured, whereas Black couples with the same purported income were shown lower quality houses in mostly Black neighborhoods. In one example, a Black couple who said that they were looking for a house in the suburbs were shown scores of houses in only one, relatively poor town. The same realtor later drove a similarly situated white couple through the same town to discourage them from buying there, saying disdainfully, "How would you like to live here?" White couples were cautioned against purchasing in the 19th Ward because "a lot of blacks have moved in."[10]

These racial and ethnic changes made no difference in terms of attempts to desegregate the schools; that time had passed. But though government and community interest in desegregation had dwindled considerably, there were still some scattered attempts to draw attention to the question. New York Education Commissioner Ewald Nyquist warned in 1975 that the city's schools were "extremely segregated" and that he intended to intervene (he never did). Two years later the Urban League of Rochester, under Executive Director Bill Johnson, issued a comprehensive report showing how racial isolation had continued to increase dramatically. From 1970 to 1975, the proportion of minority students attending majority-minority schools had increased from 56 to 77 percent. Achievement gaps, as measured by state test scores, were stark and persistent, both within the city and between the city and the suburbs. The Urban League proposed an overhaul of city school attendance zones to better balance students by race and warned that it might sue to rectify the situation. The school board, though, shrugged off the Urban League's findings of academic disparity between majority white and majority nonwhite schools and summarily rejected the idea of revisiting reorganization. "The recommendations do nothing more than flirt with the chaotic situation we had in 1971," Frank Ciaccia said. "The board should take this report, study it and reject it."[11]

Although the school board never formally took up the Urban League recommendations, it did convene a committee on integration in the same month that the report was issued, charging it with developing ideas for improving racial balance among students and teachers in the city. The Citizens Committee on Race and Education was nearly derailed before it began its work after some school board members objected to the presence of the word "race" in its name. "The word 'race' is inflammatory and it won't help the committee study what it's going to study," Louis D'Angelo said. The committee chairman, Rev. Richard Comegys of St. Stephen's Episcopal Church, ignored the criticism, and it was dropped. But the committee's initial seven-month term eventually stretched to nearly two years as it struggled to raise funds for research. "We got a lot less support than we expected from local businesses and local foundations," Comegys said. "As a result, our report will have only about one-tenth of what we had hoped to have." When it finally was released in January 1979, the Comegys report concluded that open enrollment and other voluntary programs within the district had done "essentially nothing" to stem worsening racial isolation. It instead identified the main problem as persistent "white anxiety . . . [having] more to do with perceived atmosphere than with direct threat, with tension rather than explosion." It found that specialized programs like World of Inquiry had drawn the best students, white and Black, from other schools, leaving the latter worse off. The only viable solution, it determined, was a metropolitan approach. The school board did not formally respond to the Comegys report, either. It, like the Urban League report, was mostly forgotten. "A lot of people say they support the principle of integration, but there's not a lot of people in this community who are going to work for it," Comegys concluded.[12]

In 1979, federal investigators arrived in Rochester from the Departments of Justice and Health, Education, and Welfare, and announced that they were "looking for evidence that either the city school district, other school districts, or other governmental agencies, such as zoning boards or housing authorities, took action with the intent to create segregated schools or segregated housing patterns." The investigation came in response to multiple parents' complaints about their children's lack of an equal opportunity. The investigators promised that their report would be "exhaustive," possibly leading to a settlement or lawsuit. In particular, it seemed the 1972 repeal of Herman Goldberg's reorganization plan might finally get the critical examination that the school board had then feared. If the investigators ever completed their work, though, it did not become public. The pending inquiry faded without a formal conclusion. The federal agencies involved responded to 2019 Freedom of Information Act requests by stating that no documents related to the investigation existed in their files.[13]

The city school board from 1962 to 1972 had argued ferociously over whether the district was doing enough to counteract racial segregation and its effects. In the subsequent years, board members took a much more fatalistic view. "Kids fail because they put no effort into their education," Irene Frusci said in 1978. "I've been called defeatist for saying that, but I'm a nurse, and I know that some of my patients die." Brenda Fraser, who had been a proponent of the Herman Goldberg reorganization plan before joining the school board, said that desegregation was no longer "politically feasible" and therefore not worth discussing. "If you try to make integration an issue in the campaign, not even the liberals will vote for you," she said. "Without any legal action behind you, they'll say, 'Why are you stirring up that trouble again?'"[14]

Until 1972, the Rochester City School District's grappling with the question of segregation overshadowed its mounting financial difficulties. After the reorganization plan was rescinded in 1972 by a new school board majority pledging fiscal responsibility, the question of funding rose to the forefront. Enrollment, and with it per-pupil state aid, peaked around 44,000 in 1968–69 before beginning a steady decline that has continued mostly unabated to the present—even as students' level of need has risen. As more and more middle-class families (and businesses) moved into the suburbs, the city's tax revenues began to decline. "The property tax within the corporate limits of the City of Rochester no longer will bear the crushing burden of both education and city service costs," City Manager Kermit Hill wrote to Superintendent John Franco in 1971. "Both city services and education must suffer because, by law, we now must try to squeeze both feet into this tight shoe."[15]

This situation, replicated in urban districts across New York, eventually served as the foundation for a major lawsuit, *Board of Education, Levittown Union Free School District et al. v. Ewald B. Nyquist*, challenging the prevailing, property tax–based school finance system. *Levittown* sought to establish in the state constitution the same concept that a US Supreme Court case, *San Antonio Independent School District v. Rodriguez*, had sought unsuccessfully to establish in the US Constitution—the right to approximate equity in education funding across the state, regardless of a community's real property value. After several years of litigation, the New York Court of Appeals rejected the *Levittown* plaintiffs' argument. They noted that the state constitution makes only the barest mention of education as a public duty. Critically, the court also found that the plaintiffs had not made the claim that education in any given district fell below "the statewide minimum standard of educational quality and quantity fixed by the Board of Regents." This final point would later be tested in a subsequent court case that generated decades of controversy.[16]

The city of Rochester and its school district ultimately would be rescued from their immediate revenue crisis by a sales tax–sharing arrangement with Monroe County. Before that, though, came nearly twenty years of whipsawing education budget seasons. Every year, RCSD cut hundreds of employees and then, in many cases, hired them back when funds later emerged through a variety of stop-gap budget mechanisms. During the same period, the school board decided that it needed to begin "restructuring and scaling down" the district's programs and payroll in recognition of its declining enrollment. Superintendent John Franco left for Long Island in 1980, his nine-year tenure as superintendent having bridged a massive transition in the philosophy of urban education. When he took the job in 1971, his task was to implement Goldberg's reorganization plan for racial desegregation. By the time he left, desegregation was an afterthought, and the era of school reform was underway.[17]

Franco was a Rochester native, affable and deeply connected to the community. By contrast, Laval Wilson, who stepped in as superintendent in 1980, was "an intellectual computer [with] no food, water or blood" in him, one community member complained. For the school board that hired him, this was a virtue. "We needed somebody who could come in and shake the system up internally [and] give the union a tough time," Archie Curry, vice president of the board that hired Wilson, said. "He had the little man's syndrome. . . . He came in and said, 'I'm the boss.'" Wilson was RCSD's first Black superintendent, but his appointment by no means indicated a renewed emphasis on racial equity. Instead he projected what one commentator called a "formal, bureaucratic, and essentially raceless persona."[18]

This colorblind, technocratic philosophy made Wilson a superintendent suited for his time. The national conservative tilt in education policy that began with President Richard Nixon's antipathy to busing had yielded, by the early 1980s, a widespread conviction that schooling in the classic liberal model was leading the nation far astray. This conviction was captured most influentially in "A Nation at Risk," a 1983 report from the US Department of Education. US schools, the report's authors contended, were to blame for "a rising tide of mediocrity"—in large part because they had instead been enlisted "to provide solutions to personal, social, and political problems that the home and other institutions either will not or cannot resolve." The report's call for a rededication to "the basic purposes of schooling," scrubbed of social context, echoed the conservative pushback to the movement for racial equity and desegregation in the 1960s. Now, it was rebranded as "excellence in education."[19]

The key proponents of this new movement were not fearful and economically insecure white families, but rather a nearly complete roster of the most influential business executives in the country. Industry leaders got involved "because profits depend on it," as Xerox CEO David Kearns put it. "Without it, our society will founder, and our businesses will, as well." The education reforms of the excellence in education movement, which continues in spirit to the present, were drawn largely from the pages of business school textbooks. Perhaps the most important of them was the emphasis on measuring success or failure with a new array of performance indicators. The schools that performed the best would profit by attracting more students, while those that did not would be—in the two words that best summarize the era—held accountable.[20]

For these early reformers, the universal applicability of business principles to the arena of public education was implicit. "I don't know anything about education," admitted Norman Deets, Xerox's workforce training director, who worked closely with RCSD. "But I know about how to make decisions, how to restructure management, and how to put together a quality product." Education was now seen as a product, with children as the consumers. "[Schools] must tailor their offerings to the needs of the customer, and they must believe that in a fundamental sense, the student is always the customer," Kearns wrote. To complete the metaphor, schools were education factories—not terribly well designed ones, from the viewpoint of the nation's top business minds, staffed largely by employees in dire need of retraining or replacement.[21]

In large part because of a nationally significant teachers' contract in 1987, and as one of the last payments of tribute for its mid-century industrial prowess, Rochester became an important locus for school-reform thinking. Marc Tucker, an influential academic, launched his National Center on Education and the Economy in Rochester in 1988. David Kearns would leave Xerox to become the US deputy secretary of education under George H. W. Bush. "This is the educational flagship of the United States," American Federation of Teachers president Albert Shanker said in 1988. "Everybody is looking at Rochester."[22]

The concept of magnet schools—consumer-oriented, aligned with workforce needs, and competing with one another for enrollment—fit perfectly into the vision of public education as a Darwinist marketplace. The idea has a long provenance, beginning with vocational schools such as Edison Tech and other specialized programs that draw students by choice rather than geography. In the mid-1970s, specialized schools became magnets not only for students but also, as importantly, for federal desegregation dollars. The district had a few abortive experiments with new magnet programs in the 1970s before finally striking gold in 1979 with the restructuring of Joseph C. Wilson Junior High School.[23] Wilson, the former West High School, had descended into chaos as a middle school. "That was the worst place in the world," Peter McWalters, then a mid-level administrator and later the RCSD superintendent, said plainly. Federal magnet school funding would convert Wilson into a "trilogy" of magnet programs focusing on the performing arts, college-track academics, and science and technology. The district, now led by Laval Wilson, followed up in 1981 with another large-scale plan that closed Madison High School and planted the seeds of elementary and secondary programs in buildings throughout the city.[24]

Within a few years, Wilson Magnet High School had mostly met the lofty expectations the community had set for it. Attendance and achievement were way up; students skipped lunch to learn computer programming in the state-of-the-art laboratories or to finish their Latin homework. Just as notably, violence and suspensions were way down. "When I first came here, I expected to find one bully, go fight him, and then it would be over," the captain of the school football team said in 1984. "But there's no bully here. There's no one to fight." A small number of suburban students enrolled in the school as well, an unthinkable notion before the school's conversion, and its racial demographics nearly mirrored those of the district as a whole. Wilson Magnet seemingly even kept middle-class families in the city. "The day may come when we move out of the city, if only for want of a little more space," two parents wrote in 1984. "But we will never consider such a move until our son has completed his education in the Rochester public schools."[25]

A string of accolades and achievements seemed to prove the school's success. In 1985, the state education department named Wilson Magnet one of the top ten high schools in New York. A business partnership program called Brainpower brought in top executives and engineers from Kodak and Xerox, among others, to lend expertise in writing curriculum. Students snorkeled in the Bahamas to learn about marine biology. In 1989 came a visit from President George H. W. Bush. "What you're doing is an example to the entire country," Bush told the students. "I'm going to do my level best as president to get this concept of magnet schools all over the country." In 1999 Wilson Magnet became the first school in Monroe County to offer the International Baccalaureate (IB) program, thanks to a $6 million federal grant. Unsurprisingly, Wilson Magnet, in particular its Academy of Excellence, developed a reputation as the finest academic program in the school district. "It wasn't perfect, but you were going to get educated there," said Malik Evans, a 1998 graduate who later served on both the board of education and city council. "You were pushed."[26]

Preceding Evans at Wilson Magnet by a few years was Lovely Warren. When school leaders periodically rounded up students to represent the school's grand reputation, Warren was not their choice. By the time she arrived in high school, her life had been turned upside down by the revelation that her father, a Xerox engineer, had become addicted to crack cocaine. "When life changed for him, life changed for me," she said. "I became very angry and I acted out. I would fight all the time." Family issues aside, though, Warren felt intuitively that her very presence at Wilson Magnet said something about her. "We were the smart kids, and that was known in the community," she said. "I knew that I was smart, and if I could just stop acting out I could be whatever I wanted."[27]

Wilson was the most celebrated magnet school in Rochester, but it was by no means the only one. The roster changed over the twenty years or so when magnet schools were most prominent in the city, but several proved long lasting. School of the Arts began as one of the three pathways at Wilson Magnet, then moved into space at Monroe High School and eventually to its own building on Prince Street. A law and government magnet was housed first at Jefferson High School before moving to John Marshall High School. Edison Tech and School Without Walls, the two long-standing alternative programs, were reclassified as magnets. There were also more than a dozen elementary schools labeled as magnets, including ones focused on early education, language development, and studying the Genesee River.[28]

Were Rochester's magnet schools, as Bush believed, a model worth following for both academic success and desegregation? The evidence is mixed. The district's first review, in 1984, showed that test scores at the magnet schools were no better on the whole than those in the regular comprehensive high schools. Absenteeism and student turnover were lower at magnet schools, but largely because the students who attended them were more stable to begin with. Certain magnet programs, like those at Wilson Magnet and School of the Arts, eventually drew great demand from RCSD families and became permanent institutions. At the same time, a revolving array of others—an environmental sciences magnet program at Charlotte High School, for example—proved short lived. This sink-or-swim dynamic in magnet schools would be seen again with charter schools in the twenty-first century.[29]

The results in terms of desegregation were even less encouraging. Although some Rochester magnet programs were racially balanced, they could not stop galloping white flight throughout the city. The district's nonwhite enrollment rose from 58 percent in 1979, when the first official magnet opened, to 72 percent a decade later. Just a quarter of elementary students attended "racially balanced" schools that year, defined as those within 10 percentage points of the districtwide enrollment of nonwhite students. A 1989 district report showed that just one-third of Black and Latino ninth graders were enrolled in Regents-level social studies, and that just one-third of those students passed the final Regents exam. The numbers for white students were exactly the opposite: nearly two-thirds took the more challenging course, and two-thirds passed the exam. "Magnets, then, are good for education," the *Times-Union* editorialized. "But they are not, by themselves, the answer to segregation. To say that they are is to tolerate 'separate but equal' for a long time to come."[30]

The crux of the problem was that, while attention was showered on the top-performing magnet schools, many of the nonmagnet comprehensive schools floundered. Laval Wilson and later superintendents insisted that the district remained committed to the comprehensive high schools, and all schools were technically required to enroll an equitable number of students of across differences in race, wealth, and academic performance. The sky-high recruiting budget and glowing promotional materials for the magnet schools, however, spoke for themselves, and they were eligible for federal funding that other schools were not. As McWalters later conceded: "The gifted programs were all white females and the troubled programs were all Black boys." The disparity existed even within school buildings, where magnet programs were sometimes hosted alongside regular classrooms. John Marshall High School, for example, was home to a well-regarded law and government magnet program for high-achieving students as well as an on-site childcare center for the ninety nonmagnet teenage girls—one fifth of its female enrollment—who already had children of their own.[31]

Lovely Warren captured the dynamic, half in jest, in describing how different high schools in the city had their own reputations when she was a student: "At that point in time all the schools had something," she said. "We [Wilson] were the school of knowledge. . . . East was for sports. Edison was for tech and the trades. Franklin and Josh Lofton were the schools for bad kids." Indeed, with Madison closed and Wilson reinvented, Franklin became a dumping ground for students not talented or resourceful enough to land elsewhere. It was deemed "in need of assistance" by the state in 1985, cycled through principals at an alarming rate, and ultimately landed on the state's final sanction list in 1991, a label that marked it for possible state takeover if it did not improve rapidly.[32]

Hope for improvement was based on technical fixes and, in large part, school choice for students. "We're not a pick-and-choose district," a top administrator said in 1993. "We let kids pick and choose." The result, only partially intended, was erosion of the traditional enrollment zones and dilution of the concept of a magnet school. McWalters in 1988 ended secondary-school feeder patterns, and the district enrollment office began placing more and more elementary school students outside their official "home" zones. With the strict geographic placement system stripped away, the magnet schools became less distinct. White enrollment, meanwhile, continued to plummet, putting the goal of integration even further out of reach. "It is no longer possible to redraw home school attendance area boundaries that simultaneously satisfy instructional capacity and provide for socio-economic and/or racial/ethnic diversity," the school board admitted in 2002 in a policy eliminating single-school attendance areas in favor of three "zones" for elementary schools. Five years later, the last remnant of dedicated magnet school funding in the district was folded into a block grant.[33]

Of the profusion of magnet schools that emerged in the 1980s in Rochester, only one remains—and even then, only in name. Wilson Magnet lost its three distinct magnet tracks but still offers the IB program. RCSD acknowledged in 2014, though, that barely any of its students graduated with an IB diploma and most didn't even enroll in the courses. The few suburban students once enrolled there and in other selective city schools have long since vanished. Benchmarks related to race and poverty have been abandoned. The city's three enrollment zones, the last vestige of neighborhood schools, have proven porous, with more than half of elementary school students going to a school across town from where they live.[34]

Archie Curry served on the school board from 1978 until 2005, essentially the entire magnet school era. His own children attended magnet programs at School 3, Wilson Magnet, and Edison Tech. He attributed the magnet concept's ultimate lack of success to disinterest, based partly on fear, from white families:

> At Marshall, we thought if it had a law magnet, it would be great. They had a whole courtroom and everything. No white kids came there. We said to the suburban schools, 'You can send your kids.' They didn't come. . . .
>
> Magnet schools were a way to get more white kids to stay in city schools, and then by osmosis, Black kids would be better off. . . . We destroyed neighborhood schools, and by the time we [ended], we couldn't integrate because there were no white kids left to integrate.[35]

The magnet schools movement may not have succeeded in stopping the trend of worsening racial segregation in Rochester (and Monroe County) schools, but the attempt at least acknowledged the problem. By contrast, nearly every other significant local attempt at education reform has been silent on the effects of segregation. These attempts have been frequent and unfailingly earnest. Several have been launched from the business community or else were developed with its support: the August Group, the Rump Group, the Call to Arms, the Call to Action, the Children's Zone, and Beacon

Schools. Mayor Bob Duffy fought valiantly but unsuccessfully for mayoral control of the district. All have sought to solve the problem of segregated education with a combination of coordinated supports—mentoring, social services, and health care—and structural change in the school system, with a particularly critical eye toward the elected school board.[36]

These reforms, none of them indigenous to Rochester, all are based on the same premise: that it is possible—preferable, in the opinion of some—to provide a separate but equal education for all children, no matter how massive the contrast in race and affluence from one school district to another. Indeed, the notion of equal outcomes between urban and suburban students has been either implicitly rejected or punted into the distant future. As the Rump Group, a coalition of the city's industrial leaders, wrote in "A Community at Risk," a much-discussed 2003 report: "It is unreasonable to demand that Rochester students suddenly match the performance of students in Brighton or Greece. . . . [But] it is reasonable to expect students in the Rochester City School District to perform as well as, or better than, students in any district with a predominantly low-income population."[37]

The presupposition of racial and economic segregation also underlies federal (and New York) education policy dating back to George W. Bush's No Child Left Behind. That this premise directly contradicts the decision in *Brown v. Board of Education*, perhaps the most significant and revered Supreme Court decision of the twentieth century, is by and large ignored. Indeed, the universal acceptance of the essentially conservative principles underlying the reform and accountability movement is the clearest possible proof of the decisiveness with which the debate over segregation was resolved. Much has been written about the programs of the education reform movement, both locally and nationally. The two most prominent of them will be discussed below: the landmark 1987 Rochester teachers' contract and the rise of charter schools.

A 1980 strike had left relations between RCSD and its teachers frosty throughout Laval Wilson's tenure. When Wilson left for Boston in 1985, though, he was replaced by Peter McWalters, who saw himself first as a "teacher on leave," not an administrator, and quickly made common cause with the Rochester Teachers Association. Union president Adam Urbanski, for his part, disavowed "unions as they used to be" and sold his members on the need to assume greater responsibilities.[38] In the fall of 1987, the school board and teachers ratified a three-year contract that vaulted Rochester to the forefront of the national reform movement. The basic concept, as journalist Katherine Boo put it, was "to shower money and power on teachers." It was the first part of that equation that captured headlines: a 40 percent increase in pay over three years, which resulted in the median teacher salary rising from $34,000 in 1986–87 to $46,000 in 1989–90. Rochester teachers became the highest paid in the country, a coup for Urbanski and the American Federation of Teachers. The added teacher duties, meanwhile, were mostly not spelled out in the contract but rather listed as "agreements to agree." They included programs for teacher development and remediation and the establishment of school-based decision-making bodies dominated by teachers.[39]

"It does nothing less than put Rochester in the forefront of the national educational reform movement," school board member Catherine Spoto said in voting to approve the new contract. Leading a movement, however, is not the same thing as running a school system, and implementation proved a harder lift than reform leaders had anticipated. For business-minded reform advocates and many parents, the prospect of weeding out so-called bad teachers was one of the contract's top selling points. The confidential nature of that weeding, however, made it difficult to assess. Frustrated parents were quick to point to examples where bad teachers remained untouchable. "We have teachers who fraternize—I mean, *have sex with*—teenagers, and they're still teachers," Parent Council president Marvin Jackson said in 1992. "But mostly, we just have some plain old bad teachers, and nothing ever happens to them."[40] Signs of dissent in the community had become clear by the time the labor deal expired in 1990. Academic performance had only increased marginally, the country was entering a recession, and distaste for Rochester's home-grown school reform was rising. Urbanski recalled meeting with a group of community leaders who were impatient with the pace of change in the schools. "I said, 'I know, me too. But real change takes real time,'" he recalled. "And someone responded, 'Yeah, but you took that money real quick.'"[41]

A generation after the 1987 teachers' contract, lasting evidence of the reform it heralded is difficult to see. Teacher salaries in RCSD, once the highest in the country, are now in the middle of the pack in Monroe County. School-based planning is absent from many buildings and ineffectual in others. Complaints about ineffective teachers coasting to retirement have scarcely abated. Urbanski responded: "All our efforts to improve learning outcomes for students were outpaced by the declines in the students' conditions."[42]

Archie Curry voted against the contract and laid much of the blame on McWalters for being "duped" into granting an extravagant pay raise without getting the promised returns in writing. McWalters, who left Rochester in 1991, rejected the notion that Urbanski took advantage of him. And though he went on to positions of greater influence later in his career, he admitted a wistfulness for the Rochester reform that never was. "When I arrived in Rochester [in 1970], I felt like I was in one of the most progressive places I could imagine," he said. "I distinctly remember having the sense: 'This is the place that can make that happen.' . . . But some of the stuff didn't stay long enough, get supported enough, or they just couldn't deliver it."[43]

The waning of the late-1980s reform effort marked a turning point in the relationship between RCSD and the local business community. "Nine years after Rochester's historic 'reform movement' started, there is little progress to report, despite a more than 40% increase in per-pupil expenditures," the business-heavy August Group wrote in 1994. Disillusioned, local business leaders started looking outside the district for other solutions. They found one in charter schools, a movement that began as a way to encourage teachers to experiment with pedagogy and curriculum. By 2019–20 there were fourteen charter schools in Monroe County educating about 6,700 Rochester children. Advocates point to superior state test scores and graduation rates at most charter schools compared to district schools, and the data supports them. At the highest-performing charter schools, students often best even their peers in wealthy suburban schools. Like magnet schools before them, charter schools fit neatly into a competitive, capitalistic frame of reference. "The beauty of charter schools is that, in exchange for many freedoms . . . [they] must deliver or risk closure," said Geoff Rosenberger, an investment banker and chairman of the Rochester Prep charter school board.[44]

In some cases, though, the freedom inherent in the charter school sector has led to abuses. In keeping with a national pattern, there have been numerous instances where Rochester-area charter school leaders have directed public funding into their own pockets, most often through real estate transactions. For example, the Education Success Network, an umbrella group comprising several schools along with a tutoring operation and real estate arm, created a thicket of contracts among its entities, including several where the signatories were affiliated with both parties.[45]

As with other accountability-era reforms, the charter school movement is not intended to reduce segregation, either within urban districts or across metropolitan areas. Instead, charter school advocates view poverty and racial segregation as rationalizations for failure and evidence of low expectations. It is not surprising, then, that the median Rochester-area charter school manages to surpass the median RCSD school in racial segregation, with 92 percent Black and Latino students compared to 89 percent in the district. Indeed, more than failing to address racial and socioeconomic segregation, charter schools actively deepen RCSD's concentration of other sorts of vulnerable students. The median Monroe County charter school has half as many non-English speakers and students with disabilities as RCSD.[46]

One Rochester charter school does concern itself directly with segregation. That is Genesee Community Charter School (GCCS), a small K–6 school on the campus of the Rochester Museum and Science Center on East Avenue. Its twenty-year history illustrates the potential—and the problems—of charter schools in the context of school desegregation. It was launched as "diverse by design," with demographic goals pegged to Monroe County rather than the city of Rochester. In practice, this means enrolling more middle-class and white children, and indeed GCCS has succeeded in that, perhaps too well. The school's enviable campus setting and emphasis on child-based learning have made it an instant favorite of white families living nearby in the relatively affluent southeast quadrant. In 2014–15, when its five-year charter term came up for renewal, the school had 67 percent white children and just 26 percent economically disadvantaged children. In response the board of regents asked the school to give preference to economically disadvantaged children in its lottery. The school's leaders parried the request but, after another five years of little progress in changing its demographics, agreed to create a weighted lottery.[47]

Should GCCS be celebrated as a model of school integration, where the demographics roughly mirror the metropolitan area and the curriculum is imbued with a social justice message? Or is it another parasite on RCSD, attracting away students with means and the state funding that comes along with them to the detriment of the city as a whole? The school in 2020 pledged to enroll more nonwhite and economically disadvantaged students, as well as English-language learners and students with disabilities, to more closely match the demographics of RCSD. Even while promising to pursue that goal, though, school leader Shannon Hillman questioned its wisdom. "I think it is achievable to do this major flip in our demographics and still be highly successful," she said. "The lost piece is, you wouldn't have the opportunity to grow up with kids different from you if you're in a segregated school."[48]

In a market-based conception of public education, the prospect of scalable success has become a holy grail. Schools that can point to a positive trendline, no matter how preliminary, are soon inundated with visiting educators, officials, and journalists looking for evidence of something that works. Replication, though, is a constant challenge, in part because these model programs often succeed through unacknowledged but important advantages. The paradox of GCCS was true as well of magnet schools, whose successes stemmed from the makeup of the student body as much as from the teaching the schools provided. Other charter schools are a closer match to traditional public schools but nonetheless retain important privileges—fewer students with disabilities and the ability to turn out low-performing students, for instance—that RCSD lacks. In other cases—for instance, the costly, much touted partnership between the University of Rochester and East High School beginning in 2015—the advantages include an infusion of outside resources not available to other schools. Broader reforms like the 1987 teachers' contract, meanwhile, have failed to generate systemic improvements. In no case has any meaningful desegregation occurred, racial or otherwise, in large part because school district lines have become too stiff a barrier. "We said we were going to achieve balance, but it was balancing 70 percent minority populations," Ed Cavalier said of his time as an RCSD administrators in the 1980s. Like, 'Let's make sure there's no one school that's better than another.' . . . There was no longer any way to integrate."[49]

Only once since the school board election of 1971 has there been a serious challenge to the segregated nature of education in the Rochester area. That came in 1998 in a lawsuit filed on behalf of a group of students including fifteen-year-old Amber Paynter.

Paynter was born in New Jersey, and during her childhood she and her mother moved back and forth several times between a suburban school district there and Rochester. "I remember going to second grade in Rochester and doing work I did in kindergarten in New Jersey, and my mom made a huge deal about that," Paynter said. "And that was the first time I was like: 'Oh, OK, there's something called inequality.'" By the time Paynter reached John Marshall High School she was inured to the dysfunction in the district and concentrated on keeping her head down while maintaining passing grades. Her mother, Mona Stone, helped recruit other families for the lawsuit. "She was very passionate about: 'Let's stand up for our kids and fight,'" Paynter said. "I remember her saying: 'People are so used to having less, they're not aware of what the possibility could be. . . . We can have better schools.'"[50]

The student plaintiffs were assembled by the Greater Rochester Area Coalition for Education, or GRACE.[51] The group included much of Rochester's social justice–oriented legal community as well as like-minded academics and politicians. One was county legislator Christopher Wilmot, who in 1996 unsuccessfully floated the idea of studying school district consolidation. Group members were moved to action by the vast disparity in academic outcomes in the city and suburban school districts. "Are our children being educated? The answer depends on, among other things, where you live and the economic circumstances of your family," Wilmot wrote. "Some differential is inevitable, but the existing disparity is unconscionable."[52]

The initial lawsuit, filed in September 1998 as *Paynter v. State of New York*, provided a laundry list of inequitable educational outcomes in RCSD compared to the surrounding suburbs: higher dropout rates, lower graduation rates, worse test scores. In sum, it alleged, these were evidence that Rochester children were being denied a sound, basic education. The complaint then went further, claiming that this deprivation was a direct cause of concentrated poverty in the city and that the "state laws and state policies [that] have caused and contributed" to it—in other words, de jure segregation. In particular the plaintiffs pointed to a 1973 state law that gave municipalities veto power over the siting of low-income housing developments. "Through no fault of its own, the RCSD has been saddled with tremendous educational hurdles," they concluded. "By itself, the District simply cannot overcome the educational disadvantages imposed by extreme concentration of poverty."[53]

The lawsuit sought no specific fix but rather asked the court to order the creation of a remedy and to take the parties under its supervision. In interviews, GRACE members said that they were not necessarily looking for a full metropolitan school district, even if they favored one conceptually. As Bryan Hetherington, one of the lead *Paynter* attorneys, said: "We were pretty convinced you could do a relatively non-disruptive remedy that would take advantage of the unique demographics of this community, with a combination of magnets and changing housing patterns by improving the city schools. We were always kind of vague in terms of our remedy because we wanted State Ed to listen to the local districts and see what they needed to be willing participants."[54]

Longtime observers of the district's segregation struggle may have recognized one of the names on the lawsuit. Lillian Colquhoun was the lead plaintiff in the 1970 case *Colquhoun v. Board of Education*, where she sued on behalf of her daughter Sereena Brown. By 1998 she was a grandmother and joined *Paynter* on behalf of her two grandchildren, Yancey and Yalawn Christian, of whom she had custody. Yalawn Christian recalled growing up under her grandmother's roof with a large and changing assortment of aunts, uncles, and cousins—as many as ten living together at once under Colquhoun's care. "It was really rough," she said of her time in Schools 3 and 4, both almost entirely nonwhite. "There were a lot of children with trauma and PTSD and different things going on at home, and when they got to school there weren't a lot of counselors to establish relationships."[55]

The legal framework of *Paynter* was partly inspired by a pair of contemporary education lawsuits: *Sheff v. O'Neill*, in Connecticut, and *Campaign for*

*Fiscal Equity Inc. v. State. Sheff*, first filed in 1989, alleged that educational disparities between Hartford and the state's nonurban schools violated the equal protection clause of the state constitution, specifically as a result of racial and socioeconomic isolation. After seven years of litigation, the state's highest court agreed with the plaintiffs. It ordered the creation of an interdistrict remedy that ultimately involved building dozens of magnet schools and controlling enrollment to ensure racial and socioeconomic diversity.[56]

*Sheff* raised eyebrows but had relatively little national impact because it relied on language in the Connecticut state constitution that did not exist in New York or elsewhere. The *Campaign for Fiscal Equity* (CFE) lawsuit, on the other hand, picked up where *Levittown* in New York had left off. The judges in *Levittown* had ruled that, though funding across New York school districts might be unequal, a claim of constitutional violation could not be proven unless the plaintiffs showed that the unequal funding resulted in unequal outcomes. A statewide coalition called the Campaign for Fiscal Equity filed a lawsuit in 1993 alleging that very thing: that funding disparities across districts had deprived poor students of their constitutionally guaranteed right to a "sound, basic education." A trial began in 1999.[57] *CFE* and *Paynter*, then, proceeded together through the state courts, aiming at the same broad goal through different means. Hetherington noted how the issues of funding and demographics were often cynically played against each other: "In a state where people were bringing a finance suit, the state defendants would say, 'It's concentration of poverty,'" he said. "And in states where there was a concentration of poverty suit, they'd say, 'It's financing.'" To get around this dilemma, *Paynter* proposed a novel formulation of the problem, arguing that "inputs" included not just money but also the students themselves.[58]

The initial lawsuit named only state representatives, including Education Commissioner Richard Mills. The state protested that the individual Rochester-area school districts, too, should be named, given that they inevitably would be implicated in a potential remedy. The courts agreed on appeal, meaning that the list of named defendants had ballooned by the time Judge John Ark issued the first substantive ruling in the case in November 2000. This was a strategic setback for the plaintiffs, who had counted on keeping the suburban districts sidelined and possibly engaged in a solution. "The court forced the suburban districts to come in; we didn't want them to," Feldman said. "[Once involved], they couldn't make any nuanced arguments. They had to just oppose."[59]

In his ruling, Ark agreed with the plaintiffs that "poverty concentration and racial isolation have affected the education provided to minority students in the RCSD, as in most American, and certainly New York State cities, to be inferior to that in surrounding suburban districts." Beyond this general platitude, though, he turned skeptical. He dismissed several of the plaintiffs' claims, in large part because the argument focused strictly on outcomes without tying them to a lack of "minimally acceptable educational services and facilities." The only claims Ark left standing were for civil rights violations at the state and federal level, though here as well he was skeptical. "When compared to the other school districts in Monroe County, the RCSD is separate but apparently not equal," Ark wrote. "But the courts realize they are not competent to resolve these most difficult education issues . . . [through a] court mandated solution." The state appellate division upheld Ark's ruling in December 2001 and dismissed the remaining claims as well. The last chance lay with the state court of appeals, which agreed to hear the case and scheduled a hearing for May 8, 2003.[60]

As it happened, the court of appeals heard *Paynter* the same day as *CFE*, the first in the morning session and the second in the afternoon. A single day's deliberation would set the direction of New York education policy for a generation. If *Paynter* was allowed to continue, the injurious effect of segregation might finally get a hearing at the highest level. If the *CFE* plaintiffs prevailed, the legislature would need to develop an entirely new funding policy that better accounted for student need. If both were rejected, the quest for judicial reform in New York would be dealt a mortal blow.

The decisions in both cases were released on June 26, 2003. The dismissal of *Paynter* was upheld by a 4–1 ruling. Chief Judge Judith Kaye, in the majority opinion, rejected the idea that "an Education Article claim by students against the State may consist of an abundance of terrible educational outcomes . . . with no assertion that these results are caused by any deficiency in teaching, facilities or instrumentalities of learning, or any lack of funding." This, she agreed with the lower courts, contradicted the key finding of *Levittown*, at the least.

She continued:

> The only deficient input plaintiffs allege is the composition of the student body of RCSD schools. Plaintiffs say that no matter how well the State funds their schools, if plaintiffs and their classmates fail, it is the State's responsibility to change the school population until the results improve. . . .
>
> Holding the State responsible for the demographic composition of every school district, moreover, would mean either making it responsible for where people choose to live, or holding that it must periodically redraw school district lines, negating the preferences of the residents.[61]

The *CFE* lawsuit alleging an unfair state finance system, meanwhile, won on appeal, a momentous holding that led to several more years of litigation and negotiation over how a more equitable system could be designed—and how much money the state should pour into it. A final settlement was reached in 2007 but was abandoned almost immediately because of the financial crisis of 2008. Even after the state economy recovered, Governor Andrew Cuomo declined to return to the high-priced *CFE* formula, arguing that it was not binding on the state. This bickering over the proper funding level consumed a great deal of legislative energy throughout the 2010s. From a broader perspective, though, the reduction of the argument to figures in the budget and nothing more represented a final retreat from the idea that local school districts or the state of New York—or anyone at all—bore some responsibility to address racial and socioeconomic segregation in schools.[62]

The sole dissenting opinion in *Paynter* came from George Bundy Smith, the only Black judge on the court of appeals. While enrolled in law school at Yale, Smith had volunteered as a Freedom Rider in Alabama for the Congress on Racial Equality, studying for his exams while riding on the bus. After graduation he worked for the NAACP Legal Defense and Education Fund, helping draft the appellate briefs leading to James Meredith's admission into the University of Mississippi. He also clerked for Jawn Sandifer, who in 1962 had supervised the *Aikens* desegregation lawsuit in Rochester.[63]

The bulk of Smith's lengthy *Paynter* dissent was a history lesson on the development of the education article in the New York state constitution. The clause, drafted in 1894, consists of a single unadorned sentence: "The legislature shall provide for the maintenance and support of a system of free common schools, wherein all the children of this state may be educated." Smith cited the report of the Constitutional Convention at length to show that, "while the Education Article was enacted to ensure that all the children in the State would have access to a sound education, its enactment was motivated by the plight of poor children." He contrasted the framers' emphasis on a "permanent, broad and firm" educational system with the *Paynter* plaintiffs' allegations of "shockingly inadequate education."

Smith argued that the plaintiffs should be allowed to proceed to trial to make their case that a "racially and socially separate education" violated the education article. "The Constitution does not place the responsibility of providing a sound education on local school districts, or towns, or cities," he wrote. "It places that responsibility squarely on the State." Smith dismissed the defendants' paean to local control as a "red herring" meant to divert attention from the state's overriding obligations. "Plaintiffs are not arguing for the elimination of local school boards," he wrote. "They argue that the State should not draw district lines in a manner that encircles poor and minority students, and sets them up for failure."[64]

Rhetoric aside, Smith's dissent meant little. "This case is done," Hetherington told reporters. For the families who signed up as plaintiffs, the fight was mostly forgotten. Amber Paynter said that her mother remained bitter about the lawsuit nearly twenty years after it concluded. "I think she was so upset nothing ever came of it, she won't really talk about it," Paynter said in 2020. "The lawyers basically courted poor Black moms . . . [and] I think a lot of the moms were under the assumption that this was a huge deal and it was going to affect their lives, like, right now. And I don't think that was the reality."[65]

It is noteworthy that the allegations in *Paynter* are based primarily on socioeconomic status rather than race. This was done strategically, Jonathan Feldman said, because "the Supreme Court had made race unviable in terms of federal claims." He was referring to a trio of school desegregation cases in the early 1990s where the court showed skepticism of race-based claims. Those decisions would be followed in even more dramatic fashion by another ruling in 2007 that sealed the Supreme Court's conservative turn since *Milliken v. Bradley*.[66]

Scores of cities across the United States were placed under court supervision for school desegregation during the 1960s and 1970s. Even when the political winds shifted after *Milliken*, these orders remained in effect, so that judges occasionally were required to determine whether segregation had yet been eliminated "root and branch," according to the standard set by *Green v. New Kent County* in 1968. Disputes regarding such determinations in Oklahoma, Georgia, and Missouri school districts reached the Supreme Court from 1991 to 1995. In these three cases the court jettisoned the "root and branch" standard and dramatically lowered the bar for districts seeking release from judicial supervision. The desegregation orders, the court wrote in *Oklahoma City v. Dowell*, were "not intended to operate in perpetuity, federal supervision of local school systems always having been intended as a temporary measure to remedy past discrimination."[67]

These rulings had an immediate impact in cities across the country that earlier had been subject to mandated desegregation orders, including Buffalo. Parents and activists there sued for desegregation in 1972, alleging both de facto and de jure segregation. Unlike in Rochester, the lawsuit, called *Arthur v. Nyquist*, succeeded. The state district court agreed that the current system had been "purposely segregated" and ordered the creation of a desegregation plan. That plan closed low-performing, mostly Black schools and replaced them with attractive federally funded magnet programs. Attendance patterns were redrawn and busing in many cases was made mandatory, eventually affecting about thirty thousand students. Black student achievement improved by some measures and Buffalo was hailed as a national model; one of the parent leaders of the group South Buffalo Anti-busers ended up sending her son to a magnet school across the city. Even in this best-case scenario, however, the victory was not complete. There were five times as many applicants to magnet schools as there were open slots, and teachers and families in the remaining traditional neighborhood schools complained of a short shrift.[68]

Buffalo's success had two crucial supports. First, it had the most per-pupil federal magnet school support of any district in the country. Second, the court order provided political cover and a convenient excuse for actions like closing familiar neighborhood schools. "This way, they pointed to the judge and said, 'He's a tyrant; he's making us do it,'" the supervising judge, John Curtin, said. Neither of these columns proved enduring. By 1991 Buffalo was receiving no federal magnet funding whatsoever. Then, following the trio of Supreme Court actions, the supervising judge declared in 1996 that Buffalo had achieved "unitary status," even though a third of schools remained out of compliance with demographic targets. Many magnet schools closed or lost appealing features, and applications to magnet schools decreased by one-third over four years. White flight changed from a trickle to a gusher. "Today, the progress made during the 20 years of the *Arthur v. Nyquist* desegregation order has largely been undone," a later analyst wrote.[69]

The Supreme Court decisions from 1991 to 1995 were, as one commentator put it, "a harbinger of an era of increased judicial indifference to ensuring desegregation." The impression was confirmed in 2007, when the court heard complaints from parents in the public schools of Seattle and Louisville. In both cities, parents (white parents in Seattle, Black parents in Louisville) alleged that their children had faced racial discrimination after being denied their first choice under the existing race-conscious placement policies. The defendants responded by asserting a legitimate governmental interest in maintaining racial diversity in schools.[70]

The cases were joined and came to be known as *Parents Involved in Community Schools v. Seattle School District No. 1*. Writing for a split majority, Chief Justice John Roberts came down definitively on the side of the protesting parents. Allowing race-conscious policies like those in Seattle and Louisville, he wrote, would guarantee that "race will always be relevant in American life" and "would support indefinite use of racial classifications." Except in specific remedial case, nearly any reference to race was verboten. "The way to stop discrimination on the basis of race is to stop discriminating on the basis of race," Roberts wrote in an oft-cited phrase. Justice Stephen Breyer's dissent, meanwhile, lamented that *Brown* had been reduced to mere "fine words on paper." Echoing Thurgood Marshall's famous dissent in *Milliken*, Breyer warned that *Parents Involved* in time would be "a decision that the Court and the Nation will come to regret."[71]

The years after the publication of "A Nation at Risk" in 1983 are known as the "excellence in education" era. They just as easily could be called the age of acronyms. Propelled by the demand for measurement and efficiency and constantly roiled by reform, the education field has never been more difficult to decipher. NCLB begat RTTP begat ESSA. Schools are measured on AYP via the DTSDE; teachers must hit SLOs for their APPR. New York schools classified as CSI or TSI must submit SCEP and SIG plans, part of a broader DCIP.[72]

Much of this muddle is driven by US Department of Education guidelines that state education agencies and, in turn, school districts, must follow to ensure federal funding. The burden falls most heavily on poor urban school districts like Rochester, where compliance with various oversight measures, as well as grant requirements, requires the full-time attention of several administrators who otherwise could be working on teaching and learning. "All these state requirements for urban districts, the SIG plans, the SIF plans, the SCEP plans, the quarterly reports . . . I mean, we have a whole office that just works with that stuff," interim RCSD superintendent Linda Cimusz said in 2016. "The burden of time that comes with all that, versus being able to work with principals and focus on schools—that really has a large impact."[73] An even greater escalation involves the appointment of an outside expert as a distinguished educator or monitor (Rochester has had both). These appointments are grounded in the unshakable logic of the school reform era: problems in educational achievement are a matter of pedagogy, organization, and systems management. The demographics of the student body may dictate how those technocratic knobs are tuned but are never considered remotely determinative.

For a time during the 1980s, Peter McWalters was as closely identified with this logic as any school superintendent in the country. He was one of many devotees of "A Nation at Risk," which held, in McWalters' words, that "basically the system is broken and we're sliding into mediocrity." Now, at the other end of his career, McWalters has reconsidered the premise. "After twenty-five years of test-based, standards-based accountability, tightening the screws, it hasn't been proven to be very successful," he said in 2020. Instead, he said, a "good school" is easily identified in the same way as always: mostly white, middle-class, English-speaking children, few of them with disabilities. "It absolutely is that simple," McWalters said. "It took some of us a while to realize that that simple image [in "A Nation at Risk"] has become a false promise of fixing it. It assumed things ever worked before that, but they didn't. The system was never set up to serve all kids."[74]

# Conclusion

## Three Steps toward Change

Terry Dade was young, handsome, and relentlessly upbeat. He charmed the Rochester school board in his 2019 interview for the superintendency by referring to the city as "our family" and its students as "our babies." Just three months after he was hired, however, the scope of his task changed dramatically. A routine year-end audit uncovered serious irregularities in the district's finances. It eventually emerged that the district, under the leadership of the previous superintendent, Barbara Deane-Williams, had completely exhausted its fund balance and then overspent its 2018–19 and 2019–20 budgets by about $60 million. The sum staggered the community and triggered a review by the state comptroller as well as the appointment of an outside monitor. The reckoning came in the winter and spring of 2020, when Dade was left to slash away at district spending. The district cut scores of employees in the middle of the year then hundreds more in the 2020–21 budget. Millions of dollars were taken from a special education program that had just come back from the brink of a major federal lawsuit. Social workers were reduced by more than a quarter. A last-minute emergency loan from the state legislature prevented even greater losses before the end of the 2019–20 school year. Nearly one hundred people signed up to protest at the first public budget hearing; only the COVID-19 pandemic, which forced the school board to hold meetings online, spared

Dade the spectacle of a packed and hostile room. "Someone's going to hell," one former board member said.[1]

What the public did not know was that Dade, less than a year into his three-year contract, had already found an exit door. The same week as the budget hearing, Dade interviewed for the superintendent's job in the Cornwall Central School District, a small, wealthy district on the Hudson River in Orange County, New York. Its total annual budget of $75 million was smaller than the revenue shortfall RCSD faced for 2020–21. Cornwall announced that it had hired Dade in the middle of a Rochester school board meeting before he had told anyone in Rochester, and the news spread like wildfire on social media before board members could react. "Unfortunately, I have not been able to focus on what I was brought here to do," Dade wrote later that evening in an open resignation letter. "While I will be transitioning to another school district in New York, my heart will forever be a part of the RCSD family." To reporters in Cornwall, meanwhile, Dade said he was excited about moving there "because it's the kind of district where he'd feel comfortable with his children . . . attending school."[2]

In Rochester and cities across the country, this is the reality of urban education almost a quarter of the way through the twenty-first century. Once-proud school districts stand scandalized and scorned, hemorrhaging students and money, lurching from consultant report to consultant report and on and off state sanction lists. Promising early results are never mentioned again after the pilot program loses funding. The refreshing new approach of one administration is the regrettable error of the next. Families with means find alternatives elsewhere for their children or cluster in a few select programs, whereas the children who need the most care—those with disabilities, or a lack of English proficiency, or no stable place to live—receive the least. Exhaustively compiled and disaggregated academic data show that wealthy and white children mostly do well, whereas poor and nonwhite children mostly do not.

Urban school districts find themselves in this pathetic position only at the end of generations of complacency and half-hearted calls for reform. White leaders in northern cities, content to juxtapose themselves against Birmingham and Little Rock, did not acknowledge the problem of racial segregation until it had reached a crisis level. Their initial attempts to address the issue were mostly feeble, whereas opposition, often explicitly racist, grew, finally bursting out politically in the late 1960s. It was at this fateful juncture that Rochester, for the one time in its history, faced the question of segregation squarely. Voters revolted and district leaders backed down in the face of shouted protests, ignoring other parents who urged them to carry on. Since then, with few exceptions, school and political leaders in Rochester and Monroe County have hardly dared address the problem, even as the evidence of harm to nonwhite and white children alike has become obvious.

All of this is Rochester's educational inheritance—but not the whole of it. Recall the first chapter of this book; Rochester did desegregate its schools once. Frederick Douglass is more than a totem for the city. He helped lead Black children, including his own, into white Rochester schools from which they previously had been barred. To be sure, that was a very different time. Desegregation involved a hundred or so Black children in a student body of thousands, for one thing. Still, the way it happened then is instructive for the present. Parents and strong community leaders agitated on behalf of Black children, persisting for decades despite setbacks and periods of apparent stagnation. School leaders eventually succumbed to economic pressure rather than moral pressure. Formal desegregation in the nineteenth century proved elusive for decades, from the founding of the first village schoolhouse in 1812 to the city's adolescence 38 years later, and the situation for Black children was far from perfect once it was achieved. Still, Rochester was the first city in New York, and one of the first anywhere, to desegregate its schools. Now, 150 years later, Rochester again has the opportunity to lead.

The thesis of this book is that Rochester, like most places in the United States, has always quailed when called to confront the racial and socioeconomic segregation that underlies and perpetuates its most pressing problems, education first among them; and, further, that no lasting solution to these problems is possible until segregation is addressed.

Nothing can happen overnight. There are, however, immediate steps to be taken that go beyond idle wishing. Three of them are listed below. The first would give the community a solid foundation to consider, seriously and with eyes open, the creation of a comprehensive, undivided, racially diverse educational system. The second would be an immediate and significant step toward racial equity for local school districts as currently constituted. The third would involve no immediate structural change or student transfers but would help ensure that children and teachers in the Rochester area recognize the racist past that shaped the unequal present in the schools where they study and work—an absolutely necessary precondition for change no matter when it occurs.

1. **A comprehensive report on potential major metropolitan reforms in education and other areas, including the viability of a unified countywide school system.**

The drafting of a report is not an exciting first step, but it must be done. Breaking school district lines in the name of efficiency and equality has been discussed since the 1920s, but only at a conceptual level. Proponents have never had good answers to the most basic questions: Who would pay for it? What legislation would be required? How would children be assigned to schools, and how long would they ride on the bus? In the absence of facts, speculation and fear have filled the void. The very word "metropolitan" has become a bugaboo.

A report addressing these questions would have much ground to cover. It could encompass the idea of moving revenues, rather than students, across district lines. It could revisit the concept of a federation of school districts as laid out in 1971 as part of RCSD's ineffectual 15-Point Plan. It must, too, include at last a fully fleshed-out vision of what true desegregation might look like in Monroe County as well as possible legal means to achieve it. This vision would require consideration of an overarching governing body; a mechanism for local, state, and federal funding; a framework for state legislation, including an analysis of legal obstacles; and the cost of action as well as inaction. It should have clear roles and immediate action steps for all involved parties, including school districts and the state legislature, should they choose to act. A mechanism for robust public participation would be vital, with a privileged position for the nonwhite families who have been disadvantaged for generations. This report could be completed within eighteen months. Informing and mobilizing residents, as well as passing legislation and weathering potential judicial challenges, would take longer, of course. But no work can begin until solid information is available.

Crucially, the report would be an opportunity to examine other potential areas for metropolitan collaboration as well. Inequities in housing, transportation, jobs, and public infrastructure, among other things, are equally stark and could be addressed best in concert. Researchers Jennifer Jellison Holme and Kara Finnigan laid out the case for a "regional equity framework," in their words, in their book *Striving in Common*: "Countering the powerful forces that perpetuate the geography of inequality in education and in other domains (such as housing and economic development) requires addressing the web of forces—economic, political, and personal—that weave together to sustain these inequities. The causes and effects of inequality are regional in nature, and they require a regional solution that is specifically focused on equity across multiple policy domains."[3] The framework that Holme and Finnigan have in mind is based on a model from Omaha, Nebraska, called the Learning Community. It includes some elements with clear applicability to Rochester, including more robust "mobility practices," such as greater accessibility in Urban-Suburban, as well as a regional governing body. It also calls for pooling education funding at the county level to enable fairer distribution. It is not exactly a metropolitan school district, but rather a form of "federated regionalism" with some similarities to the "voluntary cooperative federation of school districts" floated in 1971. Countywide solutions hold great promise in education, housing, and other areas, both in combating the historical effects of racism and in general municipal efficiency. Numerous guideposts already exist, including effective collaborative measures in water supply and emergency response systems. It is far past time for the same concept to be extended where it is needed most. [4]

2. **Written policies for greater equity in enrollment and participation for suburban districts in Urban-Suburban.**

Successfully developing an action plan from the report outlined in the first recommendation would take several years in the best case. Fortunately, Monroe County already has a tool in hand to create change immediately. It is written into state law and has been in place for more than fifty years. It has permanent staff and widespread public support, at least in its current incarnation. This is Urban-Suburban, and the flexibility that suburban districts long have wielded to maintain exclusivity can be used to make it more equitable, immediately.

Each participating school district has complete freedom in how it selects its students from among the hundreds of applicants each year. These policies are typically not written down; instead, autonomy is given to building administrators in choosing students for their schools. There is no reason, however, that a district's selection criteria could not be prescribed in advance by the board of education. Indeed, putting these criteria in writing would provide needed transparency and help guide a conversation about education equity for Rochester children.

One such rule should be that students are chosen at random from the entire pool of applicants, without regard for academic performance, disciplinary history, family structure, special education status, or English-language proficiency. Younger siblings of Urban-Suburban students should get automatic placement in the same district.

Students should not be exited from their suburban district for any reason other than the uncoerced desire of their parents. If children from Rochester do poorly in class, or fight at school, or require costly special services, they should receive all the support that district has to offer until they graduate or age out, just as they would if they lived in the district.

Data on Urban-Suburban students, academic and otherwise, should be disaggregated and monitored in order to flag disparities early. This does not mean that children from the city must wear a badge in the hallways. Rather, districts should abandon their color-blind philosophy and find ways to support students according to their circumstances. By the same logic, teachers, counselors, and school administrators should proactively identify and offer support to Urban-Suburban students as needed.

The basic transportation provided by the Rochester City School District should be supplemented at the suburban district's expense to ensure that Urban-Suburban students are able to partake fully in all extracurricular and social opportunities at school. This would mean extra late buses for students who stay after school for any reason. More generally, consideration would be given to how students in the city—and their parents—could attend events outside school hours (or, for parents, during school hours), including performances and games, parent-teacher conferences, and school board meetings. The districts should pledge—surely it is not asking too much—that Urban-Suburban students will not spend many hours every week sitting in the bus loop, weary from a long day of school and waiting to go home.

The Rochester school board, for its part, could pass a resolution ending its participation in the program if the above conditions are not met. It could go further and allow parents to check a box to enter the Urban-Suburban lottery on the standard kindergarten intake form. This would vastly diversify the pool of students applying for the program. As of early 2021, the program is not advertised at all, and awareness of it is only shared through word of mouth, privileging well-connected and resourceful city children over their less fortunate (or non-English-speaking) peers and further skewing the applicant pool.

Suburban districts could also design their enrollment policies in a way that creates a mutually beneficial relationship with the city rather than an extractive one. Districts in western Monroe County could select only students from zip codes on the city's west side, and similarly to the south and east. This could lead to investment from the suburban community in a particular section of the city. Examples might include student and teacher learning exchanges or neighborhood service projects. This would save money on transportation, because city students would not be crossing the county. In time, it could serve as the nucleus—or at least a data point—for more significant metropolitan cooperation.

These changes likely would have a negative impact on Urban-Suburban's current sterling academic and social reputation. This reputation, though, is ill gotten. It is based on the performance of a few students chosen against formidable odds to participate—chosen, in part, for their perceived ability to overcome stiff program-specific challenges, including a punishing daily commute and a lack of dedicated social and academic supports in their new district. If these challenges become insurmountable—or if students struggle for too long to get good grades or turn out to have a significant disability—then they are ejected from their purported home school, leaving the program's record untarnished. These hidden detriments of the program accrue exclusively to the city school district. It loses its brightest students and instead ends up with an even heavier concentration of those whom the suburban districts reject. A fairer program design would set Urban-Suburban on a path toward the lofty ideal it was designed to achieve.

**3. Intensive antiracism education for children and adults in all Rochester-area school districts.**

Much of the skepticism of metropolitan school reform in the Black community stems from the belief, borne out repeatedly over time, that white families do not want a substantial number of Black children sharing their own children's classrooms. Similarly, many Black people assume that their children would be asked to assimilate into a predominantly white environment rather than the other way around. "To be immersed in and judged by a system that fails to recognize the history, culture and needs of black students may, indeed, be worse than being excluded," Derrick Bell wrote.[5]

It is true that physical desegregation is only the necessary first step toward true social integration. Equally important is a widespread understanding of the value of the proposition. For any large-scale school integration measure to succeed in the Rochester area, children, parents, and educators everywhere, but especially in mostly white, suburban districts, must be educated. Children must learn explicitly about the harm that racism has caused and continues to cause, both around the world and in their own communities. They must learn that segregation is not naturally occurring but was willfully imposed and today is willfully maintained. They must learn that it harms them—all of them.

As James Baldwin wrote:

> White children, in the main, and whether they are rich or poor, grow up with a grasp of reality so feeble that they can very accurately be described as deluded—about themselves and the world they live in. . . . The reason for this, at bottom, is that the doctrine of white supremacy, which still controls most white people, is itself a stupendous

> delusion: but to be born black in America is an immediate, a mortal challenge. People who cling to their delusions find it difficult, if not impossible, to learn anything worth learning: a people under the necessity of creating themselves must examine everything, and soak up learning the way the roots of a tree soak up water.[6]

Of the three recommendations given here, this is the simplest and least expensive to implement. In fact, districts have already begun the work. Since at least 2017 the majority of Monroe County school districts have recognized the need for antiracist action in every facet of their operations, including the classroom. They made a collective pledge in 2020, after the killing of George Floyd in Minneapolis, to "take responsibility for educating ourselves and [be] intentional in rebuilding our educational system which has not served underrepresented student populations well."[7] Two separate teams of educators—one jointly sponsored by all Monroe County districts, another at the Pathstone Foundation, led by Rush-Henrietta teacher Shane Wiegand—have begun creating curricula that not only address racism frankly but also show its local manifestation in housing and education, among other things. Some districts are further along in these varied efforts than others, and none are close to claiming victory. Significantly, no school leaders in Rochester or its suburbs have seriously broached the question of equity across district boundaries; instead, the focus has been on better accommodating the children of color within each district, however few they may be.

Such antiracist efforts have much ground to cover and many deeply ingrained assumptions to correct. Perhaps the most damaging assumption, and the most far-reaching, is that good schools are those with mostly white students, to which Black students may be admitted as a special dispensation. This was the attitude, for instance, when RCSD launched its first iteration of open enrollment in 1963. Superintendent Herman Goldberg addressed Black parents directly in a letter: "We would like to know if you want your child to have a chance to attend a school where there are more white children."[8] It was not the company of white children, of course, that Black parents wanted for their own children. Rather it was the advantages that seemed to follow those children naturally: more money, higher expectations, greener ballfields, greater future prospects.

It is important to note that this work—not just revising curricula and discipline policies, not just hiring more nonwhite teachers, but fundamentally changing the way children and adults understand the world—is essential whether metropolitan desegregation happens or not. This means striving in our own time and place to bend the arc of the moral universe toward justice.

It means fulfilling our promise to leave a more equitable world for our children. For Rochester and for the United States, it means breaking out of the racial snares that for so long have held us back.

As a graduate of Wilson Magnet High School and the University of Rochester, as a banker, as a school board member, and as a city councilman, Malik Evans recognizes the value of racial and socioeconomic integration.* He supports the idea of metropolitan education reform and has written about the need for targeted desegregation measures before schools in Greater Rochester can serve students to their full potential. He is a believer, and so it is disheartening to hear his brusque response before the question is even fully posed to him of whether such a vision might come to pass.[9]

"Never going to happen."

The worst of Rochester's past and present is embedded in that short phrase. It encapsulates despair in the face of injustice and ingrained pessimism against even the suggestion of planned progress. Evans may be right; he certainly is not alone in his assessment. If so, the prognosis for the community and the nation is poor.

But let us look to the children. Beginning in 2016, students from high schools throughout the Rochester region began gathering twice a year to discuss racism and bias in their schools through an initiative called Roc 2 Change. Within a few years these summits were drawing more than five hundred students from nearly every high school in the area. Their enthusiasm is sustained as well through multicultural and antiracist groups that have appeared at many schools, where students have pushed for policies to better address discipline and academic opportunity but also to look more holistically at racism in their own communities. "People telling their stories made me feel it's OK to talk about racism and my experiences and how to make school more equal," one Black Penfield High School student said after a 2018 gathering. Even in the whitest suburbs, these opinions and calls for action are rapidly gaining credence and followers. Protests for racial justice in 2020, after the deaths of George Floyd in Minneapolis and Daniel Prude in Rochester, drew hundreds of Rochester-area teenagers ready to fight for change.[10]

---

*Evans won the Democratic primary election for mayor of Rochester in June 2021, making him the likely mayor beginning in January 2022.

Such efforts can be frustratingly transient. A commitment that begins with one charismatic leader or influential report fades imperceptibly, only to be reborn five, ten, or fifty years later. Roc 2 Change, for instance, bears a close resemblance to the Students Union for Integrated Education (SUIE), founded in 1968. SUIE boasted more than a hundred student members from across Monroe County who met twice a month "to discuss intercultural relations and urban-suburban education." It saw some victories—it persuaded the Brighton school board to permit a student exchange and live-in with teenagers from Madison High School in Rochester, for instance—but otherwise struggled to gain footing, then folded as its leaders graduated. One of its last, unsuccessful pushes was in support of the Woods plan for educational parks spanning district lines.[11]

"If my father had taken a few steps in this direction, things would have been a little easier for me," Glenn Edwards, a Black SUIE student leader, said in 1968. "But if I shrink before the immenseness of the problem now, my children will find it even harder."[12] Edwards and his peers did not shrink. Fifty years later, though, the immensity of the problem remains daunting. The renewed and sustained student activism apparent in Roc 2 Change is a positive development, but youthful hope has faded before. Justice in education will require more than a series of gatherings, more than one generation's burst of energy, and more than promises or pledges.

Rather, places like Rochester—their educators, their parents, their children—must acknowledge the past and tear down the walls that were built to divide them. They must forge and uphold new physical and conceptual bounds to their communities. They must consider anew their commitment to educating all children, steadfast in the face of opposition and with full faith in the worth of the investment.

# Acknowledgments

I am deeply grateful to everyone who spoke with me for this book. Their accounts of their experiences as students, educators, parents, and community leaders were vital to my understanding of the last fifty years. Several sat for more than one interview, pointed me toward other sources, or provided documents. My sincere thanks to Anne Micheaux Akwari, Arkee Allen, David Anderson, Dave Balter, Ruth Balter, Jeanette Banker, James Beard, John Bliss, Carlton Brown, Luis Burgos, William Cala, Velverly Caldwell, Terry Carbone, Marlene Caroselli, Musette Castle, Ed Cavalier, Yalawn Christian, Frank Ciaccia, Walter Cooper, Jeff Crane, Archie Curry, Mark Allan Davis, Patricia DeCaro, Tate DeCaro, Susan deFay, Bob Duffy, Malik Evans, Mark Faegre, Jonathan Feldman, Anna Ferro, Deborah Gitomer, Mary Halpin, Bryan Hetherington, Kirk Holmes, Joan Coles Howard, Jasper Huffman, Kennedy Jackson, Bill Johnson, Wayne Johnson, Suzanne Johnston, Nellie King, Roy Lane, Jessica Lewis, Charles Marshall, Sereena Martin, Peter McWalters, Dana Miller, Joe Morelle, Nicole Morris, Idonia Owens, Nydia Padilla-Rodriguez, Amber Paynter, Dorothy Pecoraro, Jonathan Perkins, Don Pryor, Andrew Ray, Vera Richardson and her niece, Vera Richardson, Faust Rossi, Bob Sagan, Djinga St. Louis, Yvette Singletary, Lynette Sparks, Danny Speer, Bob Stevenson, Adam Urbanski, Thomas Warfield, Lovely Warren, Gloria Winston Al-Sarag, Lillie Winston, John Woods, and Alice Young.

There is hardly a page in this book that does not contain at least one endnote pointing to a newspaper article. In Rochester as elsewhere, the unheralded daily work of journalists has been crucial in preserving local history. I thank and appreciate the many reporters, editors, photographers, and news assistants at the *Democrat and Chronicle*, the *Times-Union*, and other daily and weekly newspapers whose work is referenced in this book. Particular recognition is due to Frederick Douglass's *North Star*, Howard Coles's *Voice*, and James and Carolyn Blount's *about . . . time* magazine for preserving news about Rochester's Black community that white-owned newspapers failed to capture.

I include my current colleagues at the *Democrat and Chronicle* in my gratitude and appreciation. They have been a source of support and encouragement in writing this book and an inspiration as we strive to fulfill our journalistic mission in trying times. Matthew Leonard was an early and trusted advocate. Executive Editor Michael Kilian has been a tireless champion of journalism that reveals, explains, and combats structural racism in Rochester, past and present. He granted me leave to work on this book and has encouraged me in myriad ways, including by publishing an early version of chapter 2 in the February 9, 2020, edition of the newspaper.

The Rochester city historian, Christine Ridarsky, and her staff of Jay Osborne, Emily Morry, Brandon Fess, Dan Cody, and Gabe Pellegrino cumulatively walked many miles fetching stacks of books and clip folders for me. They offered, only half joking, to arrange a private office and sleeping quarters for me in the Local History and Genealogy Division reading room of the Rochester Public Library; I declined, but regardless am deeply thankful for their help and hospitality over several years. A version of chapter 1 appeared in the Rochester Public Library's journal: "Racial Segregation in Rochester Schools: 1818–1856," *Rochester History* 78, no. 2 (January 2020).

Thank you to Jessica Lacher-Feldman, Melinda Wallington, and Autumn Haag, among others, for their repeated assistance at the University of Rochester Rare Books and Special Collections division at Rush Rhees Library, and to Stephanie Ball at the Rochester Museum and Science Center. Thanks as well to the staff who helped me at other institutions: the Rochester Municipal Archives; the Rose Archives at SUNY Brockport; the Project UNIQUE Papers at Nazareth College; the Big Springs Historical Society in Caledonia, New York; the New York State Archives in Albany; the Jerome and Ruth Balter Papers at Swarthmore College in Swarthmore, PA; and the Library of Congress in Washington, DC.

Joan Coles Howard, Conor Dwyer Reynolds, Mitch Gruber, Emily Morry, Idonia Owens, Christine Ridarsky, Chris Widmaier, and Shane Wiegand all read portions of the book and offered valuable feedback; so, too, did the anonymous but appreciated peer reviewers who volunteered their time for Cornell University Press. Alana Kornaker cheerfully and skillfully drew the East High School enrollment boundary maps in chapter 3. Special thanks to Banke Awopetu for her feedback as well as her constant support and encouragement through the writing process.

At Cornell University Press, Michael McGandy had a ready answer for every question. His keen edits made for a more concise and more powerful book. Thanks as well to Mary Kate Murphy and others at the press.

My parents, Dave and Ginny Murphy, helped me in the writing of this book as they have throughout my life: generously, naturally, and invaluably.

To Kat, my wife, who made this book happen in a thousand ways: thank you, and I love you.

The book is dedicated to my children, Millie and Woody, in the faith that they will be both the builders and beneficiaries of a more just future.

# Notes

Frequently cited sources have been identified by the following abbreviations:

| | |
|---|---|
| *DC* | *Democrat and Chronicle* (Rochester, NY) |
| LOC | Library of Congress (Washington, DC) |
| NYSA | New York State Archives (Albany, NY) |
| PW | Phillis Wheatley Public Library Oral History Collection (Rochester, NY), available at http://www.rochestervoices.org/collections/african-american-oral-histories/ |
| RBSCP | Department of Rare Books, Special Collections and Preservation, University of Rochester |
| RMSC | Rochester Museum and Science Center |
| RPL | Rochester Public Library |
| *T-U* | *Times-Union* (Rochester, NY) |

## Preface

1. James Baldwin, "Notes of a Native Son," in *Baldwin: Collected Essays,* ed. Toni Morrison (New York: Library of America, [1964] 1998), 713.

## Introduction

1. *DC*, "RCSD Will Consider Renaming," May 14, 2018; author interview with Djinga St. Louis, Aug. 17, 2018.

2. *DC*, "$1.2M Effort Collapses [. . .]," Oct. 28, 2018.

3. *DC*, "City Opens 5 New Schools," Sept. 2, 1968; "Douglass Prepares to Close," May 8, 2007; "Troubled RCSD Program [. . .]," Sept. 22, 2017.

4. *North Star*, "Editorial Correspondence," April 7, 1848.

5. *North Star*, "Proscription and Oppression towards Colored Children in Rochester," Nov. 2, 1849; "Zion Church School," Nov. 9, 1849.

6. *North Star*, "Colored Schools," Aug. 17, 1849.

7. *People ex rel. King v. Gallagher* 93 NY 438, 458–66 (1883).

8. *People ex rel. King v. Gallagher*, 462.

9. *North Star*, "Proposition," Aug. 10, 1849; *DC*, "Franklin Rowdies [. . .]," Oct. 2, 1968; untitled FIGHT press release, March 19, 1969, box 4B, Franklin Florence Papers, RBSCP. The study on school violence, known as the Meagher report, is available in box X0301, Rochester Municipal Archives, Rochester, NY.

10. *T-U*, "School 30 Parents to Fight [. . .]," Nov. 22, 1963; author's notes, Spencerport Board of Education meeting, Dec. 9, 2014.

11. *DC*, "City Students Drive Revenue for Suburban Schools," June 20, 2019; New York State Temporary Commission on the Condition of the Colored Urban Population, *Second Report* (Albany, NY, February 1939), 114–15.

12. *New York Times*, "It Was Never about Busing," July 12, 2019.

13. *Anti-Masonic Enquirer*, "New York Legislature," Jan. 31, 1832; *T-U*, "Inner-City Parents Say 'No' to School Plan," Feb. 4, 1971.

14. *DC*, "The Long Way Home," Feb. 25, 1995; "Mayor's Grandfather McClary Dies," Jan. 3, 2014; author interview with Lovely Warren, Oct. 21, 2019.

15. Author interview with Lovely Warren, Oct. 21, 2019; *DC*, "Education Remains Key Issue in Battle," Sept. 7, 2017.

16. Author interview with Lovely Warren, Oct. 21, 2019.

17. Author interview with Lovely Warren, Oct. 21, 2019.

18. Derrick Bell, *Silent Covenants*: Brown v. Board of Ed. *and the Unfulfilled Hopes for Racial Reform* (New York: Oxford University Press, 2004), 113, 136.

19. Bell, *Silent Covenants*, 21–27.

20. Bell, *Silent Covenants*, 24–25.

21. "Brief of 553 Social Scientists as *Amici Curiae* in Support of Respondents," submitted in *Parents Involved in Community Schools v. Seattle School District No. 1*, 551 US 701 (2007).

22. sean f. reardon et al., "Is Separate Still Unequal? New Evidence on School Segregation and Racial Academic Achievement Gaps," working paper no. 19-06 (Stanford, CA: Stanford University Center for Education Policy Analysis, 2019).

23. Rucker Johnson, *Children of the Dream: Why School Integration Works*, with Alexander Nazaryan (New York: Basic Books, 2019), 56–65.

24. Johnson, *Children of the Dream*, 59; Gary Orfield, John Kucsera, and Genevieve Siegel-Hawley, "*E Pluribus* . . . Separation: Deepening Double Segregation for More Students" (Los Angeles: Civil Rights Project/Proyecto Derechos Civiles, September 2012); Amy Stuart Wells and Robert L. Crain, "Perpetuation Theory and the Long-Term Effects of School Desegregation," *Review of Educational Research* 64, no. 4 (Winter 1994): 531–55; Robert D. Putnam, *Our Kids: The American Dream in Crisis* (New York: Simon and Schuster, 2015), 207–16.

25. Author interview with Frank Ciaccia, June 28, 2018.

26. Rochester City School District, "An Interim Report on a Fifteen Point Plan to Reduce Racial Isolation and Provide Quality Integrated Education" (June 21, 1968), held at Local History and Genealogy Division, RPL; *Hearings before the Select Committee on Equal Educational Opportunity of the United States Senate* (Washington, DC, Oct. 7, 1971), 9039.

27. Author interview with Lovely Warren, Oct. 21, 2019; author interview with James Beard, May 31, 2019; *T-U*, "KKK Tactics Dangerous," June 24, 1971; Alberta Cason press statement, Feb. 10, 1969, folder 4B:14, Franklin Florence Papers, RBSCP.

28. *DC*, "Transfer Response Swamps Schools," Dec. 20, 1963.

29. *Democrat and Chronicle*/Rochester Area Community Foundation/Siena College Research Institute poll, Dec. 18, 2018, to Jan. 2, 2019. Seven hundred respondents, margin of error +/– 4.8 percent, available at https://www.documentcloud.org/documents/20986622-rochester-siena-poll-monroe-1218-crosstabs. The Urban-Suburban

question is from the 2015 version of the same poll (823 respondents, margin of error +/– 3.4 percent). DC, "New Siena Poll Results [. . .]," March 31, 2019.

30. Jim Antonevich, "Great Schools for All Parent Survey Summary Report," (Rochester, NY: Metrix Matrix, 2016), http://gs4a.org/wp-content/uploads/2016/05/GS4A-Summary-Survey-2016-FINAL-B.pdf; *DC*, "Parents Say They Like Magnet Schools," May 27, 2016.

31. Gary Orfield and Danielle Jarvie, "Black Segregation Matters: School Resegregation and Black Educational Opportunity" (Los Angeles: Civil Rights Project/Proyecto Derechos Civiles, December 2020).

32. Dan W. Dodson, "Educational Challenges Relating to Desegregation," Central School Boards Committee for Educational Research, 1965, folder 4:28, James E. Allen Personal Papers 1950–71, New York State Library Manuscripts and Special Collections, Albany, NY.

33. *New York Times*, "Daniel B. Dodson, 72, Retired Professor, Dies," Aug. 19, 1995; Mt. 5:41 (King James Version); Dodson, "Educational Challenges Relating to Desegregation."

34. Dodson, "Educational Challenges Relating to Desegregation."

## 1. The African School

1. Rochester city directory, 1841, RPL; Blake McKelvey, "The Physical Growth of Rochester," *Rochester History* 13, no. 4 (October 1951); *Daily Democrat*, "Board of Education," Aug. 11, 1849.

2. *Daily Democrat*, "At the Meeting of the Inhabitants [. . .]," Feb. 20, 1841.

3. Walter Henry Green, *History, Reminiscences, Anecdotes and Legends of Great Sodus Bay, Sodus Point, Sloop Landing, Sodus Village, Pultneyville, Maxwell and the Environing Regions* (Sodus, NY: Henderson-Mosher, 1947), 66–71; Blake McKelvey, "Lights and Shadows in Local Negro History," *Rochester History* 21, no. 3 (October 1959); *DC*, "Important Lessons to Learn," July 19, 2020.

4. Austin Steward, *Twenty-Two Years a Slave and Forty Years a Freeman* (Syracuse, NY: Syracuse University Press, 2002), 44.

5. Edgar J. McManus, *A History of Negro Slavery in New York* (Syracuse, NY: Syracuse University Press, 1966) 177.

6. Steward, *Twenty-Two Years*, 54–64.

7. McKelvey, "Lights and Shadows" 3–5; Thomas James, "The Wonderful Eventful Life of Rev. Thomas James, by Himself," *Rochester History* 37, no. 4 (1975), 5.

8. Austin Reed, *The Life and the Adventures of a Haunted Convict*, ed. Caleb Smith (New York: Modern Library, 2017), 5.

9. *Telegraph*, Aug. 17, 1819, cited in Blake McKelvey, *Rochester: The Water-Power City, 1812–1854* (Cambridge, MA: Harvard University Press, 1945), 100; Edward R. Foreman, "Rochester: Its Name and Its Founder," in *Centennial History of Rochester, New York*, vol. 1, ed. Edward R. Foreman (Rochester, NY: Rochester Historical Society, 1931), 262; Howard Cross, "Creating a City: The History of Rochester from 1824 to 1834" (master's thesis, University of Rochester, 1836), 98, folder 1:2, Whitney Rogers Cross Papers, RBSCP; Rochester city directory, 1834, RPL.

10. Cross, "Creating a City," 9, 323; McKelvey, *Water-Power City*, 100.

11. Whitney R. Cross, *The Burned-Over District: The Social and Intellectual History of Enthusiastic Religion in Western New York, 1800–1850* (Ithaca, NY: Cornell University Press, 1950), 55.

12. Robert S. Fletcher, *A History of Oberlin College, from Its Foundation through the Civil War*, vol. 1 (Oberlin, Ohio: Oberlin College, 1943), 18–25; Charles G. Finney, *Memoirs* (New York: A. S. Barnes), 290–91; Milton Sernett, *North Star Country: Upstate New York and the Crusade for African American Freedom* (Syracuse, NY: Syracuse University Press, 2002), 23. See also Cross, *The Burned-Over District*, 211–37.

13. Lawrence Cremin, *American Education: The National Experience, 1783–1876* (New York: Harper Torchbooks, 1988), 165.

14. Carleton Mabee, *Black Education in New York: From Colonial to Modern Times* (Syracuse, NY: Syracuse University Press, 1979), 36; Steward, *Twenty-Two Years*, 76; Henry O'Reilly, *Settlement in the West: Sketches of Rochester; with Incidental Notices of Western New-York* (Rochester, NY: William Alling, 1838), 293.

15. Cremin, *American Education*, 137–38.

16. Harlan Hoyt Horner, ed., *Education in New York State, 1754–1954* (Albany: New York State Education Department, 1954); S. A. Ellis, "A Brief History of the Public Schools of the City of Rochester," *Publications of the Rochester Historical Society* 1 (1892), 71; Blake McKelvey, "Rochester's Public Schools: A Testing Ground for Community Policies," *Rochester History* 31, no. 2 (April 1969); Henry C. Maine, ed., *Rochester in History with Portraits and Our Part in the World War* (Rochester, NY: Wegman-Walsh, 1922).

17. Leon Litwack, *North of Slavery: The Negro in the Free States, 1790–1860* (Chicago: University of Chicago Press, 1961), 126; Herbert Aptheker, *A Documentary History of the Negro People in the United States: From Colonial Times through the Civil War*, (New York: Citadel, 1973), 398–402.

18. Steward, *Twenty-Two Years*, 158.

19. *Daily Advertiser*, "Board of Education," March 27, 1850.

20. *Daily Advertiser*, March 27, 1850; *Anti-Masonic Enquirer*, "New York Legislature," Jan. 31, 1832.

21. *Rights of Man*, "The Following Is an Abstract [. . .]," April 26, 1834. Rochester city directory, 1834, RPL; O'Reilly, *Settlement in the West*, 291.

22. Mabee, *Black Education*, 70.

23. Arthur O. White, "The Black Movement against Jim Crow Education in Buffalo, New York, 1800–1900," *Phylon* 30, no. 4 (1969), 376.

24. *Daily Advertiser*, March 27, 1850; John N. Thompson, "History of the Sabbath Schools of Rochester," *Genesee Country Scrapbook* 6 (1955): 14.

25. *Daily Advertiser*, "Report on Condition of African School," Feb. 28, 1833.

26. *Rights of Man*, "The Following Is an Abstract [. . .]," April 26, 1834.

27. Steward, *Twenty-Two Years*, 147.

28. *Rights of Man*, "The Following Is an Abstract [. . .]," April 26, 1834; Musette Castle, "A Survey of the History of African Americans in Rochester, New York, 1800–1860," *Afro-Americans in New York Life and History* 13 (July 1989), 7–32.

29. *Daily Democrat*, Aug. 11, 1849.

30. *Daily Democrat*, Feb. 20, 1841.

31. *Daily Advertiser*, "City Council," July 2, 1841; "Board of Education," July 12, 1841.

32. Rochester city directory, 1844, RPL.

33. *Daily Advertiser*, March 27, 1850; *Daily Advertiser*, "Board of Education," April 9, 1846; Judith Polgar Ruchkin, "The Abolition of Colored Schools in Rochester, New York, 1832–1856," *New York History* 51, no. 4 (July 1970), 377–93.

34. *Daily Advertiser*, "Board of Education," Sept. 1, 1847; *Daily Democrat*, "Colored School Exposition," April 23, 1849; Rochester city directory, 1849, RPL.

35. *Daily Democrat*, "Address of the Colored People," March 30, 1846.

36. US Bureau of Education, "Special Report of the Commissioner of Education on the Condition and Improvement of Public Schools in the District of Columbia" (Washington, DC: US Bureau of Education, 1871), 207.

37. Frederick Douglass to Amy Post Oct. 28, 1847, Isaac and Amy Post Papers, RBSCP cited in Victoria Schmitt, "Rochester's Frederick Douglass," *Rochester History* 67, no. 3 (Summer 2005), 16.

38. Frederick Douglass, *Narrative of the Life of Frederick Douglass, 1845*, The Frederick Douglass Papers, series 2, vol. 1, eds. John W. Blassingame and John McKivigan IV (New Haven, CT: Yale University Press, 1999), 31–32.

39. Carter G. Woodson, *The Education of the Negro Prior to 1861* (New York: G. P. Putnam's Sons, 1915), 320; Cremin, *American Education*, 138.

40. William F. Peck, *Semi-Centennial History of the City of Rochester* (Syracuse, NY: D. Mason, 1884), 307; Blake McKelvey, "Private Educational Enterprise since the Mid-Century," *Rochester Historical Society Publication Fund Series* 17 (1939), 155; Schmitt, "Rochester's Frederick Douglass" 25; Leigh Fought, *Women in the World of Frederick Douglass* (New York: Oxford University Press, 2017), 157.

41. The entire below account comes from a lengthy open letter Douglass published in the *North Star*, "H.G. Warner, Esq. [. . .]," Sept. 22, 1848.

42. There is no record that Warner ever responded in writing, including in his papers stored at the University of Rochester. Douglass pressed his point several weeks later in the *North Star*: "Mr. Warner edits a paper in this city, and we naturally supposed that he would vindicate his conduct in the matter referred to in his paper. In this, however, we have been thus far mistaken; either from feelings of shame, or a conviction that his conduct admits of no defense, he has thus far remained silent." *North Star*, "H.G. Warner Esq. [. . .]," Oct. 20, 1848.

43. Schmitt, "Rochester's Frederick Douglass," 21; Rosetta Douglass Sprague, "Anna Murray-Douglass—My Mother As I Recall Her," *Journal of Negro History* 8, no. 1 (January 1923), 97; Frederick Douglass, *Life and Times of Frederick Douglass, 1881*, The Frederick Douglass Papers, series 2, vol. 1, eds. John W. Blassingame and John McKivigan IV (New Haven, CT: Yale University Press, 1999).

44. Douglass, *Life and Times,* 210; Fought, *Women in the World of Frederick Douglass*, 156–58.

45. Frederick Douglass Jr., "Frederick Douglass Jr. in Brief from 1842–1890," in *If I Survive: Frederick Douglass and Family in the Walter O. Evans Collection,* eds. Celeste-Marie Bernier and Andrews Taylor (Edinburgh, UK: Edinburgh University Press, 2018), 633; *DC*, "To Rest in Rochester," Feb. 22, 1895.

46. References to the Douglass children's public education are scattered but mostly consistent. See Charles Remond Douglass, "Some Incidents of the Home Life of Frederick Douglass," in Bernier and Taylor, *If I Survive*, 671; Douglass Jr., "Frederick Douglass Jr. in Brief from 1842–1890," in Bernier and Taylor, *If I Survive,*

633; John W. Thompson, *An Authentic History of the Douglass Monument* (Rochester, NY: Rochester Herald Press, 1903), 157; James M. Gregory, *Frederick Douglass, the Orator* (Chapel Hill: University of North Carolina at Chapel Hill, 2001 [1893]), 199–206; *DC*, "About Frederick Douglass," Oct. 8, 1922.

47. *DC*, Feb. 22, 1895; Sprague, "Anna Murray-Douglass," 98; Douglass Jr., "Frederick Douglass Jr. in Brief, from 1842–1890," in Bernier and Taylor, *If I Survive*, 633; Thompson, *An Authentic History*, 157.

48. Douglass, "Some Incidents," in Bernier and Taylor, *If I Survive*, 671.

49. McKelvey, *Water-Power City*, 285–86.

50. *North Star*, "Education Among the Colored People," Oct. 26, 1849.

51. *Daily Democrat*, Aug. 11, 1849.

52. *North Star*, "Colored Schools," Aug. 17, 1849.

53. *North Star*, "Proposition," Aug. 10, 1849; *Daily Democrat*, "Colored Schools Meeting," Dec. 24, 1849.

54. *North Star*, "Proscription and Oppression [. . .]," Nov. 2, 1849; "Zion Church School," Nov. 9, 1849.

55. *North Star*, Nov. 9, 1849; "Meeting Against Colored Schools," Dec. 21, 1849; *Daily Democrat*, "Colored School Meeting," Dec. 14, 1849.

56. *North Star*, Nov. 2, 1849; Dec. 21, 1849; *Daily Advertiser*, March 27, 1850; *Ninth Annual Report of the Superintendent of Public Schools of the City of Rochester* (Rochester, NY: A. Strong, 1852), 20–21.

57. *Daily Union*, "The Colored People and the Board of Education," Aug. 31, 1854.

58. *Daily Union*, "Board of Education," Aug. 23, 1854; Ruchkin, "The Abolition of Colored Schools"; *Twelfth Annual Report of the Superintendent of Public Schools of the City of Rochester, Presented March 26, 1855* (Rochester, NY: Lee, Mann, 1855), 20–21.

59. Lucy N. Colman, *Reminiscences* (Buffalo, NY: H. L. Green, 1891), 16.

60. *Thirteenth Annual Report of the Superintendent of Public Schools, Rochester, Presented March 24, 1856* (Rochester, NY: Daily Advertiser Press, 1856), 17.

61. *Daily Democrat*, "Board of Education," July 11, 1856.

62. White, "Black Movement"; Mabee, *Black Education*, 198–203; *People ex rel. King v. Gallagher* 93 NY 438 (1883); *People ex rel. Cisco v. School Board of the Borough of Queens* 161 NY 598 (1900); *Paynter v. New York* 98 NY 2d 644 (2002), Smith dissent.

63. Colman, *Reminiscences*, iii.

64. *North Star*, Aug. 17, 1849.

## 2. Nowhere Else to Go

1. Interview with Jesse [*sic*] James, Sept. 21, 1979, PW.

2. Interview with Jesse [*sic*] James, Sept. 21, 1979; *DC*, "'Instigator' Looks Back," Aug. 2, 1987; "Clubs 'Anchor' Blacks," April 7, 1991.

3. Blake McKelvey, "Lights and Shadows in Local Negro History," *Rochester History* 21, no. 3 (October 1959).

4. *New National Era*, "Letter from the Editor," June 13, 1872.

5. Isabel Harmon, untitled and undated document, Big Springs Historical Society, Caledonia, NY. In addition to its archives, Big Springs has an excellent permanent exhibit on the community's Black history. See also *DC*, "In Quiet Belcoda [. . .],"

April 18, 1948; "Good Pay, Good Land," July 22, 1979; *Caledonia Advertiser*, "A Bit of Harmon History," Jan. 25, 1962.

6. Benjamin Frank Harmon to Corina Brown Harmon, July 21, 1871, Big Springs Historical Society, Caledonia, NY; *DC*, "Colored Folks Went Home," Dec. 19, 1904; "Colored Men Make Good Farm Hands," Feb. 13, 1907; July 22, 1979; "The Road to Rochester," Feb. 22, 1981.

7. Interview with Evelyn Brandon, March 28, 1980, PW.

8. Blake McKelvey, "Rochester's Ethnic Transformations," *Rochester History* 25, no. 3 (July 1963), 5–24.

9. Interview with Evelyn Brandon, March 28, 1980.

10. R. Nathaniel Dett to Juanita Jackson, Aug. 26, 1936, folder I:G135, NAACP Papers, LOC; *Voice*, "Rochester as I See It," October 1934; Eunice Grier and George Grier, *Negroes in Five New York Cities: A Study of Problems, Achievements and Trends* (New York State Commission against Discrimination, Division of Research, Aug. 1958), 58.

11. New York State Temporary Commission on the Condition of the Colored Urban Population, *Second Report* (Albany, NY, February 1939), 41. See also reports of two Rochester visits, in 1926 and 1931, by National Urban League Director of Industrial Relations T. Arnold Hill, folder I:D35, National Urban League Papers, LOC.

12. Elizabeth Brayer, *George Eastman: A Biography* (Baltimore: Johns Hopkins University Press, 1995), 278.

13. Sally Parker, *Tearing Down Fences: The Life of Alice Holloway Young* (Rochester, NY: self-published, 2020), 23; Laura Warren Hill, *Strike the Hammer: The Black Freedom Struggle in Rochester, New York, 1940–1970* (Ithaca, NY: Cornell University Press, 2021), 107; Brayer, *George Eastman*, 475; Marion Gleason, "The George Eastman I Knew," *University of Rochester Library Bulletin* 26, no. 3 (Spring 1971); *DC*, "Twenty-Nine Years of Service," March 14, 1940; "Solomon Young Recalls Posh Days," Feb. 3, 1964.

14. Franklin Bock to American Civil Liberties Union, June 12, 1924, folder I:C281, NAACP Papers, LOC.

15. Irving Gray to NAACP, Aug. 31, 1924, and Walter White to Van Levy, Oct. 8, 1924, both in folder I:C281, NAACP Papers, LOC.

16. Franklin Bock to Walter White, Aug. 27, 1924, Sept. 8, 1924, folder I:C281, NAACP Papers, LOC.

17. James Rose, Charles Lunsford, and Van Levy to James Weldon Johnson, May 13, 1927; James Rose to Walter White, Sept. 21, 1930; George Burks to Walter White, Oct. 22, 1929; George Eastman to Walter White, Nov. 5, 1929; all in folder I:G135, NAACP Papers, LOC.

18. William Warfield, *My Life and My Music* (Champaign, IL: Sagamore, 1991), 51.

19. New York State Temporary Commission on the Condition of the Colored Urban Population, *Second Report*, 114; Ingrid Overacker, *The African American Church Community in Rochester, New York, 1900–1940* (Rochester: University of Rochester Press, 1998), 117; *DC*, "Group Fights Hospital Pact," Dec. 11, 1937; "Doctors Nip Move [. . .]," Dec. 22, 1937; "Fight Fails at Hospital Plan Parley," Dec. 23, 1937.

20. New York State Temporary Commission on the Condition of the Colored Urban Population, *Second Report*, 114–15; Mrs. George Hoyt Whipple, "'Key' to the Eastman Scrapbook," *University of Rochester Library Bulletin* 21, no. 1 (Fall 1965).

21. *DC*, "UR Commended [. . .]," May 7, 1943; "NAACP at UR Blasts [. . .]," Aug. 13, 1958; Interview with James Christian, April 23, 1980, PW; Michael Klein to Herbert Wright, Sept. 24, 1958, folder III:E12, NAACP Papers, LOC.

22. *T-U*, "From Sanford, Fla. [. . .]," March 10, 1969, part of a four-part series on the Great Migration in Rochester. See also Dwayne E. Walls, *The Chickenbone Special* (New York: Harcourt Brace Janovich, 1971), 167; Eugene Barrington, "New Beginnings: The Story of Five Black Entrepreneurs Who Migrated from Sanford, Florida, to Rochester, New York" (PhD diss., Syracuse University, 1976); Victoria Schmitt, "Goin' North," *Rochester History* 54, no. 1 (1992).

23. Dorothy Nelkin, *On the Season: Aspects of the Migrant Labor System* (Ithaca, NY: New York State School of Industrial and Labor Relations, Cornell University, 1970), 11.

24. William H. Metzler, *Migratory Farm Workers in the Atlantic Coast Stream: A Study in the Belle Glade Area of Florida, Circular 966* (Washington, DC: US Department of Agriculture, 1955), 3–7

25. Author interview with Walter Cooper, June 28, 2018.

26. *DC*, Dec. 19, 1904; undated clipping from Rochester *Post Express*, ca. 1918–19, in Charles W. Frazier, ed., *The Old Ship of Zion: Its History and Its People* (Rochester, NY: self-published, 1995), 219.

27. Stephen W. Jacobs, *Wayne County: The Aesthetic Heritage of a Rural Area* (Lyons, NY: Wayne County Historical Society, 1979) 31, 92–94; Genesee/Finger Lakes Regional Planning Board, "Agricultural Land Resources—Regional Survey, Report 14" (December 1972), 83, 94.

28. *DC*, "Sodus Famed as Fruit Country," Aug. 27, 1944.

29. *DC*, "154 Jamaicans Arrive [. . .]," June 21, 1944.

30. "Alex Brown," in *Migrant Farmworkers of Wayne County, New York: A Collection of Oral Histories from the Back Roads*, ed. Joyce Woelfe Lehmann (Lyons, NY: Wayne County Historical Society, 1990), 58–59.

31. Dale Wright, *They Harvest Despair: The Migrant Farm Worker* (Boston: Beacon, 1965), 147.

32. Wright, *They Harvest Despair*, 110–11.

33. Genesee/Finger Lakes Regional Planning Board, *Migrant–A Human Perspective* (1972), 65; *DC*, "Labor Camps in State Jam Workers into Filthy, Unsanitary Firetraps," Sept. 24, 1944.

34. Jeffry Hoffman and Richard Seltzer, "Migrant Farm Labor in Upstate New York," *Columbia Journal of Law and Social Problems* 4, no. 1 (1968), 30–31.

35. "Ruby McCants Ford," in Lehmann, *Migrant Farmworkers of Wayne County, New York*, 27.

36. Howard W. Coles, "Nomads from the South," unpublished manuscript, ca. 1941, 3, oversized folder 1:1, Howard W. Coles Collection, RMSC.

37. Coles, "Nomads from the South," 2–5; *T-U*, "'Imported' Negroes Stage Revolt [. . .]," Aug. 21, 1941.

38. Genesee/Finger Lakes Regional Planning Board, *Migrant*, 21.

39. Robert Coles, *Uprooted Children: The Early Life of Migrant Farm Workers* (Pittsburgh, PA: University of Pittsburgh Press, 1970), 37–38.

40. William H. Friedland and Dorothy Nelkin, *Migrant: Agricultural Workers in America's Northeast* (New York: Holt, Rinehart and Winston, 1971), 248.

41. Coles, *Uprooted Children*, 130.

42. *DC*, "Ill-Fed Children of Migrant Camps Helped by Too-Few Day Nurseries," Sept. 27, 1944; Hoffman and Seltzer, "Migrant Farm Labor in Upstate New York," 43.

43. Hoffman and Seltzer, "Migrant Farm Labor in Upstate New York," 40.

44. "Ivory Simmons," in Lehmann, *Migrant Farmworkers of Wayne County, New York*, 78.

45. Coles, *Uprooted Children*, 76.

46. *DC*, "Farm Labor Camps 'Deplorable,'" Sept. 9, 1967; "Ivory Simmons," in Lehmann, *Migrant Farmworkers of Wayne County, New York*, 81. The *Democrat and Chronicle* ran a four-part series beginning Sept. 24, 1944, and another beginning Aug. 22, 1965. The *Frederick Douglass Voice* had a compelling account on Nov. 3, 1972.

47. Barrington, "New Beginnings," 54.

48. Grier and Grier, *Negroes in Five New York Cities*, 28.

49. Undated clipping from Rochester *Post Express*, ca. 1918–19.

50. Laura Root, "An Analysis of Social Distance between the Two Negro Communities of Rochester, New York" (master's thesis, University of Rochester, 1951), 18, 64, held at RBSCP.

51. Root, "Analysis of Social Distance," 61, 79–80.

52. Root, "Analysis of Social Distance," 78.

53. Interview with Bobby Johnson, April 2, 1980, PW.

54. Robert C. Weaver, *The Negro Ghetto* (New York: Harcourt, Brace, 1948), 28–29.

55. Grier and Grier, *Negroes in Five New York Cities*, 22.

56. Douglas S. Massey and Nancy A. Denton, *American Apartheid: Segregation and the Making of the Underclass* (Cambridge, MA: Harvard University Press, 1993), 17–19.

57. Howard Coles, "Brief History of *Frederick Douglass Voice*" and "Biographical Sketch, Howard Wilson Coles," both in folder 6:4, Howard W. Coles Collection, RMSC; author interview with Joan Coles Howard, Aug. 7, 2018.

58. Howard Coles, "Preliminary Background Material on Status of Negroes in Rochester," Howard W. Coles Collection, RMSC; "A Real Property Inventory of Rochester, New York" (Rochester, NY: Rochester Bureau of Municipal Research, 1940), held at Local History and Genealogy Division, RPL.

59. Coles, "Preliminary Background Material."

60. Marvin Slotoroff, "Report of Survey of 28 Negro Families Living in Predominantly White Neighborhoods in Rochester, New York (May–June, 1960)," folder 18:4, Walter Cooper Papers, RBSCP; interview notes, folder 19:5, Walter Cooper Papers, RBSCP; see also Robert H. Rhodes, "House-Hunting in Rochester: A Case History," 1962, folder 18:4, Walter Cooper Papers, RBSCP.

61. Weaver, *The Negro Ghetto*, 217.

62. Howard Coles to F. Dow Hamblin, February 3, 1960, folder 1:28, Howard W. Coles Collection, RMSC.

63. Richard Rothstein, *The Color of Law* (New York: Liveright, 2017), 63–75; Federal Housing Administration, *Underwriting Manual* (Washington, DC: US Government Printing Office, 1939), sections 978–80.

64. Federal Housing Administration, *Underwriting Manual* (Washington, DC: US Government Printing Office, 1938), section 951.

65. "Mapping Inequality" project, University of Richmond, https://dsl.richmond.edu/panorama/redlining; *DC*, "Maps from 1930s Show Discrimination," Oct. 24, 2016; "Closed Doors," Feb. 9, 2020.

66. *DC*, "Racial Bans Pervaded in Monroe," Aug. 9, 2020; City Roots Land Trust and the Yale Environmental Law Clinic, "Confronting Racial Covenants: How They Segregated Monroe County and What to Do about Them" (2020); James A. Kushner, *Apartheid in America: An Historical and Legal Analysis of Contemporary Racial Segregation in the United States* (Arlington, VA: Carrollton, 1980), 19–20. The 1948 Supreme Court case was *Shelley v. Kraemer*, 334 US 1 (1948).

67. *T-U*, "Housing Bias Hits Hard [. . .]," June 8, 1960; Quintin Primo, *The Making of a Black Bishop* (Wilmington, DE: Cedar Tree, 1998), 70; Conor Dwyer Reynolds, "The Motives for Exclusionary Zoning" (working paper, Yale University, 2019), https://ssrn.com/abstract=3449772, 57–93.

68. Warren Hill, *Strike the Hammer*, 17; Norma Wagner to Marvin Rich, April 24, 1962; Ralph W. Barber, "The Effects of Open Enrollment on Anti-Negro and Anti-White Prejudices among Junior High School Students in Rochester, New York" (EdD diss., University of Rochester, 1968), 33.

69. Author interview with Nellie King, June 19, 2018; *DC*, "Action Vowed on Blockbusting," May 23, 1969.

70. *Voice*, "Negro Family Housing Survey Reveals Startling Facts," March 14–28, 1938; Anna Louise Staub and Vicki Schmitt, "Building an Urban Faith Community: Centennial History of St. Augustine Church, Part Two," *Rochester History* 60, no. 3 (Summer 1998), 7.

71. Interview with Evelyn Brandon, March 28, 1980.

72. Author interview with Alice Young, June 27, 2018.

73. *DC*, "Police Probe Cross Burning, KKK Cross," June 2, 1980; "White Supremacy Has a History in Rochester," Aug. 18, 2017; author interview with Jasper Huffman, Aug. 4, 2018.

74. Author interview with Walter Cooper, June 28, 2018; *DC*, "Educator, Chemist, Community Leader [. . .]," Feb. 11, 1986. See also Slotoroff, "Report of Survey of 28 Negro Families."

75. Urban League of Rochester, "Research Report No. 1, Covering Operations from September 1967 to September 1968," folder 20:16, Howard W. Coles Collection, RMSC.

76. *DC*, "Baden-Ormond Area Project Dedicated," June 15, 1951; "Hanover Homes Magic Shown at Open House," Dec. 27, 1952.

77. "FIGHT in the Seventies," undated ca. 1971, Howard W. Coles Collection, RMSC; *DC*, "Hanover Houses Must Go," Nov. 13, 1974; "Hanover Houses a Dumping Ground," Feb. 17, 1976.

78. Author interview with Luis Burgos, Sept. 27, 2018.

79. Author interview with Velverly Caldwell, Oct. 3, 2018; author interview with Luis Burgos, Sept. 27, 2018.

80. Interview with Clarence T. Ingram, May 22, 1980, PW.

81. Herman Goldberg et al., "Racial Imbalance in the Rochester Public Schools: Report to the Commissioner of Education," (Rochester, NY, Sept. 1, 1963), held at Local History and Genealogy Division, RPL.

## 3. Willing Combatants

1. Author interview with Nellie King, June 19, 2018.

2. *DC*, "Portable Classrooms Depreciate Property," Dec. 8, 1964; "Crowd of 200 Protests Use of Police Dogs," Aug. 20, 1961; author interview with Nellie King, June 19, 2018.

3. New York State Temporary Commission on the Condition of the Colored Urban Population, *Second Report* (Albany, NY, February 1939),106; *DC*, "No. 3 School One of City's Oldest," Sept. 16, 1928 (the series ran from Sept. 9, 1928, to Nov. 17, 1929, with one school featured each week).

4. William Warfield, *My Life and My Music* (Champaign, IL: Sagamore, 1991) 22, 47.

5. Ingrid Overacker, *The African American Church Community in Rochester, New York, 1900–1940* (Rochester: University of Rochester Press, 1998), 117.

6. *DC*, "A Family History of Pride, Deeds," Feb. 5, 1989.

7. New York State Temporary Commission on the Condition of the Colored Urban Population, *Second Report*, 106.

8. *Union and Advertiser*, "Small Sensation," April 8, 1895.

9. *DC*, "It Seems Conclusive," April 9, 1895.

10. *DC*, "Children in Church," June 14, 1897; "Board of Education," July 3, 1889; "Zion A.M.E. Church," June 30, 1890; "Booker Washington's Stenographer," June 8, 1902; "Cupid Records His Victories," June 30, 1904; "Will Decorate Monument," Aug. 22, 1911; *Pittsburgh Courier*, "Granddaughter of Frederick Douglass Dies in Missouri," Nov. 6, 1943.

11. *Crisis*, Sept. 1918, 241; West High School yearbook January 1916, Monroe County Library System, Rochester, New York, http://www.libraryweb.org/~digitized/yearbooks/West/1916_Jan.pdf.

12. *Weekly News* (Rochester, NY) 4, no. 42 (June 27, 1924), folder I:G135, NAACP Papers, LOC; *DC*, "Pioneers in Education," Feb. 28, 1994; "Rochester Schools Pioneer Dies at 104," Jan. 5, 2016; Rochester city directory, 1927, RPL; Adolph Dupree, "Rochester Roots/Routes Part II," *about . . . time*, Aug. 1984. Dupree is the only source to identify Sprague and Van Buren as pioneers but errs in dating their tenures.

13. New York State Temporary Commission on the Condition of the Colored Urban Population, *Second Report*, 109.

14. *DC*, "Orphans' Home at Lake Causes Disquietude," Sept. 20, 1916; "Small Farm as Site for Dorsey Home Assured," July 31, 1918; "Can Care for 35 Boys and Girls at Dorsey Home," Oct. 24, 1919; "Mrs. Dorsey, Orphans Home Founder, Dies," June 5, 1932.

15. *DC* "To Open New School for Negro Children," April 14, 1922; "'Mother' Dorsey Called to More Important Work," July 14, 1922; "Only Two Principals in 52 Years' History of 24 School," Feb. 10, 1929; "Close Home Founded by Mrs. Dorsey," March 9, 1928; Dupree, "Rochester Roots/Routes."

16. *DC*, "Manitou Beach Kingdom of Joy for Whole Day," July 28, 1921.

17. "To the Members of the Dorsey Home for Dependent Colored Children," March 19, 1928, Jean Vance Clarke Papers, Local History and Genealogy Division, RPL; *DC*, June 5, 1932.

18. *DC*, "Remember Sambo and Tigers? [. . .]," Oct. 12, 1951.

19. *DC*, "NAACP Praises Ban on 'Little Black Sambo,'" Dec. 4, 1951, "That Decision on 'Sambo'—Contrasting Comments," Dec. 9, 1951, "Thinks We're Imbeciles," Dec. 18, 1951, "Scores Intolerance," Dec. 22, 1951.

20. Patricia Sullivan, *Lift Every Voice: The NAACP and the Making of the Civil Rights Movement* (New York: New Press, 2009), 267–74.

21. Roy Wilkins, "The Negro Wants Full Equality" (1944), in Rayford W. Logan, ed., *What the Negro Wants* (Notre Dame, IN: University of Notre Dame Press, 2001), 115.

22. Mary McLeod Bethune, "Certain Unalienable Rights" (1944), in Logan, *What the Negro Wants*, 250.

23. John Hope Franklin and Alfred A. Moss, Jr., *From Slavery to Freedom: A History of African Americans*, seventh ed. (New York: Alfred A. Knopf, 1994), 465–66.

24. Davison M. Douglas, *Jim Crow Moves North: The Battle over Northern School Segregation, 1865–1954* (New York: Cambridge University Press, 2005), 225–26.

25. Richard Kluger, *Simple Justice: The History of* Brown v. Board of Education *and Black America's Struggle for Equality* (New York: Vintage, 2004), 134.

26. Ann Pointer quoted in William H. Chafe, Raymond Gavins, and Robert Korstad, eds., *Remembering Jim Crow: African Americans Tell about Life in the Segregated South* (New York: New Press, 2001), 155.

27. *Plessy v. Ferguson*, 163 US 537 (1896), 13.

28. Kluger, *Simple Justice*, 122.

29. Gunnar Myrdal, *An American Dilemma*, vol. 1: *The Negro Problem and Modern Democracy* (New Brunswick, NJ: Transaction, 1996), lxix, 519.

30. Kluger, *Simple Justice*, 260.

31. *Sweatt v. Painter*, 339 US 629 (1950); *McLaurin v. Oklahoma Board of Regents* 339 US 637 (1950).

32. Kluger, *Simple Justice*, 290.

33. James T. Patterson, Brown v. Board of Education*: A Civil Rights Milestone and Its Troubled Legacy* (New York: Oxford University Press, 2001), 25–30.

34. Ronald H. Bayor, *Race and the Shaping of Twentieth-Century Atlanta* (Chapel Hill: University of North Carolina Press, 2000), 119; Kluger, *Simple Justice*, 413.

35. Kluger, *Simple Justice*, 321; *Brown v. Board of Education of Topeka*, 347 US 483 (1954), 15.

36. *Brown v. Board of Education of Topeka*, 349 US 294 (1955).

37. *T-U*, "May 17 is a New Emancipation Day," May 18, 1954.

38. *DC*, "Dr. Anthony Jordan," Dec. 20, 1971.

39. Author interview with Anne Micheaux Akwari, March 7, 2019.

40. Eunice Grier and George Grier, *Negroes in Five New York Cities: A Study of Problems, Achievements and Trends* (New York: New York State Commission against Discrimination, 1958), 83–87.

41. Author interview with Walter Cooper, June 28, 2018.

42. Grier and Grier, *Negroes in Five New York Cities*, 31–32.

43. Interview with Frank McElrath, March 10, 1980, PW.

44. *DC*, Sept. 16, 1928; "9 City Schools More than 31 P.C. Negro," July 31, 1962; Rochester City School District, "Annual Statistical Report, 1965–66" (Rochester, NY, 1966).

45. *DC*, "New School May Not Help Overcrowding," Oct. 23, 1959; *North Star*, "Zion Church School," Nov. 9, 1849.

46. *DC*, "Negro Leaders Charge Bias [. . .]," July 8, 1960; Walter Cooper, "Presented Before the Board of Education by the Municipal Affairs Committee—July 7," folder 3A:5, Walter Cooper Papers, RBSCP.

47. *DC*, "City Ponders Upping Mobile Schools' Use," Jan. 6, 1960; July 8, 1960; "Shortened Classes Dropped [. . .]," July 16, 1960; "Official Proceedings [. . .]," Aug. 3, 1960.

48. "Regents Statement on Intercultural Relations in Education," January 28, 1960, box 4, James E. Allen Personal Papers, NYSA; *Southern School News*, "Eight Districts Outside South Plan Voluntary Desegregation," September 1962, 18.

49. *Taylor v. Board of Education of City School District*, 191 F. Supp. 181 (SDNY 1961), 30.

50. *Advocator* 3, no. 3 (April–May 1961), folder 4:14, Walter Cooper Papers, RBSCP.

51. *T-U*, "NAACP Switches its Attack to the North," May 31, 1962; *DC*, "N.Y. Policy Cited in School Suit," June 22, 1962; *Southern School News*, "13 Northern and Western School Districts Extend Desegregation," November 1962, 14; June Shagaloff, "A Review of Public School Desegregation in the North and West," *Journal of Educational Sociology* 36, no. 6 (Feb. 1963), 292–96.

52. Author interview with Walter Cooper, June 28, 2018.

53. Author interview with Walter Cooper, June 28, 2018. Cooper's papers do not contain the study to which he referred, done by UR student Jonathan Steepee. According to Cooper's 1961 annual report on the local NAACP's education committee, he completed "a comprehensive study" of de facto school segregation in Rochester and presented it to the main body on Oct. 20. But, he wrote to Jawn Sandifer, it was subsequently withdrawn "due to suspicion of collusion between some executive board members and 'downtown' politicians." Walter Cooper to Jawn Sandifer, March 22, 1962, folder 19:6, Walter Cooper Papers, RBSCP. A partial version of the Steepee study exists in the NAACP Papers at the Library of Congress and will be discussed later.

54. Author interview with Walter Cooper, Aug. 21, 2018.

55. Laura Warren Hill, *Strike the Hammer: The Black Freedom Struggle in Rochester, New York, 1940–1970* (Ithaca, NY: Cornell University Press, 2021), 25–28.

56. *DC*, "NAACP to Study Schools," March 31, 1962; "Court Action Expected on Segregation," May 5, 1962; *T-U*, "De Facto School Segregation Debated at Board Meeting," April 13, 1962.

57. The full list of child plaintiffs: Allen, Denise, and James Aikens; Charles Banks; David, Joseph, and Kathe Balter; Donna and Patricia Carroll; Arthur Crutchfield; Jan and Ross Dubin; Beth, Mark, and Susan Faegre; Ann and Lydia Micheaux; Michael Truitt; Deborah, Jeremy, and Miriam Tuttle; and Nellie Whitaker (King). The defendants were Superintendent Robert Springer, the school board, and its five members individually.

58. *Aikens v. Board of Education* (WDNY 9736), 6

59. *DC*, "Bi-Racial Suit Filed," May 29, 1962.

60. Author interview with David Balter, April 27, 2019; author interview with Ruth Balter, April 19, 2019.

61. Author interview with Susan (Faegre) deFay, May 16, 2019; author interview with Mark Faegre, May 21, 2019.

62. Author interview with Mark Allan Davis, Feb. 26, 2019; *DC,* "NAACP Names Acting President," Feb. 2, 1962; "Davis Sworn as Judge," March 12, 1967; "Supreme Court Losing Highly Praised Justice," Dec. 9, 1996; "Court System Pioneer Davis Dies," March 13, 2010.

63. *T-U,* "Segregation Suit Timing Surprises Supt. Springer," May 29, 1962.

64. *DC,* "Schools Lawsuit is a Slap," May 30, 1962.

65. *T-U,* April 13, 1962; "2 Deny Conflict of Interest," June 1, 1962; *DC,* "Cerulli Unanimously Elected . . .," May 9, 1962.

66. *DC,* "Schools to Ask Study of Segregation Issue," June 5, 1962; "City Denies Responsibility for School Segregation," June 19, 1962; *Aikens v. Board of Education* response (June 18, 1962), 4.

67. *DC,* "Negro Named School Head," May 29, 1962; author interview with Alice Young, June 27, 2018.

68. *DC,* May 29, 1962; author interview with Alice Young, June 27, 2018.

69. Author interview with Walter Cooper, June 28, 2018; *DC,* "Principal Named to Direct Aid to Deprived Children," Sept. 3, 1965.

70. *DC,* "Dr. Springer: 'Quality of Education Equal in All Schools,'" March 9, 1963; "A Catalyst for Desegregation," Nov. 7, 1969.

71. *DC,* May 29, 1962.

72. Gary Orfield, *Must We Bus? Segregated Schools and National Policy* (Washington, DC: Brookings Institution, 1978), 15–24; Matthew Delmont, *Why Busing Failed: Race, Media, and the National Resistance to School Desegregation* (Oakland: University of California Press, 2016), 123.

73. *DC,* "Overcrowded School 4 May Let Pupils Transfer," Dec. 19, 1962; March 9, 1963.

74. Form letter from Citizens' Committee on School Integration, Nov. 28, 1962, folder 3A:10, Walter Cooper Papers, RBSCP; *T-U,* "School Integration Needs Discussed," Feb. 13, 1963; *DC,* "Group Protests 'Segregation' at School 44," Dec. 17, 1962; US Commission on Civil Rights, *Hearing Before the United States Commission on Civil Rights: Hearing Held in Rochester, New York, Sept. 16–17, 1966,* held at Rush Rhees Library, University of Rochester.

75. Rochester Board of Education minutes May 21, 1953; June 18, 1953; April 21, 1955; Oct. 2, 1958; April 30, 1959; Aug. 4, 1960; Herman Goldberg et al., "Racial Imbalance in the Rochester Public Schools: Report to the Commissioner of Education," (Rochester, NY, Sept. 1, 1963), held at Local History and Genealogy Division, RPL.

76. US Commission on Civil Rights, "Staff Report on Issues Related to Racial Imbalances in the Public Schools of Rochester and Syracuse, New York," held at Rush Rhees Library, University of Rochester, 8–9; *DC,* "New School 2 to be Racially Balanced," Feb. 22, 1961; "District Change Keeps Imbalance," Dec. 5, 1963.

77. Cooper's correspondence with Steepee is in folder 3A:7, Walter Cooper Papers, RBSCP; see also Jonathan Steepee, "Racial Discrimination in the Rochester, N.Y. School District," folder V:1377–78, NAACP Papers, LOC.

78. Steepee, "Racial Discrimination."

79. Goldberg et al., "Racial Imbalance in the Rochester Public Schools"; Delmont, *Why Busing Failed*, 128; author interview with Walter Cooper, Aug. 21, 2018.

80. Rochester *Post Express*, undated ca. 1918–19, in Charles W. Frazier, ed., *The Old Ship of Zion: Its History and Its People* (Rochester: self-published, 1995), 219.

81. *T-U*, April 13, 1962; *DC*, May 30, 1962.

## 4. Six Rugged Years, All Uphill

1. *DC*, "Dr. Springer Has Heart Attack," June 1, 1963; "Goldberg Named to Fill In For Springer," June 5, 1963; "Last Rite Tomorrow for Dr. Springer," June 20, 1963.

2. *DC*, June 20, 1963.

3. Randy Goldman interview with Herman Goldberg, May 15, 1996, oral history collection, United States Holocaust Memorial Museum, https://collections.ushmm.org/search/catalog/irn504462.

4. T-U, "What Allen Ruling Means to Rochester," June 18, 1963; US Commission on Civil Rights, Hearing Before the United States Commission on Civil Rights: Hearing Held in Rochester, New York, Sept. 16–17, 1966, held at Rush Rhees Library, University of Rochester, 289.

5. Herman Goldberg et al., "Racial Imbalance in the Rochester Public Schools: Report to the Commissioner of Education" (Rochester, NY, Sept. 1, 1963), Herman Goldberg, "Grade Reorganization and Desegregation of the Rochester Public Schools: A Report to the Board of Education" (December 1969), both held at Local History and Genealogy Division, RPL.

6. *DC*, "City Schools 'Better Integrated,'" Jan. 6, 1970; *National Observer*, "Doubts Grow About School Integration," Jan. 26, 1970.

7. *DC*, Jan. 6, 1970.

8. *T-U*, June 18, 1963; *DC*, "City Schools to End Racial Imbalance," June 19, 1963.

9. *T-U*, "Here Are Proposals [. . .]," Aug. 27, 1963; "Rochester: Return of Junior Highs," Aug. 31, 1971; *DC*, June 19, 1963; "Integration OK With Board [. . .]," Aug. 28, 1963; Goldberg et al., "Racial Imbalance in the Rochester Public Schools." For more on junior high schools, see Nellie M. Love, "An Analysis of the Junior High School Movement in the City of Rochester, New York," (EdD diss., University of Rochester, 1968).

10. *DC*, Aug. 28, 1963; "School Racial Quota Plan [. . .]," Sept. 7, 1963; "NAACP Generally Favors [. . .]," Sept. 27, 1963; Goldberg et al., "Racial Imbalance in the Rochester Public Schools"; William C. Rock, "Summary of Reactions to '*Cliffs to Climb*,'" (Rochester City School District, July 15, 1963), folder 3A:13, Walter Cooper Papers, RBSCP.

11. *DC*, "Board's Imbalance Plan Aired," Oct. 9, 1963; "Parents Have Mingled Feelings [. . .]," Oct. 20, 1963; "Students Are Confident of Racial Solutions," Dec. 1, 1963; *T-U*, "Vote to Be Asked [. . .]," Dec. 6, 1963.

12. *DC*, "Integration OK With Kids," Nov. 22, 1963, "Transfer Response Swamps Schools," Dec. 20, 1963; *T-U*, "School 30 Parents to Fight [. . .]," Nov. 22,

1963; Herman Goldberg and H. Hunter Fraser to district parents, Dec. 2, 1963, folder 3A:9, Walter Cooper Papers, RBSCP.

13. *DC,* Nov. 22, 1963; "Pupil Transfer Completed," Jan. 14, 1964; Margaret M. Brazwell, "'No One Ever Asked Us:' Counterstories of the Rochester, NY Open Enrollment Process" (EdD diss., 2010, University of Rochester), 75, 89.

14. US Commission on Civil Rights, *Hearing Before the United States Commission on Civil Rights*, 98, 112, 177.

15. *Strippoli v. Bickal* 42 Misc. 2d 475 (N.Y. Misc. 1964); *DC,* "Work Repeated, Pupils Tell Court," Jan. 16, 1964; "Parents Group Will Oppose [. . .]," Feb. 5, 1964; "School Shift Foes Organize," Feb. 6, 1964.

16. *Strippoli v. Bickal; Di Sano v. Storandt*, 22 A.D.2d 6 (1964); *DC,* "City to Appeal Ban [. . .]," June 16, 1964.

17. *T-U,* "Group Will Combat School Segregation," April 9, 1964; *DC,* Nov. 22, 1963; "Princeton Plan Foes Unite," Dec. 6, 1963; Citizens' Committee on School Integration to Lloyd Storandt, March 1964, folder 3A:6, Walter Cooper Papers, RBSCP.

18. *Jewish Ledger*, "Door Opened—Not Heart," Feb. 7, 1964, reprinted in *T-U,* Feb. 20, 1964.

19. *DC,* "Crowd of 200 Protests [. . .]," Aug. 20, 1961; Carvin Eison, dir., *July '64* (Rochester, NY: ImageWordSound, 2006) 54 min.; Laura Warren Hill, *Strike the Hammer: The Black Freedom Struggle in Rochester, New York, 1940–1970* (Ithaca, NY: Cornell University Press, 2021), 53–54.

20. Simulmatics Corp., "Unrest in Rochester: A Research Report" (unpublished report, Aug. 1, 1967), folder I:156, Daniel Patrick Moynihan Papers, LOC; Nydia Padilla, "Puerto Rican Contributions to the Greater Rochester Area" (MEd thesis, State University of New York College at Brockport, 1985), 70, box 1, Nydia Padilla-Rodriguez Papers, RMSC.

21. Porter Homer, "Riots of July, 1964," (City of Rochester, Aug. 27, 1965); State Commission against Discrimination, "Greater Rochester Takes a Look," (undated pamphlet ca. 1957), Howard W. Coles Collection, RMSC; Walter Cooper, "Reflections on the Rochester Riots in Rochester, N.Y.," undated, folder 4:18, Walter Cooper Papers, RBSCP; Eison, *July '64*.

22. Homer, "Riots of July, 1964"; Thomas H. Allen, "Report on the Rochester, N.Y. Incident" (NAACP, July 1964), folder III:C106, NAACP Papers, LOC.

23. Peniel E. Joseph, *Waiting 'til the Midnight Hour: A Narrative History of Black Power in America* (New York: Henry Holt, 2006), 5–6, 111.

24. Lou Buttino and Mark Hare, *The Remaking of a City: Rochester, New York, 1964–1984* (Dubuque, IA: Kendall Hunt, 1984), 16; *DC,* "Still Fighting the Good Fight," July 21, 1985; "FIGHT Aims to Organize [. . .]," June 12, 1965.

25. S. Prakash Sethi, *Business Corporations and the Black Man: An Analysis of Social Conflict; The Kodak-FIGHT Controversy* (Scranton, PA: Chandler, 1970), 23, 51; Eison, *July '64*.

26. Sol Chaneles, "Unrest in Rochester," undated (ca. August 1967); folder I:156, Daniel Patrick Moynihan Papers, LOC; Simulmatics Corp., "Unrest in Rochester."

27. Buttino and Hare, *Remaking of a City*, 19; US Commission on Civil Rights, *Hearing Before the United States Commission on Civil Rights*; Bernard Gifford (FIGHT

education committee chairman), "Policy Statement Concerning Rochester and Area Schools," Oct. 15, 1967, folder 5:15, Walter Cooper Papers, RBSCP.

28. Jim McCain to Jimmie McDonald, July 31, 1964, folder III:C106, NAACP Papers; author interview with Walter Cooper, Aug. 21, 2018; untitled cartoon, folder 5:2, Walter Cooper Papers, RBSCP; *T-U*, May 14, 1975; author interview with Gloria Winston Al-Sarag, Sept. 20, 2018; Hill, *Strike the Hammer*, 71–73.

29. Reuben Davis letter to Jawn Sandifer, May 17, 1962; minutes, Rochester NAACP Executive Committee, November 1962, both in folders III:C105–6, NAACP Papers, LOC.

30. Jerome Balter to June Shagaloff, May 8, 1964, folder V2828:5, NAACP Papers, LOC; untitled open letter, Citizens' Committee on School Integration, November 1962, folder titled "Citizens' Committee on School Integration, 1962–66," Jerome Balter and Ruth Balter Papers, 1959–1974, Swarthmore College Peace Collection, Swarthmore, PA.

31. *DC*, "NAACP Shifts Strategy on School Balance," May 7, 1965; *T-U*, "NAACP May Drop Law Suit on Schools," April 30, 1965; minutes, Coordinating Council, March 22, 1966, folder titled "Citizens' Committee on School Integration, 1962–66," Jerome Balter and Ruth Balter Papers, 1959–1974, Swarthmore College Peace Collection, Swarthmore, PA; Gertrude Gorman to Gloster Current, March 18, 1966, folder IV:C59, NAACP Papers, LOC.

32. Theron Johnson, "Report of Special Study of Elementary School Pupils," undated (ca. October 1963), folder 2:2, New York State Education Department Bureau of School District Organization Subject and Administrative Files, New York State Library Manuscripts and Special Collections, Albany, NY.

33. *T-U*, "Drive For Balance," Aug. 26, 1963; Rochester City School District, *Cliffs to Climb*, June 20, 1963; *DC*, "Black Teachers' 'First Day' Shocking," April 13, 1970; "The Lucky Teachers Got Jobs," Sept. 17, 1972; author interview with Nydia Padilla-Rodriguez, March 5, 2021. There is no single source for historical statistics on teacher diversity; the numbers presented here are gathered from scattered press reports and other sources.

34. Author interview with Lillie (Young) Winston, Sept. 28, 2018.

35. Author interview with Lillie (Young) Winston, Sept. 28, 2018; author interview with Andrew Ray, Feb. 4, 2019.

36. Author interview with Andrew Ray, Feb. 4, 2019.

37. Bettina L. Love, *We Want to Do More Than Survive: Abolitionist Teaching and the Pursuit of Educational Freedom* (Boston: Beacon, 2019), 47–48.

38. Love, *We Want to Do More Than Survive*, 48; author interview with Musette Castle, June 21, 2018.

39. Rochester City School District, *The Negro in American Life: Teacher's Guide* (1964); *T-U*, "Someone for The Kids [. . .]," Oct. 25, 1972; US Commission on Civil Rights, *Hearing Before the United States Commission on Civil Rights*, 42; Gifford, "Policy Statement Concerning Rochester and Area Schools"; *DC*, "A Proud Heritage," March 4, 1963.

40. Author interview with Idonia Owens, Jan. 18, 2019.

41. Author interview with Jonathan Perkins, June 3, 2019.

42. Author interview with Nellie King, June 19, 2018; author interview with James Beard, May 31, 2019.

43. *DC*, "Schools Face Cut [. . .]," June 8, 1966; "More Negroes Will Be Bused," Oct. 21, 1966; *T-U*, "How City Fights [. . .]," June 21, 1966.

44. US Commission on Civil Rights, *Staff Report on Issues Related to Racial Imbalances in the Public Schools of Rochester and Syracuse, New York*, (1966), held at Rush Rhees Library, University of Rochester, 8–9.

45. Ralph W. Barber, "The Effects of Open Enrollment on Anti-Negro and Anti-White Prejudices among Junior High School Students in Rochester, New York" (EdD diss., University of Rochester, 1968), 104–8.

46. George J. Rentsch, "Open Enrollment: An Appraisal" (EdD diss., University of Rochester, 1966), 238–41; "Testimony by Minister Franklyn [*sic*] Florence, President of FIGHT, Sept. 16, 1966, before the U.S. Civil Rights Commission," box 4B, Franklin Florence Papers, RBSCP; US Commission on Civil Rights, *Hearing Before the United States Commission on Civil Rights*, 169–70.

47. Citizens' Committee for School Integration, "Ability Index Otis, Grade 5 School Mean, Rochester, N.Y. School Districts" (unpublished report), folder 3A:6, Walter Cooper Papers, RBSCP; US Commission on Civil Rights, *Staff Report*, 14–17; *DC*, "Better Schools Urged [. . .]," July 17, 1966; "Allen Urged to Speed [. . .]," Aug. 5, 1966; *T-U*, "Plea Made on School Imbalance," Sept. 8, 1966.

48. *DC*, "Goldberg Ordered to Plan [. . .]," May 20, 1966; "Metro School Districts Urged [. . .]," May 20, 1966; *T-U*, "State Readying School Plan," June 17, 1966.

49. Rochester City School District, "Desegregation of the Elementary Schools: Special Report to the Board of Education" (Feb. 1, 1967); *DC*, "School Board Studies Plans by Goldberg," Feb. 2, 1967.

50. Jerome Balter, "Statement to the Rochester Board of Education," Feb. 16, 1967, folder titled "Schools, 1967–69," Jerome Balter and Ruth Balter Papers, 1959–1974, Swarthmore College Peace Collection, Swarthmore, PA; Rozetta McDowell to Herman Goldberg, Feb. 27, 1967, folder V:1377, NAACP Papers, LOC; *DC*, "Bickal Blasted for Criticism [. . .]," March 3, 1967; "Classroom Teachers Back Rochester Plan," March 10, 1967; untitled press statement, Feb. 21, 1967; box 4B, Franklin Florence Papers, RBSCP.

51. *DC*, "Busing Plan Opposed," Jan. 24, 1967; March 3, 1967; "Tax Unit Attacks Busing," March 14, 1967.

52. *DC*, "Politicos, Parents Rap School Integration," Jan. 6, 1964.

53. US Commission on Civil Rights, *Hearing Before the United States Commission on Civil Rights*, 186; *T-U*, "The Issue of Race in Schools," July 22, 1966.

54. Transcript of Louis Cerulli comments at public hearing, Feb. 14, 1967, folder titled "Schools 1967–69," Jerome Balter and Ruth Balter Papers, 1959–1974, Swarthmore College Peace Collection, Swarthmore, PA; *DC*, "Cerulli Meets with Parents [. . .]," Feb. 15, 1967.

55. *DC*, "School Push Set by Negro Leaders," March 18, 1967; Benjamin H. Richardson, "City School Reorganization: Antecedents, Forces, and Consequences" (EdD diss., University of Rochester, 1973), 85–86.

56. Rochester Board of Education, untitled document announcing 15-Point Plan, March 16, 1967, folder 3A:9, Walter Cooper Papers, RBSCP.

57. *DC*, March 18, 1967; "Negro Groups Fight Board's School Plan," March 29, 1967; "Parents Hit Pupil Imbalance Program," July 24, 1967; Jerome Balter, "Statement to the Rochester Board of Education."

58. *T-U,* "School Desegregation Decision Due Tonight," March 17, 1967; "Roche Has Eyes on Political Future," Nov. 9, 1967; author interview with Faust Rossi, May 17, 2019.

59. *DC,* "Schools to Pay Workers [. . .]," June 30, 1967; "Inner City Assails Bus Plan," July 21, 1967; "Busing Too Successful," Sept. 22, 1967; Parents Association of Clara Barton No. 2 School to Herman Goldberg et al., July 14, 1967, folder 3A:9, Walter Cooper Papers, RBSCP.

60. Rochester City School District, "An Interim Report on a Fifteen Point Plan to Reduce Racial Isolation and Provide Quality Integrated Education," (June 21, 1968), held at Local History and Genealogy Division, RPL; *DC,* Sept. 22, 1967; *T-U,* "Parents and Principal Praise School 2 Plan," March 26, 1968; "100 White Pupils are Lined Up [. . .]," June 17, 1968; "Our Children Say" (collection of statements from children at School 2 in the 1968–69 and 1969–70 school years), folder 5:4, Harry Gove Papers, RBSCP.

61. Author interview with Dana Miller, Sept. 19, 2019.

62. Author interview with Dana Miller, Sept. 19, 2019; *T-U,* "White Response to School 2 [. . .]," Aug. 21, 1968.

63. *DC,* "Principals Urge Full Integration," March 26, 1969; "Integrationists Urge Boycott," Aug. 19, 1969; "Principals Take to Streets," Aug. 28, 1969; Franklin Florence to John Mitchell, Aug. 15, 1969, folder 4B:13, Franklin Florence Papers, RBSCP.

64. *DC,* "Desegregation Plans Demanded [. . .]," Aug. 22, 1969; "School Boycott Called Off," Sept. 6, 1969; *T-U,* "Double Targets Reflected [. . .]," Sept. 6, 1969.

65. *DC,* "Cerulli Quits City School Board," Dec. 25, 1969; "Ashford Accepts Chicago Post," Jan. 17, 1970.

66. *T-U,* "Roche Ponders Busing [. . .]," Oct. 3, 1969; *DC,* "Board Outlaws Non-Voluntary School Busing," Dec. 19, 1969; "Suit Looms on School Integration," Dec. 20, 1969; "Goldberg 'Should Have Quit Work,'" Dec. 23, 1969.

67. *DC,* Dec. 19, 1968; Dec. 20, 1969; *T-U,* "Integration Plans Shaped Despite Vote," Dec. 19, 1969; Urban League of Rochester, "Position Statement on Reorganization of Rochester Public Schools," January 1970, folder 8:5, Walter Cooper Papers, RBSCP.

68. Goldberg, "Grade Reorganization."

69. Goldberg, "Grade Reorganization"; *T-U,* "Integration Plan Would Reorganize [. . .]," Dec. 30, 1969; *DC,* "Balance Plan for Schools," Dec. 30, 1969.

70. *T-U,* "Junior Highs Finding Favor [. . .]," Jan. 6, 1970; Aug. 31, 1971; *DC,* "Verdict Toughened on Schools' Violence," March 24, 1969; "Report Urges Board Action [. . .]," June 14, 1969; "Schools: All Plans Up in Air," Dec. 31, 1969; Goldberg, "Grade Reorganization."

71. *DC,* Dec. 31, 1969; "School Board Chair Filled," Jan. 1, 1970; "Branch to Head City School Board," Dec. 29, 1970. At the time, the mayor was responsible for appointing replacement school board members. Cerulli officially resigned on December 28, allowing outgoing Democratic mayor Frank Lamb to choose Branch as his successor, whereas Roche waited until the last moment to resign, letting incoming Republican mayor Stephen May choose Serrano to replace him.

72. *T-U,* "700 Jam Parents' Meeting," Feb. 4, 1970.

73. George J. Rentsch, "Community Meetings and Conflict Management," *Integrated Education: Minority Children in Schools* 11, nos. 4–5 (1973), 48–52; see also *DC,*

"New School Program Draws Shouts [. . .]," Feb. 3, 1970; and Richardson, "City School Reorganization," 136.

74. Herman Goldberg and Phale D. Hale, "An Experiment in Community Schools: Controversy and Development" (Rochester, NY: Community School Council, 1970), held at Local History and Genealogy Division, RPL; Richardson, "City School Reorganization," 154–60; Joseph Wilson, "Statement by Joseph C. Wilson Regarding the Plan for Reorganizing and Desegregating the Rochester Public Schools," Feb. 4, 1970, folder 140:01, Joseph C. Wilson Papers, RBSCP; *DC*, "Teen-agers League Urges Integration," Jan. 18, 1970.

75. *T-U*, "Legislator Opposes Plan," Feb. 5, 1970; *DC*, "Teachers Give Sims 'No' Nod," Feb. 16, 1970.

76. *T-U*, "81 Spoke While the Board Listened," Feb. 6, 1970; "Four Days of Decision," Feb. 26, 1970; *DC*, "School Vote Stuns [. . .]," Feb. 26, 1970; Richardson, "City School Reorganization," 151–53; newsletter, Citizens for Quality Integrated Education, March 1971, folder 5:4, Harry Gove Papers, RBSCP.

77. *T-U*, Feb. 26, 1970; *DC*, "37 Teachers Call In Sick," Feb. 27, 1970; "Close 'Inquiry' for Two Days," Feb. 28, 1970; "School Boycott Called Off [. . .]," March 4, 1970. The absent teachers later were found to have instituted an illegal strike and were docked two days' pay.

78. Ewald Nyquist to Herman Goldberg, March 2, 1970, folder 20:6, Ewald B. Nyquist Subject Files, NYSA; *DC*, "Board's Solution Pleases Nobody," March 6, 1970.

79. *DC*, "City Schools Reorganized," March 6, 1970; "Schools Face Boycott Today," March 9, 1970; "Schools Back to 'Normal,'" March 11, 1970; "Board Holds Up Leaves, Tenure," April 3, 1970.

80. *DC*, "147,000 in School Today," Sept. 9, 1970; "Schools' First Day: All's Well," Sept. 10, 1970.

81. *DC*, "RNSAC Loses Officers," Sept. 15, 1970; *T-U*, "'Splinter' Group Picks Cerulli," Oct. 17, 1970.

82. *DC*, "School Board," Oct. 31, 1970; "Democrats Win School Board [. . .]," Nov. 4, 1970.

83. *DC*, "No Politics in Schools? [. . .]," Aug. 31, 1969; "School Vote Breeds Political In-Fights," March 8, 1970; "Laverne Balks [. . .]," March 21, 1971; "Non-Party Vote to Elect Board," April 23, 1971. Partisan school board elections were reinstated in 1981.

84. *DC*, "West, Madison Shifts Planned," Jan. 6, 1971; "School Plan: 2nd Time's a Charm," Jan. 31, 1971; "Crowd Delays School Vote," Feb. 5, 1971.

85. Herman Goldberg speech, Dec. 15, 1970, box X0428, Rochester Municipal Archives, Rochester, NY; *DC*, "Goldberg Quits School Job," Nov. 19, 1970; "Franco First in Line [. . .]," June 5, 1971.

86. *DC*, "Schools Support Dropped," Feb. 4, 1971; "City Schools Reorganized," March 6, 1971; *T-U*, "Inner-City Parents Say 'No' [. . .]," Feb. 4, 1971; "Petition Appeals to Wyoma Best," March 4, 1971; "Mrs. Best Defends School Reorganizing," April 19, 1971; Richardson, "City School Reorganization," 305.

87. *T-U*, "Protest Reorganization of City High Schools," Feb. 13, 1971; *DC*, "Call in Class: Boycott," Feb. 7, 1971; "2 Suspended as Pupil Boycott [. . .]," Feb 9, 1971; "School Shift Foes March," Feb. 14, 1971; March 6, 1971.

88. George Richardson to John Pellegrino, "Incident at Charlotte High School," (police report), April 20, 1971, box X0429, Rochester Municipal Archives, Rochester, NY.

89. Richardson, "City School Reorganization," 176–81; *T-U,* "Three on Board Defy Council [. . .]," April 12, 1971; "School Plan Foes Protest [. . .]," June 11, 1971; *DC,* "GOP Councilmen Reject Loan Request [. . .]," April 24, 1971; "Wood Wields Extraordinary Power [. . .]," June 13, 1971; *Hearings Before the Select Committee on Equal Educational Opportunity of the United States Senate* (Washington, Oct. 7, 1971), 9036.

90. US Dept. of Health, Education and Welfare Office of Education, *Planning Educational Change vol. 4: How Five School Systems Desegregated* (Washington, DC: US Government Printing Office, 1969); *DC,* "Schools Make U.S. Booklet," Aug. 26, 1969.

91. New York State Education Department, "Racial and Social Class Isolation in the Schools: A Report to the Board of Regents of the University of the State of New York" (Albany, NY, December 1969); *Greece Post,* "Humbly, Humanly, Commissioner Talks on Education," May 14, 1970.

92. *DC,* "School Busing on Defense [. . .]," July 27, 1969.

## 5. From Charlotte to *Milliken*

1. Benjamin H. Richardson, "City School Reorganization: Antecedents, Forces, and Consequences" (EdD diss., University of Rochester, 1973), 218–19.

2. Herman Goldberg, "New Partnerships in Education: A Truth-in-Packaging School System," annual message to staff, Sept. 23, 1970, folder 140:1, Joseph C. Wilson Papers, RBSCP.

3. Author interview with Bob Sagan, Sept. 27, 2019.

4. Richardson, "City School Reorganization," 194–96; Rochester City School District, "Policy Statement on School Disruptions," Nov. 28, 1970; *Rip Off* (publication of Concerned Youth Community), Jan. 20, 1971, folder 5:7, Harry Gove Papers, RBSCP; DC, "Most High Schools Closed After Strife," June 18, 1971.

5. *DC,* "Everyone Getting School Blame," July 23, 1972; author interview with James Beard, May 31, 2019; author interview with Marlene Caroselli, Oct. 1, 2019.

6. Richardson, "City School Reorganization," 302–6; author interview with James Beard, May 31, 2019; *T-U,* "KKK Tactics Dangerous," June 24, 1971.

7. *T-U,* "School Plan Foes Protest [. . .]," June 11, 1971.

8. *T-U,* "Protesters in Sheets [. . .]," July 15, 1971; June 24, 1971; *DC,* July 16, 1971; Richardson, "City School Reorganization," 307.

9. *T-U,* "Adults Teach Children a Bad Lesson," June 28, 1971.

10. *DC,* "90 P.C. of Students Report," Sept. 10, 1971; "Few Complaints on School Shifts," Sept. 26, 1971; *T-U,* "Smooth Start [. . .]," Oct. 1, 1971.

11. *DC,* "Whites Form Group," Oct. 6, 1971; "Report Cards 'Hooky Game' Pawns," Dec. 11, 1971; *T-U,* "Smooth Start [. . .]," Oct. 1, 1971.

12. Richardson, "City School Reorganization," 261.

13. Author interview with Ed Cavalier, Oct. 2, 2019.

14. *DC,* "School Decision Reserved," Feb. 29, 1972; Ralph W. Barber, "The Effects of Open Enrollment on Anti-Negro and Anti-White Prejudices among Junior High

School Students in Rochester, New York" (EdD diss., University of Rochester, 1968), 31, 39; author interview with Bob Sagan, Sept. 29, 2019.

15. *T-U,* Oct. 1, 1971; *DC,* "Students List Demands," Oct. 5, 1971; "Blacks Urge Boycott [. . .]," Oct. 6, 1971; "Parents Decry 'Runaround,'" Oct. 8, 1971; "Parents Ask Dean's Ouster," Oct. 19, 1971; author interview with Roy Lane, June 27, 2019; Richardson, "City School Reorganization," 192; Robert Byrnes to Rochester Police Commissioner John Mastrella, Nov. 10, 1971, folder 20:6, Ewald Nyquist Subject Files, NYSA.

16. Author interview with Bob Sagan, Sept. 29, 2019; author interview with Bob Stevenson, Oct. 1, 2019.

17. Irving Levine, "Proposal for a National Consultation on Ethnic America," in American Jewish Committee Institute of Human Relations, *The Reacting Americans: An Interim Look at the White Ethnic Lower Middle Class,* 1969, folder 20:16, Howard W. Coles Collection, RMSC; Boris Mikoji, "Race, Nationality and Politics in an Urban Community" (PhD diss., Case Western Reserve University, 1970); Simulmatics Corp., "Unrest in Rochester: A Research Report" (unpublished report, Aug. 1, 1967), folder I:156, Daniel Patrick Moynihan Papers, LOC.

18. Author interview with Bob Stevenson, Oct. 1, 2019; Richardson, "City School Reorganization," 293.

19. Jerre Mangione, *Mount Allegro* (New York: Hill and Wang, 1963), 164–65.

20. Author interview with Jasper Huffman Aug. 4, 2018.

21. Author interview with Dana Miller, Sept. 19, 2019.

22. Author interview with Nydia Padilla-Rodriguez, Aug. 22, 2019.

23. *T-U,* "Some City Parents [. . .]," Sept. 28, 1971; "How They're Teaching [. . .]," Sept. 30, 1971; *DC,* "'Block' Schools Probed," Sept. 29, 1971; "Block Schools Get Free Books," Oct. 18, 1971; "Block Schools Facing Review Monday," Dec. 18, 1971; Richardson, "City School Reorganization," 198–201. The five block schools were: Eastside Tutoring Service, 145 Parsells Avenue; the Old Schoolhouse, 492 Lyell Avenue (apparently relocated from the Italian-American Sport Club shortly after opening); Northwest Liberty School, 1322 Dewey Avenue; Lighthouse Tutoring Service, 4409 Lake Avenue; and the Open School, 266 Lyell Avenue.

24. *T-U,* Sept. 30, 1971; "Parents Create Tension in Schools," Nov. 1, 1971; "Block Schools Probed," Jan. 7, 1972.

25. *DC,* "Block Schools Pledge Fight," Dec. 3, 1971; "Move on Block Schools," March 8, 1972; "Block Schools Are Defended," May 6, 1972; *T-U,* "40 Parents Freed in School Case," May 16, 1972.

26. Author interview with Frank Ciaccia, June 29, 2018.

27. Author interview with Frank Ciaccia, June 29, 2018; *DC,* "New School Plan [. . .]," Jan. 28, 1970.

28. Author interview with Frank Ciaccia, June 29, 2018; *DC,* "Board Outlaws Non-Voluntary School Busing," Dec. 19, 1969.

29. Jerome Zukosky, "Giving Up on Integration," *Time,* Oct. 14, 1972; *T-U,* "Cerulli Hits Bus Plan," Feb. 4, 1970; Richardson, "City School Reorganization," 242–44.

30. *T-U,* "The Voters Wanted a Change," Nov. 3, 1971.

31. *T-U,* Nov. 3, 1971; *DC,* "Democrats Win School Board," Nov. 4, 1970.

32. Author interview with Ed Cavalier, Oct. 2, 2019; *T-U,* Nov. 3, 1971.

33. Ewald Nyquist to Sally Miles, Nov. 15, 1971, folder 20:6, Ewald Nyquist Subject Files, NYSA.

34. Author interview with Sereena (Brown) Martin, Dec. 27, 2019; *DC,* "Desegregation Suit Filed. . .," March 4, 1970.

35. *DC,* March 4, 1970; "Segregation Suit Charges Board," April 9, 1970; *T-U,* "A Judge on the Spot," March 15, 1972. Besides Lillian Colquhoun and her daughter, Sereena Brown, the other plaintiffs were Elizabeth Jones, her daughter Gail Jones, and her grandsons Steven and Michael Jones; and Louise Duncan and her children Edward, Kenneth, Francenia, Jeffery, and Robert Duncan. The lawsuit, *Colquhoun v. Board of Education*, CIV-1970–97 (WDNY), was converted to a class-action in April 1970.

36. *Keyes v. School District No. 1, Denver*, 413 US 189 (1973); *DC,* "Busing Shift Could Speed Integration," Nov. 8, 1971; "Board Struggles with School Plan," Jan. 18, 1972; "Alter School-Shift Plan [. . .]," Jan. 25, 1972.

37. *DC,* "Board to Drop School Reshuffle," Feb. 1, 1972; "School Shift Tab [. . .]," March 7, 1972.

38. *DC,* Feb. 1, 1972; "City School Changes OK'd," Feb. 4, 1972; "School Board's Plans Criticized," Feb. 16, 1972; *T-U,* "Farbo Rebuked on Bid to Close School 14," Feb. 8, 1972; "Parents Oppose Minority Busing," Feb. 16, 1972.

39. *DC,* "School 14: Races Mix . . . and Learn," Dec. 5, 1971; "No School Decision Now," March 15, 1972.

40. *DC,* "Block Schools Defy Franco," Jan. 11, 1972; "Busing: It's a Year of Decision," March 19, 1972; *New York Times,* "Opposition at a Fever Pitch," Nov. 14, 1971.

41. Gary Orfield, "Congress, the President and Anti-Busing Legislation, 1966–1974," in *School Busing: Constitutional and Political Developments*, vol. 2: *The Public Debate over Busing and Attempts to Restrict Its Use*, ed. Douglas Davison (New York: Garland, 1994), 5–7, 21–25, 55; Richard M. Nixon, "Message of the President of the United States Relative to Busing and Equality of Educational Opportunity," March 20, 1972, in Davison, *School Busing*, 155.

42. *DC,* "Foes Ask Voice [. . .]," March 19, 1972; "Whites Get School Choices," March 24, 1972; Morton J. Sobel to Ewald Nyquist, May 18, 1972, folder 20:6, in Ewald Nyquist Subject Files, NYSA.

43. *T-U,* "Injunction Denied on City's Schools," June 14, 1972.

44. *DC,* "Parents Endorse Separate Schools," May 17, 1972; "School Plan Satisfy All?" May 18, 1972.

45. *DC,* "Adversaries of Busing [. . .]," March 12, 1972; "Six Parents Battled Board," April 13, 1972; "DeHond Crushes Zone A," May 5, 1972; "DeHond Wins Senate Bid," Nov. 8, 1972; *T-U,* "Zone A Parents Urged [. . .]," May 18, 1972.

46. *DC,* "Incidents Mar End of Study," June 17, 1972; "Violence Shutters Schools," June 20, 1972; "9 Pupils Named in Disorder," June 21, 1972; "Community Bias [. . .]," July 20, 1972; "School Hearings Make a House Call," July 21, 1972; author interview with Ed Cavalier, Oct. 2, 2019. Much of the detail regarding the incidents on June 16 and 19 comes from a series of hearings that the school board held over the summer.

47. *DC,* June 20, 1972; June 21, 1972; author interview with Dorothy Pecoraro, Oct. 23, 2019.

48. Author interview with Marlene Caroselli, Oct. 1, 2019; author interview with Idonia Owens, Jan. 18, 2019; *DC*, July 21, 1972.

49. *DC*, "Police Role at School Criticized," July 19, 1972; author interview with James Beard, May 31, 2019.

50. *DC*, July 19, 1972; "A Trick Absolves Policeman," Aug. 19, 1972.

51. *DC*, "Dr. Cerulli Dies at 61," March 14, 1972; "Dr. Cerulli Courageous," April 6, 1972; "It's Dr. Louis Cerulli School," Dec. 20, 1974; author interview with Ed Cavalier, Oct. 2, 2019.

52. *DC*, "School Changes Bringing Gripes," July 26, 1972; "City's Students [. . .]," Aug. 29, 1972; Richardson, "City School Reorganization," 223–24, 228.

53. Richardson, "City School Reorganization," 228, 239; Jerome Balter, "Statement to the Rochester Board of Education," Feb. 16, 1967, folder titled "Schools 1967–69," Jerome Balter and Ruth Balter Papers, 1959–1974, Swarthmore College Peace Collection, Swarthmore, PA; Matthew F. Delmont, *Why Busing Failed: Race, Media, and the National Resistance to School Desegregation* (Oakland: University of California Press, 2016), 3, 174.

54. *DC*, "Parents: Drop School Action," Aug. 17, 1972; "Integration Bid Future Unclear," May 6, 1976; newsletter, Citizens for Quality Integrated Education, June 1970, folder 5:3, Harry Gove Papers, RBSCP; J. Harold Flannery to Norman Chachkin and Nathaniel Jones, June 29, 1972, folder V:1498, NAACP Papers, LOC.

55. Conrad Istock to Ewald Nyquist, Sept. 25, 1972, folder 41:17, Ewald Nyquist Subject Files, NYSA.

56. Zukosky, "Giving Up on Integration."

57. Author interview with Marlene Caroselli, Oct. 1, 2019; Richardson, "City School Reorganization," 238.

58. *DC*, "Students Promise Unity," Sept. 30, 1972.

59. Author interview with James Beard, May 31, 2019.

60. *Keyes v. School District No. 1*; Gary Orfield, Gary Orfield, *Must We Bus? Segregated Schools and National Policy* (Washington, DC: Brookings Institution, 1978), 15–19.

61. Herman Goldberg et al., "Racial Imbalance in the Rochester Public Schools: Report to the Commissioner of Education" (Rochester, NY, Sept. 1, 1963), held at Local History and Genealogy Division, RPL; Richardson, "City School Reorganization," 223–24; US Census data, 1950–70.

62. US Census data; Jeffrey Mirel, *The Rise and Fall of an Urban School System, 1907–81* (Ann Arbor: University of Michigan Press, 1993), 333.

63. *Green v. County School Board*, 391 US 430 (1968); Eleanor P. Wolf, *Trial and Error: The Detroit School Segregation Case* (Detroit: Wayne State University Press, 1981), 220–38.

64. Joyce A. Baugh, *The Detroit School Busing Case:* Milliken v. Bradley *and the Controversy over Desegregation* (Lawrence: University Press of Kansas, 2011), 145; Robert Bork and J. Stanley Pottinger, "Memorandum for the United States as Amicus Curiae," *Milliken v. Bradley*, in Douglas, ed., *School Busing: Constitutional and Political Developments, Vol 1*, 392–418.

65. Gerald Grant, *Hope and Despair in the American City: Why There Are No Bad Schools in Raleigh* (Cambridge: Harvard University Press, 2009), 150–52; *Milliken v. Bradley* (418 US 717.

66. *Milliken v. Bradley.*

67. "Milliken v. Bradley in Historical Perspective: The Supreme Court Comes Full Circle," *Northwestern University Law Review* 69 (1975), 799–801; Terrance L. Green and Mark A. Gooden, "The Shaping of Policy: Exploring the Context, Contradictions, and Contours of Privilege in *Milliken v. Bradley*, over 40 Years Later," *Teachers College Record* (March 2016), 2; *San Antonio Independent School District v. Rodriguez*, 411 US 1 (1973); *Milliken v. Bradley.*

68. *DC*, "Court's Detroit Ruling Blow to Desegregation," July 26, 1974.

69. George J. Rentsch, "Community Meetings and Conflict Management," *Integrated Education: Minority Children in Schools* 11, no. 4–5 (1973): 48–52.

## 6. Considering the Metropolis

1. Wilho Salminen to Greece Board of Education, June 22, 1966, provided to author by John Woods.

2. James Wilmot to Joseph Wilson, April 29, 1966, folder 139:7, Joseph C. Wilson Papers, RBSCP; *DC*, "Protest Planned at School Meet," April 15, 1965.

3. *DC*, "A Metropolitan School District," May 23, 1941.

4. *DC*, "Competent, Constructive," May 18, 1945; "Metropolitan District Urged [. . .]," June 3, 1947.

5. *DC*, "School Board Member for Metropolitan Plan," June 3, 1947.

6. Blake McKelvey, "Rochester's Metropolitan Prospects in Historical Perspective," *Rochester History* 19, no. 3 (July 1957): 28; Andrew J. Coulson, *School District Consolidation, Size and Spending: An Evaluation* (Mackinac Center for Public Policy, 2007). School districts in the South were more often formed in accordance with county boundaries, in part because the county was historically a more salient political unit in the South compared to the North and in part because operating parallel education systems for Black and white students across wide rural expanses was a costly endeavor and required greater geographical scale. This distinction, initially based in white supremacy in the South, ultimately made desegregation a less complex affair there compared to in the North, where politically independent districts proliferate within single metropolitan areas. For more background on the factors behind the shape of school districts across the United States, see William A. Fischel, *Making the Grade: The Economic Evolution of American School Districts* (Chicago: University of Chicago Press, 2009).

7. Joseph Barnes, "Rochester's Era of Annexations, 1901–1926" (PhD diss., State University of New York at Buffalo, 1974); *DC*, "Repeal of Charter Section Suggested [. . .]," Jan. 10, 1931.

8. *DC*, "Ask Smith to Back [. . .]," April 8, 1924; "Urges Study of Tax Phases," Jan. 8, 1925; "City Should Keep Its First Bargain [. . .]," Feb. 19, 1929; Jan. 10, 1931; May 23, 1941; May 18, 1945; "Dewey Signs Bill Giving Autonomy to School Boards, April 20, 1950; "Aex Recommends Fiscal Freedom [. . .]," Sept. 14, 1955; "School Fiscal Freedom Called Step Forward," Oct. 6, 1955; "City Puts Pressure on Free Districts," Feb. 22, 1964; "Assembly OKs Bill to Abolish Free Schools," May 1, 1975. See also A. Vincent Buzard, "Brief in Opposition to the Continuation of Free School Districts Around the City of Rochester," Feb. 26, 1972, box X0429, Rochester Municipal Archives, Rochester, NY.

9. McKelvey, "Rochester's Metropolitan Prospects," 28; *DC*, "Edison Tech Courses Advocated for Girls," Oct. 17, 1958; "Law Stymies County Control of Edison High," Feb. 10, 1960; Jonathan Steepee, "Racial Discrimination in the Rochester, N.Y. School District," folder V:1377, NAACP Papers, LOC

10. *T-U*, "Time Short for Joint School Program," Dec. 17, 1952; *DC*, "Deadline Stands, Education Board Tells Irondequoit," May 28, 1954.

11. *DC*, "The 'Why' of Waiting [. . .]," May 30, 1954; "School Bids Short of Estimates," June 10, 1964.

12. *DC*, "City is Growing!" July 9, 1940; "Metropolitan School District Needed," May 30, 1947; "City Taxpayers Built Them Up," May 31, 1947.

13. Rochester City School District, *Desegregation of the Elementary Schools* (February 1967); *DC*, "Metro School District Urged," Feb. 8, 1967; "Why Goldberg Didn't Offer Metro School Plan," Feb. 16, 1967.

14. *DC*, "Suburbs Bar Merged Schools," Dec. 13, 1966; "Long Look at Schools Pledged," Feb. 3, 1967; "Metro School Plan Essential—Allen," Jan. 18, 1967.

15. *DC*, "Call for Calmness," Feb. 9, 1967.

16. *DC*, Feb. 3, 1967; "Don't Force Busing," Feb. 25, 1971; Jerome Balter, "Statement to the Rochester Board of Education," Feb. 16, 1967, folder titled "Schools, 1967–69," Jerome Balter and Ruth Balter Papers, 1959–1974, Swarthmore College Peace Collection, Swarthmore, PA.

17. Untitled document (announcing 15-Point Plan), Rochester Board of Education, March 16, 1967.

18. Stephen H. Greenspan and Friedrich J. Grasberger, *Target: The Three E's; a Study of the Organizational and Financial Structure of Public Education in Monroe County* (Rochester, NY: Rochester Bureau of Municipal Research, February 1969).

19. The 1971 report also echoed some points that a state joint legislative committee had made in late 1968. Monroe County Educational Planning Committee, *A Proposed Model for a County Federation of School Districts* (August 1971); *DC*, "School Federation Urged," Sept. 29, 1971; Greenspan and Grasberger, *Target*; *DC*, "Merger Eyed on Special Education," Dec. 31, 1968.

20. Monroe County Educational Planning Committee, *A Proposed Model*; Nancy Orr, *A Financial Plan in Support of the Federated Intermediate Educational District* (Rochester, NY: Rochester Center for Governmental and Community Research, October 1971).

21. Author interview with Don Pryor, April 9, 2020; Monroe County Educational Planning Committee, *A Proposed Model.*

22. Author interview with Don Pryor, April 9, 2020.

23. *DC*, "City Schools Would Blend into Suburbs," May 8, 1983; "Wilson Plan Being Taken Seriously," May 9, 1983; "City Schools' Distress Signal Is Real," May 10, 1983; "Council Adopts 'Balanced' Budget," June 30, 1983; "City Fiscal Problems," Dec. 25, 1983.

24. The founding of Project UNIQUE is discussed briefly in: Rochester City School District, *World of Inquiry School* (1976), https://files.eric.ed.gov/fulltext/ED132231.pdf; *DC*, "UR Professor Liaison Aide [. . .]," Nov. 20, 1964; "Storefront School Planned," Jan. 13, 1967; "Superclasses Will Open in School 58," June 16, 1967; "Peek-a-Boo School at Sibley's," Feb. 28, 1968. See also William Young, *Project UNIQUE* (Rochester, NY: Rochester House of Printing, 1969), folder 137:9, Joseph C. Wilson Papers, RBSCP.

25. Project UNIQUE, newsletter, January 1968, Nazareth College Archives, Pittsford, NY.

26. *DC*, Jan. 13, 1967; June 16, 1967; Feb. 28, 1968; "New Tasks for Satellite School," Nov. 13, 1971; Rochester City School District, *World of Inquiry School*; Dean Corrigan, "Reflections on the Creation of the World of Inquiry School," report attached to Nov. 13, 2009, letter to Jean-Claude Brizard, provided to author by Tate DeCaro.

27. *T-U*, "West Irondequoit Schools to Take [. . .]," April 13, 1965; *DC*, "Protest Planned at School Meet," April 15, 1965; Robert Spillane to Gordon Ambach, July 12, 1979, folder 10:3, Gordon M. Ambach Subject Files, NYSA.

28. *T-U*, Old and New Merge [. . .]," Nov. 28, 1967; *DC*, "Model School to Open [. . .]," Sept. 4, 1967; Nov. 13, 1971.

29. Project UNIQUE, newsletter, January 1968; *T-U*, "More Applicants Than Capacity [. . .]," May 24, 1967; Nov. 28, 1967.

30. *DC*, "Teachers Object to Inquiry Plans," Feb. 27, 1969; "Faculty, Parents Reply to Critic," March 1, 1969.

31. *T-U*, "Panel Urges Relocation [. . .]," Feb. 2, 1977.

32. Author interview with Thomas Warfield, Sept. 17, 2019.

33. Author interview with Tate and Patricia DeCaro, Aug. 26, 2019.

34. Rochester City School District, *World of Inquiry School*; *DC*, "Removing City Limits," Feb. 8, 1995; "City Studies All-Boys School," Sept. 11, 2008; graduation rate data available from New York State Education Department, at http://data.nysed.gov; placement data obtained by author from Rochester City School District via Freedom of Information Act request, July 10, 2017.

35. Steven L. Bennett, "Our Incredible Experimental School" *Campus School Documents* 3, 2011, SUNY Brockport College Archives (online), https://digitalcommons.brockport.edu/campus_docs/3; Brockport State Teachers College, "Campus School Parent Handbook," *Campus School Documents* 1, 1964, SUNY Brockport College Archives (online), https://digitalcommons.brockport.edu/campus_docs/1.

36. Bruce Leslie interview with Andrew Virgilio, Aug. 31, 1999, SUNY Brockport, Rose Archives; *DC*, "City to Bus Inner City Pupils [. . .]," Aug. 19, 1966; "Children Learning to Work and Play [. . .]," April 7, 1981; "220 Students Must Find New Schools," Aug. 29, 1981.

37. Bennett, "Our Incredible Experimental School"; *DC*, April 7, 1981.

38. *DC*, "Some Help for New Teachers," July 7, 1966; Rochester City School District, *World of Inquiry School*; author interview with Jeannette Banker, Jan. 23, 2019.

39. Author interview with Terry Carbone, Feb. 28, 2019.

40. *DC*, "Federal Funding May Save Campus School," Feb. 28, 1976; Aug. 29, 1981; author interview with Terry Carbone, Feb. 28, 2019.

41. *DC*, "New School of Inquiry Planned," June 15, 1973; *T-U*, "Inquiry School Sept. 10," Aug. 24, 1973; "Inquiry School Enrollment Up [. . .]," Aug. 31, 1973; "Inquiry School," Sept. 4, 1973.

42. *T-U*, "Inquiry School Hailed," Feb. 21, 1974; "Inquiry School Threatened," May 28, 1974; *DC*, "School Integrated—By Choice," Sept. 22, 1975.

43. *DC*, "Don't Drop School Integration Priority," Aug. 4, 1975; "Brockport School May Be Saved," Feb. 28, 1976; "Students Sought for Integrated School," Aug. 23, 1977; *T-U*, Feb. 21, 1974.

44. Author interview with Terry Carbone, Feb. 28, 2019.

45. Author interview with Thomas Warfield, Sept. 17, 2019; author interview with Terry Carbone, Feb. 28, 2019; author interview with Jeannette Banker, Jan. 23, 2019.

46. John Woods, "Suburban-Industrial-City Cooperative Educational Plan for Disadvantaged Children for the City of Rochester," undated ca. July 1967, folder 3A:9, Walter Cooper Papers, RBSCP; *DC*, "School Park Proposal Gets Good Reception," July 11, 1967.

47. Author interview with John Woods, Jan. 14, 2019; *DC*, July 11, 1967; "Interest Grows [. . .]," July 26, 1967; "Greece Votes Aid to City Schools," Aug. 10, 1967.

48. *DC*, "Greece Voters Turn Down Busing," Feb. 27, 1967; "Greece Rejects Busing from City," June 6, 1968; "World Shown What Racism is About," March 4, 1969.

49. *DC*, "City Board Skeptical About Park School Plan," July 12, 1967; Aug. 10, 1967; *T-U*, "Rochester Rapped on Segregation," April 11, 1968.

50. Herman Goldberg to Ewald Nyquist, Feb. 3, 1970; and Nyquist to Goldberg, Feb. 24, 1970, both in folder 20:6, Ewald Nyquist Subject Files, NYSA.

51. John Bennion, "Report on the Activities of the Task Force on Reducing Racial Isolation in Monroe County during the 1970–71 School Year," May 3, 1971, attached to Craig Smith letter to Kermit Hill, Oct. 5, 1971, folder titled "Board of Education General 1971," box X0429, Rochester Municipal Archives, Rochester, NY; *Brighton-Pittsford Post*, "BCS Teachers Speak on Integration Issue," April 9, 1970.

52. Herman Goldberg to Ewald Nyquist, Feb. 3, 1970, folder 20:6, Ewald Nyquist Subject Files, NYSA; *Brighton-Pittsford Post*, "BHS Students Back Integration," April 2, 1970.

53. Author interview with William Cala, Oct. 10, 2019; *Rochester City Newspaper*, "Regional Schools," May 21, 2014; *DC*, "Cala Seeks a Metro School," Sept. 21, 2008; "The Regional Academy: History," undated document, provided to author by William Cala; "The Regional Academy Act of Two Thousand Ten," draft enabling legislation, provided to author by William Cala.

54. Author interview with Bryan Hetherington, Dec. 19, 2019; author interview with William Cala, Oct. 10, 2019.

55. *Rochester City Newspaper*, May 21, 2014; "The Regional Academy Act of Two Thousand Ten"; author interview with Bryan Hetherington, Dec. 19, 2019.

56. Author interview with William Cala, Oct. 10, 2019; author interview with Joseph Morelle, Feb. 19, 2020; author interview with Bryan Hetherington, Dec. 19, 2019; William Cala, "Why Mayoral Control Is Wrong and Doesn't Work," undated essay ca. 2010, provided to author by William Cala; *Rochester City Newspaper*, May 21, 2014.

57. Author interview with Bryan Hetherington, Dec. 19, 2019; author interview with Malik Evans, Jan. 30, 2020.

58. Author interview with Lynette Sparks and Don Pryor, Jan. 8, 2020; *Rochester City Newspaper*, "Lessons for Rochester from Raleigh," July 23, 2014.

59. Author interview with Lynette Sparks and Don Pryor, Jan. 8, 2020; "GS4A: Great Schools for All," undated brochure, provided to author by Great Schools for All.

60. Jim Antonevich, "Great Schools for All Parent Survey Summary Report" (Rochester, NY: Metrix Matrix, May 2016), http://gs4a.org/wp-content/uploads/2016/05/GS4A-Summary-Survey-2016-FINAL-B.pdf; *DC*, "Magnet Schools Supported," June 10, 2016; author interview with Lynette Sparks and Don Pryor, Jan. 8, 2020.

61. Author interview with Lynette Sparks and Don Pryor, Jan. 8, 2020.

62. Author interview with William Cala, Oct. 10, 2019; *DC*, "RCSD announces its 'Path Forward,'" Jan. 26, 2018; Rochester Board of Education, *Resolution 2016–17:899*, June 27, 2017.

63. *DC*, "Hannah-Jones Asks [. . .]," Oct. 28, 2017; author interview with Lynette Sparks and Don Pryor, Jan. 8, 2020.

64. *DC*, "Mayor Calls for Consolidations," March 5, 2002.

65. *DC*, "Merge School Districts?" Sept. 25, 1996; "Mayor Criticizes Consolidation Letter," April 19, 2002; "Reactions Split at Metro Forum," April 26, 2002; author interview with Bill Johnson, Dec. 27, 2019.

66. *DC*, "GOP hits Johnson [. . .]," July 24, 2003; "Johnson Outspends Brooks," Oct. 28, 2003; author interview with Bill Johnson, Dec. 27, 2019.

67. *DC*, "Flap over Race Roils Monroe Campaign," Oct. 3, 2003; "Johnson Stresses Experience and Vision," Oct. 19, 2003.

68. *DC*, "Brooks Soars," Nov. 5, 2003; *Rochester City Newspaper*, "Lessons from the Johnson Loss," Nov. 12, 2003; "2004 'Pollie' Award Winners" (McClean, VA: American Association of Political Consultants, 2004), https://theaapc.org/wp-content/uploads/2015/10/2004_Winners.pdf.

## 7. The Urban-Suburban Program

1. *DC*, "Indicted City Aides [. . .]," Aug. 3, 1962; "Jazz," May 29, 1977; "Pythodd Club, a Jiggling Jazz Mecca," June 21, 2015; author interview with Kirk Holmes, July 22, 2018.

2. Norman Gross, "Minority Group Isolation in Schools (Part II)," *about . . . time*, Aug. 1979, 2–3; *DC*, "W. Irondequoit Pupil Shift [. . .]," Sept. 4, 1965; "Retiring Director Fighting to Save [. . .]," May 23, 1982; Lawrence W. Heinrich, "A Descriptive Study of a Cooperative Urban-Suburban Pupil Transfer Program" (EdD diss., University of Rochester, 1969), 72.

3. *DC*, "Irondequoit to Get City 1st Graders," April 14, 1965; *T-U*, "W. Irondequoit Schools to Take [. . .]," April 13, 1965; Heinrich, "Descriptive Study," 72–77.

4. Author interview with Kirk Holmes, July 22, 2018.

5. *DC*, "Students Are Confident [. . .]," Dec. 1, 1963; "Madison's Answer to Image [. . .]," March 18, 1964; "High School Pupils Examine Prejudice," Oct. 30, 1964; US Commission on Civil Rights, *Hearing Before the United States Commission on Civil Rights: Hearing Held in Rochester, New York, Sept. 16–17, 1966*, held at Rush Rhees Library, University of Rochester, 62–65.

6. *DC*, "Teacher Salaries Proposal [. . .]," March 8, 1956; "Storandt Sees Gross [. . .]," Aug. 23, 1962; *T-U*, "Negro History Courses Pushed," July 18, 1968.

7. Author interviews with Deborah Gitomer, Oct. 17, 2018, Dec. 19, 2018.

8. *DC*, "Gross Fire Returned at Session," Oct. 17, 1968.

9. *DC*, "Narrowing the Distance," Oct. 8, 2014.

10. *Etter v. Littwitz*, 47 Misc. 2d 473, 262 NYS 2d 924 (1965); *DC*, Sept. 4, 1965; "Irondequoit Board Upheld on Accepting Negroes," Feb. 25, 1966; "Irondequoit Ponders Pursuing Busing Fight," Sept. 22, 1967; Heinrich, "Descriptive Study," 140.

11. *DC*, "West Irondequoit Elects Board 'Secrecy' Foe," June 17, 1965; *DC*, "School Budget Rejected in W. Irondequoit," May 4, 1967; Gross, "Minority Group Isolation in Schools (Part II)," 30.

12. Heinrich, "Descriptive Study," 145, 152, 162; author interview with Mary Halpin, Oct. 2, 2018.

13. Author interview with Kirk Holmes, July 22, 2018; author interview with Yvette Singletary, July 31, 2018.

14. Clement Finch Hapeman, "Teacher and Administrator Evaluations of the West Irondequoit Intercultural Enrichment Program," Spring 1967, folder 1:16, Urban-Suburban Summer School Program, Brighton, NY, Papers, RBSCP.

15. *DC*, "Concern of Few Stirs [. . .]," Aug. 17, 1966; "The History of Project U-S: 50th Anniversary Edition" (November 2015), https://www.monroe.edu/cms/lib/NY02216770/Centricity/Domain/121/US_History_50thAnnivEdition_rev4_21_16.pdf; Project UNIQUE, newsletter, January 1968, folder 2/1/16.1, Nazareth College Archives, Pittsford, NY.

16. *Brighton-Pittsford Post*, "Brighton Group to Fight 'Busing,'" Nov. 10, 1966; *Brighton-Pittsford Post*, "Busing Poll," undated clipping ca. December 1966, folder 1:12, Urban-Suburban Summer School Program, Brighton, NY, Papers, RBSCP

17. *T-U*, "Parents More Receptive to Integration," Sept. 26, 1972.

18. "A Special Report to the Board of Education of Hilton Central School on Poverty and Integration," April 25, 1967, folder 3B:12, Walter Cooper Papers, RBSCP.

19. *DC*, Oct. 17, 1968; "Sick, Says Gross of Suburban Whites," Jan. 31, 1969; "Board Rejects School Integration Plan," March 13, 1979; "Webster Poll Opposes Pupil Transfer," Feb. 22, 1979.

20. Gross, "Minority Group Isolation in Schools (Part II)."

21. *DC*, "6 take on U.S. [. . .]," May 9, 1974; "Project US," undated booklet ca. 1980, Local History and Genealogy Division, RPL; *T-U*, "The Annual Urban-Suburban Crisis," May 16, 1975; "Worry Expressed about Future of School Desegregation Program," Nov. 14, 1984; "The History of Project U-S."

22. Kara S. Finnigan and Tricia J. Stewart, "Interdistrict Choice as a Policy Solution: Examining Rochester's Urban-Suburban Interdistrict Transfer Program" (presentation at "School Choice and School Improvement: Research in State, District and Community Contexts," Vanderbilt University, October 25–27, 2009), 13–14, 26; *DC*, "Transfer Program Could Be in Danger," Sept. 3, 1980; "Urban-Suburban Program Stresses Diversity," Jan. 9, 1991; "Fairport Targets Diversity," Nov. 17, 2003.

23. Author interview with William Cala, Nov. 13, 2018.

24. Author interview with William Cala, Nov. 13, 2018; *DC*, "Fairport Mulls Pupil Transfer Plan," Feb. 26, 2003; Nov. 17, 2003.

25. "The History of Project U-S"; *DC*, "District Won't Enter Orogram," Feb. 2, 2011.

26. Author interview with William Cala, Nov. 13, 2018.

27. Spencerport Board of Education, minutes, Oct. 28, 2014; Dec. 9, 2014; Feb. 2, 2015; Feb. 24, 2015.

28. Author's notes, Spencerport Board of Education meeting, Dec. 9, 2014.

29. *DC*, "School Choice Debate Divisive," Dec. 10, 2014.

30. *DC*, "Step Up, Spencerport," Feb. 3, 2015; "District Joins Despite Rancor," Feb. 25, 2015.

31. *DC*, "Only 25 Places for 60 Kids," July 16, 1965; "W. Irondequoit Schools Take [. . .]," Sept. 8, 1965; "Learning Better When We're Together," Nov. 27, 1998.

32. *DC*, "School Turns White Girl Down," Sept. 11, 1998.

33. *DC*, "Transfer Plan at a Crossroads," Jan. 27, 1999; "Integration Program to Reopen," June 22, 2000.

34. *Hopwood v. Texas*, 78 F.3d 932 (5th Cir. 1996). The Circuit Court decision was abrogated by the US Supreme Court in 2003 in *Grutter v. Bollinger*, 539 US 306 (2003).

35. *Parent Ass'n of Andrew Jackson High Sch. v. Ambach*, 598 F.2d 705 (2d Cir.1979); *Brewer v. West Irondequoit Central School Dist.*, 32 F. Supp. 2d 619 (WDNY 1999). See also *Parent Ass'n of Andrew Jackson High Sch. v. Ambach*, 738 F.2d 574 (2d Cir.1984).

36. *DC*, "Ruling Adds to Race Debate," May 13, 2000, June 22, 2000; "Early Success in Spencerport," Dec. 30, 2016.

37. *Parents Involved in Community Schools v. Seattle School District No. 1*, 551 US 701 (2007); author interview with William Cala, Nov. 13, 2018.

38. Rush-Henrietta Board of Education, "Board of Education Position Summary: Urban-Suburban Inter-District Transfer Program" (May 25, 2016).

39. *DC*, "Program May Admit Whites," March 20, 2015; Dec. 30, 2016; "The History of Project U-S"; Author interview with Jeff Crane, Oct. 22, 2018.

40. *DC*, "Diversity of Students Sought," May 23, 2015; "Webster Schools to Take City Kids," Nov. 25, 2015; "Long Bus Ride Forces Kendall from Urban-Suburban Plan," Sept. 7, 2016; "Honeoye Falls-Lima to Offer [. . .]," Dec. 22, 2017.

41. Rochester City School District, "Urban Suburban Program," internal memo, Feb. 12, 2018; 2017–18 district data from New York State Education Department General Formula Aid Output Report database, available at stateaid.nysed.gov.

42. Author interview with Richard Stutzman, Jan. 21, 2015.

43. Honeoye Falls-Lima Urban-Suburban Committee, "Report to the HFL Board of Education" (October 24, 2017).

44. Rochester City School District operating budget, 2014–15; RCSD, "Urban Suburban Program"; *DC*, "City Students Drive Revenue for Suburban Schools," June 20, 2019; author interview with Jeff Crane, Oct. 22, 2018.

45. *Brewer v. West Irondequoit Central School Dist.*

46. William C. Young et al., *Project UNIQUE* (Rochester, NY: self-published, 1969), 50, folder 137:9, Joseph C. Wilson Papers, RBSCP.

47. Hapeman, "Teacher and Administrator Evaluations."

48. Center for Governmental Research, *Race and Education in Rochester: Successes, Problems and Opportunities* (Rochester, NY, June 1979), 120–21; *DC*, "Schools Can Improve Racial Balance: Study," Aug. 17, 1979.

49. Finnigan and Stewart, "Interdistrict Choice." See also Jennifer Jellison Holme and Kara S. Finnigan, *Striving in Common: A Regional Equity Framework for Urban Schools* (Cambridge, MA: Harvard Education Press, 2018); Kara S. Finnigan et al., "Regional Educational Policy Analysis: Rochester, Omaha, and Minneapolis' Inter-District Arrangements," *Educational Policy* 29, no. 5 (2015), 780–814.

50. West Irondequoit newsletter no. 37 (April 1965), cited in Finnigan and Stewart, "Interdistrict Choice," 24.

51. Heinrich, "Descriptive Study," 192.

52. Holme and Finnigan, *Striving in Common*, 60–63; Finnigan et al., "Regional Educational Policy Analysis"; Kara S. Finnigan and Jennifer Jellison Holme, "Learning from Inter-District School Transfer Programs," *Poverty & Race* 24, no. 4 (July/August 2015), 12.

53. Finnigan and Stewart, "Interdistrict Choice."

54. Rush-Henrietta Central School District, "Responses to Most Frequent Community Questions about the Urban-Suburban Program" (October 2016); Finnigan and Stewart, "Interdistrict Choice"; Honeoye Falls-Lima Urban-Suburban Committee, "Report."

55. Finnigan and Stewart, "Interdistrict Choice," 22.

56. Finnigan and Stewart, "Interdistrict Choice."

57. *Dennis et al. v. Board of Education of the Pittsford Central School District*, WL 696398 (WDNY 2005).

58. *DC*, "Penfield Puts New Limits on Transfers," March 24, 1994.

59. Author interview with Jessica Lewis, Sept. 27, 2018; author interview with Wayne Johnson, Aug. 4, 2018.

60. *DC*, "Removing City Limits," Feb. 8, 1995; author interview with Jessica Lewis, Sept. 27, 2018; author interview with Kennedy Jackson, Dec. 20, 2018.

61. Finnigan and Stewart, "Interdistrict Choice," 36.

62. Author interview with Jeff Crane, Oct. 22, 2018; *DC*, "Urban-Suburban's Reach at 50," Jan. 18, 2015.

63. Author interview with Jeff Crane, Oct. 22, 2018.

64. *DC*, May 23, 1982.

65. Author interview with Jeff Crane, Oct. 22, 2018.

66. US Department of Health, Education, and Welfare, Office of Education, *Planning Educational Change*, vol. 4: *How Five School Systems Desegregated* (Washington, DC: US Department of Health, Education, and Welfare, 1969); *DC*, Aug. 17, 1966.

67. Author interview with Walter Cooper, Aug. 21, 2018.

## 8. The Age of Accountability

1. *DC*, "Legal Opinion Stops Busing Resolution," Oct. 3, 1969.

2. *DC*, "Warren Calls on Community [. . .]," March 5, 2019; "Is This Off the Table?" March 7, 2019.

3. *T-U*, "City School Rolls Decline [. . .]," Dec. 29, 1970; US Census data, 1970 and 2010; student enrollment data from New York State Education Department, available at data.nysed.gov.

4. *DC*, "Puerto Ricans Quite Crowded Island for City [. . .]," Jan. 12, 1955; Karen McCally, "Building the Barrio: A Story of Rochester's Puerto Rican Pioneers," *Vocero Hispano*, April 1957, folder 1:31, Nydia Padilla-Rodriguez Papers, RMSC; Nydia Padilla, "Puerto Rican Contributions to the Greater Rochester Area" (MEd thesis, State University of New York College at Brockport, 1985), 12–15, box 1, Nydia Padilla-Rodriguez Papers, RMSC; Nydia Padilla-Rodriguez interview with Ramon Padilla, Nov. 23, 1985, folder 1:19, Nydia Padilla-Rodriguez Papers, RMSC.

5. McCally, "Building the Barrio"; *DC*, "Adelante Begins; Bilingual Studies," Aug. 19, 1969; "Rochester's Spanish Community," June 18, 1972; Manuel Rivera, "Bilingual

Education in Rochester: A Report," draft copy, Rochester City School District Department of Bilingual Education, June 1982, folder 140:14, Sue Costa Papers, RMSC; George Rentsch, "The Puerto Rican in the Rochester Public Schools," Rochester City School District, Nov. 3, 1966, folder 15:202, Sue Costa Papers, RMSC.

6. *DC*, "Vietnamese Still Dream about Going Home," Aug. 27, 1978; "Scars Linger," Aug. 8, 1981; "For Refugees, a Long Road to Prosperity," Sept. 25, 1988; enrollment data from New York State Education Department, available at data.nysed.gov.

7. Author interview with Nydia Padilla-Rodriguez, Aug. 22, 2019.

8. McCally, "Building the Barrio"; *DC*, "Asian Influx," Nov. 11, 2014.

9. Enrollment data from New York State Education Department, available at data.nysed.gov; US Census data, 1970 and 2000; author interview with Musette Castle, June 21, 2018; author interview with Gloria Winston Al-Sarag, Sept. 20, 2018; see also Gary Orfield and Susan Eaton, *Dismantling Desegregation: The Quiet Reversal of* Brown v. Board of Education (New York: New Press, 1996), 84–85.

10. Urban League of Rochester, "Monroe County Housing Audits, May 1974—December 1975," July 1976, folders 12:27–29, Sue Costa Papers, RMSC.

11. *DC*, "A Warning to City Schools on Integration," May 1, 1975; *T-U*, "Urban League Proposes Steps [. . .]," May 20, 1977; David J. Wirschem, *Racial Isolation in the Rochester Public Schools: The Problem and What To Do about It* (Urban League of Rochester, April 1977), folder III:347, National Urban League Papers, LOC.

12. *DC*, "Group's Name Inflammatory?" June 1, 1977; "School District Integration Study [. . .]," Jan. 7, 1979; "City Schools' Integration is Criticized," Jan. 30, 1979; "Report: Students Should Be Allowed to Choose School," Oct. 16, 1979.

13. *DC*, "County, City School Integration Examined," July 1, 1979. The documents are also not contained in the papers of Patricia Harris, then the Health, Education and Welfare secretary, at the Library of Congress.

14. *DC*, "Frusci: Kids Fail Because They Don't Try," July 12, 1978; July 1, 1979.

15. Lou Buttino and Mark Hare, *The Remaking of a City: Rochester, New York 1964–1984* (Dubuque, IA: Kendall Hunt, 1984), 234–35; Joel S. Berke, Margaret E. Goertz, and Richard J. Coley, *Politicians, Judges, and City Schools: Reforming School Finance in New York* (New York: Russell Sage Foundation, 1984), 163–65; Kermit Hill to John Franco, Dec. 28, 1972, box X0429, Rochester Municipal Archives, Rochester, NY.

16. *Board of Education, Levittown Union Free School District et al. v. Ewald B. Nyquist*, 57 NY2d 27, 439 NE2d 359, 453 NYS2d 643 (1982); *DC*, "School Financing: Tough Knot to Unravel," June 25, 1978; "Unequal Spending for Schools Legal," June 24, 1982; Brian J. Nickerson and Gerard M. Deenihan, "From Equity to Adequacy: The Legal Battle for Increased State Funding of Poor School Districts in New York," *Fordham Urban Law Review* 30, no. 4 (May 2003), 1361–64. The relevant section of the New York State Constitution (article 11, section 1) reads: "The legislature shall provide for the maintenance and support of a system of free common schools, wherein all the children of this state may be educated."

17. *DC*, "Franco, Board in Awkward Positions," March 2, 1980; "Franco to L.I. [. . .]," April 22, 1980; "Teachers Ratify the Pact," Sept. 12, 1980; "Teachers Union called Cohesive," May 6, 1981; Buttino and Hare, *Remaking of a City*, 236–41.

18. *T-U*, "The Change Agent," July 4, 1981; author interview with Archie Curry, March 2, 2020; Ralph Edwards and Charles V. Willie, *Black Power/White Power in Public Education* (Westport, CT: Praeger, 1998), 33.

19. "A Nation at Risk: The Imperative for Educational Reform" (Washington, DC: US Commission on Excellence in Education, 1983).

20. Denise Gelberg, *The "Business" of Reforming American Schools* (Albany: State University of New York Press, 1997), 126–27.

21. *Education Week*, Nov. 14, 1990; David Kearns and Denis Doyle, *Winning the Brain Race: A Bold Plan to Make Our Schools Competitive* (San Francisco: Institute for Contemporary Studies, 1988), 3.

22. Gerald Grant and Christine Murray, *Teaching in America: The Slow Revolution* (Cambridge, MA: Harvard University Press, 1999), 142; *DC*, "Assignment: Change," Jan. 17, 1988; "Education Must Change, and Business Can Help," Sept. 25, 1988.

23. *DC*, "School Program Lacking Support," Feb. 26, 1973; "Magnet OK Looks 'Certain,'" June 9, 1973; "Voluntary Integration Plan Okayed," Nov. 16, 1973; "Schools Plan Arts Program as Attraction," Aug. 7, 1976; *T-U*, "Magnet School Shift Planned [. . .]," June 22, 1977; Buttino and Hare, *Remaking of a City*, 233–34.

24. *DC*, "Magnet Schools: City's Main Hope for Integration," Dec. 3, 1979; "City School Board Votes 5–1 [. . .]," Dec. 7, 1979; "Big Change Proposed for Schools," Dec. 19, 1980; "School Restructuring Ok'd," May 1, 1981; *T-U*, "1 of 4 Attends 'Away' School," Dec. 19, 1979; *Rochester City Newspaper*, "Have We Found a Racial Magnet?," Sept. 6, 1979; author interview with Peter McWalters, March 9, 2020; Buttino and Hare, *Remaking of a City*, 233–34.

25. Author interview with Suzanne Johnston, Oct. 11, 2019; *T-U*, "From Tough School to Tough Standards," Jan. 24, 1984.

26. *DC*, "Parents Pleased with Magnet School," Jan. 21, 1984; "Wilson Magnet High School Proves Itself," Jan. 27, 1985; "Taste of Adventure in Learning-Trip to Bahamas," March 5, 1986; "I Won't Forget This Visit," May 19, 1989; "Federal Grant Will Aid City's Top Students," Sept. 19, 1998; author interview with Malik Evans, Jan. 30, 2020.

27. Author interview with Lovely Warren, Oct. 21, 2019.

28. *DC*, "Magnet Schools' Enrollment Down," Jan. 25, 1984; "Education Officials Praise Program [. . .]," June 21, 1988; *T-U*, "City Magnet Schools Get Their Report Card," May 8, 1984; "New Magnet Schools' Methods [. . .]," Sept. 16, 1986.

29. *T-U*, May 8, 1984; *DC*, "School Tour Finds Quick Benefactor," Feb. 21, 1983.

30. Orfield and Eaton, *Dismantling Desegregation*, 16–19; *T-U*, "Tolerating Segregation," Feb. 6, 1984; "New Definition Helps Schools' Racial Balance," June 5, 1984; "White Students Score Higher than Minorities," June 20, 1989; *DC*, "City Schools Show Racial Imbalance," Oct. 31, 1989.

31. *T-U*, "Magnets' Costs Soar," June 25, 1980; "Recruiting Drive Planned for City Magnet Schools," Dec. 20, 1983; "A Shaky Refuge from the Raw World," June 24, 1992; *DC*, "Assessing the Future of City's Magnet Schools," June 7, 1982; author interview with Peter McWalters, March 9, 2020; author interview with Suzanne Johnston, Oct. 11, 2019.

32. Author interview with Lovely Warren, Oct. 21, 2019; *DC*, "Urbanski Leads Teachers Union in Blast [. . .]," June 7, 1989; "Franklin High Added to Bad-School List," July 13, 1991; "Franklin High Principal Asks [. . .]," Aug. 6, 1991; "Rivera Says He Won't Forsake Franklin High," Oct. 29, 1991.

33. *DC*, "City Schools: The War against Attrition," Aug. 28, 1988; "District Endorses Choice," Aug. 9, 1993; Rochester School Board, "Parent Preference/Managed

Choice Policy #5153," adopted Oct. 17, 2002; Rochester City School District budgets, 1993–94 and 2007–08.

34. *DC*, "Wilson High to Restore IB Classes for All," Oct. 2, 2014; "Panel Looks at School Choice," Jan. 28, 2017.

35. Author interview with Archie Curry, March 2, 2020.

36. Mary Anna Towler, the founder of *Rochester City Newspaper* and a veteran of the fight for school desegregation, summarized these efforts nicely in "The More Things Change: 48 Years with the RCSD," a Sept. 3, 2019, column in *City*.

37. Rump Group, "A Community at Risk: Why the Failure of Rochester City Schools Is Everybody's Business" (2003).

38. *New York Times*, "Big Raises Agreed on for Rochester Teachers," May 16, 1986; Julia Koppich, "The Rocky Road to Reform in Rochester" (paper presented at the annual meeting of the American Educational Research Association, April 1992), available at https://files.eric.ed.gov/fulltext/ED346557.pdf, 10, 13; Gelberg, *The "Business" of Reforming American Schools*, 175–77.

39. *DC*, "School-Based Planning Takes Root in Rochester," Aug. 29, 1988; "Did City Schools Get What They Paid For?" May 7, 1995; *Washington Monthly*, "Reform School Confidential," October 1992; Koppich, "Rocky Road to Reform," 20–28; author interview with Adam Urbanski, March 3, 2020.

40. *DC*, "City Zapped," Sept. 8, 1987; author interview with Adam Urbanski, March 3, 2020; *Washington Monthly*, October 1992.

41. *DC*, "Teachers Contract Approved," Sept. 4, 1987; Koppich, "Rocky Road to Reform," 34–46; author interview with Adam Urbanski, March 3, 2020.

42. *DC*, May 7, 1995; author interview with Adam Urbanski, March 3, 2020.

43. *DC*, "McWalters Chosen," May 28, 1986; author interview with Archie Curry, March 2, 2020; author interview with Peter McWalters, March 9, 2020.

44. Art Aspengren et al., "For All Our Children . . . No More Excuses! A Framework for Transforming Rochester's Public Education System," (Dec. 5, 1994), also known as "The King/Johnson Report"; *DC*, "Accountability is Key," Oct. 14, 2012; "New Charter Schools Lead District Exodus," Feb. 18, 2014; "Enrollment at Charter Schools Still Booming," Nov. 21, 2017; Rochester City School District, "Budget and District Profile, 2020–21," May 7, 2020.

45. *DC*, "Charter School Leader Fired [. . .]," May 6, 2015; "Public Funding, Little Oversight," Jan. 24, 2016; "Charter School Criticized for Finances," May 26, 2017; "Public Helps Bolster Developer's Profit," Dec. 10, 2017.

46. *DC*, "Unwanted?" Nov. 10, 2019.

47. *DC*, "Regents Approve Charter School [. . .]," July 14, 2000; "To Succeed, Keep Middle-Class Students [. . .]," March 28, 2015; "Regents Make Moves against Charter Schools," May 21, 2020; Koppich, "Rocky Road to Reform," 26–27.

48. Author interview with Shannon Hillman, May 13, 2020.

49. *DC*, "RCSD Board Approves Closings [. . .]," Feb. 29, 2020; author interview with Ed Cavalier, Oct. 2, 2019.

50. Author interview with Amber Paynter, Sept. 23, 2020.

51. The full list of child plaintiffs: Amber Paynter, Desirae Morris, Yancey and Yalawn Christian, Shanika Graham, Alicia Feliciano, Taiwan and Ashley Jackson, Ryan Addamson, Nicholas Williams, Jerome Blocker, Winnie Alfred, Ashley Smith, Joshua Graham, and Eli Presha. All were school-age Black children living in the city of Rochester.

52. *DC*, "Local Lawsuit Takes Schools to Task," Aug. 27, 1998; "Helping to Even Up City and Suburban Success Rates," Sept. 30, 1998; "Suit Links Poor Grades to Poverty," Nov. 13, 2002; author interview with Bryan Hetherington and Jonathan Feldman, Dec. 19, 2019.

53. *Paynter v. State of New York*, 187 Misc. 2d 227, 720 N.Y.S.2d 712 (2000).

54. *Paynter v. New York*; author interview with Bryan Hetherington and Jonathan Feldman, Dec. 19, 2019.

55. Author interview with Yalawn Christian, Sept. 23, 2020.

56. *Sheff v. O'Neill*, 238 Conn. 1, 3 (1996).

57. *Campaign for Fiscal Equity Inc. v. State*, 86 N.Y.2d 306 (1995).

58. Author interview with Jonathan Feldman and Bryan Hetherington, Dec. 19, 2019.

59. Jane F. Morse, *A Level Playing Field: School Finance in the Northeast* (Albany: State University of New York Press, 2007), 59; author interview with Jonathan Feldman and Bryan Hetherington, Dec. 19, 2019.

60. *Paynter v. New York*; *DC*, "City Hall Says It's Backing GRACE lawsuit," March 7, 2003.

61. *Paynter v. New York*; *DC*, "Ruling Deals Mortal Blow to GRACE Suit," June 27, 2003.

62. *DC*, "School Aid Formula Gets an 'F,'" June 27, 2003; "Why NY's School-Aid Formula is Flunking," Aug. 28, 2016.

63. *New York Times*, "Judge George Bundy Smith, 80, Dies [. . .]," Aug. 10, 2017; Sandra Jefferson Grannum, Erika J. Duthiers, and Janet A. Gordon, "George Bundy Smith" (White Plains: Historical Society of the New York Courts, 2007), https://history.nycourts.gov/biography/george-bundy-smith/.

64. *Paynter v. New York.*

65. *DC*, June 27, 2003; author interview with Amber Paynter, Sept. 23, 2020.

66. Author interview with Jonathan Feldman and Bryan Hetherington, Dec. 19, 2019.

67. The cases are *Oklahoma City v. Dowell*, 111 US 630 (1991); *Freeman v. Pitts*, 503 US 467 (1992); and *Missouri v. Jenkins*, 515 US 70 (1995). See Raymond Wolters, *Race and Education, 1954–2007* (Columbia: University of Missouri Press, 2008), 265–67.

68. *Arthur v. Nyquist* 415 F. Supp. 904 (WDNY 1976); Jenna Tomasello, "Buffalo History and the Roots of School Segregation: The Rise of Buffalo's Two-Tiered School System," in *Discrimination in Elite Public Schools: Investigating Buffalo*, ed. Gary Orfield and Jennifer B. Ayscue (New York: Teachers College Press, 2018), 47–50; John Kucsera and Gary Orfield, "New York State's Extreme School Segregation: Inequality, Inaction and a Damaged Future" (Civil Rights Project/*Proyecto Derechos Civiles*, March 2014); *New York Times*, "School Integration in Buffalo is Hailed . . .," May 13, 1985; *Buffalo News*, "For Vocational High Schools [. . .]," June 8, 1997.

69. *Buffalo News*, "Magnets: Losing Their Attraction [. . .]," June 8, 1997; *New York Times*, May 13, 1985; Tomasello, "Buffalo History," 50.

70. J. John Harris et al., "The Curious Case of *Missouri v. Jenkins*: The End of the Road for Court-Ordered Desegregation?" *Journal of Negro Education* 66, no. 1 (Winter 1997), 50; *Parents Involved in Community Schools v. Seattle School District No. 1*, 551 US 701 (2007), including "Brief of 553 Social Scientists as *Amici Curiae* in Support of Respondents."

71. *Parents Involved v. Seattle.*

72. The answer key: No Child Left Behind; Race to the Top; Every Student Succeeds Act; Adequate Yearly Progress; Diagnostic Tool for School and District Effectiveness; Student Learning Outcomes; Annual Professional Performance Review; Comprehensive Support and Improvement; Targeted Support and Improvement; School Comprehensive Education Plan; School Improvement Grant; District Comprehensive Improvement Plan.

73. *DC*, "Straight Talk on City Schools," Aug. 16, 2016.

74. Author interview with Peter McWalters, March 9, 2020.

## Conclusion

1. Author interview with Melanie Funchess, April 8, 2020; *DC*, "City Probably Will Close More Schools," April 9, 2020.

2. Terry Dade to Rochester City School District Students, Families and Staff, April 23, 2020, available at https://www.documentcloud.org/documents/20986264-dade-resignation-letter; *Times Herald-Record* (Middletown, NY), "Cornwall Names New School Superintendent," May 5, 2020.

3. Jennifer Jellison Holme and Kara S. Finnigan, *Striving in Common: A Regional Equity Framework for Urban Schools* (Cambridge, MA: Harvard Education Press, 2018), 128.

4. Holme and Finnigan, *Striving in Common*, 96–114.

5. Derrick Bell, *Silent Covenants:* Brown v. Board of Ed. *and the Unfulfilled Hopes for Racial Reform* (New York: Oxford University Press, 2004), 166.

6. James Baldwin, *No Name in the Street*, in *Baldwin: Collected Essays*, ed. Toni Morrison (New York: Library of America, [1972] 1998), 431–32.

7. "Stand Against Racism," Monroe County Council of School Superintendents, June 9, 2020, available at https://fairport.org/2020/06/a-message-from-monroe-county-superintendents-stand-against-racism/; *DC*, "Suburban Struggle," Dec. 16, 2018.

8. Herman Goldberg and H. Hunter Fraser to RCSD parents, Dec. 2, 1963, folder 3A:9, Walter Cooper Papers, RBSCP.

9. *Rochester City Newspaper*, "Education . . . Means Emancipation", Feb. 13, 2019; author interview with Malik Evans, Jan. 30, 2020.

10. *DC*, "Students Confront Racial Issues," Jan. 9, 2016; Dec. 16, 2018; "Student Activists Step Up [. . .]," Oct. 16, 2020; *Rochester Business Journal*, "Local Students Leading Discussion [. . .]," July 10, 2020.

11. *DC*, "Students Fight for School Integration," Feb. 24, 1968; "MCC Students to Take Up [. . .],"April 6, 1968.

12. *DC*, Feb. 24, 1968.

# Note on Sources

Because of this book's broad scope in both time and subject matter, my research required the use of a wide variety of archival sources. Locating these documents and fitting them into my understanding of the topic was both a struggle and a joy. Here are some of the key sources and repositories I relied on.

The Rochester Public Library's Local History and Genealogy Division has a thoroughly categorized mountain of newspaper clippings for most of the twentieth century as well as a nearly complete microfilm record of all major and minor newspapers printed in the city since its founding. It also holds original copies of many Rochester City School District documents dating to the nineteenth century. The library hosts the invaluable Phillis Wheatley Public Library Oral History Collection, containing dozens of recorded interviews with Black community leaders in the late 1970s and early 1980s. These are online at http://www.rochestervoices.org/collections/african-american-oral-histories/.

The University of Rochester's Rare Books and Special Collections division at Rush Rhees Library (RBSCP) contains several collections that are indispensable to those researching the racial dynamics in Monroe County after 1950. The Walter Cooper Papers cover important parts of the early Civil Rights era, while the Franklin Florence Papers pick up mostly after the uprising in July 1964. The Joseph C. Wilson, Ruth Scott, Harry Gove, and Urban-Suburban Summer School Program, Brighton, NY, papers were also useful. The University of Rochester hosts the Rochester Black Freedom Struggle Oral History Project, a collection of interview recordings made by the historian Laura Warren Hill for her book *Strike the Hammer*. The recordings and transcripts are available online at https://rbscp.lib.rochester.edu/4489.

The Rochester Museum and Science Center (RMSC) is home to the Howard C. Coles Collection, the voluminous and wide-ranging files of the pioneering journalist, including his unpublished manuscript "Nomads from the South." Coles created an important statistical record regarding housing conditions for Black people in Rochester throughout the twentieth century. RMSC also holds several important collections relating to the growth of the Puerto Rican community in Rochester. The largest of them is the Sue Costa Collection of Hispanic/Latino Papers, while the most useful single document for my purposes was Nydia Padilla's 1985 master's thesis, "Puerto Rican Contributions to the Greater Rochester Area."

Other local libraries and repositories that I consulted include the Rochester Municipal Archives; the Rose Archives at SUNY Brockport; the Project UNIQUE Papers at Nazareth College; and the Big Springs Historical Society in Caledonia, New York. At the New York State Archives in Albany I reviewed the personal papers of Education Commissioners James E. Allen and Ewald Nyquist as well as both men's official Commissioner's Files. These collections yielded several interesting documents not intended for local consumption, most significantly the 1970 letter from Herman Goldberg to Nyquist discussing the possibility of a school operated jointly by Rochester and Brighton. The Jerome and Ruth Balter Papers at Swarthmore College in Philadelphia gave fascinating behind-the-scenes perspective on the local desegregation movement in the early 1960s.

The National Association for the Advancement of Colored People Papers at the Library of Congress in Washington, DC, were an extremely fruitful resource. They contain previously unreported information regarding race relations in the early twentieth century and the full case file of *Aikens v. Board of Education*, including a fragmentary copy of the Steepee study that was believed to have been lost. Elsewhere at the Library of Congress, the draft Simulmatics study in the Daniel P. Moynihan Papers gives a strikingly frank view of physical and social segregation in Rochester after 1964. I also found valuable information in the papers of the National Urban League.

This book relies as well on a great deal of secondary literature, both about Rochester and about other places in the country. The story of the nineteenth-century push for desegregation in Rochester schools is told well by Judith Polgar Ruchkin in "The Abolition of Colored Schools in Rochester, New York, 1832–1856," *New York History* 51, no. 4 (July 1970), 377–93. Blake McKelvey's *The Water-Power City* is a valuable overview of the first few decades of Rochester's history, while Milton Sernett's *North Star Country* describes abolitionism and nineteenth-century civil rights activities in upstate New York in general. Carleton Mabee's *Black Education in New York* gives the context of other New York school districts' struggles regarding desegregation and access to education for Black children. David Blight's biography of Frederick Douglass is the best and most comprehensive—together, of course, with Douglass's own memoirs.

The peerless history of the national Great Migration is Isabel Wilkerson, *The Warmth of Other Suns: The Epic Story of America's Great Migration*. Two massive government publications provide important data about Rochester's Black community before the Civil Rights era: the *Second Report* of the New York State Temporary Commission on the Condition of the Colored Urban Population, from 1938; and *Negroes in Five New York Cities: A Study of Problems, Achievements and Trends*, a 1958 publication of the New York State Commission against Discrimination Division of Research. Blake McKelvey's "Lights and Shadows in Local Negro History," *Rochester History* 21, no. 3 (October 1959), 1–27, is a general overview of Black history in this and other periods. Joyce Woelfe Lehmann, ed., *Migrant Farmworkers of Wayne County, New York: A Collection of Oral Histories from the Back Roads* collects interviews with some of the many men and women who picked apples and cherries in Wayne County. There are many journalistic exposés regarding working conditions for migrant workers; one of the best is Dale Wright's book *They Harvest Despair*. Laura Root's 1951 master's thesis, "An Analysis of Social Distance between the Two Negro Communities of Rochester, New York," provides a fascinating insight into the social dynamics of the Third and Seventh Wards before the Great Migration began in earnest. It is available for review in person at the University of Rochester Rare Books and Special Collections division. A good national overview of housing discrimination is Richard Rothstein's 2017 book *The Color of Law*. Patricia Sullivan's book *Lift Every Voice* illustrates the rise of the NAACP. Richard Kluger's *Simple Justice* is an excellent overview of *Brown v. Board of Education*, while *Brown v. Board of Education: A Civil Rights Milestone and Its Troubled Legacy*, by James Patterson, explores its aftermath.

As its title implies, *The Remaking of a City: Rochester, New York, 1964–1984*, by Gannett journalists Lou Buttino and Mark Hare, is an overview of the turbulent two decades after the 1964 uprising; it includes a chapter on education. The US Commission on Civil Rights held a hearing in Rochester in September 1966 that gathered firsthand testimony from several important figures in the school district. Benjamin Richardson's doctoral dissertation on RCSD reorganization was the single most important secondary source for this book, combining interviews and qualitative analysis to give an uncommonly clear narrative of those complicated years. Ralph W. Barber, too, wrote a valuable dissertation in 1968, "The Effects of Open Enrollment on Anti-Negro and Anti-White Prejudices among Junior High School Students in Rochester, New York." On the national level, Matthew Delmont's book *Why Busing Failed* provides needed framing around the political implications of the word "busing." *Trial and Error*, by Eleanor Wolf, is the best single analysis of the *Milliken v. Bradley* case.

A useful source for the early history of Urban-Suburban is Lawrence Heinrich, "A Descriptive Study of a Cooperative Urban-Suburban Pupil Transfer Program," a 1968 dissertation; so is the program office's own historical review, written on the occasion of its fiftieth anniversary. Kara Finnigan of the University of Rochester has analyzed the later years of the program with great insight, most notably in her 2009 presentation with Tricia Stewart, "Interdistrict Choice as a Policy Solution: Examining Rochester's Urban-Suburban Interdistrict Transfer Program."

Those looking for more detail on the evolution of school funding in New York should see the book *Politicians, Judges, and City Schools*, by Joel S. Berke, Margaret E. Goertz, and Richard J. Coley. Denise Gelberg's book *The "Business" of Reforming American Schools* is a review of the first fifteen years of the accountability era and includes a chapter on Rochester. Julia Koppich's 1992 paper "The Rocky Road to Reform in Rochester" is a comprehensive look at the 1987 teachers' contract.

Gary Orfield has been the most prolific and influential writer on school segregation for more than forty years; one particularly valuable book is *Dismantling Desegregation*. Rucker Johnson makes a case for school integration with a novel data set in *Children of the Dream: Why School Integration Works*. Arguing the opposing case is Derrick Bell in *Silent Covenants*.

# Index

Page numbers in *italics* refer to figures and tables.


abolitionist movement, 3, 20, 22–24, 30–31, 34
academic outcomes: of desegregated education, 11–14, 115, 120; disparities between city and suburban districts, 222–23; at magnet schools, 215, 228; of open enrollment programs, 115, 120; poverty and, 9, 11–12, 223–25; at World of Inquiry School, 169. *See also* education
Aex, Robert, 160
African Americans. *See* Black Americans
African Methodist Episcopal (AME) Zion Church, 3, 21, 27, 36, 38, 75, 85
*Aikens v. Board of Education* (1962), 89–90, 96, 98, 108–10, 151, 226
Akerly, Harold, 158–59
Alinsky, Saul, 107
Allen, James, 99–102, 115, 148, 160, 163, 183, 185
Al-Sarag, Gloria Winston, 108, 208
Amaker, Julius, 52
AME (African Methodist Episcopal) Zion Church, 3, 21, 27, 36, 38, 75, 85
Anthony, Susan B., 74
antibusing movement: federal support for, 147; 15-Point Plan aligned with, 118; leadership of, 6, 116–17, 123; rallies held for, 130; rationale of, 13, 120, 134; resolution passed in favor of, 123, 124
antiracism education, 16, 237–39
Ark, John, 224–25
*Arthur v. Nyquist* (1976), 227–28
Ashford, Laplois, 84, 121
Atwater, John, 38–39
Auld, Hugh, 30, 40
Auld, Sophia, 30

Baldwin, James, x, 237–38
Balter, David, 89, 90
Balter, Jerome, 17, 89–90, 109, 118, 151, 164
Balter, Ruth, 89–90
Banker, Jeannette, 171, 173
Barber, Ralph, 114–15, 137
Barnes, William, 37, 38
Beard, James, 113, 134, 150, 153
Bell, Derrick, 10, 237
Bennion, John, 175
Best, Wyoma, 128–30, 141, 143
Bethune, Mary McLeod, 78
Bianchi, Lewis, 143
bias. *See* discrimination
Bickal, Robert, 115, 118
bilingual education programs, 2, 207
Bishop, John, 28
Bishop, William, 26
Black Americans: advocacy by, 7–8, 19, 25, 37–40; Great Migration by, 42, 50, 57, 59, 78, 110, 207; housing for, 5, 42, 59–60, 62–68, 83; Italian American relations with, 138–39; as migrant workers, 43, 50–59; opposition to desegregation, 8–11, 14; percentages in US cities, 43–44, *44*; police relations with, 73, 105–6, 149–50; skepticism of medical profession by, 56; in suburban areas, 208; Sunday schools for, 20–21, 23, 25–27, 75; as teachers, 75, 110–12; voter registration and, 78–79. *See also* civil rights movement; discrimination; racism
Black Power movement, 46, 107, 112, 154
Black student unions (BSUs), 112–13
block schools, 140–42, 266n23
blockbusting, 66, 68, 136
Bloss, William and Celestia, 29
Board of Cooperative Educational Services (BOCES), 165–66, 171, 190, 193
*Board of Education, Levittown Union Free School District et al. v. Ewald B. Nyquist* (1982), 211, 224, 225

Bock, Franklin, 47
Bonner, Walter, 77
Boo, Katherine, 218
Boothby, Samuel, 28
Bork, Robert, 155
Bower, Frank, 141
Bracken, Gary, 192
Branch, David, 124, 127–30, 135, 141, 143
Brandon, Evelyn, 44, 45
Brewer, Laurie, 193
Breyer, Stephen, 229
Brighton Central School District, 2, 174–76, 185, 188–89, 196, 202
Brizard, Jean-Claude, 177
Brockport Center for Innovation in Education, 14, 170–73, 175, 176, 180, 182
Brockport Central School District, 159, 188
Brooks, Maggie, 180, 181
Brown, Albert, 170
Brown, Alex, 51–52
Brown, Linda, 79, 81
Brown, Regina, 185
Brown, Sereena. *See* Martin, Sereena Brown
*Brown v. Board of Education* (1954): alternative outcomes to, 10; de jure segregation disallowed by, 144; implementation of ruling, 82–83, 87, 104; modern-day disregard for, 206, 218, 229; NAACP role in, 80–82, 155; racial admissions criteria and, 195; reversal of *Plessy v. Ferguson* by, 4–5
BSUs (Black student unions), 112–13
Buffalo City School District: 19th century segregation in, 26, 39; 20th century segregation in, 85, 110, 145, 227–28. *See also Arthur v. Nyquist* (1976)
Burger, Warren, 155
Burgos, Luis, 69, 70
Burkhart, Harvey, 47
Burks, George, 48
Bush, George H. W., 214
Busing: criticisms of, 14, 146; emotionalism of, 131, 151, 172; funding for, 190, 197; national moratorium on, 147; in reorganization plan, 129, 152; school overcrowding alleviated by, 95; student responses to, 103. *See also* antibusing movement

Cala, William, 176–80, 190–91, 195
Caldwell, Velverly, 70
Camelio, Ann, 141
*Campaign for Fiscal Equity Inc. v. State* (1995), 223–26
Carbone, Terry, 171, 173
Carmichael, Stokely, 107
Caroselli, Marlene, 134, 149, 152
Carter, Robert L., 90
Cason, Alberta, 14
Castle, Musette, 111, 208
Cavalier, Ed, 136–37, 143, 149, 150, 222
Cerulli, Louis: in antibusing movement, 6, 116, 123, 130, 134; death of, 150; on desegregation initiatives, 91, 101, 117–19, 125, 204; on educational parks, 174; on metropolitan school districts, 163–64; photograph of, *117*; reorganization plan opposed by, 138, 143; resignation from school board, 121, 124, 263n71; United Schools Association and, 128, 135
Cervone, Gian Carlo and Maria, 170
Charlotte High School: Black student union at, 113; conversion to junior high school, 123, 135; magnet program at, 215; nonwhite student percentage at, 151; racist incidents at, 14, 130, 134; social class divisions at, 137; Madison High School exchange, 185; violence at, 17, 133–35, 137, 148–49
charter schools, 6, 177, 196, 215, 220–22
children: discrimination and impact on, 82; of migrant workers, 54–56, 73; orphanages for, 76–77; of refugees, 207; traumatic experiences for, 55, 56, 70. *See also* education
Christian, James, 49
Christian, Yancey and Yalawn, 223
Churchville-Chili Central School District, 191
Ciaccia, Frank, 13, 142, 156, 209
Cimusz, Linda, 229
civil rights movement: in curricular materials, 112; desegregation litigation during, 7, 79, 90, 156; educational access during, 205; migrant workers during, 57; nonwhite teacher recruitment during, 110; Urban-Suburban during, 204; Young Turks in, 83–85
Clark, Kenneth, 82, 90
Clark, Mamie, 82
Claytor, Glen, 87
Coalition of Concern, 125, 127, 129
Coles, Clayton, 60
Coles, Howard, 53–54, 60–63, *61*, 67
Coles, Joan, 60
Coles, Robert, 55, 56
Colman, Lucy, 17, 38, 39

Colquhoun, Lillian, 17, 127, 144, *145*, 153, 223
*Colquhoun v. Board of Education* (1970), 127, 145–48, 151, 223, 267n35
Comegys, Richard, 209–10
common schools, 22, 24–29, 35–37, 39, 226
community school councils, 8, 9, 127, 129, 146
Cona, David, 150
Congress of Racial Equality (CORE), 66, 84, 112, 116, 226
Conning, Mary, 29
Cooke, Frances, 89, 118
Cooper, Walter: background of, 87–88; on desegregation efforts, 94; on double-shifting plan, 86; inspiration provided by, 17; on metropolitan school districts, 204; on migrant workers, 50; as NAACP activist, 84, 88; on racial uprising in Rochester (1964), 106; on Steepee study, 96, 257n53
CORE (Congress of Racial Equality), 66, 84, 112, 116, 226
Corrigan, Dean, 167
Crane, Jeff, 192, 195, 197, 202–3
Cremin, Lawrence, 23, 24
Crewson, Walter, 184
Cromwell, David, 189
Cross, Whitney, 22
Crumb, Michael, 191
Crutchfield, Rosetta, 72, 73
Culpepper (Virginia), 42–43, 51, 60
Curran, Arthur, 91
Curry, Archie, 212, 217, 219

Dade, Terry, 231–32
Daley, Marie, 75
Danforth, George F., 4–5
D'Angelo, Louis, 209
Davis, Mark Allan, 91
Davis, Reecy, 121–23, *122*, 125, 129, 142
Davis, Reuben, 88–92, 108
de facto segregation: *Aikens* lawsuit and, 109; *Arthur* decision and, 227; *Brown* decision and, 83; de jure segregation vs., 94; educational inequality and, 79; educational parks as solution to, 173; *Keyes* decision and, 153; Panetta on, 95; RCSD response to, 91; Steepee study of, 98, 257n53; Urban-Suburban Program in reduction of, 194
de jure segregation, 82–83, 94, 144, 153, 223, 227
de Kiewiet, Cornelius, 49
Deane-Williams, Barbara, 179, 231
DeCaro family, 169
Deets, Norman, 213
DeHond, Gordon, 124, 128, 136, 141–43, 148
Deller, W. McGregor, 172
Delmont, Matthew, 151
demonstration schools, 170–71, 175
Dennis, Lorie, 201
Denton, Nancy, 59–60
desegregated education: academic outcomes of, 11–14, 115, 120; advocacy for, 7–8, 19, 25, 38–40; Black opposition to, 8–10, 14; cities under court supervision for, 227; educational parks for, 116, 173–74, 240; employment outcomes of, 13; in federation plan for school districts, 118, 164–66, 234, 235; 15-Point Plan for, 118–19, 121, 164, 234; funding for, 2, 7, 12–13, 101, 147–48; Goldberg Plan for, 123–30, *126*, 144; interdistrict partnerships for, 14, 158, 170, 173–80, 182; Italian American opposition to, 138–40; at magnet schools, 215–17, 224; in metropolitan school districts, 158–59, 161–64, 180–82, 204, 233–35; in neighborhood schools, 39, 87, 116; Princeton Plan for, 102, 103, 109, 116, 123; public polling on, 14–15, *15*; RCSD initiatives for, 13–15, 101–5, 113–25, *119*, 127–31; Rochester plan for, 116–17; structural obstacles to, 15–16; Triad Plan for, 113; white opposition to, 3, 6–7, 10, 17, 102–4, 114–18, 130–31. *See also* busing; open enrollment programs; reorganization plan; Urban-Suburban Interdistrict Transfer Program
Dett, R. Nathaniel, 45
Dick, Homer, 160, 161
Dieck, William, 174
Dinolfo, Cheryl, 206
discrimination: children impacted by, 82; in employment, 5, 45–49, 107–8, 206; in housing, 5, 42, 59–60, 62–68, 83, 94–96, 208–9; of immigrant populations, 44; NAACP response to, 46–49, 73. *See also* racism; segregated education
Dodson, Dan, 16, 17
Dorsey, Isabella, 75–77, *76*
Dorsey, Thomas, 75–76
Douglas, William, 156
Douglass, Anna Murray, 1–2, 30, 31, 33
Douglass, Charles Remond, 34
Douglass, Frederick: in abolitionist movement, 3, 30; on education, 3, 30–31, 34–40, 85, 233; letter to Warner, 32, 33, 249n42; on liberalism in Rochester, 42; schools named after, 2–3, 135

Douglass, Frederick, Jr., 33, 34
Douglass, Rosetta, 31–34, 75
Doyle, Jack, 180–81
Duffy, Bob, 218

East High School, 74, 96, 97, 123, 127, 135–36, 222
East Irondequoit Central School District, x, 161, 185, 195
East Rochester (New York), 67
East Rochester Union Free School District, 189, 195, 196
Eastman, George, 46–48
Eastman Kodak Company, 45–48, 65, 107–8
Easton, William, 104
Edison Technical and Industrial High School, 160–61, 213, 215, 217
education: antiracism, 16, 237–39; bilingual programs, 2, 207; block schools, 140–42, 266n23; charter schools, 6, 177, 196, 215, 220–22; common schools, 22, 24–29, 35–37, 39, 226; curriculum for, 77, 88, 108, 111–12, 184, 188, 237–39; demonstration schools, 170–71, 175; on discrimination, 16; federation plan for school districts, 118, 164–66, 234, 235; gifted programs, 2, 118–20, 216; inequality in, 3–4, 15, 79, 234; metropolitan school districts, 158–59, 161–64, 180–82, 204, 233–35; for migrant children, 54–56, 73; open classroom concept, 124, 153, 172, 173; private schools, 9, 29, 141, 188–89, 201; reform efforts, 5, 176, 205, 212–13, 217–22, 229, 233–40; school district formation in US, 269n6; slaves prohibited from, 2, 30; special education services, 165, 201, 202, 231; Sunday schools, 20–21, 23, 25–27, 75. *See also* academic outcomes; desegregated education; magnet schools; segregated education; teachers
educational parks: Herman Goldberg plan for, 116, 173; John Woods plan for, 173–74, 240
Edwards, Glenn, 240
Elins, Herbert, 175
employment: desegregated education and, 13; discrimination in, 5, 45–49, 107–8, 206; of migrant workers, 43, 50–59
Erie Canal, 22, 23
Essley, Peter, 175
Etter, Doyle O., 185
eugenics movement, 46
Evans, Malik, 178, 214, 239
excellence in education movement, 212–13, 229

Faegre, Mark and Susan, 90
Fair Housing Act of 1968, 59, 208
Fairport Central School District, 176, 177, 190–91, 202
Farbo, Joseph, 145, 146
Farley, Elizabeth, 143, 146
Federal Housing Administration (FHA), 59, 64
federation plan for school districts, 118, 164–66, 234, 235
Feldman, Jonathan, 224, 227
15-Point Plan, 118–19, 121, 164, 234
FIGHT organization, 69, 85, 107–8, 110–13, 116, 125, 137
Finney, Charles Grandison, 22
Finnigan, Kara, 198–202, 234
Fish, George and Hal, 49–50
Flannery, J. Harold, 151
Florence, Franklin: on desegregation efforts, 121; on employment discrimination, 107; on 15-Point Plan, 118; as FIGHT president, 6, 85, 100, 107; on nonmilitant activists, 108; on open enrollment programs, 115; on racial uprising in Rochester (1964), 106; student boycott supported by, 128
Floyd, George, 238, 239
Ford, Ruby McCants, 53
Fourteenth Amendment, 79, 80
Franco, John, 14, 129, 141, 153, 212
Franklin High School, 17, 123, 134–36, 139, 149, 161, 216
Fraser, Brenda, 210–11
Freeman, Zenas, 21
Frey, Thomas, 124, 127–30, 145, 176–78
Frusci, Irene, 210
Fullager, William, 167

Garrison, William Henry, 31
Gates Chili Central School District, x, 163
Genesee Community Charter School (GCCS), 221
Gerst, Wilbur, 125
Gibson, John, 50
Gifford, Bernard, 8, 127, 129, 168
gifted programs, 2, 118–20, 216
Gitelman, Jacob, 86, 91
Gitomer, Deborah, 185
Goldberg, Herman: background of, 100; on Black teacher recruitment, 110; on educational parks, 116, 173, 174; 15-Point Plan promoted by, 118–19; on interdistrict partnerships, 175, 176; on metropolitan school districts, 163; on open enrollment programs, 101, 115, 238;

photograph of, *122*; Project UNIQUE and, 167; reorganization plan of, 123–30, *126*, 144; on resources for Black schools, 96, 98; Rochester plan promoted by, 116–17; as superintendent, 99, 133; transfer plan initiated by, 102–4
Grant, Gerald, 178
Gray, Irving, 47
Great Migration, 42, 50, 57, 59, 78, 110, 207
Great Schools for All, 158, 178–80, 182
Greater Rochester Area Coalition for Education (GRACE), 222, 223. *See also* *Paynter v. New York* (2002)
Greece Central School District, 110, 157, 166, 173, 174
*Green v. County School Board* (1968), 154
Gross, Norman, 17, 170–72, 185–90, *186*, 193, 198, 203

Haak, Jessica, 193–94, 197
Halpin, Mary, 187
Hannah-Jones, Nikole, 7–8, 180
Hanover Houses, 68–70, 144
Hare, Mark, 178
Harmon, Benjamin Franklin, 43
Harris, Katherine Jordan, 83
Harrison, Richard, *122*
Heiligman, Warren, 146
Helm, William, 19–20
Helmer, Earle, 185
Henderson, John, 144, 146–48, 154
Hetherington, Bryan, 176–78, 223, 224, 227
Hill, Kermit, 211
Hillman, Shannon, 221
Hilton Central School District, 189, 191, 195
Holme, Jennifer Jellison, 234
Holmes, Kirk, 183, 184, 187
Home Owners' Loan Corporation (HOLC), 64
Homer, Porter, 106
Honeoye Falls-Lima Central School District, 191, 196, 200
*Hopwood v. Texas* (1996), 194
housing: discrimination in, 5, 42, 59–60, 62–68, 83, 94–96, 208–9; for migrant workers, 51–54, 57; poverty and, 69, 70; public housing projects, 68–70, 88; redlined communities, 42, 64–65; restrictive covenants and, 5, 48, 64, 65, 68; segregated education and, 5, 42, 59, 64, 71, 86, 94–96; in suburbs, 15, 65, 67, 208
Howard, Joan Coles, 60
Huffman, Jasper, 67, 139

immigrant populations, 44, 138, 170, 207–8
Ingram, Clarence, 70–71
integrated education. *See* desegregated education
interdistrict partnerships, 14, 158, 170, 173–80, 182. *See also* Urban-Suburban Interdistrict Transfer Program
Irondequoit (New York): housing discrimination in, 65; Ku Klux Klan activity in, 67. *See also* East Irondequoit Central School District; West Irondequoit Central School District
Istock, Conrad, 148, 152
Italian Americans, 44, 96, 135, 137–40, 150

Jackson, Marvin, 219
Jackson, Trent, Jr., 105
James, Jessie, 41–42
James, Thomas, 21, 23, 27, 29
Jarvie, Danielle, 15
Javits, Jacob, 57
Jefferson High School, 17, 123, 135, 137–40, 148–50
jobs. *See* employment
Johnson, Bill, 180–82, 209
Johnson, Bobby, 58–59
Johnson, Rucker, 12, 13
Johnson, Wayne, 201
Jones, Reuben, 33–34, 37, 38
Jordan, Anthony and Katherine Harris, 83
Josh Lofton High School, 216

Kaufman, Irving, 87
Kaye, Judith, 225
Kearns, David, 212, 213
Kelly, Alfred, 81
Kennedy, Anthony, 195
Kennedy, Robert, 57
*Keyes v. School District No. 1, Denver* (1973), 144, 153–54
King, Martin Luther, Jr., 107
King, Nellie Whitaker, 66, 72–73, 113
Kluger, Richard, 79
Knox, William Jacob, 68
Kodak. *See* Eastman Kodak Company
Kriegsfeld, Irving, 68
Ku Klux Klan, 52, 67–68

labor force. *See* employment
Lamb, Frank, 106, 263n71
Lang, Perry, 150
Larimer, David, 193–94
Learning Community model, 234–35
Lee, Rachel, 159
Levy, Van, 47

Lewis, Jessica, 201, 202
Littwitz, James, 185
Lofton, Josh, 149–50
Lonsberry, Bob, 181
Love, Bettina, 111
Lunsford, Charles, 45, 47–49, 84, 88
lynchings, 74, 77

Mace, Richard, 201
Madison High School, 104, 115, 123, 135, 146, 151, 184–85
magnet schools: academic outcomes at, 215, 228; desegregation at, 215–17, 224; in 15-Point Plan, 118, 119; interdistrict, 179, 204; poverty of students at, 179; public polling on, 15; Wilson Magnet High School, 9, 213–17. *See also* World of Inquiry School
Major Achievement Program (MAP), 119–20
Malcolm X, 107
Mangione, Jerre, 138–39
Mann, Horace, 24
MAP (Major Achievement Program), 119–20
Marshall, Elihu, 26–27
Marshall, Thurgood, 80, 81, 90, 107, 155–56
Marshall High School, 115, 123, 135, 184, 216
Martin, Sereena Brown, 144, *145*, 223
Massey, Douglas, 59–60
Mastrella, John, 150
McClary, Cecil, 8
McDonald, John, 25–26
McElrath, Frank, 84–85
*McLaurin v. Oklahoma Board of Regents* (1950), 80–81
McWalters, Peter, 213, 216, 218–20, 229–30
medical profession, Black skepticism of, 56
Merrill, Arch, 51
metropolitan school districts, 158–59, 161–64, 180–82, 204, 233–35
Metropolitan World of Inquiry School, 14, 170–72, 180
Micheaux, Anne, 83
migrant workers, 43, 50–59
Miller, Dana, 120–21, 139
Miller, Dean, 141
*Milliken v. Bradley* (1974), 155–56, 227
Minarik, Stephen, 181–82
Miner, Myrtilla, 29
Mitchell, Constance, 66, 84, 107
Mitchell, John, 66, 84, 121
Monroe County (New York): Board of Cooperative Educational Services in, 165–66, 171, 190, 193; charter schools in, 220–22; Educational Planning Committee, 164–65, 175; executive race in (2003), 180–82; federation plan for school districts in, 164–66, 234, 235; Human Relations Commission, 89, 102, 115; metropolitan school districts for, 158–59, 161–64, 180–82, 204, 233–35; Non-Partisan Political League in, 83; population by geographic area, *63*; public polling on desegregation initiatives, 15, *15*; restrictive covenants utilized by, 65
Monroe High School, 67, 123, 135
Moore, Isaac, 29
Moore, Joan, 74
Morelle, Joseph, 177–78
Morris, Jacob, 28
Mumford (New York), 42–43, 53, 60
Murray, Anna. *See* Douglass, Anna Murray
Myrdal, Gunnar, 80

National Association for the Advancement of Colored People (NAACP): on Black teacher recruitment, 110; *Brown v. Board of Education* and, 80–82, 155; desegregation initiatives supported by, 116; on discrimination, 46–49, 73; history and growth of, 78–79; lawsuits filed against RCSD, 73, 89–92, 108–10, 203; Legal Defense and Education Fund, 10, 151, 226; Princeton Plan supported by, 102; school curriculum concerns, 77; on segregative containment mechanisms, 155; University of Rochester chapter, 49, 88; Youth Council of, 73
National Association of Real Estate Boards, 62–63
neighborhood schools: desegregation of, 39, 87, 116; expansion of, 19; gerrymandering and, 87; housing practices and, 71; open enrollment as threat to, 104; overcrowding in, 85; preservation of, 119, 142, 146, 150, 156; reluctance to leave, 14, 136; renewed support for, 9
Nelkin, Dorothy, 50
Ness, Mildred, 148
Nicolosi, Mary, 128, 135
Nixon, Richard, 131, 147, 155, 212
No Child Left Behind Act of 2001, 218
NorthSTAR program, 2
Norton, Herbert, 151

Nothnagle, John, 62
Nyquist, Ewald, 127, 131, 141, 143–46, 148, 175–76, 209

*Oklahoma City v. Dowell* (1991), 227
open classroom concept, 124, 153, 172, 173
open enrollment programs: academic outcomes of, 115, 120; characteristics of, 102, 238; criticisms of, 101, 104–5, 115; participation in, 14, 103, 113; reverse initiatives, 118–20, 131; student responses to, 114, *114*; Urban-Suburban Program as extension of, 167, 184; white opposition to, 103–4, 114, 115
Orfield, Gary, 12, 15
Ouimet, Jeremy and Rachel, 192
Owens, Idonia, 113, 149

Padilla, Juan, 105
Padilla, Nydia, 110, 139–40, 207
Padilla, Ramon, 206
Panetta, Leon, 95
*Parent Ass'n of Andrew Jackson High Sch. v. Ambach* (1979), 194
*Parents Involved in Community Schools v. Seattle School District No. 1* (2007), 11, 209, 228–29
Parker, Fred I., 197, 198
paternalism, 44, 74, 106, 107
Patti, Santo, 149
Paynter, Amber, 222, 227
*Paynter v. New York* (2002), 176, 223–27
Peck, Nancy, 127
Pecoraro, Dorothy, 149
Penfield Central School District, 172, 188, 201, 204, 239
*People ex rel. King v. Gallagher* (1883), 4–5
Perkins, Jonathan, 113
Phillips, Dorothy, 123, 124, 127, 129, 145
Pittsford Central School District, 169, 188, 189, 196, 201, 208
*Plessy v. Ferguson* (1896), 4–5, 10, 79–81
police-community relations. *See* Rochester Police Department
Post, Amy, 30, 39
poverty: academic outcomes and, 9, 11–12, 223–25; charter schools and, 220; federal antipoverty funding, 94, 124, 174, 190; housing conditions and, 69, 70; of magnet school students, 179; of migrant workers, 55; of Regional Academy students, 177; Urban-Suburban and, 195
prejudice. *See* discrimination
Primo, Quintin, 65, 88, 91, 96
Princeton Plan, 102, 103, 109, 116, 123
private schools, 9, 29, 141, 188–89, 201
Project UNIQUE, 110, 131, 167–68, 189
Prude, Daniel, 239
Pryor, Don, 165, 166, 178–79
public education. *See* education
public housing projects, 68–70, 88
Puerto Rican community, 69, 105–6, 125, 129, 139–40, 146, 206–7
Pugh, William, 168
Putnam, Robert, 13

Quakers, 20, 30, 31, 33
Quigley, Joseph, 76
Quinn, John, 36

race riots (national), 78, 107. *See also* racial uprising in Rochester (1964); violence
racial uprising in Rochester (1964), 48, 65, 69–71, 101, 105–7, 166–67
racism: antiracism education, 16, 237–39; at Charlotte High School, 14, 130, 134; in curriculum, 77, 88; eugenics movement and, 46; of Ku Klux Klan, 52, 67–68; as learned behavior, 9; as obstacle to metropolitan school districts, 161, 182; root causes of, 16; of teachers, 74, 75, 187; in Urban-Suburban, 187, 188, 190–93, 202. *See also* discrimination; segregated education
Ray, Andrew, 111
Ray, Phebe, 17, 28–30, 39
RCSD. *See* Rochester City School District
reardon, sean, 11–13
redlining, 42, 64–65
Reed, Austin, 21
refugees, 170, 207
Regional Academy, 176–80, 182. *See also* Cala, William
Rentsch, George, 124–25
reorganization plan: block schools as alternative to, 140–42; components of, 123–24, 132, 135; implementation of, 129–30, 136, 144; opposition to, 125–30, *126*, 133–43; rescinding of, 133, 142–50, 210, 211; student and teacher responses to, 152–53
restrictive covenants, 5, 48, 64, 65, 68
Richardson, Benjamin, 134, 153
Ridley, Letha, 75
Risingh, Leonard, 28
RNSAC (Rochester Neighborhood School Associations Council), 125, 127–28

Roberts, John, 195, 228–29
Robinson, David, 166
Robinson, Jackie, 16
Robinson, Joseph, 20
Roc 2 Change initiative, 239, 240
Roche, Michael, 119–21, 123, 124, 130, 263n71
Rochester City School District (RCSD): budget gaps facing, 166; desegregation initiatives, 13–15, 101–5, 113–25, *119*, 127–31; double-shifting plan of, 85–86; financial challenges for, 211–12, 231; free school districts within, 159–60; interdistrict partnerships and, 14, 158, 170, 173–80, 182; NAACP lawsuit against, 73, 89–92, 108–10, 203; per-pupil funding allotment in, 196, 197; segregated education perpetuated by, 94–96, 98; students by race and ethnicity in, 207, *208*; suburban students attending schools in, 160, 168, 169. *See also* open enrollment programs; reorganization plan; Urban-Suburban Interdistrict Transfer Program; *specific schools*
Rochester International Academy, 207
Rochester Neighborhood School Associations Council (RNSAC), 125, 127–28
Rochester plan, 116–17
Rochester Police Department, 73, 105–6, 149–50
Rochester Teachers Association (RTA), 116, 125, 127, 218
Rochester (New York): abolitionist movement in, 22–24, 34; annexation of outlying towns, 159–60; common schools in, 24–29, 35–37; employment discrimination in, 5, 45–49, 107–8, 206; Great Migration in, 42, 50, 57, 59, 110, 207; history of segregated education in, 19, 25–39, 94; housing discrimination in, 5, 42, 59–60, 62–68, 83, 94, 208–9; immigrant populations in, 44, 138, 170, 207–8; incorporation of, 22, 27; Ku Klux Klan activity in, 67–68; migrant workers in, 43, 50–59; population by race and ethnicity, 42–44, *43*, 83, 154, 206–7; public polling on desegregation initiatives, 14–15, *15*; racial uprising in (1964), 48, 65, 69–71, 101, 105–6, 166–67; social movements in, 22–24, 34–35; Sunday schools in, 20–21, 23, 25–27, 75; urban renewal projects in, 66, 68–69, 207.
Rock, William, 135, 141
Root, Laura, 58
Rosenberger, Geoff, 220
Rossi, Faust, 115, 118, 119, 121, 174
Roth, Stephen, 154, 155
Rounds, Stephen, 187
Rowe, Trevyan, 1–2
RTA (Rochester Teachers Association), 116, 125, 127, 218
Rush-Henrietta Central School District, x, 195, 196, 200, 208, 238

Sagan, Bob, 133, 137–38
St. Louis, Djinga, 2
Salminen, Wilho, 157
*San Antonio Independent School District v. Rodriguez* (1973), 156, 211
Sandifer, Jawn, 90, 226
Sanford (Florida), 41, 49, 72, 73, 161
schools. *See* education
Scott, Elsie, 74
Scott, Evelyn, 201
segregated education: *Brown* decision on, 82–83; de jure segregation, 82–83, 94, 144, 153, 223, 227; history of, 19, 25–39, 94; housing practices and, 5, 42, 59, 64, 71, 86, 94–96; inequality resulting from, 3–4; *Milliken* decision on, 155–56; RCSD perpetuation of, 94–96, 98; "separate but equal" doctrine and, 4, 10, 39, 79–82, 216, 218. *See also* de facto segregation; desegregated education; neighborhood schools
Sellers, Helen, 75
"separate but equal" doctrine, 4, 10, 39, 79–82, 216, 218. *See also Plessy v. Ferguson* (1896)
Sepulzeda, Cero, 146
Sernett, Milton, 22–23
Serrano, Emilio, 124, 128, 263n71
Sette, Alfred, 205
Seward, Sarah, 31
Seymour, Howard, 85, 160
Shagaloff, June, 87
Shanker, Albert, 213
*Sheff v. O'Neill* (1996), 223–24
Simmons, Ivory, 56
Sims, James, Jr., 125, 127, 128
Singletary, Yvette, 187
Slavery and enslaved people: education prohibited for, 2, 30; as migrant workers, 43; role-playing activities involving, 202. *See also* abolitionist movement
Smith, George Bundy, 226–27
Smith, James W., 26–27

Sparks, Lynette, 179, 180
special education services, 165, 201, 202, 231
Spencer, John, 19, 27–28
Spencerport Central School District, 7, 191–93, 195, 197, 202
Spinning, James, 77
Spoto, Catherine, 219
Sprague, Florence, 75
Springer, Robert, 91, 92, 94–96, 99
Steepee, Jonathan, 96, 98, 257n53
Stevenson, Bob, 138
Steward, Austin, 19–21, 23, 25, 27–29, 39
Storrs, Hannah, 84, 112
Straub, Chester, 194
Strippoli, Christopher, 104
Students Union for Integrated Education (SUIE), 240
Stutzman, Richard, 196
suburbs: Black Americans in, 208; housing in, 15, 65, 67, 208; opposition to metropolitan school districts, 163; public polling on desegregation initiatives, 15, *15*; racist incidents in schools in, 14; RCSD acceptance of students from, 160, 168, 169; Regional Academy opposed by, 177; white flight to, 4, 67, 154, 157, 206. *See also* individual town and district names; Urban-Suburban Interdistrict Transfer Program
Suffoletto, Mike, 202
SUIE (Students Union for Integrated Education), 240
Sunday schools, 20–21, 23, 25–27, 75
SUNY Brockport. *See* Brockport Center for Innovation in Education
*Swann v. Charlotte-Mecklenberg Board of Education* (1971), 147, 155
*Sweatt v. Painter* (1950), 80–81

teachers: contract negotiations (1987), 218–19; decline in quality of, 9; in demonstration schools, 170, 171; nonwhite, 75, 110–12, *112*; Project UNIQUE and, 167; racist attitudes of, 74, 75, 187; on reorganization plan, 152–53; of Sunday schools, 23, 75. *See also* Rochester Teachers Association
Thayer, Phebe, 33
Thomas, Stanley and Dolores, 183
Towler, Mary Anna, 182
Tracy, Lucilia, 31, 32
Triad Plan, 113
Tucker, Marc, 213
Tuskegee Institute, 46, 75

United Council on Education and Taxation, 141, 143, 148
United Federation of Inner-City Parents, 121, 125
United Schools Association, 128, 135, 140–41, 150
University of Rochester (UR): desegregation at, 7; discrimination at, 48–49; East High School partnership with, 222; educational parks and, 173; on federation plan for school districts, 165; NAACP chapter at, 49, 88; Project UNIQUE and, 167
Urban League, 68, 84, 121, 123, 128–29, 208–10
urban renewal projects, 66, 68–69, 207
Urbanski, Adam, 218, 219
Urban-Suburban Interdistrict Transfer Program, 183–204; attrition rate in, 200–201; enrollment criteria, 193–95, 199–200, 235–37; funding for, 169–71, 190, 193, 204; level of interest in, 14; objectives of, 193, 195, 198, 203; opposition to, 7, 157–58, 174, 185, 187, 189–93; origins of, 183–85; Project UNIQUE and, 167, 189; reform recommendations, 202; revenue benefits for member districts, 196–97; student responses to, 187–88, 198, 201–2

Van Buren, Viola, 75
violence: by Ku Klux Klan, 67; lynchings, 74, 77; near public housing projects, 70; in schools, 6, 13, 17, 133–37, 148–50, 154; threat of, 65, 67, 70, 103, 114, 124–25, 134, 135, 140, 153, 210. *See also* race riots, racial uprising in Rochester (1964)
Virgilio, Andrew, 170
voter registration, 78–79

Walls, Bessie, 75
Warfield, Thomas, 168–69, 173
Warfield, William, 48, 73–74
Warner, Horatio Gates, 32, 33, 249n42
Warren, Earl, 82
Warren, Lovely, 8–10, 14, 206, 214–16
Washington, Booker T., 46, 75
Wayne County (New York), 49, 51, 52, 53, 56, 57, 98
Webster Central School District, 110, 171, 172, 189, 196, 202
Weller, Earl, 160, 161
Wells, Ida B., 74
West High School, 75, 113, 116, 123, 135–37, 146, 149. *See also* Wilson Magnet High School

West Irondequoit Central School District, 172, 183–85, 187–89, 191–99, 201
Wheatland-Chili Central School District, 188
Whipple, George, 47–49
Whitaker, Nellie. *See* King, Nellie Whitaker
White, Van, 2
White, Walter, 47–48
Wilkins, Roy, 78, 87
Williamson, Obadiah, 84
Wilmot, Christopher, 180, 222–23
Wilmot, James, 158
Wilson, Joseph, 125, 158
Wilson, Laval, 166, 212, 214, 216, 218
Wilson Magnet High School, 9, 213–17. *See also* West High School
Wiltsey, Glenn, 118
Woodland, Jeannette, 86
Woods, John, 173–75, 240
Woodson, Theresa, 192
workers. *See* employment
World of Inquiry School: academic outcomes at, 169; boycott organized against, 127; funding for, 169–70; impact on city schools, 210; instruction style at, 168; racial integration at, 168, 173; student and teacher responses to, 182. *See also* Metropolitan World of Inquiry School
Wright, Dale, 52

Young, Alice Holloway, 67, 68, 92–94, *93*, 103
Young, James, 67, 68
Young, Lillie, 110–11
Young, Solomon, 46
Young, William, 110, 167
Young Turks, 83–85, 108

Zuber, Paul, 98
Zukosky, Jerome, 152

CPSIA information can be obtained
at www.ICGtesting.com
Printed in the USA
LVHW101337110422
715883LV00007B/38/J